They Called Him
STONEWALL

★★★

A LIFE OF LT. GENERAL T. J. JACKSON, C.S.A.

Burke Davis

 BURFORD BOOKS

Grateful acknowledgment is made to the publishers and copyright owners who have so generously granted permission for the use of excerpts from their publications; especially to:

Houghton Mifflin Company, Boston, Massachusetts, for permission to reprint selections from THE LIFE AND LETTERS OF MARGARET J. PRESTON, edited by Elizabeth Preston Allan, copyright, 1903, by Elizabeth Preston Allan.

Fleming H. Revell Company, Westwood, New Jersey, for permission to reprint excerpts from EARLY LIFE AND LETTERS OF GENERAL THOMAS J. (STONEWALL) JACKSON, by T. J. Arnold, copyright, 1916, by Fleming H. Revell Company.

Charles Scribner's Sons, New York, New York, for permission to adapt and reprint excerpts from WAR YEARS WITH JEB STUART, by W. W. Blackford, copyright, 1945, by Charles Scribner' Sons.

The University of North Carolina Press, Chapel Hill, North Carolina, for permission to reprint excerpts from NATURAL BENT, by Paul Barringer, copyright, 1949, by Anna Barringer; I RODE WITH STONEWALL, by R. K. Douglas, copyright, 1940, by The University of North Carolina Press; FOREIGNERS IN THE CONFEDERACY, by Ella Lonn, copyright, 1945, by The University of North Carolina Press; and RUSTICS IN REBELLION, by G. A. Townsend, copyright, 1950, by The University of North Carolina Press.

Printed in the United States of America

10 9 8 7 6 5 4 3 2

Library of Congress Cataloging-in-Publication Data
Davis, Burke.
    They called him Stonewall : a life of Lt. General T. J. Jackson, C.S.A. / Burke Davis.
        p.   cm.
    Originally published: New York : Rinehart, 1954. With new introduction by the author.
    Includes bibliographical references and index.
    ISBN 1-58080-029-7 (pb : alk. paper)
    1. Jackson, Stonewall, 1824–1863.   2. Generals—Confederate States of America
Biography.   3. Confederate States of America. Army Biography.   4. United States—
History—Civil War, 1861–1865—Campaigns.   I. Title.
E467.1.J15D27   1999
973.7'3'092—dc21
[B]   99-21661
                                                                                              CIP

to Angela

Acknowledgment

For aid in writing this book, I am indebted to my wife, Evangeline, critic, goad and typist; to Lettie Rogers, grammarian, stylist and indispensable consultant; to Carroll G. Bowen and Mattie Straughan, who proposed it; to Robert D. Loomis, its enthusiastic editor; to the Confederate Museum and the Valentine Museum of Richmond; to the Southern Historical Collection of the University of North Carolina Library; to the North Carolina Department of Archives and History; to the Greensboro Public Library, in particular Olivia Burwell and Irene Hester; to the libraries of the Woman's College, University of North Carolina, and of Guilford College.

I am also indebted to North Carolinians who opened their private libraries to allow use of valuable books or manuscripts, among them: Keith F. Cooper, Mrs. Edgar C. Garber, Mrs. C. T. Lipscomb, Mrs. Mary R. Lomax and Mrs. Henry Myers.

For contributions neither literary nor historical, I am indebted to my neighbors, Eve and Floyd Hugh Craft of Melwood; to Joseph B. Stevens, M.D., and his elixir for burdened writers; and to Miles H. Wolff, a helpful and understanding newspaper editor.

Burke Davis

Cornwallis House,
Guilford College, N.C.
April 21, 1954

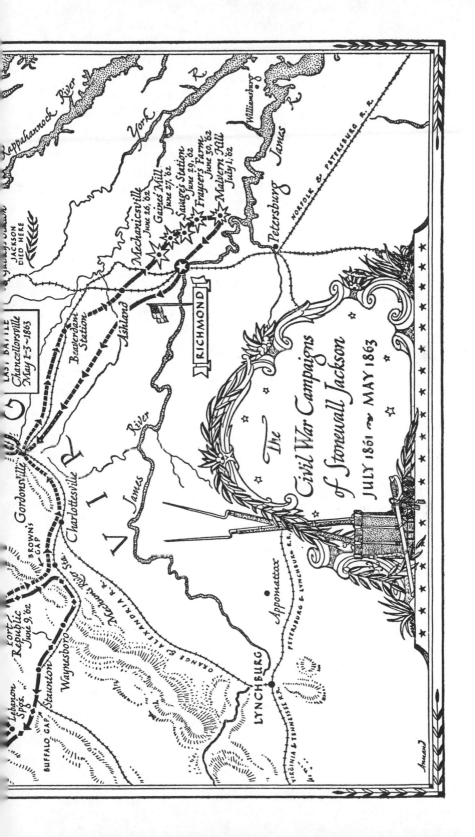

The
Civil War Campaigns
of Stonewall Jackson
JULY 1861 ~ MAY 1863

RICHMOND

Rappahannock River
York R.
James R.
Williamsburg

Mechanicsville
June 26, '62
Gaines' Mill
June 27, '62
Savage's Station
June 29, '62
Frayser's Farm
June 30, '62
Malvern Hill
July 1, '62

Petersburg

NORFOLK & PETERSBURG R.R.

JACKSON
DIED HERE

LAST BATTLE
Chancellorsville
May 1-3, 1863

Beaverdam
Station
Ashland

Gordonsville

BROWN'S
GAP

Charlottesville

James River

VIRGINIA

Appomattox

ORANGE & ALEXANDRIA R.R.

PETERSBURG & LYNCHBURG R.R.

LYNCHBURG

VIRGINIA & TENNESSEE R.R.

Port
Republic
June 9, '62

Lebanon
Spgs.

Staunton

Waynesboro

BUFFALO GAP

Introduction

★★★ TO THE 1999 EDITION

The tactical genius displayed by Lieutenant Thomas Jonathan Jackson in the early stages of the Civil War was unsurpassed in that bitter conflict which established the modern United States.

The lightening blows struck by Jackson's troops on a succession of battlefields were notable more for their sheer audacity and the impassioned resolve of their commander than for the unorthodoxy of conception. The classic maneuvers upon which Jackson's durable fame rests also owed much to his religious faith.

Jackson certainly thought of himself as a Christian soldier and was persuaded that his stern Presbyterian God had blessed the Confederate Cause. His was a faith that never wavered, even in the darkness of a spring night in 1863 when having completed the most celebrated of his exploits, he was gunned down by his own men. Eight days later he was dead, when the South still celebrated the triumph at Chancellorsville, and Robert E. Lee began planning a second invasion of the North, which ended at Gettysburg.

Jackson's untimely death probably deprived the Confederacy of its only realistic opportunity to force an end to the war, with a peace upon terms favorable to the rebellious states.

That, at least, is an article of faith shared by thousands of today's Civil War enthusiasts, lost in dreams of what Lee might have accomplished at Gettysburg and beyond, had Jackson been at his side to seize the high ground and to conceive and execute flanking marches and enveloping movements and stunning, unexpected assaults.

Some modern observers have concluded that Jackson could not be accepted in today's armed forces because of the quirks of his personality. Yet it was surely this array of personal traits from which his military outlook was formed. A recent, and highly respected, biographer seeks to minimize the eccentricities evident in Jackson's behavior—though these are attested to by a host of contemporary observers.

Comment in striking terms was made throughout Jackson's career. The boy soldiers who observed his strange ways as a professor at Virginia Military Institute called him Tom Fool. A number of war-time veterans of the Stonewall Brigade noted his odd behavior in letters and journals, and some eminent Confederate general officers made plain their astonishment in their first service with Stonewall.

General Richard Taylor, son of President Zachary Taylor, left a detailed and engaging sketch of Jackson's appearance and behavior at a moment during the Shenandoah Valley Campaign. At almost the same time General Richard Ewell, summoned with his troops to join this unfolding military miracle, told a fellow officer, "I tell you, sir, General Jackson is as crazy as a March hare." This was the outburst of an accomplished officer driven to a frenzy of frustration by Jackson's cryptic orders and his passion for military secrecy.

Ewell soon learned, of course, that Stonewall's apparent lunacy was merely a manifestation of genius at work—for during the next few days at Jackson's side he took part in the incredible Victories in the Valley, when "the March hare" with his small, outnumbered force, defeated four Federal armies in rapid succession and cleared the Shenandoah of Jackson's enemies.

By the time Stonewall was summoned eastward by Lee to aid in the defense of Richmond, the conqueror from the Valley was already the leading figure in the Confederate pantheon of heroes.

This war-time biography appeared in 1954, half a century after the definitive work by the British Historian G. F. R. Henderson. *They Called Him Stonewall* remained in print for almost forty-five years. I am pleased its life will be extended by this new edition.

—BURKE DAVIS
April, 1999

Contents

BOOK THREE

Book One:

☆☆☆ *If this valley is lost, Virginia is lost.*

—JACKSON

★★★ JOHN BROWN'S BODY

It had been a long wait on the hill, with the crowd shivering under a wind from upriver, but at last, just before noon, there was a stir on the porch of the jail.

An ugly old man appeared there, shuffling in carpet slippers, wearing a long-tailed coat and black hat, blinking in the light of the sun, which had just emerged. Men standing near by caught the odor of him and his time in the jail.

The prisoner walked stiffly, and was drawn forward by the pain of a kidney ailment, so that his step seemed tentative and doddering. He handed a folded bit of paper to his jailer, who rustled it as if to read it, but the old man spoke, and the jailer thrust the note into his pocket.

The old man craned his wattled neck to peer at soldiers moving in the roadway beneath—three infantry companies wheeling into line. Other troops waited beyond.

"I had no idea Governor Wise thought my murder so important," the prisoner said. The nasal voice was unhurried and bitter; the set of the cracked lips betrayed no fear.

He went forward as if accompanied by friends, down a flight of stairs with his jailer on one arm and the sheriff on the other. They clambered into a waiting wagon, and when the old man had

3

settled himself on a coffin between the seats, the driver snapped his whip over the rumps of two white farm horses. The prisoner paid no heed to the box on which he sat, and all about, at their distance, the troops watched with covert curiosity the stiff-backed old man who bore himself as if impatient to die. The wagon crawled behind the militia infantry, its wheels strewing the merest dust, and the coffin trailing an odor of fresh lumber.

The wagon went up toward the crest of the hill, where the gallows were.

"A man couldn't have asked prettier weather," old Brown said. Neither the sheriff nor the jailer looked at the prisoner.

The old man's hatchet face had a pleasant, almost happy, expression as he gazed around at the country under the dull sky. Hills tumbled to the west, incredibly blue in the distance; to the east, where the waters of the Shenandoah and the Potomac met, the river banks loomed in vast shoulders. The prisoner saw above these the smoke of Harpers Ferry, where ruin had come to him.

The wagon turned into a hollow square of troops, one thousand of them, and went past a piece of artillery which gaped toward the gallows with gunners at attention. The old man raised his head once more to the valley of the Shenandoah.

"This is a beautiful country," he said. "I never truly had the pleasure of seeing it before."

"None like it," the sheriff said.

The prisoner was first to mount the scaffold, and when he stood above the crowd, he snatched off his dusty hat, which he dropped at his feet. His hair rose in an unkempt gray shock.

Two men fitted the white hood over his head and adjusted the rope. In the last glimpse of light, the prisoner caught sight of the red and gray uniforms of cadets of the Virginia Military Institute who stood between the regiments of militia. Once the hood was on, the jailer stirred his feet, as if adapting himself to a new sense of relief.

Half a dozen hands thrust over the scaffold, groping for the prisoner's fallen hat, and one of them dragged it off, evading the jailer's vicious kicks. Subdued sounds came from below, where unseen men fought over the souvenir.

The old man's voice was muffled by the hood. "I can't see, gentlemen. You must lead me."

The sheriff and a guard led him to the trap, where he stood in the broken slippers, waiting. The militia stamped endlessly in the dust below, going back to its places in the square.

"You want a private signal, now, just before?" the sheriff asked.

"It's no matter to me. If only they would not keep me waiting so long."

The sheriff and the jailer did not now recognize the old voice they knew so well; it was formal and somehow remote. It was the first slight sign of fear or remorse or even hesitation the old man had shown them, and the two officers exchanged glances of veiled triumph.

The militia was ten minutes at its stumbling, while the old man waited, now and then bending his knees to make himself comfortable. Each of the other figures on the scaffold seemed to grow more rigid as time passed. The sheriff looked far down the hill on every hand, creasing his brow over an expression of childlike earnestness, as if he entertained the fear that someone might storm the hilltop, crowned as it was with a mass of troops, in an effort to deliver the old man.

The very young men of the Virginia Military Institute smirked at the awkward militia; but their smiles were fleeting, and hidden from the bearded officer who sat his horse on their right front, as if daydreaming. The commander was a sorry figure, clasped tightly in a shabby coat. He was the obscure Professor of Natural and Experimental Philosophy and Artillery Tactics from the Institute in Lexington.

"Lookit old Tom Fool," one of the cadets whispered. "Another wink, and he's asleep."

"Giving orders to God," another scoffed. "We heard him last night, apraying for old Brown's soul like a damned niggerlover."

Major Thomas Jonathan Jackson, almost as if he had heard the words of the child soldiers, stirred and turned his gaze down the line. "Gentlemen," he piped. The cadets fell silent.

From the ranks of the Richmond militia across the square, a thin-shouldered infantryman glared at the hooded figure on the scaffold. The militiaman's eyes were dark with excitement, as if he had quite lost himself in the spectacle. He was Private John Wilkes Booth.

Major Jackson galloped between the companies, herding them into order, and then settled once more, head lowered, withdrawing into his wrinkled uniform. Already he was thinking of writing a letter to his wife, a description of old Brown's end. A few nights earlier he had reassured her:

> Charlestown, Nov. 28, 1859
> I reached here last night in good health and spirits. Seven of us slept in the same room. I am much more pleased than I expected to be; the people appear to be very kind. There are about 1,000 troops here, and everything is quiet so far. We don't expect any trouble. The excitement is confined to more distant points. Do not give yourself any concern about me. I am comfortable, for a temporary military post.

There was at length an end to the shuffling of feet in the field, and on the scaffold there were slight movements. The prisoner muttered to his jailer, "Be quick, Avis."

The jailer tightened the noose, stepped backward, and the sheriff took a hatchet from a guard. The glinting blade parted a rope, thumped into the wood, and the old man dropped through the platform. The rope whipped back and forth, spinning, rasping against the scaffold, and then began to slow its motion. No sound came from the field where the watchers stood.

After an interval, Major J. T. L. Preston, the Institute Latin professor, shouted, as if he read from a paper—so loudly that all of them heard:

"So perish all such enemies of Virginia! All such enemies of the Union! All such enemies of the human race!"

The troops were ordered at ease, and stood in the square for half an hour longer, while the dark bundle stilled on the scaffold. A band of men went there, and the body was cut down.

The soldiers moved off, and behind them rose the clatter of hammers on the coffin case.

The jailer, thrusting a hand into his pocket, drew forth the paper on which the old man had written. He read its trembling script.

Charlestown, Va., 2nd December, 1859.
I John Brown am now quite certain that the crimes of this guilty land; will never be purged away; but with Blood . . .

The jailer shook his head, grinning uncertainly, and passed the paper to the sheriff, who was to deliver it to the widow.

It was no later than twelve thirty, but the shadow of the gallows already lay across the dust of the slope, where the Virginia soldiers had marched and the horses of their officers had torn the cold turf.

Major Jackson rose directly from supper and sat down to the writing of a letter to his wife. With his bluff manner of detachment, he closed his mind to the passage of the others in his room:

December 2nd. John Brown was hung today at about half-past eleven A.M. He behaved with unflinching firmness. . . . The coffin was of black walnut, enclosed in a box of poplar. . . . He was dressed in a black frock coat, black pantaloons, black vest, black slouch hat, white socks, and slippers of predominating red. There was nothing about his neck but his shirt collar. . . .

Brown fell through about five inches, his knees falling on a level with the position occupied by his feet before the rope was cut. With the fall his arms, below the elbows, flew up horizontally, his hands clinched; and his arms gradually fell, but by spasmodic motions. There was very little motion of his person for several moments, and soon the wind blew his lifeless body to and fro.

His face, upon the scaffold, was turned a little east of south, and in front of him were the cadets, commanded by Major Gilham. My command was still in front of the cadets, all facing south . . . altogether it was an imposing but very solemn scene.

I was much impressed with the thought that before me stood a man in the full vigor of health, who must in a few

moments enter eternity. I sent up the petition that he might
be saved. Awful was the thought that he might in a few
minutes receive the sentence, "Depart ye wicked, into everlasting fire!" I hope that he was prepared to die, but I am
doubtful. He refused to have a minister with him. His wife
visited him last evening.

His body was taken to the jail, and at six o'clock P.M.
was sent to his wife at Harpers Ferry. When it arrived,
the coffin was opened, and his wife saw the remains, after
which it was again opened at the depot before leaving for
Baltimore, lest there should be an imposition. We leave for
home via Richmond tomorrow.

★★★ IS GIDEON QUITE SANE?

Roosting on the fence in the early May sun, he was more scarecrow than man, an effigy from the hands of some rustic humorist of this hill country. He was a joke of some sort; otherwise he defied belief.

He sat, incongruously sucking a lemon, on the outskirts of the village of New Market, Virginia, this spring day of 1862, surrounded by his troops, who rested after a brief noon meal. Wry-faced and pensive, he dealt with his everlasting lemon, evidently oblivious to all else.

No one knew where the fruit came from, but it was always on hand. He spent half his time with one of the yellow skins gleaming in his beard, and his men had been waved into combat with his half-sucked lemons, as if by the batons of some imperial marshal. None other among the millions caught up in the great war seemed to be supplied with lemons, as this one was. The fruit had surely come from afar, through the blockade which was beginning to strangle his country—and whose leaks were a scandal on both sides of the Potomac. Yet the grim, warring deacon, T. J. Jackson, affected lemons. It was one of the least of his mysteries, vaguely connected with the nerv-

9

ous indigestion and cold feet of which he complained.

Last night, in the midst of his troubles, he had made the first confession of his suffering, to Kyd Douglas, the cub of his staff. Douglas, reading a Richmond newspaper to his commander, had laughed at the report of a man who had committed suicide because of his dyspepsia. Jackson wagged his head.

"Ah, you don't understand, young man. I have been in agony from it for twenty years, and I'll never again risk its horrors. I can think of nothing more likely to drive a man to suicide than dyspepsia."

Hence, the staff presumed, lemons, and the curious meals: raspberries, milk and bread. But the officers exchanged no amused glances before him. It was not precisely fear which ruled his headquarters, but there was little time for levity.

Today he wore, as he had since anyone could remember, the old coat of a major, a grimy, dusty, threadbare and single-breasted survivor of the Mexican War, permanently wrinkled into the General's inelegant mold by its sixteen years of service. The most urbane of his officers could describe the General's cap only as "mangy." Now, as ever, it rode far down his nose, the visor all but touching the beard. The coat was stained with the rusty watermarks of years; everything about him seemed in disrepair. So awkwardly did he crouch on his fence that he created the impression that, if he should fall, he might clatter to earth in three or four sections.

Unnoticed now by his men or his staff, he fell into one of his customary five-minute naps, having taken at least a dozen during the day. In that moment, nothing could have been more ludicrous than the suggestion that this man and these troops stood on the very threshold of military immortality. There was scarcely a soul on hand who recalled with any pride, just now, that the weather-beaten figure hanging on the fence rails had won passing fame last summer at Bull Run, as well as a curious nickname, Stonewall.

He had been up most of the night with new worries, these the most embarrassing of all. Some troopers of Turner Ashby —Ashby, the dashing leader of his cavalry—had got drunk on duty, from sampling applejack of the country. The enemy, of course, had seized that moment to drive them in, killing a few, capturing others, and driving the survivors into the hill fastnesses, God knew where. It had not been long, either, since the General had stamped out a rebellion of the mountain people, shot some deserters, and fought a couple of unfortunate battles. Yet his plain face wore that serene somnolence.

His troops were by no means unaware that he was a strange one, for he gave daily demonstrations of his character. Lately, when he had snappishly inquired the whereabouts of a courier who had been serving him faithfully, he was told that the boy was dead, a few moments earlier killed in line of duty. Jackson had muttered in his distracted voice, "Very commendable. Very commendable."

Nothing that came in the path of this little army seemed normal or within reason. Yesterday, for example. The troops were fresh from a bloody little brush with the enemy on a bluff hill called Bull Pasture Mountain, a victory, their commander assured them, after the Federals had abandoned the village of McDowell. They did not fathom the strategy in his mind and his elation at driving apart the twin armies of the enemy. They knew only that the Yanks of the Ohio and West Virginia regiments had fought like furies, and that the gray columns had lost more heavily than the enemy. The men in Jackson's ranks would remember the march home. Its route, they noted profanely, took them on a detour—in the path of the enemy, who was just now satanically clever.

All day the Confederates had plodded in a blue fog of smoke, coughing, spluttering. It was a bitter cloud that pressed over them on the mountain roadway. For the Federals had set fire to the hill forests to cover their retreat, winning praise even from Jackson for the stratagem. The pillars of smoke and fire lay far ahead, blotting out the vistas to the eye and telescope. The army stumbled forward, all but blind.

The Federals were not yet content. They lay on hidden bluffs with their horse artillery and, when the army of Jackson appeared in good range, poured concentrated fire down upon it from the masked batteries, scattering the files. It was slow, painful work: creeping forward, falling flat under fire, lying

while the front files flanked out the big guns, then on to meet
the next entertainment arranged by the Yankees. The skirmishers
burned their feet in smoking woods, for they were driven out
of the road by officers in an effort to prevent ambush. It went
on until after dark. And so, on this May day, they were in no
mood for heroics from anyone, not even their fierce commander.

He declared a half-holiday for them, and they rested, but
they made bitter jokes about his being forced to march on
Sunday, which must have tortured his God-fearing heart. And
when they were enjoined by officers to celebrate a day of thanksgiving with fasting and prayer, they howled in mingled pain and
amusement. Many had not eaten well since marching on Mc-
Dowell—for then, as usual, they had been told to prepare for
action by cooking three days' rations, which they had done, and
then eaten all, knowing that hundreds of them might not survive the third day, and that rations carried easier in the belly
than in the knapsack. They laughed, and complained, and yet
they somehow loved the commander who drove them like a
madman; they would not have exchanged him.

One of his officers wrote home what many were thinking:
"General Lee is the handsomest person I ever saw. . . . This
is not the case with Jackson. He is ever monosyllabic and receives and delivers orders as if the bearer of a conduct pipe from
one ear to the other. There is a magnetism in Jackson, but it
is not personal . . . no one could love the man for himself.
He seems to be cut off from his fellow men and to commune
with his own spirit only, or with spirits of which we know not.
Yet the men are almost as enthusiastic over him as over
Lee. . . ."

This morning, there had been some who were not so enthusiastic. A few companies of the Twenty-seventh Virginia Regiment had come to the end of their voluntary enlistment; they
had signed in for a year, and that was up today. Their officers
would not allow them to leave. The Conscription Act was now
in force, and by law they must remain in the ranks. The men
swore they would not fight one more day. Their colonel came
to Jackson, who refused even to see him and, with the stern face
set like stone, said, "Why does Colonel Grigsby refer to me to

learn how to deal with mutineers? He should shoot them where they stand." That was all.

The mutiny went down. The entire regiment, under harsh orders, aimed muskets at the reluctant companies, which were given their choice: die on the spot, or take up their duties, immediately. Jackson had not even to watch it to make his iron will felt among the insubordinate troops. They surrendered.

It had been a turbulent passage of days, but he seemed resigned to that. Surely nothing disturbed him today as he sat on his fence.

Jackson was thirty-eight years old. Beyond a certain notoriety as an eccentric, he was now almost without reputation, though in the North they still frightened children with his name. He had few intimate friends, and but few, though select, admirers. He had not quite twelve months to live, a prospect which probably would not have caused him to panic if it had been revealed to him.

"My religious belief teaches me to feel as safe in battle as in bed," he had said. "God has fixed the time for my death. I do not concern myself about that."

In officers' quarters his friends sometimes defended him when he was attacked as a bumpkin Presbyterian fatalist, but some of his views made his case difficult for them. Long ago, when the war was only a dark vision looming over them all, he had chided those who feared secession was coming: "Why should Christians be disturbed about the dissolution of the Union? It can come only if by God's permission, and will be permitted only if for His people's good."

His troops gave him plentiful attention today, at their distance, but they had no conception of him as a Christian hero. They thought of their hides, trying to puzzle out what he would next ask of them. They still laughed a little over his message of congratulations on the little victory. That was fare for the draft dodgers and politicians in Richmond. They wondered, too, what he had been up to in the night. They knew that some of the engineers and a cavalry troop had been out in the storm, tearing down bridges, destroying culverts, rolling boulders down into, and felling trees across roads, for more than a mile at a stretch. They puzzled, unable to discern that their commander had already effectively blocked a junction of the three Federal armies in the region and set the stage for an assault upon General N. P. Banks and his army. It was too early to see that the enemy was already helpless.

The General remained alone on this afternoon, and not one of his staff officers approached him. It was a singular staff. Some of them men of skill and experience, though not military men —an excellent map maker, a fine physician, a wagoner who knew his business from long training, a lawyer or two of promise, and a veteran theologian. But none were assistant generals. These were little more than errand boys, not consulted about the decisions of war, and seldom given more than glimpses of plans in the mind of Jackson. The staff was seldom enlightened until the driving marches were over, and the astonished Army of the Valley looked down upon its victims, the thunderstruck enemy.

It was like Jackson to have chosen a preacher as his chief of staff. This one, the Reverend R. L. Dabney, was a major, a good enough camp officer, but with no military experience; and the younger men thought him stiff and a bit sour and less than able. There was constant talk among the boys of the staff that old Dabney should be retired. Sandie Pendleton did all the work of chief anyway. But Jackson fancied ministers, and he found Dabney good company, a distinguished Bible scholar, and an efficient chief, as well. The General left few details for others to attend to in the management of his little army.

The General roused from his brief lethargy on the fence, instantly awake, pulling once more at his lemon. In the roadway, advancing toward him, was a sight such as he had never seen. Parade ground soldiers these were, filling the turnpike, more than three thousand of them, neat in new gray uniforms, flashing white gaiters, passing by the drab lines of his mountain-worn men. The General told himself that the newcomers could not have marched five miles this day, to be so fresh.

They were a brigade of Louisiana troops, called to him from General Ewell's command, about half of them Irish, half Creoles. Their boots fell as one on the sandy road, and the regiments wheeled off into the camping grounds, watched by Jackson's open-mouthed troops. Almost before they had broken ranks, the new soldiers gathered about their regimental bands, which began to play polkas. The Army of the Valley crowded in to investigate its comrades in arms, shouting catcalls.

A young officer approached Jackson, having been directed to the fence. He was not an ordinary soldier, this commander of the Louisiana Brigade, General Richard Taylor, only son of the late President, Zachary Taylor. He was a promising officer who had studied at Yale and Harvard, Edinburgh and Paris. A bayou planter and politician and already a man of wealth and influence.

Taylor saluted Jackson.

"Brigadier General Taylor, sir. Sixth, Seventh, Eighth, Ninth Louisiana."

A long pause ensued, with Jackson pulling at the lemon. Taylor gazed at the unkempt, sunburned beard, the thin, sharp nose and pallid lips, the tiny blue eyes set deeply, clouded as if with fatigue. Only those and the largest pair of cavalry boots he had ever seen. The voice, at last, was a squeaking drawl, like that of a woman.

"How far have you come today?"

"Keazletown Road. Twenty-six miles over the mountain."

"You seem to have no stragglers."

"Never allow them."

"You must teach my people. They straggle badly." There was a subtle edge of irony, bespeaking disbelief.

Taylor nodded courteously. Jackson's glance wandered to the new brigade across the field, now dancing to the music of their bands, their arms around the waists of their partners, capering in polkas.

"Thoughtless fellows for serious work," Jackson said.

"I hope our part of it can be done none the less well, for a little gaiety."

Jackson sucked at the lemon, glanced at Taylor and made no reply. The interview was over.

When the General swung down from his perch, the new troops

could see the remarkable gait of their commander, a graceless plodding step, as if he strode across a ploughed field. The impression was heightened as he rode out from headquarters.

The horse was in its way as striking as the master; it contributed much to the general awkwardness of the pair. It was close-coupled and short, powerfully built, with a neck ludicrously large for so compact an animal; the coat needed attention, but in the May sunlight it gleamed in light tones. Little Sorrel, the troops called him; the staff called him Fancy, perhaps in irony. In his way of going he looked like a farm horse, but his gait was comfortable, and the General rode him without effort. The animal had huge, intelligent eyes, and was treated like a house pet. He had a habit of lying down like a dog on halts in the marching; Jackson often fed him apples at such times.

Sorrel was a piece of war booty, taken from a trainload of Union mounts at Harpers Ferry the year before. He had been the General's favorite horse from the first and was in use almost daily.

This afternoon the horse gave the old troops an opportunity to initiate the strangers to the ritual of life in Jackson's camp. The old troops raised a chorus of throbbing cries, halloos of greeting which swept from company to company, until the camp rang with them. At the outburst, Sorrel broke from his rolling gait into a canter. Jackson rode on as if he had heard nothing, giving no sign of pleasure or displeasure. The noise increased.

The appearance of Jackson was the only sight which could call forth this particular wild medley, though the camp was full of calls. The hungry men would always drop their duties, even if in ranks, and burst over the fields to chase a stray rabbit which bobbed into sight, and then they shouted in a similar way; thus there was the familiar saw in camp: "There goes Old Jack—or a rabbit."

Now, whether stirred by Jackson's brief appearance or the impressionable new audience, the Valley army began to roar through its rowdy calls in earnest. At sight of an officer in new jack boots—though he had been about most of the day—the troops now began to shout: "Come on outa there! We can see

yer arms stickin' out! T'aint time to go in winter quarters!" Or
they would spot a victim in a large hat, and scream: "Come on
down outa there! Y' ain't hidin'! Yer legs is hanging out!" Or
at the passing of a mustached man, the hoots would follow:
"Take them mice outa yer mouth. See their tails drooping out!"
Or: "Get on up outa that bunch of hair. We can see your ears
aworkin'!" The gusts of crude humor swept the camp for an
hour or more, ending in a furious storm of sound as the troops
echoed through the woodland the calls of chickens, ducks and
animals.

Despite the presence of several ministers this week, there was
the usual gambling. Visitors to the camp met dozens of men
in the roadway: "Chance on a raffle, mister? Take a chance on
a watch? Somebody's gonter win a fine one." In the grove were
games of poker and chuckaluck, to which men turned avidly as
soon as duty allowed. About the gambling games were the
most profane of the foul-mouthed army, about which many a
tender soldier was even now writing to his people back home.
One soldier warned his wife never to come to the camp of the
army: "Don't never come here as long as you can ceep away,
for you will smell hell here."

One chaplain complained he had never before heard such
foul language, and that the very air seemed to swear. There was
drinking, and gambling, and a few filthy, tousle-haired, slovenly
women tagged along. Most of this was kept from Old Jack, who
fought sinfulness with rigid bans, and his revivals.

His soldiers, though they were not aware of it, were much
like other regiments, both North and South; only their leader
was different, and his talents had not yet become apparent. But
it remained that he was molding them in his way, though there
were particulars in which nothing could change them.

They were lean and becoming leaner, and would carry no
superfluous weight, for whatever reason. They slept in twos,
each furnishing a blanket and an oilcloth, which they carried in
rolls over their shoulders. Their bed, warm in any weather,
consisted of an oilcloth on the ground and one on the top, with
two blankets between.

There were no overcoats, for they had long since been found

unworthy of the effort of carrying them through good weather; they wore short gray jackets, many of them torn off raggedly at the hips. Beneath, they wore white cotton garments, for in these the lice were easier to control; and when the underclothes were taken off, it was forever. Washing seldom helped, since Jackson, with his swift movements, gave them little chance to prepare hot water.

Officers could make the the men keep bayonets only by constant vigilance, and many went into battle without the blades of which their commander was so fond. They kept little else— no canteens, for tin cups tied to the belt were easier, quicker, lighter, more practical. Boxes for caps and cartridges went into the bushes, too; and revolvers, found useless, were sold, gambled away, or sent home.

No soldiers ever marched in lighter order, for there was seldom anything in the thin blanket rolls but a few berries, persimmons or apples in season, and perhaps a bit of soap. They were ragged, vermin-infested, thin, pestered by the itch—but durable, and of a fierce, unbreakable morale. No one knew how, but they gained in confidence each week. They were not downcast even by Jackson's painful "victory" at McDowell.

Now, with the coming of General Ewell, they would be almost seventeen thousand strong. In Jackson's own division, a dozen regiments, plus Ashby's Seventh Virginia Cavalry, and five batteries of artillery. Ewell brought seventeen regiments of infantry, and two of cavalry, plus a few guns. Up the Valley, too, was General Edward Johnson, watching the enemy with twenty-five hundred men, ready to join an attack.

Of these infantry regiments, seventeen were Virginian. There were five from Louisiana, two from Georgia, and one each from North Carolina, Alabama, Mississippi and Maryland.

By Union standards they were indifferently armed, with a bewildering variety of muskets and rifles and old household guns which had been converted the year before into modern weapons (by removal of the flintlock mechanism and drilling the barrels anew). There were already a few Yankee weapons scattered among the ranks, and in some brigades, where state governments or rich men had seen to their needs, there were shining new guns.

As Jackson galloped to his cavalry screen, where he might see for himself what lay ahead, he carried in his pocket a dispatch from General Lee which might change the current of their affairs. And high time, Jackson thought. The words of the order were uppermost in his mind today:

> Whatever movement you make against Banks, do it speedily, and if successful drive him back towards the Potomac, and create the impression, as far as possible, that you design threatening that line. . . .

Lee's selection of a victim for Jackson referred to General Nathaniel Prentiss Banks, an energetic volunteer from a life of politics, former Congressman and Governor of Massachusetts. He was already a victim of a Jackson assault, and though courageous, he was something less than an imaginative student of war. He lay now at the town of Strasburg, behind entrenchments, his force cut in half by the transfer of General Shields to Fredericksburg. General Frémont, his little army once mauled by Jackson, was reorganizing to the westward. Altogether, the enemy could count fifty thousand to sixty thousand men—if they could be concentrated.

This was a week in which it seemed that the Federal armies could do no wrong, and that no dangers were great enough to cause the Union anxiety. The rebellion seemed beyond the aid of its armies, let alone the puny force under Jackson. New Orleans had just fallen. The line of the Mississippi had crumbled along most of its length, with the bloody repulse of the Confederates at Shiloh. And Albert Sidney Johnston was dead, too. A vast army was creeping up the tidewater rivers toward Richmond, and Federal warships could actually be sighted from the city. It was growing late everywhere, it seemed.

Jefferson Davis had decided to abandon the capital. Military stores were being evacuated, and the records of the Confederacy were packed for flight. Lee could see only a forlorn hope, that

Jackson, if reinforced, might so menace Washington as to panic Lincoln and Stanton and the rest of the amateur war makers of the North, and induce them to relax their strangling coils. The eloquent implication was in Lee's order to Jackson. There was not a word of the prospect to anyone else. Not an officer in Jackson's command had an inkling of the stakes for which the army was to play.

Jackson's troops could not know what was afoot, but they guessed shrewdly why they lay in this spot, a crossroads vital in the Shenandoah Valley terrain. One road led eastward over the mountains toward Warrenton and Culpeper; the other northward toward Strasburg and Winchester. The men understood that their commander intended to keep them guessing. He was already far in advance of Federal intelligence, which still had him placed near Harrisonburg, three long marches to the south. The Union high command was so confident, in this moment, that General McDowell, with his forty thousand troops at their Potomac base on Aquia Creek, was launching a drive southward; he was to join McClellan before Richmond. That would be fatal to the Confederacy.

Jackson moved through the short remainder of the day as if unaware of the guessing game he inspired. He had already sown confusion among his own people, as well as the enemy. Now approaching him in the Valley, for example, was his new lieutenant, General Dick Ewell, who was indulging in a high-pitched rage unusual even for him. Jackson had called him over the Blue Ridge from his camp near Culpeper, and after night-and-day marches, he had arrived at Conrad's Store, a village rendezvous. But when he arrived, proud of the men who had suffered the forbidding roads, Jackson was gone—no one knew where. Ewell burst into flights of profanity that revealed his decided gift for the art. His coming had been colorful.

The troops were cold, for freezing rains had fallen overnight; yet they came down into Hawksbill Valley, led by Louisiana men under the Pelican flags, with bands blaring away at "Listen to the Mocking Bird."

Ewell was in such a state that he could listen to nothing.

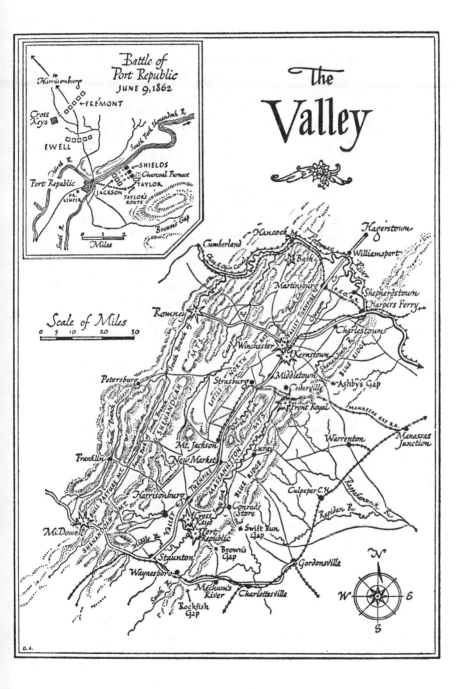

The
Valley

Battle of
Port Republic
JUNE 9, 1862

Scale of Miles
0   5   10   20   30

Major General Richard Stoddert Ewell—the army knew no other like him. An erstwhile cavalry captain in the Old Army with long service in the West, an untamed Indian fighter who preserved some of the atmosphere of the plains. Wherever he went, there tagged at his heels an overgrown Apache boy, whom Ewell called Friday, the bane of the army's existence, hailed on all sides as the most accomplished thief among a band of professionals.

Ewell sprang of a prominent Georgetown family and was descended of a hero of the Revolution. His appearance belied his gentle heritage and his West Point training as well. Small and short, bald as an egg, with a sharp, high-domed head and a wistful face with a long, swooping nose, he reminded almost everyone of a ridiculous bird. He had a habit of cocking his head on one side and then the other, as he cried out in his peeping voice. He lisped badly. In the midst of a rational conversation he was known to interrupt, squealing, "Now why do you suppose President Davis made me a major general anyway?"

He had, like Jackson, a perverse intestinal ailment, as a result of which he would eat but one dish—the wheat cereal, frumenty. He was explosive, fearless, and a soldier who saw warfare as a simple matter, much as it had been on the plains. He knew Jackson slightly, had seen him in Mexico, and thought him a queer bird; he was aware that the Valley commander had enjoyed a reputation as a goose of sorts at the Virginia Military Institute. He thought, now, that he was beginning to understand.

One of Jackson's colonels, James A. Walker of the Thirteenth Virginia, rode to Ewell's headquarters, at Conrad's Store, on a visit. He found General Ewell in such a state that he could not transact his business, and he was on the point of leaving when Ewell caught him.

"Colonel Walker, did it ever occur to you that General Jackson is crazy?"

"I don't know, General. We used to call him Tom Fool at the Institute, but I don't suppose he is really crazy."

"I tell you, sir, he is as crazy as a March hare. He has gone away, I don't know where, and left me here with some instructions to stay until he returns, but Banks' whole army is advancing on me and I haven't the most remote idea where to communicate with General Jackson. I tell you, sir, he is crazy and I will just march my division away from here. I do not mean to have it cut to pieces at the behest of a crazy man."

Ewell's cavalry chief, Colonel T. T. Munford, brought in a Federal prisoner, and Ewell questioned him almost savagely. He found that General Shields, with some eight thousand troops, was on the march east to join General McDowell at Fredericksburg, and would pass so near that he could be struck. Ewell was beside himself with the desire to attack Shields but could not do so until he had permission from Jackson. In growing excitement, he directed Munford to take his troopers and a couple of guns and impede the march of Shields by burning bridges, laying ambuscades, hitting at his wagon train—anything. He ordered Munford to report to him before leaving, at midnight.

Munford left a record of it: "He asked me to hand him a map and with the aid of a miserable lard lamp he attempted to show me where General Jackson was. Before I knew what he was after he sprang out of bed, with only a night shirt on—no carpet on the floor—and down on his knees he went; his bones fairly rattled. His bald head and long beard made him look more like a witch than a general. He became much excited, pointed out Jackson's position, General Shields' and General McDowell's . . .

"Then with an ugly oath, he said, 'This great wagon-hunter is after a Dutchman, the old fool. General Lee at Richmond will have little use for wagons if all these people close in around him; we are left out here in the cold. Why I could crush Shields before night if I could move from here. This man Jackson is certainly a crazy fool, an idiot. Now look at this.'

"Handing me a small piece of paper upon which was written, 'Headquarters, Valley District, May 1862, General R. S. Ewell: Your dispatch received. Hold your position. Don't move. I have driven Gen. Milroy from McDowell. Through God's assistance have captured most of his wagon train . . . Respectfully, T. J. Jackson, Major General'

"Ewell jumped to his feet, ran all over the room and said, 'What has Providence to do with Milroy's wagon train? Mark my words, if this old fool keeps this thing up and Shields joins McDowell we will go up at Richmond! I'll stay here but you do all you can to keep these people from getting together.' "

This explosion was scarcely over when Ewell was once more roused from his bed, this time by a courier in search of his colonel. He came up the steps, his saber banging at his side, and rapped on the door, calling for his officer.

"Come in and light the lamp," Ewell yelled. "Look under the bed. Do you see him there? Do you know how many steps you came up?"

"No, sir."

"Well, I do, by God. By every lick you gave them with that thing you have hanging about your feet—which you'll hook up when you come to my quarters. Do you know how many ears you have? You'll leave here with one less and maybe two, if you ever wake me again this time of night, looking for your damned colonel."

Ewell descended at last from his rage when Colonel Ashby arrived.

"I've been in hell for three days, Ashby. Hell. What's the news from General Jackson?"

Ashby could report details of the victory, which cheered Ewell, and he warmed with the prospect of action in some rational campaign. He was to have another day or so of confusion. He had orders from Jackson to stay where he was—but these were superseded by surprising dispatches from Richmond. General Joseph E. Johnston, their commander, ordered Ewell to move back to the east, to face the threat to Richmond.

Thus Ewell, in a dilemma, taking with him his beloved Friday and a handful of officers, went forth to find Jackson. He rode from Swift Run Gap, across the Valley, and met his new chief. The commander was more than sane.

Jackson relieved Ewell's distress with an appeal to Lee, who agreed to leave Ewell in the Valley, and also proposed once more an attack on Banks. And Jackson wrote out, at Ewell's in-

sistence, an order to protect his lieutenant from possible censure
of the high command. Ewell, in fact, wrote the order, and Jackson copied and signed it:

> . . . As you are in the Valley District, you constitute
> a part of my command. Should you receive orders different
> than those sent from these headquarters please advise
> me. . . .
> You will please move your command so as to encamp
> between New Market and Mount Jackson on next Wednes-
> day night unless you receive orders from a superior
> officer. . . .

Telegrams to Lee explained the details, and Ewell went back
to his command, to bring the men forward. With confusion
ended for the moment, the army was to prepare for action.
Ewell and Jackson had studied each other with care and had
parted friends; they found themselves more alike than seemed
possible. Jackson frowned, shaking his head, at each outbreak
of Ewell's profanity, which dwindled away during the interview. But he was attracted by the little man's impatient prodding; he was spoiling for a fight, and he would ask no quarter,
Jackson judged.

Ewell revealed the kinship of spirit in orders to one of his
brigadiers, General L. O'B. Branch: "You can't bring tents;
tent flies without poles, if you must, or tents cut down to that
size, and only as few as are indispensable. No mess-chests or
trunks. It is better to leave these things where you are than to
throw them away after starting. We can get along without anything but food and ammunition. The road to glory cannot be
followed with much baggage."

Ewell was ready to bring all of his troops to Jackson, and
though the dratted war plans were secret, he had a fair idea of
what lay ahead. He gave the impression that he was to enjoy it.

General Jackson's body servant was a large, handsome mulatto of about the General's own age, by the name of Jim. When
Jackson was in headquarters, Jim was constantly about. Tonight, as the camp darkened at New Market, Jim had work. He
prepared a full supper for the men of the staff and carried to

Jackson only a crust of cornbread and a pitcher of milk. The General would not eat until he had been given the nightly treatment of cold towels placed across his naked chest and abdomen, which he found helpful. He then took his simple food and remained standing where he had eaten. Jim understood his painfully erect position: The General believed that his organs functioned properly only when he stood, that their normal position was possible only when he held himself bolt upright. He did not waste these moments. Jim could hear Jackson's muttering and knew that he was at work.

The General was committing to memory a chart of the Valley geography, and he knew in an instant the road mileage separating any two towns of the area. He called them off now in the same way he had, last summer, memorized an artillery chart, charges, size of shot and range. These grew out of long-established mental habits, by now inflexible.

When the General finished his strange work, and had knelt in prayer for a time, Jim disappeared. He was a man of high spirits, a favorite of Jackson's staff, and one who lived dangerously.

"My General is one hard man on this temperance business," he had told the officers. "But you know it don't carry over to me. No, sir, it don't apply on old Jim. Somebody's got to do the General's drinkin' for him, and most of his laughin', too."

Jim had expanded visibly in the General's service during the war, and lorded it over his friends among the servants and the occasional women he met on the route. He became a companion hero in the legends of the General which he spread continually.

Jackson strayed into the camp. He made his way to General Taylor and sat quietly beside him, staring at the Louisiana troops as if he could not make them out. He asked a few questions about them, admired their orderly ways, sucked a couple of lemons, accepted a piece of hardtack from an officer, drank a bit of water and wandered off. He left an order with Taylor: The Louisiana troops were to lead the army. Before dawn. He would not tell him which road to take. That would be revealed in the morning. Taylor grumbled curses as the commander went away in the darkness.

One of Taylor's men had gaped at Stonewall from his fireside, in wonder, committing his image to memory. He was to write his impression: "He was dressed in a suit of gray homespun with a brimmed cap. He looked like a good driving overseer or manager with plenty of hard horse sense, but no accomplishments or other talents, nothing but plain direct sense. It was because his manners had so little of the man of the world or because he repressed all expression that he had the appearance of being a man of not above average ability. The remark was made by one of us after staring at him a long time, that there must be some mistake about him, if he was an able man, he showed it less than any man any of us had ever seen."

The campfires burned down in the groves, and it grew colder. Only the pickets could be heard. Fog rolled in as morning came. It was May twenty-first, gray and unpromising.

Jackson had scarcely slept, but there was no trace of fatigue; instead, he was unusually animated. He trotted to the Louisiana headquarters and sent Taylor's columns northward on the pike, in the vanguard of the army. After less than a mile, Jackson countermanded his order. He turned Taylor's men to their right, heading east, and the men, who had assumed they were to assault the town of Strasburg, found themselves on the road which climbed the lone passable gap over the fifty-mile barrier of the Massanutton Mountains, that singular range which lies like a fortress between the forks of the Shenandoah.

Within two hours the army had disappeared from the Valley people, who could not imagine its destination. Perhaps they were to be deserted to the enemy. It had happened before. The troops were driven from dawn to dusk, for two days in succession, passing over the mountain road Ewell's men had used just a few days before. In the ranks they cursed and shook their heads. It was unanimous, almost. This commander was mad. He marched their legs off to get them to his side, and then, evading the enemy, he marched them back again.

Jackson rode in the front of the column, not far behind Ashby's cavalry screen, which cut them off from the world. He went along as always, on that shambling little sorrel horse, his huge feet thrust outward in the stirrups, suffering the gait of his mount, his expression wooden. General Taylor thought, charitably, that Jackson had a poet's soul and was demonstrating the beauties of the Valley in spring with tours of its charms. The men wished they were down on the Peninsula, facing McClellan, where there was a war.

The column poured down into the Luray Valley, just east of the Massanutton screen, and turned north once more. Far ahead lay the town of Front Royal, and there, by special edict of Lincoln's Secretary of War, one Union regiment held the bridges of the Shenandoah.

2

★★★ FRONT ROYAL

May twenty-third dawned in unseasonable warmth, and by midmorning the distances of the Valley country shimmered with heat. Jackson's columns suffered despite the shade of the almost unbroken forests of Luray which swept upward on either side of the army, along the mountain spurs. The eastern Valley lay quiet, rich with bird song, and beginning to steam under the brilliant sky. There was nothing to signal the opening of a bold bid by the little army of Jackson, whose aim was no less than the expulsion of the Federal host from the Shenandoah.

Jackson had divulged nothing, as usual. He had prayed, and sent his bidding to Ewell: "Let us, relying upon God, prepare for attacking Banks. . . ." The commander had spent the night in the open, and near-by troops had heard singing from his headquarters as he worshiped with some of his numerous preachers. One of the hymns was a favorite of the General's: "There Is a Fountain Filled with Blood." The orders issued to the infantry seemed dull and routine: The column to continue to the north, Ewell's division leading, just as before. Jackson was busy with the cavalry, however. He called Ashby back from Strasburg in the northwest, where he had been blinding General

Banks for several days. Ashby was to cross the rough foothills of the Massanuttons and come into Jackson's front, to cut the road and telegraph between Front Royal and Strasburg.

Munford with the Second Virginia was cutting the railroad bridges to the east of Front Royal, and yet another cavalry patrol was cutting the wires linking the town with Washington. It was not long after the sun rose that Jackson, unknown even to all of his staff, had insured the isolation of Front Royal from the world, just as if he were a surgeon preparing to remove some malignant growth.

The troops paced on through the morning. Since McDowell, they had been hurried 120 miles, but they now seemed fresh. They were also undetected by the enemy, whose latest information placed Jackson sixty miles to the southwest lying quietly in front of Banks.

Some of the final orders of the night past were a bit disturbing, especially to the private soldiers, whose nose for bloodshed was infallible: Knapsacks to be left behind. Not a tent to be allowed. While the men were debating the seriousness of these orders, Jackson handled a complaint from a chaplain, a Catholic priest who declared that he could not hold services without the privacy of a tent. Jackson permitted this single exception to his order.

Ewell had spent the night just ten miles from Front Royal, and he now got orders from Jackson which enlightened him as to the commander's intentions. The column was abruptly wheeled off the main road into town, which was exposed at the foot of river cliffs and under Union guns. The men went eastward over rough country to a ruder track called the Gooney Manor Road, which entered Front Royal from the south.

The troops at last learned the identity of their intended victims—the Federal First Maryland, which held the town, the bridges and approaches. Ewell halted the column to call up his own First Maryland, under Colonel Bradley Johnson. The troops, who had lately joined complaints against harsh regulations as to enlistees, now stepped through at swagger step, and men resting by the roadside cheered them as they went to the front. Noon drew near.

At Strasburg, General Banks, the Union commander, was oblivious to the gathering storm before his outpost. With the assistance of meddlers from Washington who blithely moved his troops by telegraph as if they were chess pieces, Banks had managed to spread himself thin, so that he lay in ideal condition for crippling attacks. He was himself lulled to sleep.

In Washington, the rebellion was so nearly over, it seemed, that recruiting offices had been closed, and the capital abandoned itself to unofficial celebration. Banks complained, in fact, that there was little prospect of his seeing action, much as he relished the scent of burning powder.

He had been stripped of the forces of General Shields, now out of the Valley. The troops he had left to him were placed in an almost perfect triangle, the base of which lay across the northern face of the Massanutton range.

Banks himself held the western end of the triangle at Strasburg, with its southward-facing trenches and huge piles of stores. He had sixty-four hundred men posted in that town. The eastern end, at Front Royal, was manned by the one thousand troops of Colonel John R. Kenly, with a couple of cannon. The northern tip was Winchester, where 1,450 Federal troops held the position.

Kenly had not been inactive at Front Royal, though he was severely limited. He had sent into the Luray Valley a patrol of horsemen and infantry, which had captured a single Confederate. From this prisoner, Kenly learned that Rebel columns were expected—a report which was lost on Banks, who disregarded it and even ordered to Strasburg the few horsemen of the little expedition. Front Royal was thus left blinded.

Kenly had thrown his pickets a mile and a half south of the village, with two infantry companies in support. Another company guarded a railroad at some distance from the town, and the bulk of his force, six companies, lay in camp near the big wagon bridge. Two companies of the Twenty-ninth Pennsylvania lay between the forks of the Shenandoah to cover the railroad bridges. The only artillery on hand was good—a pair of Parrott ten-pounders, superior in range and accuracy to Confederate smooth-bores. Kenly, though more alert than his superiors, was not uninfected by their lassitude; it seemed incredible that he could be struck by any other than a tiny guerrilla force. Most of his men drowsed in a siesta.

At 1 P.M. the Confederate advance appeared on heights south of Front Royal, and officers halted the leading troops, which spread in formation, still hidden from the Federals. They were the First Maryland of Johnson's, and the Louisiana Tigers under Major Rob Wheat. They waited while General Ewell and his staff examined the country.

The tents of the enemy were plain on the river bottom, and smoke went up from their fires. Immediately at hand was the outlying Federal picket. A couple of men slumped in the shade, but only one figure was in full view—a young sentry stretched beneath a rail shelter, who rose on an elbow and stared, at first in curiosity, as four horsemen appeared on the slope above him: Generals Ewell, Taylor, Steuart and Edward Johnson. Despite their impressive uniforms, he did not appear alarmed for several moments. He at last came to his feet, fired at the riders and turned to flee. Other blue-clad men ran behind him.

The sentries fled in vain, for a group of Jackson's horsemen cut them off at the rear and captured the entire post. The cavalry reached these men only seconds before the first companies of the Maryland regiment pounded past, on their way to charge the village. The muskets set Federal drums to throbbing, and bugle calls rang in the little valley.

Jackson was some distance away, riding toward the scene with Kyd Douglas and others of his staff. Douglas saw a woman in a white dress running desperately from the town and into a ravine, as if to hide from those in the village. Douglas went out to meet her; she waved a bonnet to him, and when he came near she astonished him by calling out his name. He recognized her as Belle Boyd, a tall, somewhat long-faced brunette with prominent teeth. Douglas took her to the General. The young woman panted, red-faced.

"I knew it must be Stonewall when I heard the guns," she said. "Their force is small—just the Maryland boys and some guns and cavalry. Their guns cover the railroad bridge, but not the wagon bridge. Charge now, and you will get them all. Good-bye, and give my love to the boys." She was off.

Jackson stared after her, beginning to smile as she called back to Douglas, "If you see me in the town, remember, you haven't seen me today."

General Taylor watched the meeting in surprise and, as the woman talked, saw that Jackson not only trusted her, but that her information was not new to him. Taylor's Valley education had commenced in earnest. He wrote of the scene:

"Jackson was possessed of these facts before he left New Market; but, as he never told anything, it was news to me, and gave me an idea of the strategic value of the Massanutton [the mountain range they had just crossed and flanked]—pointed out, indeed, by Washington before the Revolution. There also dawned on me quite another view of our leader than the one from which I had been regarding him for two days past."

Isabelle Boyd, just past her eighteenth birthday, was already celebrated as a Confederate spy. She had shot, and allegedly killed, a Federal soldier who had insulted her in the family home at Martinsburg. Two months before she had been arrested and taken to Baltimore as a spy, only to be released.

She was the daughter of a Martinsburg storekeeper who was now a private in the Second Virginia of the Stonewall Brigade, an attractive, if not handsome, girl of high spirits. She was educated at Mount Washington Female College in Balti-more, but had more lately been given to passing secret messages to Turner Ashby and to stealing, and sending to the South, guns and swords of Federal troops. She had been under constant sus-picion, but today had stolen past the Front Royal sentries—though when she appeared in the open, pickets fired at her, and artillery was turned in her direction.

There was little time now for reflection upon the attributes of the commander or his spies; the Confederate vanguard was already under heavy fire in Front Royal. From the hill, Jack-son saw the opening scenes of a brief pitched battle: Federals streamed across the meadows out of the town, to take up a strong position on the road to Winchester. Women and chil-dren called and waved in joy from the houses of the town, and

some danced on the porches as the freed Negroes and Federal
soldiers ran past them. Cannon began to roll. Jackson was reassured by what he saw: the position was clearly indefensible
before a determined attack. But at this moment his front ranks
were being cut down. He took over direction of the assault.

The Marylanders and the Tigers drove down from the east,
jogging through the streets of Front Royal; they had a vicious
few moments in driving a knot of Federals who had taken post
in a hospital building, and as they ran on, a number of gray-
clad bodies lay in the sunshine. The action boiled on into the
road to Winchester. There the rifled Federal guns were driving
men to cover and ripping apart formations. Some of Ewell's
guns, brought up in haste, were outranged, and there was a
frantic search for better cannon. It developed that the entire
division carried only three rifled cannon, and while these were
being dragged from the rear, the infantry suffered.

The infantry fanned out like veterans; there was a frontal
assault, and, with precise timing, the Sixth Louisana flanked
the enemy by crossing one of the rail bridges, and others of
Taylor's brigade swept wide to the west, in a second flanking
movement. The guns were in danger from the Rebel advance,
and Colonel Kenly became anxious. Within moments he saw
a band of Confederate cavalry already across the bridge of the
Shenandoah's South Fork. If it reached the North Fork as well,
his only means of escape was gone. His men fired their last
rounds at the charging Marylanders in their front, then went at
a run, following their guns in rapid retreat. Several companies
of the Federals began firing their camp, and tents, stores, wagons
went up in sheets of flame and white smoke. The retreating
enemy fired two bridges, and on their heels came the men of
Jackson.

The General yelled until he was hoarse, urging men forward.
Louisianans and Virginians did not hesitate. They drove across
the smoking bridges almost on the heels of the Yankees, and a
company plunged into the rain-swollen stream, ordered to ex-
tinguish the flames at the opposite end of the bridge; two or
three men who could not swim were drowned, but the troops
pushed on. Cavalry hammered overhead. Among the first horse-

men was Jackson, who emerged soot-covered, his beard and uniform singed. Men burned their hands flinging burning brands from the bridge into the water. The chase formed up.

Jackson found pitifully little support, but in a fury hastened his handful of horsemen forward. He soon had them beyond the smoke screen laid by the burning enemy camp, and for a few moments the river was dark with swimming horses. The Sixth Virginia went up with Jackson. It was then too late, for the General rode to an eminence and saw below the long blue column of Kenly, almost running toward safety on the Winchester road. His opportunity for annihilation was gone.

The General groaned, "Oh, what an opportunity for artillery. Oh, if my guns were here!" He snapped to a staff officer, "Get to the rear and order up every rifled gun and every brigade in the army. Hurry!"

The Sixth Virginia dashed ahead of him toward the enemy. Ewell joined Jackson, to watch the impending clash of horsemen and the mass of well-armed infantry. The Virginians went in like centaurs. They swiftly brushed aside a screen of New York cavalry, and sent to the rear the frightened town boys, who were actually strapped to their saddles and wore breastplates. The Virginians left them far behind and slashed at the writhing end of the Federal column, now strung out for two miles along the road.

At first there was murder of the horses and riders at the village of Cedarville, for the Virginians drove in four abreast, at top speed, crowded between rail fences, and the volleys cut down the first ranks. Then the horses threshed in and were bayoneted, and men speared. But the men on foot could not long bear it; companies broke into bits, and men who had been tearing down rail fences to give them room to receive the Rebel infantry now fled. The units were surrounded by swooping horsemen, slashed with sabers, dropped by revolver fire, and harried until the last of them went into rout, through orchards and down creek banks. Their commander was himself cut down with deep wounds. The big guns were soon given up; one went into Rebel hands on the ground, and another was dragged some distance up the road, where two enterprising Rebels spotted it, borrowed farm horses from a near-by field and dragged it home.

Jackson had stayed near the front most of the time. Once two horsemen in his path heard his angry shout: "Get out of the way of my men!"

Jackson and Ewell shouted lavish praise.

"I have never seen such a charge of cavalry," Jackson said.

"The most gallant passage at arms I ever saw," Ewell shouted.

They watched the first prisoners coming in. More than six hundred were captives, including all the artillerymen of the post. The Federals had 32 dead and 122 wounded. Jackson's forces had lost 11 dead, 15 wounded.

In the crowded town, Kyd Douglas came upon Belle Boyd, pink-cheeked from her recent run. She greeted him as if the meeting were a delightful surprise and pinned a rose on his lapel.

"Remember that it's blood-red," she said, "and that it's my colors."

The final stroke, delivered at Jackson's order in the moment when the opportunity seemed gone, had been delivered by 250 Virginia horsemen. One of the prisoners said they had estimated the furious band of pursuers at three thousand. The Virginians had paid a price, for two of their most promising leaders— Captains George F. Sheetz and John Fletcher—were dead.

Jackson seemed satisfied with the day's work but pressed his investigation of the artillery's troubles with a scowling face, and, when he had found his error, made plans to improve his methods. He had a group of young riders as his orderlies during the battle, recruits from one of Ashby's undisciplined troops. In the midst of the fighting, when he had sent back for his big guns, he told one of these boys to urge the artillerymen to come in quickly over the well-used main road into the town rather than over the rough track the infantry had taken. The boy disappeared, not to be heard from again; the guns were hauled forward laboriously, painfully slow, over Jackson's original path, and much time had been lost. The General resolved that henceforth he would use a picked corps of orderlies who were worthy of his trust, so that he would not again lose his chance to blow to bits his cornered enemies.

Jackson gave his men little time to care for the dead and wounded, or to glut themselves on the captured stores. He sent them to sleep early and forbade them to light fires in the exposed places.

He went into the lowlands where the fogs now rose, to sit by a fire with General Taylor. He told the Louisianan they would march together in the morning, but said little else. Taylor, tired and upset by the death of friends, was quiet. "I fancied he looked at me kindly," Taylor wrote, "and interpreted it into an approval of the conduct of the brigade."

Jackson sat for hours, without speaking, his gaze lost in the fire. Taylor thought he might have been praying as he laid plans to overtake the shattered wing of the army of Banks, and to fall upon that commander himself.

When he was interrupted, the news was good. Ashby, ranging far up toward Winchester, had captured two locomotives, and Jackson already had all of Kenly's wagons.

He also had a problem to ponder: What would General Banks do now, since his flank had been turned? The General made clear his thinking in one of his rare, but careful, records:

> In the event of Banks leaving Strasburg he might escape toward the Potomac, or if we moved directly to Winchester he might move via Front Royal toward Washington. In order to watch both directions, and at the same time advance upon him if he remained at Strasburg, I determined, with the main body of the army, to strike the turnpike near Middletown.

But no one knew of his decision to move to this halfway point on the Winchester road. Even Ewell, as yet, knew nothing of tomorrow's plans.

Just twelve miles away to the west, at Strasburg, Banks gave a curious demonstration of a man of war whose courage and caution were hopelessly, and dangerously, mixed. By four in the afternoon, Banks had a report of the attack at Front Royal, but he did little about it, pushing out a regiment with two guns to make an investigation. He still entertained the thought that Front Royal had been struck by a small raiding party, since he knew Jackson to be far away from that spot, on the word of his most clever spies. By nightfall, Banks was persuaded that something more serious was afoot. He wired Stanton in Washington: "5,000 Rebels have driven Kenly back to Middletown. This force has been gathering in the mountains, it is said, since Wednesday."

But this did not seem to alarm Banks. He sat, amid the vast stacks of army stores he had gathered in the village, as if there were no prospect that he might be cut off.

General G. H. Gordon, a veteran who had been at West Point with Jackson, now undertook to point out to Banks the danger of their position. Gordon went to headquarters after supper and spent some hours in explaining that Banks had a compelling duty to retreat toward Winchester.

"You must get together all the possible stores, General, and load the sick and wounded, and destroy what we can't carry," Gordon said. He made his pleas in vain.

Soon Banks was advised of the return of the regiment he had sent toward Front Royal, and he got the report: All roads leading toward the Rebel positions were closed tight. A cavalry screen lay everywhere. Still Banks did not take action.

Gordon tried him further: "It is not a retreat, General. It's a perfectly honorable military movement to avoid being cut off, to keep your stores and your wounded from falling to the enemy."

That seemed to sting Banks, and the dignified politician, becoming angry, rose rapidly to his feet.

"I must develop the force of the enemy! By God, Sir, I will not retreat! We have more to fear from the opinions of our friends than the bayonets of our enemies!"

"That is not a sound military reason to occupy a false position," Gordon said.

He walked through the Federal camp, now at 11 P.M., seeing that everything was as usual. The sutlers were still cadging the dollars from the troops with their sharp bargains, and traveling actors raising tumults of laughter in their tented stalls. There was music, and laughter, and the army seemed determined to stay up through the night. Gordon thought to himself as he went to his tent: Tomorrow will see some merriment—Jackson.

Gordon took steps to save his own troops and had them packing their baggage wagons through most of the night; they were soon on the road to Winchester, and safety. He had a start of some hours on the rest of the army, it developed.

At midnight the situation became unmistakable, even to Banks. One of the survivors of Front Royal puffed into camp with the news: Kenly was dead, his command cut to pieces, the First Maryland decimated, the cavalry vanished. The Rebels were from fifteen thousand to twenty thousand strong—and already well on their way to Strasburg.

There followed some confusing messages to Washington, and then Banks, upon hearing the name of Jackson, jumped into furious action. He hustled his command northward toward Winchester, aware that Jackson was somewhere in his path.

Before dawn the weather broke, and a hard rain fell upon the armies.

3

★★★ WINCHESTER

Jackson's troops were miserable in the night, huddling in the rain, having forgotten victory and Yankees as well, except for the spoils which came in with skulkers and Negro camp servants from the battlefield.

Soon after midnight, the first troops were ordered to prepare for the march once more, and straggled into formations; but it was to require long, costly hours before all was ready for the road. At any rate, there was no need for the buglers on this dull, roaring, wet morning, nor for the familiar flies, either. One of the recruits had lately written his family:

"When we open our eyes in the morning we find the canvas roofs and walls of our tents black with them. It needs no morning reveille then to rouse the soldier. . . . The tickling sensations about the ears, eyes, mouth, nose . . . will awaken a regiment of men from innocent sleep to wide-awake profanity more promptly than the near beat of the alarming drum."

The men whom Jackson drove in pursuit of the enemy were still under his strict discipline, willing, orderly, ready to fight, but worn by yesterday's exertions and the long marches of the month, which were now beginning to tell. Most of them were

40

volunteers, with the familiar contempt for the drafted men who were sprinkled through the ranks; but the latter were striving desperately to win acceptance, and morale was thus high.

In the darkness, sergeants of the Louisiana regiments bawled out in French, to the continuing wonder of Jackson's Virginia mountain men. One Rebel had shouted: "That-there furriner calls out er lot of gibberish, and them Dagoes maneuvers like hell beatin' tanbark—jest like he was talkin' good sense!" The Creoles were among the first on the road that morning.

There were few aristocrats and slaveowners in these ranks. Most of them were from little towns and villages, tenants and laborers. But, as everywhere in the army, there was conflict between gentleman and commoner. One corporal had exploded when challenged by his officer for violation of a camp rule: "God damn you, I own niggers up the country!" And another, ordered under arrest, had cried, "I'll not do it. I was a gentleman before I joined your damned company and by God you want to make a damned slave of me!"

The seat of learning, such as it was, lay in the Rockbridge Artillery, whose First Company boasted four Masters of Arts, twenty graduates of Washington College, and some forty students from Washington and the University of Virginia. More typical were the North Carolina troops. In one company, thirty-six of sixty had signed muster rolls with their X; in another, fifty-four of one hundred were illiterate. The average was 40 per cent who could neither read nor write.

All could understand Old Jack this day, or thought they could; and, before dawn, going slowly in the road, halting, waiting, moving on again, they advanced from Front Royal toward the enemy.

After daylight, as if to increase their burdens, hail fell from the murky sky. A burial party had just sloshed in from its muddy chore when the storm broke.

Jackson had ironclad rules about the marching of his men, but today neither he nor any man could put them into effect. In the bad weather and confusion, conflicting reports from the front, and the weariness of the men, it was absurd to think of marching fifty minutes in each hour, halting smartly to stack arms at each resting spot, with a brief hour for lunch. On most marching days, Jackson sought to hurry them, up and down the columns, with his familiar "Close up, men. Hurry up. Close up." General A. R. Lawton, who became intimately familiar with him in battle, was to describe Jackson's state of mind, as he rode past his lean columns:

"He had small sympathy with human infirmity. He was a one-idea-ed man. He looked upon the broken down men and stragglers as the same thing. He classed all who were weak and weary, who fainted by the wayside, as men wanting in patriotism. If a man's face was as white as cotton and his pulse so low you could scarcely feel it, he looked upon him merely as an inefficient soldier and rode off impatiently. He was the true type of all great soldiers . . . he did not value human life when he had an object to accomplish. He could order men to their death as a matter of course."

Through the previous night, and on this unpleasant Saturday morning, he had devoted himself to the problem of hurling his men against the enemy. Once Jackson had determined to march so as to check any possible maneuver of General Banks's, he puzzled out for himself the moves he must make—with as little help as possible from the staff. Even so, those officers were busy, including the sedate chief, the Reverend Dabney, who was by now clad in regulation Confederate gray, and was no longer embarrassed when he appeared in camp with his rolled umbrella and tall beaver hat and frock coat. (The men had a habit of screeching at the reverend, "Get on out of that bee gum. We see your feet's amoving.")

One of the night's most voluble, blasphemous laborers was Major John Harman—Old John—the brassy-voiced quartermaster, who was all but carrying Jackson's columns on his back over the poor Valley roads, heaving forward with his work gangs and squads of impressed soldiers the stupendous loads of ammunition and supplies. He had spent his civilian life as master of a line of drays and stagecoaches, and he knew the country as well as his work. Even in Jackson's command he was a power unto himself, defiant of restricting authority, though devoted to the commander and the sacred calling of Yankee extermination. Tonight the lines were strung out for more than twenty miles behind the army, the heavy trains at the mercy of the elements in the boggy roads.

Just before daylight, Jackson held a brief conference with Ewell, whose forces were to continue as the army's vanguard. Jackson had puzzled for hours over the character of Banks as it related to the map of the rugged country about them and the move he was now likely to make. But of all this, not a word to Ewell.

Ashby with his cavalry was to strike for Middletown at daybreak. And here Jackson was forced to reveal to Ewell more than a glimpse of his plans, for he had decided during the night to make a change in command. He had admired the hell-for-leather charge of Lieutenant Colonel Flournoy and his Virginia troopers about Cedarville, for the daring of that thrust had won the day for him. But he reasoned that a veteran like Brigadier General George H. Steuart of the Marylanders, with more than ten years in the old cavalry, would make better use of the mounted troops.

Thus Jackson told Ewell that he was placing two of his cavalry regiments under Steuart, and ordered them to depart soon after Ashby, striking for Newtown, a point just above Middletown.

General Taylor was to follow with his brigade, ready for action. Jackson's main force was behind, but would come up as soon as possible. The entire command, in short, was to concentrate on the route from Strasburg northward to Winchester, in hope that the Federals would choose that alley of retreat.

Jackson went with the vanguard, in a curious, impatient humor. Taylor assigned about one hundred men of the Louisiana Tigers to go with him, and they began to outdistance the larger column. Jackson no longer plagued the marching officers with commands to hurry forward. Instead, this morning, he seemed unsure of himself, and, when he reached Cedarville, sat by the road, looking as if he feared to leave the bridges which might offer Banks the chance to escape through Manassas Gap, if the Federal could summon courage for that bold move. At about

nine o'clock Jackson had word from Steuart: Banks was preparing to leave Strasburg.

Soon, with a battery of artillery and the gay Tigers of Rob
Wheat at his heels, Jackson rode within sound of firing. It was
not yet heavy, but it came through screens of woodland which
filled this Valley almost as far as the turnpike to Winchester. The
Tigers went up and were caught in the skirmishing. Prisoners
told Jackson that he was facing a part of the Twenty-ninth Pennsylvania, and that a handful of New England cavalry—the First
Maine and First Vermont—were fighting a delaying action.
Halts became frequent, and the Federal carbines took their toll
as the column pushed on.

At last Jackson looked over fields and their stone fences to
Middletown and a stunning spectacle, for as far as he could
see, north and south along the pike, was a dust canopy, and
beneath it flowed the dark column of the enemy, in full retreat
toward Winchester. Jackson and his vanguard had taken six
hours to cover the seven miles to Middletown. Banks was already
ahead of him. How far, he could not yet know. But he did not
hesitate.

Before he knew whether he faced overwhelming infantry, or
simply a wagon train on the move, Jackson dashed forward with
his few men. The guns went to work, blazing from behind a
fence. A party of Ashby's wild cavalry cut the procession at the
right, at the edge of the town, and Jackson saw the enemy train
in convulsions. It broke in a thousand places, with wagons turning out, and small parties of men turning back on one another.
Those who were able fled. Ashby went to the north, driving
remnants of the enemy ahead of him. Smoke began to mount
as Federals sought to burn their stores, but the Rebels were
too quick. The Tigers were soon at the looting, diving in and
out of the wagons like practiced despoilers, though at the approach of General Taylor they ceased and went sedately into
line.

Jackson could not know that there was already failure in the
road to the north of him, that the experiment with Steuart was
not working out as it should. Steuart had cut this same long
column, at Newtown, but in small force, and was even now being

driven off at the appearance of a relief party sent by Banks.

Jackson had no time for reflection, for a strange, broken, confusing battle was developing, as his men rounded up parties of the enemy and probed north and south, meeting tiny knots of resistance. Then, at a little after noon, Federal cavalry thundered into Middletown, two thousand strong, with a couple of guns behind. Their commander halted at first glimpse of the chaos along the road, but waved his men into a trot, and they came with drawn sabers.

Jackson's head was turned for this moment. He was off in the fields placing a couple of artillery pieces so as to cut off the Federals at the north. Kyd Douglas summoned Jackson's bodyguard, which the General had evaded, and these men crouched behind a stone wall at the roadside. Someone dragged a wagon across the pike. Near by, artillery trained batteries on the solid blue column of horsemen, and Taylor's Louisianans, now coming up, charged at a run. The village became a slaughter pen whose sight was to remain a memory with Jackson for life.

The Union riders dashed into storms of flying metal; at the close quarters none could miss the massed targets, and, in a screaming of horses and men flailing in the trap, the Federal cavalry disintegrated.

Jackson had returned to look at the scene, and, months later, when he made out his report, the vision of it crept in:

> In a few moments the turnpike, which had just before teemed with life, presented a most appalling spectacle of carnage and destruction. The road was literally obstructed with the mangled and confused mass of struggling and dying horses and riders.

The Confederates found more of the pitiful novice cavalrymen in the gory roadway, boys who had died strapped to their saddles, their antique breastplates torn with shell. The sight sickened even young Douglas, who confessed to a regret that he had ordered the slaughter.

The rear guard of the cavalry, now frightened and confused, milled in the roadway, turning as if to go back to Strasburg. At that instant Turner Ashby rode up, the swaggering cavalry chief on a sweat-gleaming black stallion, who within reach of Douglas and Jackson whipped out his saber, spurred the horse and sailed over the fence. He drove up the road, charging with his blade the two hundred or more enemy cavalrymen. Douglas thought he rode to certain death, but the sight of the reckless horseman seemed to demoralize the Federals. They fled with Ashby's sword beating about at their rear, tumbling more than one man to the ground. The flight broke in many directions. Ashby trotted back with a squad of prisoners herded before him.

Jackson turned on Ashby in an attempt at reprimand. "Ashby, you risk the success of the army with such foolish exposure—you must remember who you are, man."

Douglas grinned, and the cavalryman almost dared it, hearing in the commander's voice the reluctance with which he denounced such bravery. Jackson turned from the scolding with a sheepish expression on the long cheeks.

The General was now forced to an instant decision amid perplexing signs. To the south was the smudge of burning magazines and stores at Strasburg, fired by the Federals; to the north the enemy wagon train was disappearing. There was the frenzy of chase on every hand, as survivors of ruined wagons ran for safety. But where was Banks's infantry? If it was behind the cavalry, and still to pass Middletown, Jackson must call up his main force and prepare for battle; if the bulk of the enemy force had gone north, then pursuit must be hurried. Jackson ordered a number of townspeople brought to him for questioning, and from their stories concluded that the regiments of Banks had moved toward Winchester. He turned into the Valley Pike, pushing up his artillery and Taylor's brigade.

Through the afternoon he continued the slow, halting push until now, riding in fading daylight, he was less than a dozen miles from Winchester, still passing the litter of the Federal army at the roadside: wagons intact and ruined, Bibles, kettles, blankets, playing cards, letters, photographs, canned food, songbooks. It was the debris of a panic-stricken opponent.

Jackson was in a hopeful mood despite the escape of the enemy for the second day in succession. He looked forward to greater booty ahead, confident that his cavalry was playing havoc with the head of the Federal wagon train.

As he went to the north he stopped but once, to dismount and take a cracker from a Federal wagon, brushing half-heartedly at its unclean surface, and he rode, crunching the hard bread, like a Quixote on a slow-moving Rosinante, though utterly unaware that some of his classical-minded staff had compared him to the comic Spanish knight.

A fresh disappointment met him at the village of Newtown. He approached the place convinced that Banks, if he reached Winchester at all, would limp in without a wagon train, and thus be ready for the kill.

Jackson already planned the coup.

The rising growl of an artillery duel startled him, and he urged Sorrel into a gallop. He found two guns of the Rockbridge Artillery engaging the enemy at the village. The guns, he saw, were without infantry support.

His artillery chief, Colonel Stapleton Crutchfield, was in a rage over a wasted opportunity. He shouted his explanation to Jackson:

Ashby's men had fallen upon the leading section of Banks's train here and with a few wild shots had thrown it into flight. The wagons of sutlers were among the stores and were crammed with luxuries. The undisciplined troopers could not then be driven forward to strike the enemy. They turned aside by the hundred, to eat, or take horses, some of them swarming away like gypsy bands, leading stolen horses by the reins. Some infantrymen had come up at last, but when they sighted the wagons it was all over with them as well.

They went to the looting, and the guns were left without support. The running fight from Middletown had brought confusion, the advance was slowed and dissipated. Even now, as he sought Ashby, Jackson could find only fifty of the troopers; their commander was forced to admit that the rest had flown. It was to be weeks before some returned from their homes, where they had taken the horses.

Jackson had the looters driven from the wagons, but there was little time to deal with undisciplined men; the General made a mental note to have these troops punished in one of his strange morale-building ways: they were no longer to march in the van of the Army of the Valley.

Men grumbled behind his back at manifestations of his concern for the wagons: "Damned old wagon-hunter don't care for our bellies—all he's looking is his durned lemons." There were many who referred to him thereafter by a wry nickname: Lemon Squeezer.

Even his rage this evening did not prevent his remarkable and familiar gesture when an officer called a joke to him: Stonewall replied by throwing back his head with an exaggerated snap and gaping his mouth in a silent, tight-lipped mask of laughter.

The approach of the Stonewall Brigade drove the Federal artillery from the road, and as darkness fell the route-step battle became a nightmare for the weary troops. The Federals fought their rear-guard action with skill. There were frequent halts while skirmishers turned out to unroll a new line of battle. Each volley from the front threatened panic, and the leaders were driven back upon the column. Many veterans were to speak of the night as the most trying experience of the war; casualties were few, but the action was constant, and halts continued until dawn. In each brief halt, the troops sought rest. Men fell asleep holding to their muskets. Hundreds fell away in the darkness.

Jackson rode with Taylor for much of the way. The young officer overheard the conversation between Jackson and Old John Harman, when the quartermaster came up to report. Harman said the army's wagons were far back in the valley and that a bad road blocked his every effort to move them up.

There was quick anxiety in Jackson's voice.

"The ammunition wagons?"

"All right, General. They're here. I put double teams on them and brought them through."

A sigh of relief. "Ahhh." As if Jackson had no concern for other supplies.

Taylor sought to make a joke of it, saying to Harman, "Never mind the wagons, John. There are stores aplenty in Winchester, and the General has invited me to breakfast there tomorrow."

Taylor felt a quick, restraining hand on his sleeve, a warning from Jackson, who feared to tell anyone the least of his plans, and could not understand the jest. Remembering, Taylor wrote: "Without physical wants himself, he forgot that others were differently constituted, and paid little heed to commissariat, but woe to the man who failed to bring up ammunition. In advance his trains were left behind. In retreat he would fight for a wheelbarrow."

It was a remarkable group which rode about Jackson—the commander and his staff, in the forefront of an army in night fighting, passed wagons put to the torch by the Federals, which would signal the people of Winchester of Jackson's coming. Of the riders with Stonewall, only Ashby was alert, stiffly erect; this swarthy man with something of the Arab about his face was called the Black Knight by the younger officers. There was an unnatural grimness in him, understood only by those who knew of his vow to avenge the death of his brother at Federal hands. Sandie Pendleton, as always when sleepy, was irritable and snappish; Colonel Crutchfield, one of the army's leading devotees of sleep, muttered his disgust: "This is uncivilized." Dr. Hunter McGuire, the surgeon, said nothing, lost in his concern for his Winchester home. Douglas gave his attention to remaining awake.

Fire flashed through the night, almost in their faces. Horses reared. Yankee skirmishers had ambushed them, lying behind a wall as Jackson's party came. These men fled, to make another stand in the night. Jackson was sitting with some cavalry when a volley came. The horsemen reined in.

"Charge them! Charge!" Old Jack yelled. And when the riders broke for the rear under another volley, all but riding down Jackson, his thin voice rose even higher in anguish: "Shameful! Did you see anybody struck, sir? Did you see a man hurt? Surely they need not have run, at least until they were hurt?"

The way became easier until Kernstown, a village where Jackson had fought once before—tonight there was only a skirmish there. Officers came to Jackson frequently now, asking for a respite. Jackson refused to halt the column for the night.

At last, long after 1 A.M., Colonel Sam Fulkerson found Jackson:

"General, if I may be permitted to make a suggestion, I think the troops had better be rested for an hour or so; my men are falling by the roadside from fatigue and loss of sleep. Unless they are rested, I'll not be able to put up more than a thin line tomorrow."

Every time his command halted, this officer said, it left dozens of men behind, fallen asleep in fence corners and brush heaps.

Jackson did not cease to resist even then, though he was exceptionally fond of this brigade commander.

"Colonel, I do not yield even to you in my feeling for these gallant men. But I am obliged to sweat them tonight, sir, so that I can save their blood tomorrow.

"Just south of Winchester there is a line of hills—they must not be occupied by the enemy artillery. Our people must be there, and by daylight. I will give you two hours' rest."

When the order was passed, the men fell into the road.

Jackson agreed to leave Fulkerson's men behind, and to take forward his own old brigade; but when he saw the men drop in their tracks, he changed his mind. The entire army fell asleep. Jackson himself was almost the lone exception.

He dashed off a note to Ewell, who read it up front, on a parallel road, within sight of Federal pickets. It was only a rough sketch of the roads, streams and woods of country surrounding Winchester. In heavy outline was drawn the position of the troops of Banks, as well as Jackson's own position on the pike. Under this drawing was the laconic message:

"Attack at daylight."

With his orders finished, Jackson took over the guard. Men who stirred in sleep saw him. He stood in front of the sleeping vanguard, without a coat to protect him from the heavy dew. For about an hour he stood—and could bear it no longer. He woke his officers and passed the word to march.

Jackson's task this Sunday was simple, but by no means easy. He was confident that Ewell, with his troops on the road from Front Royal to the east, would come in on his right as he stormed the town. He suspected that Banks would have taken the commanding heights, and that would mean serious fighting.

The men were weary, but they went forward. They crossed a stream called Abraham's Creek when it was scarcely daylight, with the stars fading over them, and approached the hills. Jackson was one of the first to see shadowy figures of Federals on the slopes.

The timing was perfect. Ewell, with his one brigade and ten guns, swept down on the Federal positions just as Jackson was giving General Charles Winder his unmistakable orders: "You must occupy that hill."

The skirmish lines fanned up the slope, here and there driven back by savage blasts of artillery fire. Jackson's guns came up, and for half an hour challenged the heavier Federals. Many batteries were blasted; some of the Rockbridge guns remained in place until their wheels were gone, and the horses dead, and few men were left to serve the hot barrels. But in the end the Union guns were overcome. It was Taylor's men who finished them off.

Jackson first heard Ewell throw his men forward just as the sun was driving the mist from the field. There the First Maryland and the Twenty-first North Carolina were out front; the General then advanced his own brigade, and asked Douglas to take him to General Taylor. When he reached the Louisianan, the hot artillery duel was at its peak, and the Federal gunners, ever alert, had taken position by a stone wall running perpendicular to Jackson's position.

As Jackson rode through, the men began to cheer, but the order was passed quieting them, so that the enemy would not be signaled of the coming assault. The men then took off their hats, and Jackson removed his as well. The officers interpreted this as a touching tribute, but Douglas noted that the General drew the keen, searching glances of the privates, who sought in his face the signs of coming trouble.

Jackson greeted Taylor.

"General, can your brigade charge a battery?"

"It can try," Taylor said.

"Good. It must. Get the men forward." He pointed out the guns which were tearing holes in his infantry columns and beating down his own artillery. Taylor said no more. He took the men over the creek, and as they came onto the slope they walked into a shallow depression, where they were fully exposed to the enemy cannon above them. Men dropped in their files.

Taylor saw Jackson riding beside him and shouted that this was no place for the commander. Jackson went on as if he had not heard him. He was apparently unaware that he was under fire.

Taylor saw men ducking and darting in his column and shouted, "What the hell are you dodging for? If there's any more of it, you'll be halted under this fire for an hour." The men straightened up a bit and stormed forward.

Jackson halted to put a hand on Taylor's shoulder. "I'm afraid you're a wicked fellow."

Taylor's brigade swarmed into the open and the sun fell upon it; watching officers would recall the scene, a stirring picture of men walking in cadence under fire, halting to drive a party of cavalry from their flank, and then going on behind bright bayonets.

Taylor, many years later, said that his most vivid memory was of a bluebird swooping across the field, bearing a worm in its beak. The sight of the charging Rebels shook the men on the crest, and Jackson's tactics now promised success. Ewell had struck and held on the right, and the blow at the flank, after serious early losses by the Confederates, was beginning to panic the enemy. The artillery Jackson had placed in the open was for the most part in ruins—one battery had been abandoned, surrounded with bodies, its survivors crouching in safety to the rear, while Federal shells blasted at the forlorn guns. But not for long.

Taylor's charge was a novel spectacle to the Army of the Valley; the troops went in perfect order, with Taylor riding in their front like a toy horseman with a charmed life. The men went upward into musket fire with casualties along the length of the lines, but the brigade did not falter. About halfway up the slope, when the watching army expected to hear orders to fire, Taylor coolly called for a charge, and the men jumped forward over the rocky ground and reached the crest. Now the Federals fled in earnest and the ridge was in Confederate hands.

In the final moments of that charge, coming from everywhere—back on the pike, where massed reserves waited, and in the low ground where Ewell's North Carolinians and Marylanders had been driven back, and in the charging Louisiana ranks—there rose a tremulous, quavering, ear-splitting cry. It was the first Rebel Yell from the Army of the Valley.

It seemed to startle the commander—almost as much as did the final victorious drive of the Louisiana troops—who were now joined by the Stonewall Brigade, and the men of General Arnold Elzey, who had been lying down out of the fire, in reserve. At last, all of Jackson's ten thousand infantry charged in mass.

The General seemed astonished by the rapidity with which the victory had swung to him. He sent Douglas across the fields: "Order forward the whole line. The battle's won."

The men of Taylor and Winder went past at a trot, and Jackson forgot himself. He waved his old cap over his head, shouting like a child. "Very good! Now let's holler!" The roar of the army swept down into Winchester, where the Federals were in headlong flight.

An officer pressed close to the General, evidently with the idea of restraining him, but Jackson only yelled joyously, "Go back and tell the whole army to press forward to the Potomac!"

At sight of Taylor, Jackson was again seized by emotion but did not speak. He leaned from his saddle and grasped the hand of the young Louisianan, wringing it with savage strength, grinning that glint-eyed grimace that the army was to see often in battle.

It was seven thirty in the morning, and Jackson went into a frenzy organizing the last chase of Banks. He had little assistance. The enemy, going back in order at first, had broken as the ranks passed through the town, and now there was a landscape of fleeing bluecoats, stretching to the horizon. The few Confederate infantrymen who were near enough to the enemy dropped to shaking knees and fired, but if they inflicted damage, Jackson could not see it.

He sought the cavalry, but there was none. He had seen

no considerable body of horsemen since the early morning; he
supposed most of Ashby's men were still missing, just when
the great opportunity of the war called for them. General Steuart
had two regiments of the Virginia riders, just a few hundred
yards away on Ewell's front, but where were they?

Jackson shouted in exasperation, and perhaps stronger language than Preacher Dabney was to recall: "Never was there
such a chance for cavalry! Oh, that my cavalry were in place!"
This bitterness was to be reflected in his official report, when
he lamented the switch in command, from Flournoy to Steuart.
He was swept into the town by the army.

Someone suggested artillery be brought against the Federals,
and the General shouted the order for all possible guns to be
brought up, and on they came, a few rickety, battle-worn guns,
dragged by exhausted horses which panted on the incline. Beside them came more of the infantry, scarcely able to walk,
living on the strength of delirious excitement. The army clustered
about the town, where buildings sent up towers of smoke, as
Federal stores burned. Jackson pressed on, though women,
children and old men literally besieged him as he appeared in
the streets. He went toward the river, thirty-five miles away,
which was, in his mind, the border of his country, and into
which he thought he must drive the enemy.

He got five miles north of Winchester, with his few cannoneers
more weary at each step and horses falling in their harnesses,
until at last his guns were alone, without support. In fear of
ambush, he was forced to halt pursuit, but he made one last
effort and called for mounted volunteers to chase the enemy.
When he saw the pitiful spectacle of the handful of men astride
the worn-out horses, even Jackson gave up. It was only in this
moment, after three days of the most punishing grind, that Jackson seemed to take into account the condition of his army, which
he had worn to the limit of its endurance.

Just two hours after Jackson turned from the pursuit with a
scowl, the fresh regiments of General Steuart came pounding
by, raising a magnificent dust, on the trail of the enemy who
could not now be overtaken; had Steuart been on time, Jackson
would have wiped out, rather than defeated, the army of Banks,

and perhaps have sent the Massachusetts commander to Richmond as a trophy.

Sandie Pendleton, whom Jackson had sent with peremptory orders to bring Steuart forward, came to headquarters with a maddening report: He had found the cavalrymen at ease, their horses munching clover, just a little over two miles away. Steuart stood on army regulations. He would take orders only from his immediate superior. Jackson could have no cavalry until General Ewell ordered him forward. He forced Pendleton to gallop two more miles to find an astonished Ewell and return with an order to advance. Steuart then had assembly calls played, and the cavalry belatedly, uselessly, went toward the Potomac.

The cavalry drove as far north as Martinsburg, twenty-two miles away, but had no chance to hit at the Federals; they brought back loot from abandoned magazines, and shiny new U.S. saddles and bridles appeared in the Jackson camp. There was also much-needed material—ammunition, medical supplies, food. The enemy crossed the Potomac after dark, at Williamsport, by use of the ford, ferry and pontoons.

Jackson enjoyed the remainder of the Sabbath by calling at the manse where he and his wife had stayed most of the previous winter with the Reverend James Graham and his family. He went to services in one of the brigades, too, and still found time to have his staff set up headquarters in the Taylor Hotel. He forced himself to his usual observation of Sunday, though he had regrettably been obliged to do battle that day. He waited until Monday to write his formal order to his troops, in which he recounted the events of a month past, praised his men, and then wrote of his own feelings:

But his chief duty, and that of the army, is to recognize devoutly the hand of a protecting Providence in the brilliant successes of the last three days—which have given us the results of a great victory without great losses—and to make the oblation of our thanks to God for His mercies to us and our country in heartfelt acts of religious worship.

He set aside the day for prayer and rest. He then wrote to his wife:

My Precious Darling, an ever-kind Providence blest us with success at Front Royal on Friday, between Strasburg and Winchester on Saturday, and here with a successful engagement on yesterday. I do not remember having seen such rejoicing as was manifested by the people of Winchester. . . . Our entrance was one of the most stirring scenes of my life. . . . Time forbids a longer letter, but it does not forbid my loving my *esposita*.

Jackson had literally wrecked a Federal corps. Banks belittled his own losses, but reports showed they were severe—about 40 per cent of his force. Jackson had burned or seized hundreds of thousands of dollars worth of supplies, including 9,300 small arms, 2 cannon, and countless wagons. He had taken three thousand prisoners.

The Confederate losses were insignificant: 68 killed, 329 wounded, 3 missing.

Jackson could not know the reactions he had set off in the North, which were unchecked for several panic-stricken days even by the soaring rhetoric of Banks, who began to issue victory bulletins as he crossed the Potomac:

It is seldom that a river-crossing of such magnitude is achieved with greater success. . . . There were never more grateful hearts than when we stood on the opposite shore . . . we had not suffered an attack or a rout, but had accomplished a premeditated march of near 60 miles in the face of the enemy, defeating his plans, and giving him battle wherever he was found.

Banks did not deceive Washington. President Lincoln wired General McDowell, canceling plans to send his troops to Richmond and ordering, instead, a detachment of twenty thousand hurried to the Shenandoah, to trap Jackson.

Newspaper headlines screamed of the defeat of Banks and warned that Jackson was about to fall upon Washington. The Government took over railroad lines; a new reserve corps of fifty thousand was created to defend the capital city; in a single day almost five hundred thousand volunteers pledged themselves to enter the army. The panic waned in a day or two, and calm returned to housewives who had burned and thrown away kitchen supplies and utensils, and jumpy military commanders who had destroyed arms. It was, after all, only some faraway maneuvering in the Shenandoah Valley of Virginia. Still, McDowell was prevented from joining the Richmond expedition, and many of his finest troops were hustled to the west.

Jackson sent a quiet report to Richmond. Its familiar theme: "God has blessed our arms."

After dinner the staff gathered, happy but weary, and for an hour or more Jackson listened, seldom speaking, to the talk of the young officers. Fresh newspapers were brought in from Richmond, where contraband dealers had got them through the lines, and though the General no longer read any newspapers, out of disgust with the liberties they took with him and the truth, he asked Sandie Pendleton to read him the worth-while news.

Pendleton browsed through the flimsy sheets, reading dispatches from the fighting fronts; and the staff found the war all but unrecognizable in those paragraphs.

"Here's an amusing thing in the New York *Mercury*," Pendleton said. "It will help you digest your dinner, General."

Jackson grinned. "Go on, Captain, let's hear it, if it will make us laugh at all."

"The life and character of the rebel General, Stonewall Jackson," Pendleton began.

Jackson got to his feet. "I don't want to hear that. Not at all."

"It is only a parody, General. Hold on a minute. There is nothing objectionable—you will enjoy it." And as the General sat, uncertainty on his face, Pendleton read: "He traces his ancestry to Jack, the giant-killer . . . no mortal man, his abstemiousness enables him to live for a fortnight on two crackers and a barrel of whisky."

There was more about the curious traits of his character, moral, mental and religious, and a humorous account of his wild boyhood. The General grinned more broadly, and was finally roaring with the others. Douglas remembered it as the loudest laugh of Jackson's career, but it was the last time, the staff recalled, that the General ever gave an ear to press comments on him.

4

★★★ THE VICTOR RETREATS

For a couple of nights, Jackson's staff reveled in the luxury of hotel rooms in Winchester, with Sandie Pendleton the complaining watchdog for headquarters. On the night of Tuesday, May twenty-seventh, this twenty-two-year-old officer lay in one of the outer rooms, where he was infrequently aroused by incoming dispatches. Jackson admired this boy, who was the son of an old friend, the erstwhile rector of Grace Episcopal Church in Lexington, General W. N. Pendleton. The father was commander of the Rockbridge Artillery, and soon to become Lee's chief of heavy ordnance.

Near midnight an orderly intruded upon Sandie's sleep.

"There's some old man here, come a long ways. Says he's got important word for the General. It won't keep, and he won't go away."

Pendleton muttered. "I've got no idea of getting up, short of fire or the Yankees. Bring him in." His weary voice did not conceal his disgust at the prospect of hearing another of the hundreds of excited civilians tell tales he thought might win the war.

This civilian was different. An aging man, already gray, who entered with dignity, and told a calm, intelligible story. Douglas and other officers came in to hear him.

"You've raised havoc in Washington," he said. "The talk is that your army is big enough to storm the city." He paused to explain his own movements.

"I have come almost 50 miles today, because I thought the news might be important to General Jackson. I passed Federals on the mountain road.

"They have sent some of General McDowell's men after you, fresh troops out of Fredericksburg. I did not at first believe it myself—until I went by them on the road, miles of them.

"I was told that they were troops of General Shields, with 10,000 already marching, and those just the vanguard.

"Young men, they are already less than a day's march from Front Royal, behind you in the Valley. Now, it's up to you. If you think it's worth telling the General . . ."

The old man said he had pushed his horse since passing the Federal troops and had run almost all the way into Winchester. He looked it, and Pendleton did not question him; it was clear from the old man's manner that he told the truth. Pendleton had a bed made for him in an adjoining room, after debating briefly the wisdom of waking the General. There was some talk of the dangerous position of the army.

"Shields is already nearer Strasburg than we are," one of them said. "If he moves in there, we can't get back down the Valley. Where the devil could we go?"

"We could fall back into Maryland and live off Yankee country," another said.

"Don't talk like that. Didn't you hear old man Ewell squealing around here the other day—I never saw such a hilarious thing. He'd dance around, bobbing that egg head, yelling, 'Damn this Valley to hell. Every time I look up there's another of his dratted couriers. And every time I expect another order from old Jackson to do some fool thing. I tell you, every day I keep looking for an order to storm the North Pole!' "

Pendleton turned back to his bed, saying that he would tell the General in the morning and leave the matter to him. Morning brought fresh consternation to the staff, for after the General had questioned the old man, he astonished the officers with a calm order—to put the troops in marching array. He intended to strike toward the Potomac, at Martinsburg and Harpers Ferry. The staff puzzled over it during the day, and there were new complaints that Old Jack had gone mad. The Yankees were gathering behind them, everyone knew by now: Shields from the eastern flank and Frémont from the west. Within a few days they could be cut off along the Valley pike by as many as fifty thousand Federals. And yet, heedless of this gathering storm, their maniac commander plunged north on a raid.

The troops themselves were not nearly so mystified. They had long since concluded that Old Jack would somehow find the most galling duties for them and give them the worst of everything, but in the end would pull them through, most of them. Already, today, the Lemon Squeezer had given the men a sign that he was still alive.

The army got but two days to sate its hunger from the captured stores and recover from the bone-jarring marches against Banks. And Jackson had blighted even this holiday by robbing them of their booty. He sent out a stern order, calling attention to the regulations against stealing Confederate property, which included spoils of war. All those fine U.S. boots, belts, pants, coats, hats must come off, the order said. Men who wore blue uniforms or parts thereof would be forced to prove they were not Union soldiers. There was a mournful shedding of garments gleaned from the battlefield, but many a piece was secreted in the blanket rolls, to appear later, down the days of marching and bleeding.

That was not the only complaint. Without warning came another of the General's fool orders. The men were to resume drill, four hours a day of the prancing and halting and wheeling. It was beyond belief, fresh as they were from his killing drive out of the Valley. But they were forced to work once more, growling and unwilling.

Jackson was in close touch with Richmond now, and he sensed vastly increased interest in his little army by headquarters strategists. He had suggestive orders to make a show of strength toward the Potomac if the chance arose. Headquarters saw the prospect of striking fear into the North. General Joseph E. Johnston was almost deferential in orders. His language by no means commanded Jackson to disregard the trap now being built in his rear: "If you can threaten Baltimore and Washington, do so," the order read. "It may produce an important diversion." But it continued: "Your movements, of course, depend upon the enemy's strength in your neighborhood."

So, despite growing dangers, Jackson hastened to further provoke the Federals, and sent his men to throw the Yankees from Harpers Ferry. During planning of the thrust he revealed taut nerves.

He was discussing the movement with Arnold Elzey, one of his most effective general officers. Elzey passed on to Jackson the report of some guerrillas, that the enemy had placed big guns, naval Dahlgren guns, on the heights at Harpers Ferry. Jackson snapped at him.

"Are you afraid of heavy guns?"

The commander of the brave Maryland troops flushed, but held his tongue, and went with his men to Harpers Ferry where, after an artillery duel and a brief skirmish, the Yankees were driven off, and Jackson's column pursued as far as the village of Halltown. Here, at last, they were turned south for a retreat down the Shenandoah Valley.

There was one more bit of gallantry on the part of Turner Ashby to be reported to the commander: When the Federals had shot down his artillerymen, and a party of the enemy charged his field pieces, Ashby dismounted and, seizing a sponge-staff, loaded a gun and fired it into the midst of the oncoming men, until the survivors fled.

Jackson turned his attention to the wagons, for he had captured stores priceless to the Confederacy: quartermaster's and sutler's goods valued at $150,000; an endless array of medical supplies; thirty-four thousand pounds of food—bacon, flour, salt, sugar, hard bread, cheese; one hundred cattle, and hundreds of army horses. This in addition to the ninety-three hundred stands of small arms, chiefly new rifles, and the three thousand prisoners, seven hundred of whom he released on parole.

Thus, though the people of the region were in the midst of harvest, he was forced to seize from them every vehicle capable of rolling, and down the Valley went his wagon train, twelve long miles of it.

On Friday of the same week, Jackson's army was already moving back toward Winchester. It was a sultry, rain-swept day; and in the afternoon, when the General became sleepy, he lay under a big tree to escape the showers. He woke to find at his side Colonel Alec R. Boteler, a unique and valuable servant of the army.

Boteler was Jackson's chief link with Richmond, and a man of influence. He divided his time between Jackson's staff, of which he was an informal member, and the Confederate Congress, where he held a seat. He was an old friend, well educated, and a man of parts. Jackson trusted him in all matters.

The General, having stirred from sleep, saw Boteler roughing in a pencil sketch of him stretched beneath the tree. The artist left a description of the scene.

"Let me see what you have been doing there," Jackson said. And he took the sketch, his eye wandering over it, indifferent to the quality of the drawing. He said nothing of the picture, the artist noted a bit ruefully, but said only, "My hardest tasks at West Point were the drawing lessons, and I could never do anything in that line to satisfy myself, or, indeed, anyone else."

He then turned to the business at hand, and inviting Boteler to sit beside him, he began:

"I want you to go to Richmond for me, for more men. Banks is across the river at Williamsport, being reinforced from Pennsylvania. Saxton is in front of me, getting reinforcements from the railroad. I have just learned that Shields is near Front Royal, and Frémont is moving. You can see, I am nearly surrounded by a large force."

Boteler asked the size of Jackson's army, and without hesitation the General explained the disposition of his fifteen thousand men, and his hopes of being able, even now, to defeat the Federal forces nearest him. He then asked Botcler to press for heavy reinforcements from Richmond.

"If they will send me more men, to bring my force to 40,000, I can cross the Potomac, lift the seige of Richmond, and change the fighting front from the Potomac to the Susquehanna."

Boteler prepared to leave for Richmond, going as far as Winchester in one of the army's railroad cars, with Jackson at his side. They bumped along on the route of the army's swarming retreat to the southward, until the General was aroused from his sleep in the afternoon to take a dispatch from the front. It was sobering news.

The troops he had left at Front Royal, the Twelfth Georgia, under Colonel Z. T. Conner, had been attacked by the men of General Shields, and had fallen back, after setting fire to three hundred thousand dollars' worth of captured stores Jackson had accumulated with such care. Nor was that the worst of it. Colonel Conner had abandoned his command and had ridden to the rear as swiftly as possible. Fortunately one fearless officer was on hand, a sixty-year-old captain, William F. Brown, who, undismayed, marched the command away from the overwhelming Federal advance, to safety.

Jackson stared sleepily at the dispatch, crumpled it in his hand, and stared for a moment into the rain beyond the dirty windowpane. Well, Shields had cut the Valley pike at Front Royal, and that escape route was gone. The Federal was only twelve miles from Strasburg, too, and Jackson's troops were at least forty-four miles from that point. He might well be caught between two strong armies, but if he doubted his ability to outmarch the enemy, he gave no indication. He went back to sleep.

Later, he revealed flashes of the grim humor which settled upon him.

As he rode among the troops in Winchester, Jackson passed near a boy lieutenant of Ashby's cavalry who could not suppress his curiosity.

"General," the lieutenant asked, "are the troops going back?"

"Don't you see them?"

"Are they all going?"

This was too much for the suspicious commander. "Arrest that man as a spy," he called to a colonel at his elbow.

The astounded boy seemed on the verge of fainting, when Colonel Ashby came up and saved him with a word: "He ain't got much sense anyway, General."

In the evening, back in his hotel room, Jackson dealt with Colonel Conner.

"How many men did you have killed, Colonel?"

"None."

"And how many wounded?"

"None."

Then, sharply, betraying some of the anger he felt at being robbed of the stores from the victories of Front Royal, Middletown and the Valley pike, Jackson cried, "Do you call that a fight, man? You're under arrest."

Jackson turned to the details of a march which, if it could be accomplished, would be recorded as another of his miracles. His rear guard was almost sixty miles from Strasburg, where safety lay. The enemy's vanguard was some fifty miles nearer that town. In addition to the vastly longer march he must make, Jackson had also to protect his wagons and his twenty-three hundred marching prisoners.

He sent out Ashby with sweeping orders: Cut off the Federal view at every roadway, every lane, every ford; engage the pickets, drive off cavalry, do all possible to confuse Shields and Frémont and to delay their junction. The horse artillery was to fight at every opportunity. In the flying horsemen and their guns he put his faith that his infantry could outmarch the enemy, five miles to one. Already, as he went to his room in Winchester for the evening, flashes of coming battle played in the country to the south.

Boteler said farewell to Jackson that night as he came by to get some papers meant for Richmond delivery. The colonel had ordered the hotel to send up a couple of glasses of whisky, which caused Jackson some concern.

"No, Colonel," he said. "You must excuse me. I never drink intoxicating liquors."

"I know, General, but this is a time when a stimulant will do both of us good. Make an exception and join me."

Finally Jackson sipped once or twice at the glass and asked,

"Boteler, do you know why I abstain from drinking liquor?"

"No."

"Because I like the taste of it so much. When I found that out, I made up my mind to do without it."

Jackson left Winchester only when the army was far in front of him, at 2:30 P.M. Douglas thought the men looked sullen as they tramped along the macadamized road to the south, halting for their ten minutes in each hour and lying flat in the road, for Old Jack forced them to make the most of their rests, and would not permit sitting or standing.

The Maryland troops marched until 10 P.M. in the rain, without food, and had only dry crackers for breakfast. The Stonewall Brigade made thirty-five miles before halting at midnight, when the troops fell to the ground, exhausted. Jackson spent most of the night by General Taylor's campfire. Taylor remembered:

"He was more communicative than I remember him before or after. He said Frémont, with a large force, was three miles west, and must be defeated in the morning. Shields was moving up Luray Valley, and might cross Massanutton to New Market, or continue south until he turned the mountain to fall upon our trains near Harrisonburg. The importance of preserving the immense trains, filled with captured stores, was great, and would engage much of his personal attention; while he relied on the army, under Ewell's direction, to deal promptly with Frémont. This he told me in a low, gentle voice, and with many interruptions to afford time, as I thought and believe, for inward prayer."

Dawn on Sunday, June first, was wet, fog-swept and lashed by occasional squalls of rain. There was sharp skirmishing through the day, but the enemy was slow and puzzling. Ewell's men stabbed into the heavy woods where cannon smoke drifted low in the trees, to find only retreating Federals. Ewell growled, "I'm completely puzzled. Those damned fellers. I have driven back everything as far as their main body. . . . Jackson told me not to commit myself. I wish he were here now. . . . I'm sick of this fiddling about."

Jackson pushed the troops on south, convinced that the enemy which fired on them from cover had no serious intentions of attack. He put Taylor's men in the rear with orders to show no lights after nightfall.

The General had word from Winchester that Banks had crept back into that town, but the Federal could not possibly attack the rear of Jackson's force that night. Frémont would wait until tomorrow; Shields had not yet threatened from the direction of Front Royal. It looked as if Jackson, with an audacity possible only because he gauged so well the enemy generals, had managed to drive down the Valley between the two armies of the Federals and might escape. Frémont was following Jackson down the west side of the Massanuttons, while Shields sped down the east side.

Late in the day, Jackson knew he was safe, for down the hills, all but wobbling on weary legs, came the rear guard of General Winder's men, who had covered thirty-six miles in the day. Now there was nothing in the rear but Ashby's cavalry screen. The Army of the Valley had concentrated in the face of the enemy. If the trap were sprung now, Shields and Frémont would catch nothing.

The Sunday night was terrible, however. Jackson drove the army along, determined to move into some new position known only to him. Orders went out to press toward New Market, for the race was on against the Federals, down opposite sides of the Massanutton range. Jackson heard no complaints, but these were plentiful in the ranks as the troops moved in a driving storm. The General met one officer whose command had become strung out in the hectic march.

"Colonel, why don't you get your brigade together, keep it together, and move on?"

"It's impossible, General. I can't do it!"

"Don't say impossible! Turn your command over to the next officer. If he can't do it, I'll find someone who can, if I have to take him from the ranks."

The rear guard was charged by the enemy time and again, and there were occasional stampedes. Ewell's division came down hillsides so steep—they were ankle-deep in mud—that the troops locked arms in ranks, to prevent falling. These men marched all night, until they reached Woodstock.

Taylor wrote long after: "The darkness was so intense that the road could not have been found but for the white limestone. . . . The white of the pike alone guided us along. Owls could not have found their way across the fields."

The next day was scorching and the men suffered, for there was little water along the roadway now, and Old Jack pressed them without mercy.

After waiting once more for the Sabbath to pass, so that he would not desecrate it by causing mail to be carried, he wrote his wife:

> I am again retiring before the enemy. They endeavored to get in my rear by moving on both flanks of my gallant army, but our God has been my guide and saved me from their grasp. You must not expect long letters from me in such busy times, but always believe that your husband never forgets his little darling.

Jackson had escaped the enemy pincers. He now began to entertain bold ideas once more. But before he could deal with either force of the Federals, he had to attend to an unpleasant detail. The cavalry was in trouble—the same old trouble.

The rear-guard actions had been severe as Jackson's trailing regiments brushed across Frémont's front. For several hours General Winder, with the Stonewall Brigade, had fought for his life against swarms of Union horsemen. Taylor had offered to countermarch to his aid, but Winder beat off the attacks, and finally Ashby came in with his troopers and ended the threat.

General Steuart, who had gone through such humiliating experiences about Winchester, had fought at Ashby's side, and this time, more of his men had quailed, simply because they were poorly led. For one thing, the Twenty-seventh Virginia Regiment, mistaking the Second Virginia horsemen for Federals, poured a heavy fire into them, causing severe casualties.

Two colonels, Munford and Flournoy, went to General Ewell in indignation. They asked transfer of their regiments to Ashby's command and, with Ewell's approval, Jackson agreed. Without ceremony Steuart's cavalry was placed under Ashby. Steuart was given an infantry brigade.

Jackson took one final precaution against a surprise attack by the Federals. He sent Colonel Stapleton Crutchfield, his new chief of ordnance, over the Massanuttons to see to the burning of two bridges over swift mountain streams. Jackson had the utmost confidence in this young man, a brilliant graduate of V.M.I., who performed his duties with a running fire of droll and witty comment, frequently spiced with Latin quotations. When Crutchfield reported the lone mountain crossing closed to the enemy, Jackson could relax for a time. The Union troops could not now surprise him with a thrust over the ridge, but would be forced to march the long way around, turning the mountain range at the south. And Jackson was already making plans to prevent their linking even there, by engaging each force in its turn.

Old Jack spent the night after the grueling march in a house near the village of Hawkinsville, and here had his final report of the rear-guard action from Colonel J. M. Patton. The officer reported that only one of the last attacking Federal party had escaped death or capture.

"I hate to see them shot down like that," Patton said.

Jackson seemed not to notice this sentiment, and put several questions about the little skirmish. Finally, in his quiet drawl, he asked, "Colonel, why do you say that you saw those Federals fall with regret?"

They were so much braver than usual, Patton said. He had wished their lives could be spared.

There was fire in Jackson's voice. "No. Shoot them all. I do not wish them to be brave."

The General and his staff dried their uniforms before a fire, and as their clothing steamed, the young men smoked and ate and took quick drinks of whisky. Ashby entered, and the staff enjoyed him; he had just got his commission as brigadier general. Sandie Pendleton said seriously that Ashby should now expose himself less often, and give up his reckless manner of leading every charge.

Just a day before Ashby had led them a merry chase. Jackson had been handed a message late in the afternoon saying that the enemy had come upon the cavalry chief and were seriously threatening him. Jackson ran to his horse and, with a flying staff at his heels, went to the rear and at last came upon Ashby, who jogged unconcernedly in the road.

"Where is the enemy, Ashby?" Jackson asked.

The cavalryman said he supposed they had halted for the night; he had not seen a bluecoat for hours. Jackson showed him the dispatch which had brought them tearing through the rain to his aid. Ashby said that note had been written at eight o'clock in the morning, when he was indeed in trouble, but that he had long since driven off the attackers. The staff determined that the blame lay with an irresponsible courier who had carried the note all day before passing it to an innocent soldier for delivery. Jackson did not flame into anger as the staff expected.

"A water haul," he said, and no more.

Ashby joked about the incident at headquarters; and when Pendleton continued to warn him against useless exposure in battle, Ashby said, "I don't agree. I'm not the least afraid of any ball fired directly at me. They always miss. I'm afraid of the random shots—they always hit men for whom they're not intended."

The army moved along. One night Jackson, to the dismay of the staff, refused the offer of a big, comfortable house as head quarters because his soldiers had already pitched his tent. He tented in a lowland, and rain returned in the night. The General emerged long-faced in the morning, his uniform less presentable than usual, with shoes, papers and hats afloat in the currents of his tent. He went thankfully into a house for the next night.

5

★★★ CROSS KEYS

Jackson slowed his pace as he crossed the North Fork of the Shenandoah near the village of Mount Jackson, where he burned the only bridge on the main north-south road. The river was rising rapidly, and the pursuing Frémont, though he arrived with a bulky pontoon train, could not cross. The Federals had their bridge tossing on the current for a short time, but fresh rains drove them off with only a few troops put over, and Frémont was forced to cut his bridge and halt the chase.

The Confederates had a full day of rest from skirmishing, the first time since Front Royal they had been out of the sound of guns. Jackson felt safe enough, for the rivers were higher than they had been for twenty years, according to his topographical engineer, J. K. Boswell.

The General took out the map of Virginia given to him by Crutchfield. It was already speckled with small inked circles Jackson had drawn about the Valley villages. He circled the tiny town of Port Republic, just south of the Massanuttons, a position to his liking. Just now this was the finest spot on the chessboard, lying between the routes of Shields and Frémont, commanding the only near-by bridge; it was as strong as a fortress, and from the hills Jackson could force Shields to move up so that the latter would be open to attack. The position gave the Confederates inner lines and a good route of retreat into the hill country in case of disaster. Jackson led his men in that direction.

The world began to break in upon Old Jack, even in the remote foothills. First a Yankee reporter who had been taken at Front Royal got an interview with the General, and managed to get a pass through the lines by describing in glowing terms the charge of Jackson's cavalry at Front Royal and the blood-curdling yells with which the horsemen had swept forward. The reporter went home to write a fanciful story about the General which amused headquarters for several days.

There were the Richmond papers, filling with praise of the Valley army, and even the *Whig*, which cried: "This man Jackson must be suppressed, or else he will change the humane and Christian policy of the war, and demoralize the Government." It was clear from the bundles of newspapers that the little army was titillating the Confederacy. There was also a message from President Jefferson Davis, styling Jackson's running duel with the enemy as a "brilliant campaign."

Stonewall now had some welcome news from Captain Jedediah Hotchkiss, an engineer with a particular genius for terrain. Jed Hotchkiss had climbed to the crest of the Massanuttons (he could ride once over a bit of country and leave with its topography so fixed in his mind that he could render it accurately on a map).

From the mountaintop Hotchkiss saw the column of General Shields. The enemy was in camp, foiled by the boggy roads. They were still miles away, so that it was probable that Jackson would have time to fight off Frémont's force before Shields could arrive, though this delicate matter of timing would have to be arranged while the two enemy generals were in the sound of each other's guns.

Jackson knew that he could depend upon Hotchkiss as he could upon most of his unusual staff, civilians chosen for their talents rather than reputations. Hotchkiss was an interesting example, a transplanted Northerner, born in Windsor, New York, and educated in New York schools. He had fallen in love with Western Virginia on a walking trip when he was a youth of nineteen, had settled there and opened an academy for young people. He was now thirty-two years old, enjoying to the fullest his daily work of map making, which had heretofore been his hobby. Only now was the staff overcoming its early habit of calling him "Professor Hotchkiss."

Jackson, above almost all Confederate officers, seemed to appreciate the value of active, pliant, nonmilitary minds. He withheld his officers from his decisions, but he kept them at work.

On June sixth, just as he was ready to clash with the enemy in decisive fighting, Jackson was robbed of his most dashing commander. On the rear of the army, as daylight began to fail, the cavalry staged a bizarre, tragic incident, of the sort which seemed to dog the steps of this irrepressible service.

General Ashby's troopers were near Harrisonburg, resting at the roadside, when they were surprised by the approach of the First New Jersey Cavalry, which had crossed the river undetected. Ashby in his usual fashion ordered men into saddles and charged upon the Federals. The bold dash netted him sixty-four of the enemy; one of the prisoners was a spectacular bird indeed. Taylor saw him as "a stalwart man with huge mustaches, cavalry boots adorned with spurs worthy of a *caballero,* slouched hat and plume." He was the regiment's colonel, Sir Percy Wyndham, a British soldier of fortune who had fought in Austria and Italy. He had had his horse shot from under him that day and went on foot along a road crowded with Confederates, who laughed at his exotic costume and yelled, "Lookit the Yankee colonel!" The epithet "Yankee" seemed to pain him more than his predicament. He cursed the shooting of his horse, and the cowardice of his troopers who, he said, deserted him.

Major Rob Wheat, chief of the Louisiana Tigers, leaned against a rail fence, and as Wyndham passed, Wheat sprang into the road to greet the foreigner.

"Percy, old boy!" Wheat shouted.

"Why, Rob!"

There was a brief reunion of the soldiers who had fought under Garibaldi in the birth throes of the Italian republic, and Wyndham, as a distinguished visitor, was taken to Jackson's headquarters.

As Jackson and his guest talked, the skirmishing went on, a brief inconclusive meeting of men in a roadway, so insignificant an action that it was to bear no name. Ashby caught sight of a party of Federal infantry just after the clash with the Jersey troopers and persuaded Ewell to give him the loan of three regiments of his infantry. Ewell went along himself. They met a crack outfit, the Pennsylvania Bucktails, and captured the commander, Lieutenant Colonel Thomas Kane, brother of an eminent Arctic explorer and himself a prominent Philadelphian. Kane was effusive in praise of Ashby and his charging troopers. He told one of his captors:

"Today I saved the life of one of the most gallant men in either army—General Ashby—a man I admire as much as you do."

Kane said he had seen Ashby within fifty yards of his line during the afternoon and had knocked aside the rifles of his men when they were raised to shoot the unsuspecting Confederate.

But by that hour, Ashby was dead.

He had led Ewell's men into stubborn Federal troops whose rifle volleys broke the Confederate charge time after time. At last, Ewell had sent up Colonel Bradley Johnson and his Marylanders: "Charge, Colonel, charge and end this matter."

There was still bitter fighting, and at least twenty men of the Maryland regiment went down in one volley. Johnson's horse fell dead. Ashby's horse tumbled (it was the same mount General Jackson had used at Bull Run, when he was wounded in the hand). Ashby then went ahead on foot, leading the infantrymen; they routed the Pennsylvanians. It was not soon enough for Ashby. He fell under a volley at point-blank range.

The cavalryman died in the arms of Lieutenant James Thomson, one of his most devoted followers. And Ashby's last words, called to the men of the Fifty-eighth Virginia Regiment, were: "Charge, men! For God's sake, charge!"

The troopers took Ashby's body into camp on a cavalry horse and prepared for the funeral. There were strange scenes in the camp that night—scores of the cavalrymen were openly sobbing.

Jackson was told the news as he talked with Wyndham, and could scarcely accept it. He sent the English visitor away, saying, "I cannot see him further tonight." Jackson remained alone for a time and then went to see Ashby's body. He stared at the dark face—so dark that one Federal, when attacked by Ashby, had thought he was being shot at by a Negro. Ashby had brought Jackson trouble and sometimes indiscipline, but only once had he brought false information. The horseman had, as the troops said, fought the Yankees as if he had a contract with President Davis to go at the enemy twenty-four hours daily. The cavalry screen of the army in the Valley had fought endlessly under Ashby.

The first of the army's legends began to arise that night as the body of the aristocrat-turned-horseman lay in state. Men talked of the spectacle of Ashby on his magnificent horses, always either jet black or spotlessly white, riding like an ancient knight with his black beard and flowing hair. Men began to see him as invincible in battle and to praise his gentle spirit, which had been so aroused by the invaders that he fought a record thirty-five battles within the last twenty-eight days. The most romantic of the soldiers began to speak of the army's "Paladin," which was what Ashby had become. His death at thirty-four gave the Valley army its first lesson in mourning a hero.

Jackson put the memory of him into his records:

> An official report is not an appropriate place for more than a passing notice of the distinguished dead, but the close relations which General Ashby bore to my command, for most of the previous twelve months, will justify me in saying that as a partisan officer I never knew his superior. His daring was proverbial, his tone of character heroic, his power of endurance almost incredible, and his sagacity almost intuitive in divining the purposes and movements of the enemy.

Ashby's body went off by a crude hearse to Charlottesville, trailed by many of his men with reversed arms, his horse, a sobbing body servant, and a number of hangers-on. Even Yankee prisoners at the roadside grieved at the passage, one diarist recalled.

Another casualty came forcibly to the notice of the Valley army, with new implications as to the place of Jackson's force in the greater Confederate scheme. General Joseph E. Johnston had been wounded in a battle near Richmond, a place called Seven Pines, where the big army had met the Yankees under General McClellan. Jackson's officers speculated on the logical successor to the commander in chief.

Many thought Stonewall would be called from them to take over direction of all the Southern armies. Others thought General Beauregard was the man. Ewell had another idea. "No, sir," he shrieked. "I don't know who they'll pick—but I wouldn't be scared if the choice fell on General Lee."

It was not long until word came: Lee had assumed command and would direct the Confederate military effort in Virginia. Jackson was evidently pleased, but he said nothing. His thoughts, however, had turned more often to Richmond and the fighting in eastern Virginia. And in one of his dispatches he had gone so far as to suggest that he could bring his little army to aid in the defense of the capital, if necessary.

Just now, however, events pressed upon him at Port Republic, whence he had moved his troops on the day after Ashby's death. Frémont and Shields moved toward him by parallel roads on either side of the Massanutton ridge, at the Southern tip of which lay a complex bit of terrain:

The village of Port Republic stood in the arms of the North and South Rivers, near their junction, where they formed the South Fork of the Shenandoah. The bottom lands of the rivers were open and commanded by abrupt ridges rising over them. There was a single bridge north of the village; otherwise, the streams were to be crossed only by fords, impracticable for troops when the water was high.

On Saturday, June seventh, under clearing skies, Ewell and his troops were placed about four miles northwest of Port Republic, at a place called Cross Keys from a tavern of that name. There was a junction of roads here, and near by was a Dunker church. Ewell put his five thousand men on high ground and waited.

Jackson took the balance of the force back to Port Republic

itself, where it camped on the dominating ridge. All day Jackson sought to lure Frémont to attack by the exposure of Ewell's men at Cross Keys, but the Federals seemed timid. There were a few shots at sunset, but no charge came. Jackson continued his wait. He began to despair of an opportunity for action.

He sent a message to Lee: "At present I do not see that I can do much more than rest my command and devote its time to drilling."

The situation was to change swiftly.

The next morning Jackson was in his headquarters at the home of a Dr. Kemper in Port Republic, piecing together the vague bits of information he had on the enemy. Major Dabney bustled in, asking if the army would fight on this day.

The General replied firmly. "No. You know that I always try to keep the Sabbath if the enemy will let me."

Dabney left him, and was on his way to preach the usual sermon to the troops, when an excited courier burst into headquarters with bad news. Federals were pouring into Port Republic from the east, crossing the lower ford of South River.

The General had no time for orders. "Go back and fight them," he said.

And he hurried off. Jim brought up Sorrel, and Jackson galloped toward the bridge leading to safety. The Union horsemen made prisoners of two staff officers, Colonel Crutchfield and Lieutenant Edward Willis. Jackson escaped handily and sent an urgent message to General Taylor at Cross Keys, asking for help. Within an hour, however, the Southerners had cleared the few Federals from Port Republic and the reinforcements were halted. It became clear that the day's formal action would be limited to Cross Keys—good news, since it meant that Jackson could meet the twin enemy forces in turn.

For an hour, a confused artillery duel raged about the town, and there was some skirmishing. The enemy soon pulled back, however. The work required little of Jackson's skill. He brought up two infantry brigades to guard the bridge and the affair was almost over. In the final moments Jackson had a personal brush with the enemy.

Some of his artillerymen had recently got new uniforms; and

when Jackson saw a cannon pull into position by the bridge below him, he could not be sure whether the artillerymen serving the gun were the enemy or his own men; he had just ordered Captain W. T. Poague toward the bridge with one of the Rockbridge guns.

Poague, seeing the new and mysterious gun himself, turned to Jackson: "That can't be my gun, sir. They've not had time to set it up yet. It may be one of Carrington's."

Jackson studied the cannon's crew, and as he sat his horse by one of Poague's guns, he shouted to the men at the bridge, his womanish voice carrying through the town: "Bring up that gun! Bring it up here!" There was no reply. He stood in his stirrups. "Bring that gun up here, I say!"

The strange gun crew then moved, but only to turn the mouth of the cannon so as to bear on Poague, Jackson and the artillery piece at their side. They were Federals. Jackson's reaction was immediate. "Let 'em have it."

His own gun blasted at the enemy crew, driving it from the bridge. Jackson sent infantrymen down the hill with bayonets. As the troops rushed ahead of him, Jackson threw up his hands, posing as if in prayer. The men shouted and soon cleared the enemy from the village.

At this moment, Old Jack heard big guns. Ewell was going into action. Jackson sent reinforcements but did not go to Cross Keys himself. He would leave direction of that phase to Ewell and remain in Port Republic to guard against the second enemy army.

He looked about at his positions on the grim hills. His officers were wondering if they were to fight two armies this morning, conjecturing that General Shields would now drive in to join the attack with Frémont. In the midst of such talk, Jackson spoke dramatically, "No, sir! No!" He gestured to the ranked batteries on the hillside. "He cannot do it. I should tear him to pieces!"

Colonel Crutchfield and Lieutenant Willis now returned, Willis bringing a Yankee prisoner with him; Crutchfield had been abandoned as the enemy was driven from the village. They brought a reassuring report on enemy artillery: Four guns had been captured, three of them left in the swampy roadway across the river.

Quiet fell in the town. The roar of battle from Cross Keys came in quite clearly.

At about this moment, in near-by Federal headquarters, General Shields was sending a dispatch to General Frémont:

> I write by your scout. I think by this time there will be 12 pieces of artillery opposite Jackson's wagon trains at Port Republic. . . . I hope to have two brigades at Port Republic today. . . . If the enemy . . . attempts to force a passage . . . I hope you will thunder down on his rear. . . . I think Jackson is caught this time.

Frémont was finding life as an apprentice thunderer difficult indeed.

Early in the sunny morning, his skirmish line went toward the ridge held by Ewell's veterans. The Federals first met the Eighteenth Alabama of General Ike Trimble's command. This gallant old soldier had gone through early troubles with Ewell, but was now highly regarded. This morning, to be sure, he had been wounded by a Jackson joke. Trimble wore a black army hat adorned with cord and feathers; and today, when someone mentioned "fancy soldiers" to Jackson, Stonewall had waved to Trimble, saying, "There's the only fancy soldier in my command."

The enemy had a rousing reception from Trimble's outposts and under the warming sun floundered through grainfields for a mile, until they finally pushed the Alabamans across a field of buckwheat which lay before Trimble's main force. Here the Confederate retreat halted. The Federals had no luck with Trimble's front, for it was shrewdly chosen.

The fine Union guns blazed at the Rebel center, and when this furore died down, blue infantry bobbed up in the buckwheat. They were going to storm Trimble's position. For two or three minutes in the rustling and crumping sounds of boots in the grainfield the Yankees came on, seeing nothing in front of them. The first files took the slope in orderly, drill-field fashion. Near the peak of the ridge, Trimble's muskets roared; in the smoke the torn Federal line attempted to form on its surviving officers, but under a second volley the remnants fell back down the hill. Through the rest of the action wounded men cried from the face of that hill and in the day's increasing heat begged for water. These were the survivors of the Eighth New York Regiment, all but annihilated by Trimble's fire—with more than five hundred casualties.

Frémont again turned to his artillery, and the guns raked the Confederate front, doing great damage in some quarters. General Elzey, for one, was wounded, and could no longer direct the answering fire. General Steuart received a shoulder wound.

The day dragged on. There was infrequent firing from blue-coats in thick woods across a ravine, but little more. Ewell kept shifting his strength impatiently. On a report that the enemy was gathering on the right, he sent fresh brigades two miles down the line. He fretted over the passing chance at action, but Jackson's orders forbade an attack in view of the situation in Port Republic, where a new battle might develop at any moment. Afternoon drew on with Ewell holding stubbornly to his ridge.

Ewell would not sit still, and in the late hours of the day ordered his skirmish line forward, until it lay in the position the enemy had occupied during the night. Frémont was behaving strangely, and seeming to invite attack, but it could not be delivered. Ewell, already nettled by his dilemma, was galled by the fury with which old Trimble beset him.

Trimble had been garrulously urging an attack all day, and he besieged Ewell with pleas for a night assault. When Ewell refused permission, Trimble went to Jackson, who said only, "Consult General Ewell and be guided by him." Ewell again shook his head, telling Trimble that he had fought well during the day, and attempting to explain the army's holding action. Trimble shouted: "Drive Frémont tonight, or he's going to press the army in the morning. You'd better fight one army at the time." He went off muttering about Jackson's hare-brained plans to time his blows against first one foe and then the other. He was almost the last sound of the night, growling his discontent.

The staff had a closer look at Jackson's spirit in the waning hours of fighting, near by at Cross Keys. Sitting his horse above the landscape of Port Republic, watching and waiting, the General turned to the Reverend Dabney.

"Wouldn't it be a blessed thing if the Lord would give us a glorious victory today?"

No one heard Dabney's reply, but a boy lieutenant who gazed in fascination wrote:

"Jackson's expression was that of a child hoping to receive some favor."

The General had little time for prayer or recapitulation tonight. He knew his casualties were light, and that the army was still ready for battle. (It developed that Ewell's loss was 287 men, only 48 dead; the Federals reported 664 casualties.)

Jackson stayed up late, studying means of assisting the Lord. His thoughts roved over the predicament of General Frémont, who had withdrawn so gingerly when smashed on one flank. And he dwelt, with greater respect, on the situation of the approaching General Shields. If he could concentrate the army tomorrow, by hurriedly withdrawing Ewell across the river, he might be able to whip Shields here at Port Republic. It would require some soldiering.

6

★★★ PORT REPUBLIC

Near daylight of June ninth, Jim heard Jackson at his prayers. The General soon rose and went in person to see his orders carried out, for he had conceived a swift double blow, which must be executed with precision because of the nearness of the enemy and the looping of the rivers.

Jackson ordered Ewell to begin shifting his men at the first light of day, from Cross Keys across the bridge of North River, through Port Republic, and thence over a temporary bridge of wagons on South River—so that they could be flung against Shields, who approached from the east. To check the hesitant Frémont in Ewell's rear, Jackson left a small force at Cross Keys —Trimble's brigade and two regiments under Colonel J. M. Patton, whom Old Jack had so lately scolded for his admiration of enemy gallantry.

The leading force against Shields would be the men of the old Stonewall Brigade, under General Winder. If all went well, Jackson would defeat Shields in the morning and, by afternoon, could wheel about once more and fall upon Frémont. They could thus destroy the two Union armies.

Jackson was careful to add, however, that the rear guard of

81

Trimble and Patton, if pushed by Frémont, should burn the North River bridge behind them, retreating slowly into Port Republic.

When he had given orders to Ewell, Jackson sent the wagon train over the hard trail into the mountains—except for the wagons needed for the bridging of the river. He had watched the sleepy troops at their work in the dark, hurtling water. The men stripped the bodies from the wagons and hooked their beds together until there was a bridge over the stream. It looked a bit rickety, but it should serve.

Near 2 A.M. Jackson had seen Colonel Patton and given him specific orders for the rear-guard fighting.

"I want you to throw out all your men as skirmishers, if necessary, Patton. Make a great show, and make the enemy think you have the whole army behind you. Hold your position if you can, and if he forces you back, take another and defend it the same way. And I will be back with you in the morning."

"The brigade is small, General, and there's precious little cover for it between here and the river. How long do you think I must hold?"

"By the blessing of Providence I hope to be back by ten o'clock," Jackson said.

The General went to the river, as if fascinated by the work of the men on the bridge. Some of his officers saw him sitting Sorrel in the moonlight, absorbed in the progress of the work. He was late getting to bed and was then disturbed.

Colonel John D. Imboden, chief of one of Jackson's experimental mountain artillery units—a mule battery—visited headquarters in the early morning. He tiptoed through the upper hall of the house where Jackson's staff slept. A sentry had directed him to a room where he might find Sandie Pendleton. Instead, when he opened the door, Imboden saw Jackson stretched on a bed in full dress, still wearing a sword and boots. A stubby candle cast dim light. Imboden was withdrawing when Jackson spoke.

"Who's that?"

The officer identified himself and apologized.

"That's all right, Imboden. It's time to be up. I'm glad to see you. Were the men up as you passed camp?"

"Yes, General. And cooking."

"Good. That's right. We move at daybreak. Sit down. I want to talk to you."

Jackson then spoke with emotion of Ashby's death, his voice trailing off into silence.

"General, you made a most glorious winding up of your month's work yesterday."

"Yes. God blessed our army again yesterday, and I hope with His protection to do even better today."

He then astonished Imboden by giving him a detailed plan of battle. Jackson ended by ordering him to take his mule battery to a ravine on the Luray road, where the enemy might pass if forced back. In that event, Imboden could tear the Federal lines with shell where Jackson would otherwise be unable to reach them. Old Jack then rose and went to the front.

General E. B. Tyler's blue lines lay atop the second ridge which rose beyond the Shenandoah, with his right in open fields by the river and his left in a deep woodland, high on the hilltop, near an old charcoal furnace. His men held dominating ground on all parts of the line; the flanks were well covered, and on the left a six-gun battery waited for indiscreet Rebels.

Jackson's men moved to assault this position in the cool early morning, their commander riding in their midst. He was going today as a guide, for he had refused to give even General Winder specific directions. When Winder asked for orders to fight Jackson's battle, Old Jack said only, "I will lead you."

For a mile and a half they went on, leaving Port Republic behind. They came into sight of the Federal center at a place known as The Lewis Farm. Soaring above them were two tall mountain terraces, the second higher than the first. Blue uniforms were fleetingly exposed over the face of the rear slope. From the first glance, the troops knew that bloody work was ahead.

Jackson's men drove off the Union skirmishers, but soon found that these men on the hills were not to be confused with the skittish Germans of General Frémont. Tyler, a civilian fur dealer, commanded tough Western troops from Ohio and West Virginia, with a heavy sprinkling of Irishmen. They were not overawed by the appearance of Jackson, and in the first serious brush they tore apart the lines of the old Stonewall Brigade. The Federal guns from the charcoal clearing swept the open, and the musket fire was as fierce as any the Army of the Valley ever faced. Some outfits began to waver. Jackson held on, however; he gave no sign of regret that he had not waited until his support was at hand. The fresh brigades of Ewell were still not within sight.

Taylor and his men heard the firing while they were at breakfast, and he brought them forward. The Louisianan took his first look at the field:

"From the mountain, clothed to its base with undergrowth and timber, a level—clear, open and smooth—extended to the river. Half a mile north, a gorge, through which flowed a small stream, cut the mountain at right angle . . . and on an elevated plateau of the shoulder were placed six guns. . . . Federal lines, their right touching the river, were advancing steadily, with banners flying and arms gleaming in the sun. A gallant show, they came on. Winder's and another brigade, with a battery, opposed them. This small force was suffering cruelly, and its skirmishers were driven in on their thin supporting line."

Just as the Union troops were countercharging, Taylor met Jackson. The commander was in a curious pose, Taylor recorded: his reins loose, his head down as if in prayer. Jackson looked up.

"Delightful excitement," he said.

"I'm glad you're enjoying yourself, General, but you may have an indigestion of fun if that big battery is not silenced."

Jackson beckoned Jed Hotchkiss and sent him to guide Taylor and his men up the slope, where they might take the Union guns in the flank.

Jackson moved on. He passed the few men of Imboden in their ravine and saw that they were having "a remarkable time." At each passing shell, the mules went wild, plunging and screaming and lashing so with their heels that it took three or four men to hold one of the heavily loaded beasts.

Once or twice Imboden tried to fire the mountain guns from the backs of the animals—but the mules would have none of it. With the report, they plunged into the air and fell to the ground, rolling until they rid themselves of the guns. The battery could hit no targets, and the men were enraged by the solemn questions of infantrymen who were enjoying the sight: "Now, what's supposed to go off first, the guns, or the mules?"

Jackson peered into the ravine while the mule rebellion was at its height. "Colonel, you seem to be having some sort of trouble down there." The ravine echoed with laughter. Jackson went on, leaving an order to take the distraught animals up the mountain.

The General then galloped toward the river, where his old brigade, now under Winder, was in serious trouble. He went into the ranks as if the enemy did not exist, waving his hat, shouting, "The Stonewall Brigade never retreats! Follow me!" The men went to their old position.

It was not long since an Alabama private had written home, scorning the Yankees: "We whip them every time we meet, no matter how great their numbers, or how few ours. The infernal scoundrels can't stand the bayonet—they scamper like a herd of cattle."

There was none of that today. It was hand to hand, a murderous surging of the blue and gray files. For the first time Jackson's men found themselves outnumbered at the crucial point of a battlefield, and they grappled with troops who asked no quarter. Dozens of Rebels fell under fire of the guns on the charcoal clearing above. Captain Poague's teams galloped into a wheat field, guns were unlimbered, and Jackson's artillery blazed in reply. But only two of the guns were of sufficient range to reach the Union cannon on the hill and the rest were withdrawn. The troops fought on at a grave disadvantage; Jackson sent two Virginia regiments up the hillside in a second effort to silence the guns. A battery attempted to follow the climbing men, but was forced to turn back by a tangle of laurel and rhododendron. For several minutes Jackson watched his line take the punishment, helpless to drive back the enemy. If he did not have the long-overdue support, Winder's brigade might be driven from the field.

At the rear, where Jackson sent officers to hurry reinforcements, the advance was slower than ever. The Reverend Dabney was there, shouting vainly in an effort to speed the men. Officers defied him, refusing to make their men wade the breast-deep stream as he commanded; the maddeningly slow crossing continued, the troops slipping in single file over the wagons.

After half an hour at the front, Jackson still had not heard from his flanking parties on the hill, and Winder's men were driven back. The Federals were on the point of victory.

Winder got a depressing message from Colonel Allen, who had taken the Second and Fourth Virginia regiments up the mountainside. They had reached the enemy flank but had flushed three strong Federal regiments which had charged, scattering the Virginians so badly that they were withdrawn to reform.

It was already too late to carry out Jackson's design of battle. It was ten thirty. He could no longer hope to overcome Shields and then fall back upon Frémont—only good fortune would save his army this morning. Taylor was the lone hope.

Taylor and the Louisianans found serious climbing on the steep slopes, plunging in and out of ravines. At last they stumbled within sight of the enemy guns. Taylor ordered an attack. His men crossed a ravine in the face of cannon fire, swarmed about the guns and clashed with Federal infantry, but could not hold on. They were thrown back again and were once more bled until they disappeared in the laurel thickets. But they were not through. Taylor led them back twice more. In the second attack, Taylor used the last man of his reserves, even the musicians, who had scant use for their instruments today. A drummer boy joined the melee about the cannon, where men fought with fists, knives, stones against the Federal artillerymen with their flailing sponge-staffs.

As Taylor turned the captured guns down the solid blue lines now exposed to him, General Ewell came galloping up from the rear at the head of a large body of troops. The Federals on the hill, however, had a few moments respite, for Taylor was thrown back from the captured guns once more.

Taylor saw "the enemy, arrested in his advance by our attack . . . had countermarched, and . . . came into full view of our situation. Wheeling to the right, with colors advanced, like a solid wall he marched straight upon us. There seemed nothing left but to set our backs to the mountain and die hard."

Jackson and Winder were alert, however, and threw all the men on the field against the Federal flank. It was then that Ewell emerged, bringing with him men of the Forty-fourth and Fifty-eighth Virginia regiments, which had been earlier driven off. Ewell had burned the North River bridge in the face of the timid Frémont.

In this instant, with co-ordination as precise as if it had been planned in Jackson's headquarters the night previous, three assaults fell upon the Federals, and the fierce, skillful fighting of the men of Shields over the five hours went for naught.

Taylor jumped forward with the Louisiana troops, Ewell came in next to him, and Jackson hurried Winder forward with the main force. The Yankee lines wavered. They did not flee, but stumbled off over the rows of dead, toward the route of retreat. Within ten minutes, Jackson's defeat had become an overwhelming victory.

Despite heavy casualties in his crack regiments, Jackson was delighted. Behind him lay Frémont, baffled, beaten with the scantiest of fighting; and in front of him was Shields, the most formidable of his Valley opponents, going into retreat.

Not only had Jackson escaped the trap the Union had built for him; he had severely mauled the two hunters. The twin coup he had planned for today had been impossible; but his army, after all, had accomplished miracles.

He must have been aware, at the moment of victory on this backwoods field, that the eyes of the nation were turning upon him, the lone general in the year's bloody panorama on Virginia soil who seemed to know what he was about. In the heady music of the Rebel Yell raised by his troops on this battlefield, the General who had sought so avidly to curb his ambition must have realized that the Confederacy was beginning to chant a new battle cry which gave it new hope in the unequal struggle: Jackson is invincible.

The people of the South made him overnight into a legendary hero; hardly one of them had more than an inkling of the true nature of the man behind the intriguing nickname.

7

Nothing in the making of Tom Jackson had been easy.
His first American ancestor of record was a huge Irishman, one
John Jackson, who emigrated from obscurity to Cecil County,
Maryland, in 1748, and was shunted toward the wilderness. By
1769, he had staked a tomahawk claim—blazing his boundaries
on the virgin bark of giant trees—along the Buckhannon River
and Turkey Run, not far from what was to become the town of
Weston, West Virginia. Buffalo destroyed his first corn patch,
but John returned to settle. With two sons he fought in the Revolution, helped to clear out the Indian tribes, and left large tracts
of land to his heirs.

Edward, son of John, was the grandfather of General Thomas
J. Jackson, and it was in Edward's time that the family began to
prosper. Jackson men were Congressmen and judges and tax col-
lectors. Edward was a county surveyor and sat in the Virginia
legislature; a brother, John G. Jackson, married Mary Payne, the
sister of Dolly Madison.

Years later, before he had cloaked his ambition with discretion, young Tom Jackson was to look back on these times when
he declared to a kinsman:

88

"I have some hopes that our ancient reputation may be revived."

Edward Jackson's son Jonathan, a young lawyer of Clarksburg, (West) Virginia, was, in view of his father's property, a man of promise. He married Julia Beckwith Neale from a near-by farm in 1818. Julia was said to have ancestors who were soldiers in the service of the British Crown—professionals; but there were no records. Jonathan had begun well: A basic education at the Randolph Academy in Clarksburg, and a reading of law in the office of his uncle, the judge who had married into the Madison Administration. Admitted to the bar at twenty, Jonathan was for a time a Federal tax collector. He had raised a company of cavalry for the War of 1812, but was not called to duty.

Four children were born to Jonathan and Julia: Elizabeth, Warren, Thomas, Laura. Thomas was born January 21, 1824, in Clarksburg, with Dr. James McCalley in attendance. The mother named him for her father, Thomas Neale. He was to reach manhood before adding the name of his own father.

The boy was three when Elizabeth died of an undiagnosed fever. The father tended her, contracted the disease, and within two weeks was dead, leaving his family penniless because of his unfortunate way with money and property, and a weakness for signing the notes of friends. The widow clung to her cottage home in Clarksburg by operating a little private school and by sewing for her neighbors. She gave this up after two years and married an even less successful lawyer, Captain Blake Woodson. Her new husband caught on as clerk of court in Fayette County to the west and took her with him.

Out of concern for the mother's health, the children were scattered: Warren to her brother, Alfred Neale, near Parkersburg, where he prepared for a brief life of teaching school; Thomas and Laura to the country home of their grandmother, Edward Jackson's widow. The grandmother lived near the village of Jane Lew, not far from the original site where old John Jackson had fought Indians and buffalo. The departure for this home marks the beginning of the T. J. Jackson legend.

It is a family tradition that the five-year-old Tom, displaying the fearless spirit of an incipient lieutenant general, ran into the woods and hid from a bachelor uncle sent to fetch him, and returned only at night. After two days of bribery and persuasion, the children agreed to leave their mother and went to the big home on the West Fork of the Monongahela, where they were to spend many happy years with the grandmother, a couple of maiden aunts and a clutch of high-spirited, godless bachelor uncles.

Julia Jackson died in Tom's sixth year, and shortly after the parting from her the children were carried to her deathbed for a scene of prayer and blessing that made a deep impression on the boy; the children returned immediately to the farm. The grandmother died in 1835, and Tom was sent to the home of a cousin, William Brake, near Clarksburg, on the theory that the old homestead was no longer a fit place to raise children, since the maiden aunts had married and the matriarch was gone. Tom could not bear the new home for long. He ran away into Clarksburg; he told relatives in a firm, young voice, "I have disagreed with Uncle Brake. I have left him, and I'm not going back." He got a riotous welcome on his return to the home of the bachelor Jacksons—in particular from Uncle Cummins, who was the head of the horse-loving, fox-hunting, race-crazy clan.

There followed a boyhood idyll. Tom grew up on the ample farm, dividing his time between a jockey's saddle on the four-mile track of the place and the farm chores; he is said to have directed crews of Negroes at felling timber, to have worked with millers in the family gristmill, tended sheep, flailed the flax crop, caught monstrous fish in the clear streams, gone coon hunting and boating on the West Fork, and, though probably inconstantly, attended a country school.

One summer, according to the legend, he and Warren drifted down the Ohio in a log canoe, spending some time with relatives; and then, striking out for themselves, they passed the winter and spring on an island in the Mississippi, far down in Kentucky. They cut firewood for passing boats, and they returned by steamer with nothing to show for their labors but new trunks, though Warren soon developed tuberculosis, as his mother had before him. At nineteen Warren was dead.

The Jacksons remembered Tom's devotion to learning, and

that he lay on the floor to study while a slave held a blazing pine knot over his head—the bargain being that, as Tom learned, and the slave held the hissing light, the boy would pass on the knowledge and both become educated. It is said that the slave learned enough to enable him to escape via the Underground Railway.

In 1838, when Tom was fourteen, he had his first job, and his first contact with the church which was to mean so much to him. He worked on the Parkersburg-Staunton Turnpike and each Sunday walked three miles to hear a neighborhood minister. There is no more than a hint as to why he did so; perhaps he was in unconscious protest against the godless home of his uncles. In any event, this and other signs of strong character so impressed a local squire, Colonel Alexander Withers, that in 1841 he got for Tom a constable's post. His duties were inconsiderable: the serving of legal papers for the most part. It is likely that Uncle Cummins and others of his kin, numerous in the county, helped to put Tom on the public payroll.

The first instance of Jackson's lifelong concern over his health was an attack of dyspepsia at this period. He thought life on horseback might improve his condition, even as he rode through the hills bringing tidings of trouble to neighbors and kin. He had a reputation as a steady, dependable boy, far from brilliant, with no signs of eccentricity.

His Uncle Cummins evidently gave him free rein; the nephew was to write in later years: "Times are very different from what they were when I was at my adopted home. None to give their mandates, none for me to obey but as I chose, surrounded by my playmates and relatives, all apparently eager to promote my happiness."

The shade of Cummins which lingers indicates a vigorous character, a man whose love for litigation, a family failing, caused him feuds with prominent men of the area and consumed much of his income in court; a citizen of influence and a king-maker whose blessing launched many a political career. He was one of the thousands who died in California in the turbulent Gold Fever of '49. Tom, when told of the death of Cummins, was to write: "This is news which goes to my heart. Uncle was like a father to me."

In 1842, Tom was struck by the accidental good fortune which was to mold his life. A boy from his district, having won a place at West Point, withdrew, and there was a vacancy for Western Virginia. Tom, who learned overnight of the glories of the Academy and the military life, determined to have the place. There is no evidence that he had yearned to be a soldier, nor even that he had ever seen one; his interest in military matters, so the family memories run, had been limited to marching at the head of playmates as a child, imagining himself at war. In any event, West Point seemed a glittering opportunity to better himself, and Tom bent his every effort toward going there.

Cummins was a major help, for Samuel S. Hayes, the district Congressman, was a friend, and Hayes wrote from Washington that he would give all possible help. Hayes was probably astonished to see Tom walk into his office a few days later on the strength of nothing more than a kindly letter to an influential constituent. There is a legend that Tom hurried to Washington much as he was to hurry his columns of riflemen in later years, and that he rode desperately across country to overtake a stagecoach which he had missed at Clarksburg, sending home a slave with his winded horse.

To Congressman Hayes as to Cummins and all others, the grim-faced boy confessed a lack of training to fit him for West Point, but threatened such application to duty that he would be able to remain in the Academy. The session had already begun, and there was probably scant competition for the post. Hayes took young Jackson to the Secretary of War, who approved the candidate despite his shortcomings, and after a brief tour of Washington, including a peek at the city from atop the half-built Capitol, the impatient Tom was off for West Point. He arrived on the historic plain, July 1, 1842.

Jackson's entrance was observed by a little group of cadets which included three future Confederate generals: A. P. Hill, George Pickett and Dabney H. Maury. In later years, Maury wrote:

"A cadet sergeant came by us conducting a newly-arrived cadet to his quarters. This newcomer attracted our attention at once. He was apparently about 20 years of age, was well-grown; his figure was angular and clumsy; his gait was awkward. He was clad in old-fashioned Virginia homespun woolen cloth; he bore across his shoulders a pair of weather-stained saddle bags, and his hat was one of those heavy, low-crowned, broad-brimmed wool hats usually worn in those days by overseers, county constables, wagoners, etc. He tramped along by the side of the sergeant, with an air of resolution, and his stolid look added to the inflexible determination of his whole aspect, so that one of us remarked, 'That fellow has come here to stay.'

"So much did he impress me that I made inquiry at once about him, and found he was from Virginia. I then sought him out and endeavored to show him some especial interest, and to let him know that he was not without friends in that strange land. He was not at all demonstrative, however, and seemed determined to hew out his own career."

Jackson stayed at West Point, but he was for long uncomfortable and the butt of many cadet pranks because of the irresistible combination of country inelegance and grave earnestness which he offered to tormentors.

The Academy tradition is that he studied long after lights out by banking coals upon his fire and lying before it, boning up on subjects in which he found himself years behind, particularly algebra and geometry.

General John Gibbon recalled for a biographer a scene of Jackson at the blackboard in a classroom, so ill at ease that he squirmed in pain, smeared chalk over hands, face and uniform, and sweated so freely that he was for years a marvel to his mates. The boys called him "The General."

Jackson soon won the sympathy of instructors. He had a frank, manly approach to his ignorance, and often confessed that he could not recite the day's lesson since he was months behind and had not mastered earlier assignments.

He found life no easier outside the walls. Despite his training as a jockey, he was an ungainly figure on a dragoon's saddle, and never achieved the form required in taking jumps on cavalry horses.

Jackson began with the most lowly group of his class, which the Point called The Immortals, and it appeared that he would drop even below them and into oblivion at the end of his first year. But his struggles were valiant and endless. He later said, "I do not remember having spoken to a lady while I was at West Point"— and he evidently did little else but wage his uphill battle for belated learning. This was most severe in the study of French, but serious on every front. His grade standing at the end of the first year was precarious, but he clung on: Of a class of 72, he stood 70 in French, 51 in general merit, 45 in mathematics. He drew 15 demerits.

A few stories accumulated about him during his stay. One was that a fellow cadet substituted his uncleaned musket for that of Jackson, when inspection was imminent. Jackson was known to be scrupulously neat, but he accepted the demerits without protest, refusing to report the incident to his officers. But when he discovered the identity of the culprit, he had to be sat upon to prevent his taking the case directly to the commandant. Jackson insisted that the scoundrel be dismissed for conduct unbecoming a gentleman.

Another story was that his roommate, acting as orderly-sergeant, offered Jackson immunity from answering roll calls in the chill dawn. But despite his urging, and assurances that his absence would not be reported, Jackson steadfastly refused, and met the painful duty each day.

Most of the stories have about them an air of having been conceived, or enlarged, after Jackson's rise to fame. Some of the developing signs of character, however, are unmistakable. Here, for example, Jackson began the curious health regimen which was to lead him over the country in search of relief for his vague ills. Here he began his habit of sitting bolt upright, to protect the natural alignment of his internal organs. He also wrote a book of maxims, boyish and derivative, but indicative of his cast of mind. A few samples:

Disregard public opinion when it interferes with your duty.
Sacrifice your life rather than your word.
You may be whatever you resolve to be.
Lose no time; be always employed in something useful; cut off unnecessary actions.
Be not disturbed at trifles, nor at accidents.

The tough young mind, yet unformed, seemed to be groping for a rigid creed.

At the end of the second year his standing had improved: 52 in French, 18 in mathematics, 30 in general merit. He drew only 11 fresh demerits. But a pair of new menaces had risen: in drawing he was 68; in engineering, 55.

In a letter to his sister Laura, in January, 1844, he spoke of his health, his examinations, his improved rank, and then:

> I am almost homesick, and expect to continue so until I can have a view of my native mountains . . . my pay when I leave this institution will be about $1,000 a year; though fate may decree that I shall graduate in the lower part of my class, in which case I shall have to go into the infantry, and would receive only $750 a year. . . . But be that as it may, I intend to remain in the army no longer than I can get rid of it with honor, and means to commence some professional business at home.

At the end of his third year, Jackson had risen further: 11 in philosophy, 25 in chemistry, 59 in drawing, 20 in general merit. And, he added: "In conduct, one."

In letters to Laura at this period he wrote:

> I am enjoying myself very well, considering that I am deprived of the blessings of a home. . . . I have before me two courses. The first would be to follow the profession of arms; the second, that of a civil pursuit, as law. If I should adopt the first I could live independently and surrounded by friends whom I have already made, and have no fear of want. . . . If I adopt the latter . . . my exertions would have to be great in order to acquire a name. This course is most congenial to my taste, and I expect to adopt it, after spending a few years in pursuing the former.

And:

> My constitution has received a severe shock, but I believe I am gradually recovering. My exercises this year with the broadsword as well as the small are well calculated to strengthen the chest and the muscles. So that I have some reason to believe that they will have the desired effect of restoring me to perfect health. . . .

And, in April, 1846:

> . . . Rumor appears to indicate a rupture between our
> government and the Mexican. If such should be the case
> the probability is that I will be ordered to join the army
> of occupation immediately, and, if so, will hardly see home
> until after my return, and the next letter that you will re-
> ceive from me may be dated from Texas or Mexico. . . .

Tom graduated in July with a distinguished class that had
dwindled to sixty members. He ranked 17 in general merit, 12
in engineering, 5 in ethics, 11 in artillery, 11 in mineralogy and
geology, with 7 demerits for the year. He made his lowest rank—
21—in the study of infantry tactics.

In his class were Union generals of the future: McClellan,
Stoneman, Couch, Gibbon, Foster, Reno. There were distin-
guished Confederates as well: A. P. Hill, Pickett and Maury, and
D. R. Jones, W. D. Smith, and C. M. Wilcox.

Jackson got a brevet lieutenant's commission, in artillery, July
1, 1846. He left West Point with a reputation as a shy young
soldier of sound mind, "but not quick."

Sylvanus White, a cousin, recalled that Tom stopped at home
for a few days this summer before going to Mexico, and that he
condescended to drill with the home guard. A Colonel McKinley
persuaded Tom to take over a company and insisted, even when
the fledgling soldier protested that he would not understand the
Colonel's commands. True to that prediction, the first company
of Jackson's career took off on a false course at an improper
order, and went off the parade-ground, through the town. Tom
marched it on, obeying orders to the letter.

He was then off to war by a long route. He made his way from
Fort Hamilton, on Long Island, to Pittsburgh, a four-hundred-
mile journey, and then took a boat to New Orleans. He was thirty-
six days on this trip, and K Company, First Artillery, was still
far from the fighting. Jackson went to Monterrey, and then to
Saltillo, reporting for duty; but even this invasion of Mexican soil
did not suffice. On the eve of the battle of Buena Vista, he was
ordered to join General Winfield Scott, who was ready to storm
Vera Cruz.

Jackson thought he would never see action. His impatience was recorded by D. H. Hill, an officer who was to become his brother-in-law.

"I really envy you men who have been in action," Jackson told Hill. "I should like to be in one battle."

Hill added: "His face lighted up, and eyes sparkled as he spoke, and the shy, hesitating manner gave way to the frank enthusiasm of the soldier."

On March 9, 1847, when he was barely twenty-three, Jackson had his first glimpse of war—and it was like a page from an Oriental fairy tale, a pageantry of color and high drama he would mention often, and never forget. He stood on one of the ships lying offshore as the armada of tiny surfboats swept for the beach. Jackson was near the island of Los Sacrificios, where Cortez had landed more than three hundred years earlier. The army's bands blared over the water as the miniature boats hit the dazzling sands, and the figures of men crawled ashore like insects.

Just a mile inland were the white walls of Vera Cruz, but there was no sign of life or resistance, and the American force quickly went ashore. By noon, almost all of Scott's troops were strung out in their sandy camp, some 13,500 strong. At sunset, the gruff commander had completed his council of war and was ready to invest the city. It would probably fall to an assault since it was defended by no more than four thousand Mexicans and had been deserted by Santa Anna; but Scott would use caution. For nine days he dug trenches, and for four days more he waited for heavy guns. Jackson at last saw fighting.

He commanded a light battery and his were among the first guns fired. He was busy through the five days of bombardment before the rather informal defending army surrendered the city; the light battery's guns were kept hot, and Jackson almost never left them. The result of his work came in a later promotion to the permanent rank of second lieutenant, "for gallant and meritorious conduct at the siege of Vera Cruz."

It was not all martial pomp for Jackson, however. Much later he was to confess a weakness on this battlefield to a woman friend, who wrote: "He has told me that his first sight of a

mangled and swollen corpse on a Mexican battlefield as he rode
over it the morning after the conflict, filled him with as much sickening dismay as if he had been a woman."

This weakness was not to endure.

Vera Cruz surrendered its garrison, four hundred cannon and
all its stores. Scott had lost but sixty-four men. Jackson was excited by victory, but there was a detachment of mind as he wrote
to Laura of the details:

> The capitulation occurred yesterday. . . . The troops
> march out under the condition of not serving against us
> during the present war unless exchanged. . . . This capitu-
> lation . . . a regular siege . . . must in my opinion excel
> any military operations known in the history of our country.
>
> I approve of all except allowing the enemy to retire; that
> I cannot approve of . . . we had them secure, and could
> have taken them unconditionally.
>
> While I was at the advanced batteries, a cannon ball
> came in about five steps of me. I presume you think my
> name ought to appear in the papers, but when you consider
> the composition of our army, you will entertain a different
> view . . . only those who have independent commands
> are as a general rule spoken of. . . .
>
> You will take particular care that neither this nor any
> subsequent letter gets into a newspaper.

The season dragged into April, and as Scott waited for more
supplies, Santa Anna climbed into a forbidding position astride
the highway to Mexico City, in a mountain gap called Cerro
Gordo. Scott's engineers studied it with concern, for the two
armies were now of equal size, and it might be costly to attack
the hill fortress. The Americans advanced slowly through a
country of broad forests. For a few days young Jackson had an
opportunity to look at the country.

He found it "mostly a barren waste, cities excepted," with
"but two seasons, wet and dry." For a time he lived in a Mexican
house which charmed him: "With a large back lot, which contained a beautiful orange orchard. Also in this lot was a fine
bathing establishment, the pool being about 25 by 30 feet."

Wandering, he found a church, "the most highly ornamented in the interior of any edifice" he had ever seen. He was

. . . struck by the gaudy appearance on every side, but most especially the opposite end from the entrance, which appears to be gilded. At the base is a magnificent silver altar, and on each side are statues to attract the astonished beholder. The music is of the highest character. The priests are robed in the most gorgeous apparel. The inhabitants take off their hats on approaching the church and do not replace them until they have passed it. One day while I was near the building I observed a senora (lady) gradually approaching the door. Upon another occasion I saw a female looking at a statue and weeping like a child.

The words revealed a Jackson more than fascinated by his first glimpse of the Catholic Church. His letters to Laura hinted that he was smitten with the primitive life of Mexico, which drew him strangely, though it must have seemed irrevocably sinful and heathen to young Tom.

On April seventeenth, rescued from what threatened to become an exotic interlude, he joined the army in the attack at Cerro Gordo. Here he had his first lesson in flank assault. His instructor was one of Scott's engineers, Captain Robert E. Lee. For Lee uncovered the unsuspected weakness of the Mexican line and proposed a blow across the face of precipitous rocks. Scott launched his attack. Twice the Mexicans drove back the Americans in the front, but at the climax, when every gun blazed from the beetling hill, Scott's cannon came up over Lee's rough road, crushed the western flank, rolled the Mexicans back and routed them. More than twelve hundred Mexicans fell, and Santa Anna lost all his guns, as well as three thousand prisoners. Once more, however, Scott loosed his prisoners and plodded on in the path of the enemy. Jackson's K Company was not engaged in the attack, but was held in reserve. The company came into action as Santa Anna fled through the mountains, and the light guns sped the retreat.

It was not enough for Jackson "to give them a few shots from the battery"; he was again critical of Scott's methods in a private letter: "They succeeded in effecting their escape for want of our dragoons."

Jackson wrote that his commander, Captain Taylor, "has spoken of me very flatteringly in his report to General Twiggs." But as the army pushed on toward Mexico City, Jackson was left behind. He wrote ruefully to Laura:

> I have the mortification of being left. . . . Notwithstanding my present situation I have some hope of getting forward by and by. . . . But all this is with General Scott.
> I throw myself into the hands of an all-wise God, and hope that it may yet be for the better. It may have been one of His means of diminishing my excessive ambition. . . .

Laura may have been puzzled at the expression of a fatalism new to Tom's character, and even more by the air of marked humility. This first fulsome religious expression followed his casual acquaintance with the Catholic Church. His mention of God, characteristically linked with a confession of his ambitions, seemed to set a pattern for young Tom in which God, war and ambition were inextricably mingled. He was to add other elements.

He wrote Laura further. "I am in fine quarters and making rapid progress in the Spanish language, and have an idea of making some lady acquaintances shortly."

Now he literally called himself to duty. A vacancy in a light artillery battery under Captain John Magruder lured him. Magruder was shunned by other young officers, for he had a reputation as a hard taskmaster, was hot-tempered, and always sought the hottest of fighting. Handsome John would be satisfied with nothing less than perfection in his subordinates. Jackson applied for the post.

"I wanted to see active service," he said. "To be near the enemy . . . and when I heard that John Magruder had got his battery, I bent all my energies to be with him; for I knew that if any fighting was to be done Magruder would be on hand."

Jackson chased Magruder across wild country, from his garrison post at Jalapa to Puebla. At last, when Scott thought himself ready for the field again—in August—the army pushed forward.

The offensive interrupted at least one army feud. Magruder issued a challenge to a duel to General Franklin Pierce, who was so soon to become President. It was Jackson who carried the challenge for his superior officer.

The big push also overrode other interruptions, one of them vividly described by Dick Ewell's brother, Tom, who was to die in battle in this strange country:

"The water here, unless well qualified with brandy, has a very peculiar effect on one—it opens the bowels like a melting tat. General Scott came to see us the other day. He complimented Major Sumner very warmly on our improvements, and especially on the extraordinary vigilance of our scouts who, as he said, were peering at him from behind every bush as he approached the camp. To those aware of the disease prevalent here, the mistake of the General is extremely ludicrous. When we go to drill, the men have to leave ranks by the dozens, and as the plain is bare as a table, they make an exposé of the whole affair. The effect is unique as they squat in rows about a hundred yards from the battalion, and when we deploy as skirmishers we run right over them."

Dysentery and other ailments filled Scott's crude hospitals, and as he strove to throw forward every possible man, he lost entire regiments. Volunteers whose enlistments expired trudged off home. In the face of all handicaps, the army entered the valley of Mexico City on August tenth, and, while still charmed with the view of one of the earth's loveliest cities, was driven to the attack.

Once more Scott found Santa Anna in an almost impregnable position. He had dug in at a place known as San Antonio, which he had covered with guns and laced with trenches. One flank was guarded by an impassable bog; the other, almost as forbidding to the eye, was called the Pedregal, a waste of volcanic stones, cruelly sharp, piled in endless heaps and defiles.

Dick Ewell was writing home about this time, and he was a more imaginative correspondent than Jackson: "I really think one of the most talented men connected with this army is Captain Lee of the Engineers (that was Robert E.). By his daring reconnaissances pushed up to the cannon's mouth, he has enabled

General Scott to fight his battles almost without leaving his tent."

It was now Lee who gave the army and Jackson a second lesson in flank attack. Lee pierced the awesome Pedregal. His hand struck the Mexicans from their fine position and drove them to the walls of their capital. In the doing, however, there was grim work for American troops, including Jackson and Ewell, the commander and lieutenant of the future.

Captain Lee found a mule path over the Pedregal and work parties widened it into a road. The army streamed over the gigantic rock pile. After crossing the Pedregal, the Americans faced a ridge held by General Valencia and his troops, whose twenty-two guns outranged those of Magruder. Of this, Ewell wrote home:

> We went out with General Scott and staff, who stood on a hill overlooking the scene. . . . Valencia from his works kept up an incessant fire of heavy artillery . . . now and then blazing away with his six thousand muskets as though our troops were within fifty yards (Mexican fashion). . . . The Mexicans were so surprised at not being at once driven off that they thought a great victory had been gained. They commenced a jubilee that night, among other things their bands would strike up, "Hail Columbia," play about half through it and stop.
>
> Valencia brevetted some of his officers and was crazy with joy. Santa Anna knew something more of the Yankees and ordered Valencia that night, by an aide, to strike his pieces and retire. "Pshaw, pshaw," said the latter, "Tell Santa Anna to go to hell. I have saved the Republic."

Jackson fought through these hours with no other evident thought than to serve his battery, to attract attention of his superiors, and survive. If he noted the Mexican music, he made no mention of it. Jackson was part of an army unit which was pinned into an angle of the Pedregal by superior Mexican shellfire.

The isolated American segment seemed in distress as darkness fell, for huge columns of marching Mexicans had approached during the last hours of day. The bulk of Scott's force was five miles away, over the Pedregal. After dark, rain fell in torrents and all but drowned the voices of officers in a desperate conference of war at a church in the village of Contreras. The council came to the reckless decision that the enemy should be flanked once more, by holding twelve thousand men with a handful of regular troops, while the storming party circled the position. Captain Lee was sent to advise General Scott. Lee went alone on horseback, without even a guide, through a rainstorm breaking over the Pedregal, which was now infested with bands of Mexican irregulars. He somehow went through, and Scott branded his ride, "the greatest feat of physical and moral courage" of the campaign.

Lee and other engineers led a storming party through the dark to the Mexican flank, and at daybreak the American attack again broke Santa Anna's army. A pell-mell retreat packed the road into the city, and there was slaughter at the gates. Santa Anna lost another 3,000 as prisoners, and 3,250 in dead and wounded.

The action brought Jackson a citation for gallantry from Magruder:

> My fire was opened and continued with great rapidity for about an hour. In a few moments Lieutenant Jackson, commanding the second section of the battery, advanced in handsome style, and kept up the fire with great briskness and effect. . . . Lieutenant Jackson's conduct was equally conspicuous throughout the whole day, and I cannot too highly commend him to the major-general's favorable consideration.

High praise indeed—and this report was sent to an adjutant whom Jackson would meet again one day: Captain Joseph Hooker.

After a lull, in which Scott sought an armistice and Santa Anna, delaying, called up reinforcements, the fighting was resumed. On September fifth, a savage assault carried an outpost of the city, Molino del Rey. Scott then threw his columns at Chapultepec, the citadel of Mexico. The troops hurried in over narrow, gun-swept causeways. Here the climactic scene of the war unfolded. It seemed almost as if it had been staged to display Jackson's talents.

The lieutenant took his guns behind the Fourteenth Infantry

Regiment, up the hill under fire. Jackson challenged a big gun in a breastwork above him and drew the concentrated fire of a whole section of the Mexican line. The guns had obviously been trained on the causeway in advance. The barrage killed Jackson's horses and dropped fifteen of his men. At the last there was only Jackson and a sergeant. But with the lieutenant handling the sponge-staff and the sergeant firing, the single surviving gun answered the enemy.

Gunners ran past Jackson toward the rear, and many infantrymen joined the retreat. Jackson tried in vain to halt them. He strutted in the open, shouting, "This is nothing, men! Come on. They can't hurt me. You can stand it!" The men fled on to the rear.

A messenger came up. Jackson was to pull off his gun, if possible, and come to the rear. Jackson refused to obey the order. Magruder appeared and Jackson turned on him in blazing anger. Give him fifty men, he shouted, and he could hold the position. He argued that it was more dangerous to withdraw, as General Worth had ordered, than to push ahead. Magruder agreed.

A fresh brigade came and Jackson swung a second gun into position. The combined fire began to tell and the charging brigade found an opening in the entrenchments above. One breastwork fell, and then another, and advancing parties chased Mexicans upward with ladders, from post to post, until the citadel was taken. This unprecedented battle spectacle did not end it, for the majority of the Mexican forces had fled and were now caught in the slow eddies of thronging humanity in the streets and causeways of Mexico City. Dashing American artillery pieces found good hunting in the packed masses. Jackson ranged well out in front.

The lieutenant had hitched his guns to wagon limbers and run into the center of the city, blasting the retreating peons. Magruder followed closely, with ammunition in his flying caissons. The two argued: Magruder, the army's noted daredevil, seeking to prevent Jackson from pushing too far in advance of the army, lest he be cut off. This singular discussion was overheard by two young officers, both South Carolinians: D. H. Hill, already known to Jackson; and Barnard E. Bee. The Jackson-Magruder incident was one of the final actions of the war.

The praise which official reports heaped upon him must have contented even Jackson. His name appeared twice in Scott's report. General Worth wrote: ". . . The gallant Lieutenant Jackson, who, although he had lost most of his horses and many of his men, continued chivalrously at his post, combating with noble courage." General Pillow wrote: ". . . His brave lieutenant, Jackson, in the face of a galling fire from the enemy's entrenched positions, did valuable service . . ."

Magruder gave his lieutenant full credit: "I beg leave to call the attention of the major-general commanding to the conduct of Lieutenant Jackson of the First Artillery. If devotion, industry, talent and gallantry are the highest qualities of a soldier, then he is entitled to the distinction which their profession confers."

That was enough for the commander. Jackson got his rank as a major for gallantry at Chapultepec. There was scarcely a hint of modesty in Jackson's reaction, when friends crowded about with congratulations.

Did he feel no trepidation, they asked, when other men were falling all around him?

Not at all. His only fear, Jackson earnestly confessed, was that he would not be able to get into enough of the dangerous action to draw the attention of superior officers, so that he might not be able to make his conduct under fire as notable as he would like!

He gave no further sign that he was pleased with himself, but he appeared as a remarkably single-minded young man who, having won renown on the field, was disposed to accept honors with gravity. He had passed his test as a good soldier, but there was in him none of the detachment with which Ewell, for example, looked upon the war. To Ewell the affair with the Mexicans, bloody though it was, had about it the air of comic opera. Jackson saw only the beckoning of glory.

Jackson did not stop even with complaining of the lack of opportunity under fire. He expounded the beauties of battle to his friends. It was always exalting to him, he said. Something happened to him in the gun smoke. He could not express it with precision, but: "I seem to have a more perfect command of my faculties, in the midst of fighting."

Jackson remained in Mexico until the following spring, furthering his education in assorted matters. He had fought his last battle of youth. Fourteen years of peace lay ahead of him.

Mexico had not only whetted his appetite for glory. There were stern lessons in supply and strategy and the pinch of privation, and in the very essence of victory in battle—mobility. He also broadened his acquaintance with the military aristocracy of the nation, such as it was to be in the coming years of neglect. In addition to Lee and the distinguished young men of Scott's staff, there were future Confederate generals on every hand: Ewell and Jubal Early, A. P. Hill and D. H. Hill, Joseph E. Johnston, Huger. There were also embryo Federal commanders: Grant, Hooker, McDowell, McClellan, Pope, Shields.

There were no letters about such companions. Instead, Jackson learned to dance, and became acquainted with some Mexican women. There are faint hues of a colorful season in letters to Laura:

> As I believe that this country is destined to be reformed by ours, I think that probably I shall spend many years here and may possibly conclude (though I have not yet) to make my life more natural by sharing it with some amiable Senorita. . . .

And:

> Do not allow my words about marrying in Mexico to disturb you. I have sometimes thought of staying here, and again of going home. I have no tie in this country equal to you. . . . My pay while with Captain Magruder was one hundred and four dollars per month, and I expect it will soon be the same here; but at present it is only about ninety; yet I have plenty of money. . . . I dress as a gentleman should who wishes to be received as such. I do not gamble, nor spend my money, as I think, foolishly. . . .

And:

The morning hours I occupy in studies and business, and generally taking a walk after dinner, and sometimes a ride on the Paseo or elsewhere in the evening.

The Paseo is a wide road on the southwest of the city and about half a mile in length, with a beautiful fountain in the centre, and is a place of fashionable resort. Families of wealth appear there in their carriages at sunset, partly if not entirely for show. . . . I purpose on riding . . . this evening hoping to see something there more attractive than at home.

When not on duty I generally pay a visit after supper or tea. Among those families which I visit are some of the first in the republic, as Don Lucas Alleman, Martinez del Rio. . . .

The book I am now studying is Lord Chesterfield's letters to his son translated into Spanish; so that whilst I am obtaining his thoughts, I am also acquiring a knowledge of the Spanish tongue. . . . Subsequent to this I shall study Shakespeare's works, which I purchased a few days since. . . .

There was less reserve here than in any letter Jackson wrote concerning the women of his life, and yet there was not enough to convince Laura or other readers that he was involved with a Mexican woman. He was to say much less, in his coy fashion, when it came to announcement of his actual marriage; but of the Mexican romance there remains only conjecture, based on the mild hint. Whatever the fact, some deep experience impressed him in this period, and its impact seems to speak from his letters.

In these pages to Laura, he, for the last time, gave an unstudied and natural image of himself in relations with women. The opposite sex was, for him, shortly to be merged in the powerful whirlpool of God-ambition-war-sacrifice, which appeared to grow within him.

Jackson studied in these months, but even so, thought, "I pass my time more agreeably than the greater portion of the officers," because of his Mexican friendships. He reported to Laura that his health was good. He read Humboldt's history of Mexico when the rainy season interrupted his schedule of social calls. He suggested to Laura that the American army was destroying the superstitious nature of the natives, except in one respect: "The natives still, with uncovered heads, drop on their knees at the approach of the Archbishop's carriage, which is recognized by its being drawn by two spotted mules."

Jackson was strongly attracted to the colorful figure of the clergyman. In a manner he did not explain, he became friendly with a number of priests in Mexico City, and probably tried to improve his Spanish among them. He was on such terms with these men that he spent some time in their quarters. He was as deeply impressed by the luxury of their lives as he had been by the obeisance of the church's worshipers, and wrote in obvious awe of the servants who waited upon the priests, and the rich foods of their table.

Through these friends he got an audience with the archbishop, to investigate the Catholic Church for himself; but though he saw the cleric several times, their talks passed without written record. For some reason, Jackson seemed to find the church lacking in appeal. He may—or may not—have been impelled to investigate the church by the prospect of marrying in Mexico.

He was now abruptly transferred back to the United States, and the impression left upon him by the months in Mexico was to be revealed only in the most casual and widely separated references. Beyond the use of Spanish terms of endearment to his future wife, the Mexican life seemed not to endure.

The army had ordered Jackson to a vastly different scene: a dull artillery post on Long Island, Fort Hamilton. He gave every indication that he had forgotten his experiences in the south. There remained from that war only the uniform.

Jackson's concern with religion grew. At Fort Hamilton, his commanding officer was Colonel Frank Taylor, a devout churchman who had been his superior in the First Artillery during the war. Taylor led Jackson into baptism.

Major Jackson had frequent talks with the colonel over his religious status. It seemed to trouble him that he could not ascertain whether he had been baptized as an infant. He went to a near-by chapel—it happened to have been Episcopal—and was baptized. He was careful to specify that the act merely welcomed him into the Christian fold, without binding him to become a member of any particular sect.

The Major settled into a new routine. He went on a long tour of court-martial duty: Carlisle Barracks, Pennsylvania; Fort Ontario, New York; West Point. He vacationed for a few days in upper New York State, to take a water cure. This was the first of a series of visits to hydropathic establishments, which he thought improved his health. He was forever writing Laura of his infirmities. Once his eyes failed for a few days, and light in his face was so painful that he was forced to mask even his mirror.

Jackson's doctor introduced him to a Spartan diet of stale bread and unseasoned meat, and the soldier wrote as if he gloried in this addition to his rigid code of self-denial: "The other evening I tasted a piece of bread with butter on it, and then the bread without it, and rather gave my preference to the unbuttered bread; and hence I may never taste any more of this once much relished seasoning."

He offered domineering advice to Laura on diet: "The yolk of one or two eggs—the white is hardly worth the eating as it requires digestion and affords but little nutrition. For dinner the same kind of bread and meat, one vegetable only, say peas, beans, or this year's potatoes, and for drink, plain water."

He warned her in a command which may have revealed more than he intended: "Taste nothing of which you are fond—except such things as I have mentioned. If you commence on this diet, remember that it is like a man joining the temperance society; if he afterwards tastes liquor he is gone."

Jackson seemed admirably suited by temperament to the new field of dieting. He confessed, honestly enough, that his various ailments could probably be traced to dyspepsia. His health improved. His weight rose from 133 to 166 pounds, and after two years at Fort Hamilton he was heavier than he had ever been. He sounded almost boastful: "My muscles have become quite solid. My exercises are of a violent character, when the chilblains on my feet do not prevent it."

Near the end of his stay at this post, he wrote to Laura in words which made the course of his religious development unmistakable:

"Yes, my dear sister, rather than wilfully violate the known will of God, I would forfeit my life; it may seem strange to you, yet nevertheless such a resolution I have taken, and I will by it abide. My daily prayers are for your salvation."

He was now, as abruptly as before, transferred to a new post—this time southward, to Fort Meade, Florida, where he was to spend brief and unhappy months, complaining that his scouting expeditions brought him no contact with the hostile Indians. He wrote more often of his religion and of war:

My opinion is that every one should honestly and carefully investigate the Bible, and then if he can believe it to be the word of God, to follow its teachings. . . . It is doubtful whether I shall ever relinquish the military profession, as I am very partial to it.

He wrote fondly of the Florida landscape and its vast stretches of pineland wilderness, with rides of "more than one hundred miles without seeing a house." Then, without warning, in the midst of recounting to Laura the high cost of groceries on the army post, he mentioned a letter he had received from the superintendent of the Virginia Military Institute, advising him of a vacancy on the staff, the chair of Natural and Experimental Philosophy. He had expressed interest, he said, but there was formidable competition: George B. McClellan, W. S. Rosecrans, and G. W. Smith, all comrades of Mexico. With this affair in the wind, Jackson revealed a new facet: "Philosophy is my favorite subject," he wrote.

In Lexington, Virginia, while Jackson waited and fought Florida fevers, his acquaintance, D. H. Hill, who now taught mathematics at Washington College in the little Virginia town, was telling the people of the Institute of Jackson's talents. He couldn't be sure about the philosophy, but Jackson was a crack gunner who behaved as if he had invented artillery. Not only had he shone in Mexico, but had been a determined cadet at West Point, who, if the term had been a year longer, would likely have led his class.

On March 28, 1851, Jackson was appointed: "Professor of Natural and Experimental Philosophy—and Artillery Tactics." He made a miraculous recovery from his fevers and packed for home. He wrote Laura:

"I expect to leave for home next week . . . my health is better than it has been for years, except my eyes, which are still weak."

8

★★★ THE PROFESSOR

It was spring of 1851 when Jackson arrived at Lexington in the Virginia hills. He was twenty-seven and already set in his ways, some of them quickly noted as curious by the natives. The life of the town was centered about two schools: ancient Washington College, and the twelve-year-old Institute, the latter a Southern replica of West Point, adapted to training young men for civilian life.

Before entering the classroom, Jackson had business with the hydropaths; and spent July and August on Lake Ontario, taking the baths. He reported that he "recruited very rapidly." He then went to Warm Springs, Virginia, to take over some of the cadet corps in summer encampment; and he found time to visit other spas, which then abounded in the country. He bathed at Rockbridge Alum Springs and Bath Alum Springs, and perhaps others.

He picked up an interest in science, as well, and began a collection of fossils and shells—neither of which he continued. He did not forget his Lord. In November, he joined the First Presbyterian Church, but only after attending for several Sundays and conferring with the minister, then a leading Lexington divine, Dr. William S. White. He began extended exercises in Christian logic under his pastor's direction, with results like this passage from a family letter:

> The best plan that I can conceive for an unbeliever in God . . . is to first consider things with reference merely to expediency . . . let us examine whether it is safer to be a Christian or an infidel.
>
> Suppose two persons, one a Christian and the other an infidel, to be closing their earthly existences. And suppose the infidel is right, and the Christian wrong; they will then after death be upon an equality.
>
> But instead of the infidel being·right, suppose him to be wrong, and the Christian right; then will the state of the latter after death be inestimably superior. . . .

He had begun the practice of tithing and was evidently thrifty. He acquired over these years a few of the tokens of moderately substantial position, including a couple of slaves and half a dozen shares of stock in the Bank of the Commonwealth of Virginia.

God began to dominate his thoughts now. He could scarcely separate religion from his artillery courses, which included optics and astronomy, fields in which the cadets found him dull. Some of the brighter students left complaints: Jackson was thorough, but slow and narrow-minded. He would allow pupils to reach conclusions only through his orthodox methods, and would accept no variants, however brilliant. There were deep-seated reasons for his uncompromising nature.

He gave more than a hint of this in a reply to a friend who wondered how Jackson dared accept the faculty post despite poor health, and who asked if the Major were not presumptuous. "Not in the least," Jackson said. "The appointment came unsought, and was therefore providential; and I knew that if Providence set me a task, He would give me the power to perform it. So I resolved to get well, and you see I have. What I willed to do, I could do."

This iron will could not keep him awake in church, however. He had a "predisposition to drowsiness" which often overcame him. Margaret Junkin Preston, a poet who knew him intimately in Lexington, wrote:

"Especially in church would this infirmity beset him. . . . Still he could not be persuaded to relax his perfectly erect posture. . . . When playfully pleaded with to lean back in the pew, for the reason that he could be less conspicuous, and the cadets opposite him in the gallery would be in less danger of being injured by his example . . . his constant reply to our badinage was,

" 'I will do nothing to superinduce sleep by putting myself at ease, or making myself more comfortable; if, however, in spite of my resistance I yield to my infirmity, then I deserve to be laughed at, and accept as punishment the mortification I feel.' "

He approached his church duties with a singleness of mind that passed in some quarters as fanatic zeal. Once he said to a fellow deacon who was absent from a meeting of church officers: "I don't see how, at this hour, we can possibly lack time for this meeting, or can have time for anything else, seeing it is set apart for this business."

He made regular reports to Dr. White on his own progress in piety. He sometimes managed to sound like a minister at work in letters to Laura:

> We are all children of suffering and sorrow in this world. Whilst it has many pleasures, it is not nor will not be divested of its cares. Amid affliction let us hope for happiness. . . . No earthly calamity can shake my hope in the future so long as God is my friend.

He wrote to his aunt, Mrs. Alfred Neale, in Parkersburg, Virginia, suggesting that he might hear the call to the pulpit himself.

> The subject of becoming a herald of the cross has often seriously engaged my attention, and I regard it as the most noble of all professions. . . . I should not be surprised were I to die upon a foreign field, clad in ministerial armor, fighting under the banner of Jesus.

He ended this letter, however, with the thought that he believed he could best serve the Lord in Lexington, and he wrote with evident fervor:

> Within the last few days I have felt an unusual religious joy. I do rejoice to walk in the love of God. . . . My Heavenly Father has condescended to use me as an instru-

ment for setting up a large Sabbath-school for the Negroes here.

Jackson's interest in the Negro Sunday school grew, and his own slaves were ordered to attend it with regularity. His stern code also governed here, and any late-comer to the services found the door locked, which the sponsor thought severe punishment.

Jackson seemed determined that he would not shed the uniform he had worn to fame in Mexico. Throughout his time in the village, he wore the garments of that war, topped by the cadet's cap which endured almost to the end of his life. He developed a rigid routine, too, and watches could be set in Lexington by his appearance. He left home at a precise moment for his stiff-limbed walk to the Institute campus. He returned by the identical route, with the same regularity. His meals were eaten at the exact same moment each day, and always opened with prayer—a schedule which never varied, and no one could interrupt.

Jackson was acutely embarrassed in a public role, but his will drove him to lead church meetings. Dr. White urged his flock to this service, and Jackson called upon the minister to ask if he, too, should attempt it. Encouraged, he made the effort when White called on him for a few words at prayer meeting.

Jackson stuttered some inanities, remaining stubbornly on his feet through long moments of silence, paining himself and the audience as well. White did not call him again until the Major, yet determined, insisted that he be given another chance. This time the prayers were said more smoothly, and he eventually became an accomplished prayer-leader. "My comfort or discomfort is not the question," he told White. "If it is my duty to lead in prayer, then I must persevere."

He carried this war against himself to the point of joining a village debating society—"The Franklin"—and belabored its members with awkward efforts in his screeching voice; even here he made improvement.

The Institute began to circulate similar tales of the inflexible purpose of this man, which seemed to rule every moment of his life. The cadets thought of him as a multiplication table in breeches.

One of the stories described the Institute superintendent's trials with Jackson. The commandant, Colonel Francis H. Smith, called Jackson into his office one afternoon and asked him to be seated in an anteroom while he attended to another matter. Smith then forgot Jackson entirely, left the building by another way, and went to his home for the night, with Jackson still seated in the foyer. It was there that the superintendent, to his eternal astonishment, found Jackson the next morning—with the explanation: "It never occurred to me to leave the spot of duty, where my superior told me to stay."

Relations with cadets were in this vein. One winter night, V.M.I. tradition has it, Jackson was unable to sleep because he had strongly scolded a cadet during the day for giving what Old Jack thought to be a false answer to a problem. Jackson tossed in bed, thinking of the incident, when it occurred to him that the cadet had been right, after all. The Major rose and dressed, walked through the cold night over the Institute grounds to a dormitory, where he had the wondering cadet called from sleep to accept an apology.

He is also pictured as rising another night, to walk more than a mile through a rainstorm, only to knock at the door of a friend with another explanation, this time that Jackson had made a misstatement in some minor detail of conversation during the day. The friends and cadets did not forget. Jackson's common name on the campus became "Tom Fool."

He had a wide acquaintance in the state, however, despite his piquancies and his inability to accept ordinary society. He was seldom invited to village parties, and when he did appear, and was confronted with food or drink, he refused with the cryptic reply: "I have no genius for seeming."

His reputation as an eccentric grew steadily, though within his church and school he was respected by leaders as a man of principle and talent. Yet there were touches of the exotic to puzzle the village.

There was once a lively report that a cadet whom he had helped to expel from the Institute had sworn to kill Jackson, and that he was the wild sort of boy who might well make an attempt on the Major's life. Jackson is said to have met this enraged cadet on the campus, and as the young man glared at him from his hiding place, Jackson only turned on him a calm stare—which was enough to make the cadet flee the place of contemplated murder. Lexington, to the last man, woman and child, began to know Jackson.

His reputation had a deceptive simplicity, however, for in his correspondence he revealed a certain sensitivity. He wrote an aquaintance:

> The kind of friends to whom I am most attached are those with whom I feel at home, and to whom I can go at all proper times, and informally tell them the object of my call . . . without the marred pleasure from a conviction that afterwards all my conduct must undergo a judicial investigation before 'Judge Etiquette', and that for every violation of his code I must be censured, if not socially ostracized.

Jackson was unfailingly polite, particularly to women. One woman observer left her impression: "There was a peculiarity about him which at once attracted your attention. Dignified and rather stiff, as military men are apt to be, he was as frank and unassuming as possible, and was perfectly natural and unaffected. He always sat bolt upright in his chair, never lounged, never crossed his legs, or made an unnecessary movement."

He was still a faithful correspondent with Laura, and wrote of such diverse matters as these:

> We have had green peas for some time, and the strawberries are . . . beginning to disappear, but the cherries are coming in.
>
> I wish that you could see our Institute, for I consider that it is the most tasty edifice in the state. . . . The weather is delightful. . . . I derive much pleasure from morning walks, in which is to be enjoyed the pure sweetness of carolling birds. . . .
>
> My appetite and digestion have improved . . .
>
> I have for months back admired Lexington, but now, for the first time, have I truly and fully appreciated it. Of all places that have come under my observation in the United States, this little village is the most beautiful. . . .

In taking a retrospective view of my own life, each year has opened . . . with increased promise. . . . I too have crosses, and am at times deeply afflicted . . . but I am improved by the ordeal . . . by throwing myself upon the protection of Him whose law book is the wonderful Bible. I would not part with this book for countless universes.

He made frequent mention of his health, and his abiding concern for tribulation, which he seemed to relish, as in the striking phrase, "I am a man of trouble."

In April, 1853, he stunned Laura with a line in a letter: "I am invited to a large party tonight, and among the scramble, expect to come in for my share of fun." Not even this prepared her for the news, however, for Major Tom, sworn to secrecy by his fiancée, had hoodwinked Lexington with a brief courtship of Eleanor Junkin, a daughter of Dr. George Junkin, a Northerner, Presbyterian minister, and president of Washington College.

Eleanor's older sister, Margaret, the poet, was her inseparable companion; the girls had twin interests, dressed identically, and were much alike, except that Eleanor was less shy and a bit the prettier. That did not prevent Margaret from going on the honeymoon with Eleanor and Jackson—through New York City, to Niagara Falls, into Canada, back through Boston, West Point, and other places.

Margaret left almost the only record of the wedding trip. Once, she recalled, on a Sunday afternoon in Montreal, "it was a matter of surprise to the rest of us to find Jackson going out on Sunday afternoon to witness the drill of a Highland regiment. When the matter was reverted to . . . he defended himself stoutly for having done so, giving as a reason . . . that if anything was right and good in itself, and . . . he could not avail himself of it any time but Sunday, it was not wrong for him to do so."

Eleanor disagreed, "quietly but firmly," branding Jackson's reasoning as sophistry, until Jackson said, "It is possible that my premises are wrong; when I get home I will go carefully over all this ground, and decide the matter for myself."

The result was a rigid observance of Sunday quiet which was to be interrupted only by war, and then only under the most extenuating circumstances.

Margaret also left a vivid glimpse into Jackson's nature, a moment on the honeymoon when "the military enthusiasm of Jackson's character first revealed itself to me. My sister and I stood with him one magnificent August evening, on the Plains of Abraham, at the foot of the monument erected to General Wolfe. As he approached the monument, he took off his cap, as if he were in the presence of some sacred shrine . . . he stood a-tiptoe . . . appearing much taller than usual . . . thin, sensitive nostrils quivering with emotion, and his lips parting . . . as he turned his face toward the setting sun, swept his arm with a passionate movement around the plain, and exclaimed, quoting Wolfe's dying words, 'I die content!' "

" 'To die as he died, who would not die content!' "

Of the marriage, Jackson had warned his family only with an inscrutable sentence: "Tell Miss Eliza that she must be on the lookout for something in relation to me."

Jackson paused on the honeymoon to write a physician friend from The Revere House in Boston, announcing his news thus: "I was married on the 4th instant to an intellectual, pure and lovely lady."

The couple returned to Lexington in the fall, where Jackson took over the drilling of the enlarged cadet corps, and wrote his sister: "My wife is a great source of happiness. She has those requisites of which I used to speak to you."

He sent Laura a lock of Eleanor's hair, commenting, "This she reluctantly parts with because of its color, which she hopes may prove more acceptable to your taste than it has ever been to hers."

Jackson and his wife visited often in the home of her parents. The Major found himself in agreement with Dr. Junkin, who was a strong Union man, and expressed decided ideas in discussions of politics, which were now charged with sectional conflict. In early 1854, Eleanor's mother died. Jackson wrote of her passing: "She said she was not afraid to die, and that she found Jesus precious to her soul. . . . She asked us to kiss her and told her children to live near Jesus and to be kind to one another. Her death was no leaping into the dark."

In the meager records left, Eleanor and "The Major," as she

called him, appear to have led a quiet, happy, normal life, with close relations to each of their families. During this time, for all his love of the Institute, Tom tried to land the chair of mathematics at the University of Virginia. He failed, even though he had a recommendation from Colonel R. E. Lee, the commandant at West Point.

Eleanor took a jolting stagecoach ride to visit Jackson's relatives in Western Virginia in November, 1854, and when she returned went immediately to bed. She died in childbirth; the child was stillborn. Jackson announced her death to his family:

> She has now gone on a glorious visit, though through a gloomy portal. . . . I look forward with delight to the day when I shall join her. Religion is all that I desire it to be. I am reconciled for my loss and have joy and hope of a future reunion where the wicked cease from troubling and the weary are at rest.

A bit later he wrote of her as "pure and lovely companion of my happier days. . . . We loved each other on earth; and shall that love be diminished in eternity?"

For a year he busied himself with the cadets, the church, the concerns of his numerous cousins, and real estate; he bought a farm outside the village. He revealed the growing tension in the country when he wrote to Laura of a kinsman: "Say to him that I design following out his idea of locating some land in a Northern state, but that I am a little afraid to put much there for fear that in the event of a dissolution of the Union that the property of Southerners may be confiscated."

Abruptly, in July of 1856, he changed his plans in a way to surprise all who knew him. He dropped his land ventures and went off to Europe. He had been promised leave the preceding year, for a European tour, and the postponed vacation was now offered by the Institute. He also wrote Laura that he could not get Eleanor out of his mind: "Yet even with you I would be reminded of the loss of that happiness which I once enjoyed with dear Ellie."

His passport described him: "Stature 5 feet 9 and three-quarter inches, English; forehead full, eyes gray, nose aquiline; mouth small; chin oval; hair dark brown; face oval, complexion dark." He then weighed about 175 pounds.

He sailed on the steamship *Asia* for Liverpool, on July ninth, intending to return in October. He began with a resolution to keep a journal, but lost that habit in England, where he toured the Lake Country, Scotland, and all accessible cathedrals and abbeys. In a letter to a friend, he sounded as if he recited from a travel folder with his account of that summer: "The Rhine, with its castellated banks and luxuriant vineyards; the sublime scenery of Switzerland, with her lofty Mont Blanc and massive Mer de Glace; the vestiges of Venetian beauty; the sculpture and paintings of Italy; the ruins of Rome; the beautiful Bay of Naples, illuminated by Vesuvius; and lovely France, with her gay capital." Thus the savings intended for investment in Western lands went into these spectacles, which in assortment seem to have almost numbed the traveling Major.

He once wrote another friend: "I would advise you never to name my European trip to me unless you are blest with a superabundance of patience, as its very mention is calculated to bring up with it an almost inexhaustible assemblage of grand and beautiful associations." He went on in such flowery terms about the glories of Florentine paintings and sculpture.

Among his visits, however, was one to Waterloo, where he went over the ground. He wrote no letters of this spot, but it is clear from his tireless study of former years that he knew the movements of Napoleon's campaigns almost as well as his own marches through Lexington. He picked up a smattering of French on his tour, and afterward opened the mornings of his household by reading the Scriptures from a French Testament.

His ship was late in reaching New York on the return voyage, and for several days Jackson was overdue in Lexington. On his arrival a friend asked if he were not afflicted with impatience, in view of his habitual punctuality. "Not at all," Jackson said. "I did all in my power to be here at the appointed time; but when the steamer was delayed by Providence, my responsibility was at an end."

He returned to work with renewed vigor, but did not forget Eleanor; he was often seen standing over her grave. And he continued to live in the home of Dr. Junkin. Margaret wrote:

"After the death of my sister, it became the established custom that, at nine o'clock . . . I should go to his study for an hour or two of relaxation and chat. But if I knocked before the clock had struck, I would find him standing before his shaded light . . . silent . . . and dumb. Not one moment before the ninth stroke had died away, would he fling aside his shade, wheel around his easy chair, and give himself up to such delightful nonchalance that one questioned whether this could be the same man. . . . I came to know the man as never before. His early life . . . furnished material for endless reminiscence. The blow of his wife's death was a terrible one to him, and when I would hear him say, 'Ah, if it might only please God to let me go now!' I marveled at the depth of his grief. And yet his resignation was very perfect, and to wear the aspect of cheerfulness became a fixed principle.

". . . He would tell amusing stories, and be so carried away with them himself, as almost to roll from his chair in laughter. He used to tell of hungry raids upon Mexican gardens, where . . . officers would make their supper on raw quinces. . . . He was very fond of dancing at this time (in Mexico), and had no hesitation in being present at Sunday night balls. When surprise would be expressed at this, he would say, 'Remember, I lived then up to all the light I had, and therefore I did not then, nor do I now reproach myself.'

"It was very evident that the charms of society never had so strong a hold upon him as when he was mingling freely with those beautiful Mexican women."

It was not long before Jackson again electrified the town— with his second marriage. Just before his wedding to Eleanor he had met, in the home of his friend D. H. Hill, two interesting young women from North Carolina, Eugenia and Mary Anna Morrison, also daughters of a Presbyterian minister and college president.

Mary Anna recalled these days:

"We knew that he was soon to be married. He was very intimate at the house of Major Hill, and was the first gentleman to call on us. . . . His greeting was most cordial, and he very soon offered his services . . . saying . . . we must call upon him as we would upon a brother."

Anna recalled that her pretty younger sister more often had dates, and thus Anna had the Major's arm to herself; she called it "the brotherly wing"—when they went to church. She had a strong first impression of him:

"More soldierly-looking than anything else, his erect bearing and military dress being quite striking; but upon engaging in conversation, his open, animated countenance, and his clear complexion, tinged with the ruddy glow of health, were still more pleasing. . . . His head was a splendid one, large and finely formed, and covered with soft, dark-brown hair, which, if allowed to grow to any length, curled; but he had a horror of long hair for a man . . . he was at all times manly and noble-looking, and when in robust health he was a handsome man."

She admitted that her description of him differed from that of others, but there is no indication that she was at first smitten with the Major, whom she saw go off on his honeymoon with Eleanor Junkin. The Morrison girls left Lexington, as did Major Hill, and they heard nothing from Jackson beyond the fact that his wife had died, until the Major shocked Anna with a letter full of such fond recollections of their acquaintance that the family knew she was in for a visit from Jackson.

Anna professed to be incredulous on the day she looked out the window of her father's house in Lincoln County, North Carolina, and saw Jackson's awkward figure approaching, unannounced.

Jackson had requested a leave of absence in the middle of the academic term, once he had determined to marry Anna—without notice to her. He got on well with Anna's father, the retired president and founder of Davidson College, and a man connected with several of the leading families of North Carolina.

After the visit came tender letters, and an engagement. Jackson wrote:

In my daily walks I think much of you. I love to stroll abroad after the labors of the day are over, and indulge feelings of gratitude to God for all the sources of natural beauty with which he has adorned the earth. . . . As my mind dwells on you, I love to give it a devotional turn, by thinking of you as a gift from our Heavenly Father.

He followed this with one of the most revealing of all his letters.

I wish I could be with you tomorrow at your communion . . . my prayer will be for your growth in every Christian grace. . . . It is to me a great satisfaction that our Heavenly Father has so manifestly ordered our union. . . . When in prayer for you last Sabbath, the tears came to my eyes and I realized an unusual degree of emotional tenderness. I have not yet fully analyzed my feelings to my satisfaction, so as to arrive at the cause of such emotions; but I am disposed to think that it consisted in the idea of the intimate relation existing between you, as the object of my tender affection, and God, to whom I looked up as my Heavenly Father. I felt that as if it were a communion day for myself.

He did not forget the stern nature of his Lord, however. He wrote Anna upon news of the death of Major Hill's son: "I was not surprised that little M. was taken away, as I have long regarded his father's attachment for him as too strong; that is, so strong that he would be unwilling to give him up, though God should call for his own."

They were married in July, 1857, at Cottage Home, the Morrison house in North Carolina. Anna had some bad moments, for her New York trousseau arrived just before the ceremony, and she had been forced to devise an emergency gown. She thought the minister gave an ominous ring to the phrase "indulgent husband" when he exacted promises of Jackson; the bridegroom, she recalled, was frozen stiff with fear.

He had been like a boy, almost childish, in advising Laura of the engagement:

I have an invitation for you; and what do you think it is? and who from? . . . I suppose you begin to think, Well, what does he mean? Why doesn't he tell me at once and be done with it? Well, you see I have finished the first page of my letter . . . so that if I don't tell you soon, you will hardly get it at all from this sheet. Well, now, having

cultivated your patience a little, as all women are said to
have curiosity, I will tell you that Miss Mary Anna Morrison, a friend of mine, in the western part of North Carolina . . . is engaged to be married to an acquaintance of
yours living in this village, and she had requested me to
urge you to attend her wedding in July next. . . .

Jackson gave Anna a gold watch and a set of seed pearls, and
took her on a trip to Richmond, Baltimore, Philadelphia, New
York, Saratoga, and Niagara, some of the scenes of his first
honeymoon. They did not neglect to stop at several watering
places, for the health of the groom. Anna's most vivid recorded
memory was of climbing the Trinity Church spire in New York,
to gaze down on the harbor, though she seemed to enjoy rowing
about on a lake at Saratoga, poking through the water lilies with
the Major at the oars.

Anna developed an enlarged gland in her neck, and Jackson
took her to Virginia, to Rockbridge Alum Springs; the health of
both improved. They returned to Lexington for the opening of a
new school year, and Jackson installed her in a hotel, but he expressed a longing in a letter to a friend:

I hope we shall be able to call some house our home.
. . . I shall never be content until I am at the head of an
establishment in which my friends can feel at home in Lexington. I have taken the first important step by securing a
wife capable of making a happy home, and the next thing
is to give her an opportunity.

Within a year he bought, on a side street, a big old house whose
front steps crouched over the public walk; he spent time and
money in renovation, and moved in two or three Negro servants,
some plain furniture, and Anna. Mrs. Jackson brought with her
a slave woman from North Carolina, one Hetty.

Jackson succumbed to domesticity. He studied a popular book,
Buist's *Kitchen Garden,* and with the aid of the Negroes produced
huge vegetable crops on his farm outside the village.

He and Anna memorized the Shorter Catechism as a Sunday
afternoon diversion since he had not learned it in youth. That
was the mere beginning of tasks he set for his memory. He now

made greater use of his walks to and from the campus by performing feats of mental exercise. He would begin as he left the door of his home, solving a series of complex mathematical problems, until he came to a final conclusion—as if he strode along tossing food to a trained animal. He became more expert at the solution of a variety of puzzles; in later years, he was to look upon terrain covered with combat troops, able in an intuitive flash to solve the difficulties presented. He traced the talent to his mental training in Lexington.

Anna was quickly made aware of the Jackson routine.

Jackson was up at 6 A.M., and knelt for private prayer. He then took a cold bath, every morning without exception. Next, a brisk walk, in rain or shine; in bad weather, he wore rubber cavalry boots and a heavy cloak.

At 7 A.M., family prayers, "which he required all his servants to attend promptly and regularly," Anna recalled. "He never waited for anyone, not even his wife "

Next, breakfast, and Jackson was off for the Institute, where classes began at eight. He returned home at 11 A.M., done with his classroom duties.

Until 1 P.M. he was alone in his study, standing at a high table, for there was no chair. He stood in order to keep perfect the alignment of his organs. He first read his Bible, using a commentary, poring over the pages, marking frequently with a pencil. He then studied his textbooks, and went to lunch.

After the meal, he gave himself half an hour for leisure, which Anna thought "one of the brightest periods in the home life." Many afternoons he drove to the farm with Anna, and she waited under a shade tree while he worked in the fields with a Negro helper. They went for occasional moonlight drives in the Valley.

There was no night study of books, for artificial light, Jackson thought, harmed his eyesight. He then "formed the habit of studying mentally for an hour or so without a book," reviewing the morning's lessons. He left Anna with a distinct memory of these hours: "He would, if alone with his wife, ask that he not be disturbed by any conversation, and he would then take his seat with his face to the wall, and remain in perfect abstraction until he finished his mental task, when he would emerge with a bright and cheerful face into social enjoyment again."

He became fond of having Anna read to him, and in that way they passed many evenings. Now and then, especially when she read Shakespeare, he would interrupt with a brief command: "Mark that!"

He moved his study into the living room and worked there under Anna's eye, at his tall custom-made desk, or "sat with face to the wall, as silent and as dumb as the Sphinx," among his small library of history, religion and science.

Early in 1858, Anna bore a daughter, whom they named Mary Graham; the infant died after a few weeks. Jackson wrote to a niece: "My little daughter was called from this world of sin to enjoy the heavenly happiness of Paradise. She died of Jaundice on the 25 of May. Whilst your Aunt Anna and myself feel our loss, yet we know that God has taken her away in love."

Jackson continued to suffer his vague and various ailments. He complained of an inflammation of an ear and his throat, and of neuralgia. He dosed himself with these: "chloroform liniment, a preparation of ammonia, glycerine, nitrate of silver." But after months of treatment, he wrote: "My disease is not understood by my physicians here, and I have nearly, if not entirely, lost my hearing in my right ear, and my left ear is diseased and my nose is also internally affected."

He took Anna north for the summer, and in New York he found "a physician by the name of Carnochan," in a medical college, who treated him for an inflamed tonsil and complications of the lung, by "paring off part of the tonsil."

There was some time for diversions on this trip. Jackson dutifully inspected Fortress Monroe, and for a few days bathed in the surf at Cape May, New Jersey, where Anna pictured him as "luxuriating." She dismissed his tonsillitis as "a slight bronchial trouble," and enjoyed sight-seeing with him. In New York, however, he left her alone in the mornings, striding forth from their hotel on long and unexplained walks. They went occasionally to the Dusseldorf Art Gallery, where Jackson studied paintings, gravely and at length.

Back in Lexington for the last of his undisturbed sessions with his cadets, Jackson seemed even more firmly fixed in the routine of his life. Colonel Smith reported that Jackson more than once paced up and down outside his Institute office in a pouring rain —because it was yet a few minutes prior to the customary time for presentation of his weekly report to the superintendent. He would not enter until the precise moment.

He was the butt of many a cadet joke, but there were times when Jackson could laugh with the young men who were so shortly to become soldiers. One afternoon, the drill field was especially resonant with mockery of his high, thin voice; every cadet officer was mimicking Jackson, and the drawls became so ridiculous that the companies could hardly remain together, for the laughter of cadets. The cadet adjutant, emboldened by the uninterrupted horseplay, asked Jackson how he liked the drill.

"Very much, sir," Jackson replied. "The officers gave very fine commands this afternoon."

Cadet artillerymen enjoyed a few moments of hilarity with Jackson one day by mounting a hidden bell inside the limber box of an artillery caisson, which tinkled at every movement of the battery. Jackson halted the guns time and again, seeking the source of the tinkling which gave the cadets such amusement, but if he found it, no recorded punishment was meted out.

He was perplexed by a failure of one of his scientific experiments. Jackson marched his class to the parade ground one afternoon, announced that the Institute's clock was incorrect, and that he would show them how to determine the time by observation with his instruments. It was shortly past noon at the time, but Jackson, after a series of calculations, announced the hour as 7 P.M., and cadets fell all about him, howling in laughter at the error made ludicrous by the man of legend Jackson had become. The Major joined in the laughter, but was careful to inspect his instruments and pronounce them out of working order.

Among other things his cadets recalled was the motionless, intent figure seated in the classroom, hearing recitations without a book before him, and correcting students from memory, quoting long passages of text.

To Anna he seemed to lead a double life, and she was to insist into her old age that the people of Lexington never knew her husband, because they could not fathom the change that came over him when he entered his home. There, she said, he was so gay and carefree by contrast that strangers could not have recognized him.

She recalled occasions when he tumbled on the floors with visiting small children, and a kinsman carried to manhood the recollection of Jackson saying solemnly to a young child:

"I had a little pig
And I fed him on clover.
And when he died,
He died all over."

The Major spent much time in good-humored teasing of the plump, brown-eyed little North Carolina girl he had married. He invariably used Spanish terms of endearment, and referred to himself as *esposo* and to her as *esposa* or *esposita*. He found her uncle, William Graham, amusing, a gentleman Whig from the old days who wore antique knee breeches and ruffled shirts, and silk stockings with silver buckles. He teased his wife about the Morrison clan, too, a tribe which had come from the Isle of Lewis, fishermen of the Outer Hebrides, and he likely repeated the family legend about old Jim Morrison, the first of the American branch: "He killed more red Indians and more red liquor than any man in Pennsylvania." Old Jim's sons had run strongly to Presbyterian ministers.

Anna's elder sister, Isabella, had married D. H. Hill, who was to become a Confederate general; Eugenia, the younger girl, married another such officer of the future, Rufus Barringer of North Carolina.

There were evidently some items which the Major kept from his wife:

A West Point companion, D. H. Maury, saw him just before he went to Lexington and had the chance to observe him closely. Maury wrote: "He had then become hypochondriacal. He had queer ideas about his health; he thought one side of him was heavier than the other, and sometimes he would raise one hand up to the arm's length to let the blood flow downward and lighten that arm."

The major certainly concealed nothing of his character by design, for he seemed to regard it as his duty to confess every thought passing his mind and to explain his compulsions in some detail.

Once he fell to discussing with a church friend the difficulty of obeying the injunction of the Bible, "Pray without ceasing." Jackson held that such obedience was simple.

"When we take our meals, there is grace. When I take a draught of water I always pause, as my palate receives the refreshment, to lift up my heart to God in thanks and prayer. . . . Whenever I drop a letter into the box at the post office I send a petition along with it for God's blessing upon its mission, and upon the person to whom it is sent. When I break the seal upon a letter, I stop to pray to God that he might prepare me for its contents, and make it a messenger of good. When I go to the classroom, and wait for the arrangement of the cadets in their places, that is my time to intercede with God for them. And so of every familiar act of the day."

"But don't you often forget them—coming so frequently?"

"No. I have made the practice habitual to me; and I can no more forget it than to forget to drink when I am thirsty. The habit has become as delightful as regular."

His household, molded to such an inflexible form, operated smoothly and with punctuality. Anna recalled one of Jackson's habits of outwitting his errant servants. "When a servant left a room without closing a door, he would wait until he had reached the kitchen, and then call him back to shut it, thereby giving him extra trouble, which generally insured his remembrance next time. His training made the colored servants as polite and punctual as that race is capable of being."

His wife recorded one "playful endearment" staged by Jackson:

"One morning he returned from a very early artillery drill, for which he had donned full regimentals, as it was during commencement time, and he never looked more noble and handsome than when he entered his chamber, sword in hand. He playfully began to brandish the sword over his wife's head, looking as ferocious and terrible as a veritable Bluebeard, and asking her if she was not afraid. His acting was so realistic that, for a moment, the timid little woman did quail, which he no sooner saw than he threw down his sword, and, in a perfect outburst of glee, speedily transformed himself into the very antipode of a wife-killer."

The major, she said, would often hide behind a door when he heard her approaching, and spring out "to greet her with a startling caress."

Anna was in New York for medical treatment for a few days, and Jackson's letters were full of such sentiments as: "Home is not home without my little dove. I love to talk to you as though you were here. . . . You are somebody's sunshine . . . my little dove, my little pet. . . . Try to live near to Jesus, and secure that peace which flows like a river. . . . You are very precious to somebody's heart."

Shortly after, when he had gone to White Sulphur Springs for the baths, he wrote her: "I am tired of this place. . . . I want to go and stay with my little woman. As yet I am not certain whether the waters are beneficial."

In November, 1859, he was ordered to Charlestown, where he commanded troops at the hanging of John Brown. He returned from that scene with a head cold, of which he complained.

War was now coming obviously closer to them, but the Major seems to have avoided the arguments then waxing in Lexington as in every other village and town. He let it be known that he favored the Union and insisted that Virginia could get her rights inside better than without. But he left no doubt as to where his sympathies lay. At the approach of 1860, he wrote his aunt, Mrs. Alfred Neale:

> What do you think about the state of the country? Viewing things at Washington from human appearances, I think we have great reason for alarm, but my trust is in God; and I cannot think that He will permit the madness of men to interfere so materially with the Christian labors of this country at home and abroad.

In June, the summer before the election of Lincoln, Jackson's letters showed more concern for such matters as a new piano, and the planting of Silesia lettuce, and a trip to the North, than for affairs of politics.

Anna and Jackson took the baths at Brattleboro, Vermont, and Northampton, Massachusetts, that summer, and in the latter town, at a place called the Round Hill Water Cure, Jackson made a firm friend of a Baptist minister who was an Abolitionist—to the astonishment of Anna. Her husband, she said, listened to the arguments over slavery and the secession issue, but did not enter them. Anna was herself lured to the water cure:

"I had gone there without a particle of faith in hydropathy, but as I was not strong, my husband persuaded me to try it, and it was astonishing how rapidly my strength developed. From not being able to walk a mile on arrival, by degrees I came to walking five miles a day with ease, and kept it up."

Back home, in an atmosphere becoming more tense each day, with South Carolina in outright rebellion and other states following, Jackson continued to live quietly. His first recorded mention of the day's crisis, in any detail, was in a line to Laura. After he had asked, "What is being done for The Redeemer's cause?" in her town in Western Virginia, he wrote:

I am looking forward with great interest to the 4th of January when the Christian people of this land will lift their united prayer as incense to the Throne of God in supplication for our unhappy country. (A national day of prayer for peace). What is the feeling about Beverly respecting secession? I am strong for the Union at present, and if things become no worse I hope to continue so. I think the majority in this country are for the Union, but in counties bordering on us there is a strong secession feeling.

A Washington peace conference brought a momentary lull in the gathering storm; when it failed, Jackson talked over the situation with his minister, Dr. White:

"If the Federal Government persists in these measures, there must be war. It is painful to see with what unconcern they talk war—they do not know its horrors. I have seen enough of it to know it as the sum of all evils. . . . But if they take the threatened step, we must fight."

Writing a nephew, T. J. Arnold, in Western Virginia, Jackson set down more fully his thoughts on the coming whirlwind.

. . . I am in favor of making a thorough trial for peace, and if we fail in this, and the state is invaded, to defend it with a terrific resistance. . . .

I desire to see the state use every influence . . . to procure an honorable adjustment of our troubles, but . . . if the free states, instead of permitting us to enjoy the rights guaranteed to us by the Constitution . . . should endeavor to subjugate us, and thus excite our slaves to servile insurrection in which our families would be murdered without quarter or mercy, it becomes us to wage such a war as will bring hostilities to a speedy close.

People who are anxious to bring on war don't know what they are bargaining for; they don't see all the horrors that must accompany such an event.

For myself I have never as yet been induced to believe that Virginia will even have to leave the Union. I feel pretty well satisfied that the Northern people love the Union more than they do their peculiar notions of slavery, and that they will prove it to us when satisfied that we are in earnest about leaving the Confederacy unless they do us justice.

He wrote later to another correspondent: "If I know myself, all I am and have is at the service of my country." He meant Virginia, not the United States.

Before Virginia's Secession Convention, an incident threatened bloodshed in Lexington. In the absence of officers, a group of cadets fired on a United States flag in the village, ripped it down and replaced it with a state flag. The town's volunteer militiamen drove off the cadet guard and went about restoring the American flag. Drums beat the alarm on the Institute campus, and most of the corps poured out the gates, ready for a skirmish. Only the sudden arrival of Colonel Smith halted it. The cadets were marched back to their barracks, where, in an exciting scene, they were harangued by their officers on the nation's crisis.

After several men had spoken, cadets began to call for Jackson, and the tradition is that, this time, with all traces of his customary shyness gone, he shouted:

"I admire the spirit you have shown in rushing to the defense of your comrades; and I commend the way in which you obeyed the commands of your superior officer. The time may come, young gentlemen, when your state will need your services, and if that time comes, draw your swords and throw away your scabbards."

April twelfth brought Fort Sumter; April fourteenth, Lincoln's call for seventy-five thousand men to defend the Union; April seventeenth, Virginia's secession.

Little else that Jackson said in these times is left. He was heard to agree with the theme of Jefferson Davis that the South was not in revolt, but that she was seeking to maintain the liberties won in the Revolution. This theory was much in vogue at the moment.

Virginia's secession came with Jackson in the midst of a Presbyterian synod meeting in Lexington, when his house literally crawled with visiting ministers. He found no time for church sessions, for he was on almost constant duty at the Institute, where war had already come.

Governor Letcher had sent an order from Richmond: The V.M.I. cadets of the upper classes, those best qualified, were to come at once to the capital. Jackson was to command them.

Late Saturday night, April 20, alone with Anna, he sighed the hope that he would at least be given tomorrow for rest and church affairs. It was not quite dawn when boots thumped on his steps and a messenger hammered on the door—the orders to move to Richmond. Jackson went to the campus without breakfast and worked most of the morning to prepare his young men for the road. He set 1 P.M. as their time of departure, and went home to Anna and a delayed breakfast.

He sent Dr. White to the barracks to pray over the young soldiers. Jackson then closed the door of his bedroom and sat down with Anna, taking his Bible and reading from the fifth chapter of Second Corinthians words which deeply moved his wife:

"For we know that if our earthly house of this tabernacle be dissolved, we have a building of God, a house not made with hands, eternal in the heavens . . ."

The Major read the entire chapter, and then prayed for the

country, for peace, and for Anna, her home and servants—and went out the door to war.

He found the cadets waiting at the Institute, with every strap in place. After a brief devotional service by Dr. White, they were impatient to take the road. An officer came to Jackson, saying that all was ready and that the corps should move.

Jackson nodded to the clock on the barracks wall, which indicated a few minutes before one. The young soldiers were forced to stand, silent and frowning, until their exact commander gave the word. Precisely at one o'clock they were off. They were quickly out of sight, on their way to Staunton and the railroad. Jackson was to return only in death.

9

★★★ HE HAS FOUGHT BEFORE

Jackson led his cadets toward a Richmond gone mad.
He put them into camp at the Fair Grounds, a little over a mile
from the center of the city, and was then caught in the currents
of war which swirled more rapidly each day. He was well known
among the leaders of Virginia's war effort. R. E. Lee, who had
so strongly recommended him for a new job, seven years before,
was commander of the Virginia troops. Of this, Jackson wrote
Anna: "Colonel Robert E. Lee . . . has been made major general. This I regard as of more value to us than to have General
Scott as commander. . . . I regard him as a better officer than
General Scott."

Old Winfield Scott, now vainly puffing in his effort to preside
over a similar scene in Washington, had not long since agreed: "If
I were on my death bed, and the President should tell me that a
great battle was to be fought for the liberty or slavery of the
country, and asked my judgment as to the ability of a commander,
I would say with my dying breath, let it be Robert E. Lee."

But it was not Lee whose eye first glimpsed Jackson in the
melee of politicians and speculators, last-minute Yankee trades-
men and swarming Virginia boys come in to war. John Letcher,

136

the professional politician who was now governor, came from Rockbridge County, and knew Jackson well. Letcher had just appointed a military commission to guide the State Convention, one member of which was Colonel Francis Smith, the Institute superintendent. Even so, Jackson was not immediately rescued.

His cadets were snapped up, and were busy drilling newcomers in every vacant lot and up and down the streets, leaving Jackson without an occupation. For a day or two—the record is not clear—he was stuck away in a draughtsman's office as a topographical engineer. But the Confederacy had not yet moved in, and the Virginia bureaus of war had not become so proficient in the use of red tape as to hold him from the field, and Jackson escaped.

Smith mentioned his name to Letcher, who, without hesitation, proposed Jackson for the rank of colonel, to command Virginia infantry. Jackson was sent to Lee, who gave him a sincere welcome. He told Jackson in bald terms of the strategic situation and approved Letcher's suggestion that this new colonel be sent to Harpers Ferry, where a mob of Virginians had burned the Federal armory. Lee and Jackson discussed this Potomac post, which could not be long defended because of surrounding hills, but must be held as long as possible, to secure the river line against Federal invasion. Jackson was to hold the town, begin training of troops, and send to Richmond the guns and armsmaking machinery found there.

A natural question had arisen when Jackson's name was presented to the State Convention, along with those of other colonels: "Who is this man Jackson?" That was too much for the patriotic pride of S. M. Moore, the delegate from Rockbridge County, who shouted, "He's a man we can order to hold a post, and know he'll never leave it alive to be taken by the enemy." Jackson's reputation as a Lexington eccentric was forever changed.

This rhetoric was enough, with the backing of friends, to get convention approval of Jackson's colonelcy and his post on the frontier where war might flare at any moment.

Soon Jackson was in Winchester, on the way to the post, wearing the drab, worn Institute uniform, with no mark of rank. He had so undistinguished a look that one recruit blandly asked him to teach him the manual of arms, which Jackson did. He could not stifle his pride. He wrote to Anna:

On last Saturday the Governor handed me my commission as Colonel of Virginia volunteers, the post I prefer above all others. . . . Little one, you must not expect to hear from me very often, as I expect to have more work than I have ever had in the same length of time before.

He got from Harpers Ferry about the reception which would have been given a Yankee shell. Virginia had just removed from service her swaggering volunteer officers above the grade of captain; the border village had been full of generals and colonels, all enthusiastic civilians whose conception of war was to dash about the village to the cheers of lounging troops. These favorites banished, the two thousand ill-assorted Virginia soldiers found in their place only this stern and uninspiring officer, Colonel Jackson. Not a fleck of gold on his shoulder nor a plume on his hat, yet he put troops to work as if they were laborers, or slaves. He kept rails and roads filled with cars of machinery and captured guns going back to Richmond. The easiest of the routes was to Winchester by rail, then a painful overland transfer to the Manassas Gap Railroad at Strasburg, and then eastward to the Orange and Alexandria tracks at Manassas Junction, and so to Richmond. The arms-making machinery got an almost hysterical welcome in the capital.

Jackson brought discipline to his garrison; he brought in more volunteers, established pickets and supervised endless training. He had little to say, even to his officers, and sometimes rode incognito on inspections of his outposts. He found some able men in the village, and some old friends: John Imboden, a gifted artilleryman; Colonel W. N. Pendleton, the Episcopal rector from Lexington whose Rockbridge Artillery was housed in a church (his gunners, chiefly from seminaries, christened his guns Matthew, Mark, Luke and John); there was also Major J. L. T. Preston, from the Institute, who had married Margaret Junkin.

A visiting band from the Maryland legislature called on Jackson, and though it was important to woo these neutrals, the colonel could not unbend. When the guests indiscreetly asked him of his strength, Jackson barked, "I should be glad if President Lincoln thought I had 50,000 men."

Anna learned little more through the mails: "I haven't time now to do more than tell you how much I love you. . . . You say that your husband never writes you any news. . . . What do you want with military news? Don't you know that it is unmilitary . . . to write news respecting one's post?"

One of Jackson's chief works at Harpers Ferry was perhaps the most devious ruse of his career—the virtual kidnaping of a railroad. The Baltimore & Ohio tracks lay through his lines, and though Richmond forbade him to tear up the road for fear of repercussions, he plotted to capture its priceless rolling stock by guile. Traffic was heavy since the road was hauling great loads of coal from the mountains. Jackson played for the fine locomotives and cars as if in a chess game.

He complained to John W. Garrett of Baltimore, president of the railroad, that trains disturbed his men at night, and must be routed through Harpers Ferry at about noon; the railroad agreed, though it was a troublesome chore. Garrett was hardly in position to argue with a Confederate officer who held the big bridge over the Potomac.

John Imboden, who helped in the capture, wrote: "But since the 'empties' were sent up the road at night, Jackson complained that the nuisance was as great as ever, and, as the road had two tracks, said he must insist that the west-bound trains should pass during the same hour as those going east. Again he was obliged, and we then had, for two hours every day, the liveliest railroad in America."

Jackson was then ready to close his trap. He sent Imboden to Point of Rocks, across the Potomac, with orders to halt all east-bound trains, and pass all those heading west. At Martinsburg, a few miles upriver, he reversed the order. At twelve o'clock, as Jackson ordered, the lines were closed at each end of the double-track area, and the Confederacy had netted fifty-six locomotives and more than three hundred cars.

This coup was soon a source of torment to Jackson, however. He was able to shift four of the smaller locomotives across the Shenandoah bridges to Winchester by the Winchester and Po-

tomac Railroad, but this line was light and could not accommo-
date the huge engines he had captured; further, there was no rail
line to the south of Winchester.

That was not the worst of it. Within a few days, when strategy
dictated a withdrawal from this town, Jackson was forced to
blow up the Potomac bridge and run his captive engines into the
river, or leave them charred and burning for the enemy to discover. A Washington reporter was to count over forty ruined
locomotives in a line: "Red and blistered with heat. The destruction is fearful to contemplate."

Not even John Garrett could have more bitterly rued the destruction than did Jackson, who fully understood the value of
this rail stock and was saddened to see it lost to the Confederacy.

A Richmond newspaper, the first to salute Jackson's fame,
wrote that week:

"The commanding officer at Harpers Ferry is worthy of the
name he bears, for 'Old Hickory' himself was not a more determined, iron-nerved man than he. Born in Virginia, educated
at West Point, trained in the Mexican War, occupied since at the
pet military institution of the Old Dominion, his whole life has
been a preparation for this struggle.

"A brother officer says of him, 'He does not know fear!' Above
all, he is a devoted Christian, and the strongest man becomes
stronger when his heart is pure and his hands are clean."

In the glow of this tribute, Jackson lost his command. One
morning Joseph E. Johnston appeared in Harpers Ferry announcing that he was to relieve Jackson. Old Jack quietly declined to surrender the post until Johnston, fumbling through
his papers, found an order from Lee which satisfied the ever-
soldierly Jackson that the transfer was proper. He then stepped
aside.

He was given some Virginia troops, five regiments from the
Shenandoah country, for the most part tough mountain men. In
the moment, however, Jackson could see no future glories, and
there were tones of chagrin in letters to Anna:

My precious darling, I suppose you have heard that
General Joseph E. Johnston, of the Confederate Army, has

been placed in command here. You must not concern yourself about the change. . . . I hope to have more time, as
long as I am not in command of a post, to write longer letters
to my darling pet.

Federal troops appeared in Western Virginia, and Johnston,
saying, "The want of ammunition has made me very timid,"
burned bridges and public buildings, and abandoned Harpers
Ferry. Before he got out of the town, Jackson took a couple of
captured horses. One of them was the stout Sorrel, or Fancy, the
mount that was to become famous with him.

On the day he left the smoking town, he wrote Anna: "You
speak of others knowing more about me than my darling does,
and you say you have heard through others that I am a brigadier
general. By this time I suppose you have found out that the report
owes its origin to Madam Rumor."

This wounded pride was short-lived, however, for three days
later, on June seventeenth, he was made a brigadier, with ten
other Confederates; among them: Magruder, commanding on
the Peninsula below Richmond; Dick Ewell and Colonel Barnard
E. Bee of South Carolina, known to Jackson in Mexico—and
now serving at his side, under Johnston.

A new hero now streaked across Virginia like a meteor: Pierre
Gustave Toutant Beauregard, the conqueror of Fort Sumter, a
genuine, war-tested scourge of the Yankees. He passed rapidly
northward, through a cheering Richmond, and, as if intuitively
migrant, settled at Manassas Junction. This spot was less than
thirty miles from Washington, an important rail junction, a way
point on a Federal invasion route to Richmond, and a convenient
spot to link the Confederate armies of the east and west. Beauregard began to collect troops, to the number of about twenty
thousand, and to spin elaborate plans of war.

Jackson had his hands full. He had already shown a kinship
with Lee in his plea that Harpers Ferry be held—and an unspoken contempt for the timid Johnston:

"I am of the opinion," he had written Lee, "that this place
should be defended with the spirit which actuated the defenders
of Thermopylae. . . . The fall of this place would . . . result
in the loss of the northwestern part of the state, and who can

estimate the moral power thus gained to the enemy and lost to ourselves?"

Lee had agreed, but was forced to leave Johnston to his own devices. In any event, the deed was done, and Johnston's force was patrolling south of the Potomac in the western quarter, waiting for war to come.

Jackson went through marches and countermarches, up to Charlestown, and out toward the enemy camp at Martinsburg. It seemed to Old Jack that Johnston moved to no purpose, or was frightened by shadows. He left a hint of this in a letter to Anna: "I hope the general will do something soon. . . . I trust that through the blessing of God we shall soon be given an opportunity of driving the invaders from this region."

To the east, in the Tidewater country beyond Richmond, the war had already started with a little brush at Big Bethel Church, an affair in which Jackson's brother-in-law, D. H. Hill, had come to the fore as a commander. His name was on many lips, though he had left many gray-clad bodies on the field of victory.

In the west, Jackson got no more than an occasional sniff of the enemy. He once reported one of his men shot in the abdomen but said, "I am inclined to think it was done by a Virginian rather than a Northerner."

It was at this time that he acquired a new man on his staff: Sandie Pendleton, an affable son of the rector, who was made ordnance officer and adjutant general. Despite his youth, Pendleton became the real, if untitled, chief of staff to Jackson.

Old Jack also met here a fascinating comrade in arms, a warrior so irrepressibly gay that Jackson could not keep his eyes off him: James Ewell Brown Stuart, lieutenant colonel of cavalry, just in from the Western plains. Stuart had three hundred troopers galloping the dusty roads, riding circles around the dazed Federals. The look of him was enough to stun Jackson.

Stuart dismounted from one of his punishing rides, sweeping back a soiled cloak to reveal a faultless Confederate-gray coat lined in scarlet silk; he wore tiny golden spurs, and there was a floppy black ostrich plume in his big hat. His French saber was hooked over a golden silk sash. There was a red rose in his lapel, and he wore white buckskin gloves. The solemn Jackson was dazed.

At Stuart's back rode a curious man with a banjo strapped to his shoulder, one Joe Sweeny, an old minstrel-show man who fell to making music, in which all these incredible horsemen joined:

"The years creep slowly by, Lorena,
The snow is on the grass again;
The sun's low down the sky, Lorena,
The frost gleams where the flowers have been. . . ."

Or, without warning, the fey company would howl a parody of a tune becoming popular in all camps:

"Just before the battle, mother,
I was drinkin' mountain dew.
When I saw the Yanks amarchin',
To the rear I quickly flew."

But Jackson understood Stuart immediately, for the horseman divined the true meaning of orders and carried them out like a military artisan, with creative improvements of his own. Stuart was a strong temperance man, too; he behaved as if he were perpetually inspired, but this was from natural causes, for he was a teetotaler. He, like Jackson, was a stern Sabbath-keeper, if the enemy permitted. And he worked hard with his command; Stuart did not ask the troopers to ride where he dared not go himself.

Jackson liked the ring of Stuart's words: "If we oppose force to force we cannot win, for their resources are greater than ours. . . . We must substitute *esprit* for numbers. Therefore I strive to inculcate in my men the spirit of the chase." Jackson understood him.

The two worked together as Jackson had his first formal meeting with the enemy, at a place called Falling Waters, on July 2, 1861. General Robert Patterson of the Union army pushed across the Potomac and began to probe the Rebel lines, in this case an error. Patterson was still crossing the river when Stuart advised Jackson of the move, and Old Jack rushed forward with one regiment and a few guns. He had timid orders from Johnston to feel out the enemy and fall back under cavalry cover. Jackson and Stuart managed to accomplish much more, though without breaking orders.

Jackson found the Federals near a church just south of the Potomac and put his men to wait for their advance over open fields; the unpracticed bluecoats met staggering musket fire, and then Jackson charged them. He was taking a heavy toll when superior numbers forced him to fall back. The Federals misinterpreted this move as a rout. The Union volunteers were hurried along an open highway in column, a perfect target for the Reverend Pendleton, who came up with his big guns. Tradition pictures him as raising his bushy head and praying, "Lord have mercy on their souls," before he tore apart the Union formation with a single gun.

Jackson went back slowly, so alert that he actually counted his artillery shells: "My cannon fired only eight times, while the enemy fired about 35 times; but the first fire of Captain Pendleton's battery was probably worth more than all of theirs." Jackson lost twenty-five men. "My officers and men behaved beautifully," he said.

Stuart came off well, with a string of prisoners (fifty of which he took singlehandedly). The cavalryman had closed roads on all sides of the enemy and helped to confuse Patterson so thoroughly that the latter thought he faced thirty-five hundred Rebels, rather than the band of under five hundred Jackson actually commanded. The Federals settled down in Martinsburg.

Jackson wrote Anna: "The enemy are celebrating the 4th of July . . . but we are not observing the day." He spoke once more of his recent brigadier general's commission: "It was beyond what I anticipated. . . . I have had all that I ought to desire in the line of promotion."

Affairs, however, were swirling toward a rapid climax, and he was about to step into the center of the stage of war.

Soon after midnight, July eighteenth, General Johnston was aroused in his Winchester headquarters. The main Federal army was sweeping toward Manassas Junction. He was to elude the enemy in his region and rush his men to the east. General Beauregard was attacked by an overwhelming force.

Officers woke the men, and with Stuart behind to hoodwink General Patterson, the infantry started south through Winchester, turned eastward, and in the dark road paused while officers read orders: "The Commanding General hopes that his troops will step out like men, and make a forced march to save the country." There were cheers, and the green troops tried, but were pitifully inept. Johnston long remembered "the discouragement of that day's march, to one accustomed to the steady gait of regular soldiers."

The troops reached the Blue Ridge at dark, after almost eighteen hours on the move, and early in the night forded the chest-deep Shenandoah. During the night, Johnston's army crossed Ashby's Gap. They had a rest at 2 A.M., after going twenty miles. Men fell asleep in their tracks without a thought for pickets. Jackson refused to have the exhausted men aroused for sentry duty, and he alone stood guard over the sleeping brigade. Just before daylight an officer persuaded him to lie down, while he substituted for him, and Jackson took a few moments of rest.

Stuart's cavalry passed at dawn, reporting a quiet enemy in the rear. When the infantry reached Piedmont, at the foot of the mountains, trains were waiting to carry them to Manassas. By midafternoon they were on the field of Bull Run. Few Federals came in sight of Jackson's men, but there was far cannon fire, and the stories were fearful: General McDowell was across the stream, everywhere, with thirty-five thousand men; no one had ever seen such an army. Already the country was filled with stragglers. The lines of wagons and big guns were endless, and there were carriages, too, with Congressmen and their ladies and society people out to see the sport.

A Union private, Warren Lee Goss, remembered the experience of the naïve soldiers coming down into Rebel territory: "They gave us rations of salt junk, hard-tack, sugar and coffee. Each man carried his rubber and woolen blanket, 40 rounds of cartridges, a canteen, his gun and equipments, and most of us a patent drinking tube. I hadn't been on the march an hour before I realized that it might not be such fun, after all. . . . The weather was scorching hot, but the most trying thing was the jerky way they marched us. Sometimes they'd double-quick us, and again they'd keep us standing in the road waiting in the hot sun . . . we saw carriages and barouches which contained civilians who had driven out from Washington. . . . We thought it wasn't a bad idea to have the great men . . . come out and see us thrash the Rebs. Every one of us expected to have our names in the papers when we got home."

William T. Sherman was there with the Federals, too, and wrote: "The march demonstrated the general laxity of discipline; for with all my personal efforts I could not prevent the men from straggling for water, blackberries or anything on the way that they fancied. Our men had been told often at home that all they had to do was to make a bold appearance, and the Rebels would run."

There was anxiety on the Confederate side. Lee paced in Richmond, waiting, while the sickly Jefferson Davis hung about field headquarters at Manassas, looking from the soulful hound's eyes of Beauregard to the prim little face of Joe Johnston, seeking reassurance. Lee had chosen the ground for defense, and it was good; he had labored to get troops to the site, too. Unfortunately for the Rebels, not all of Johnston's troops had yet arrived from the west. A pair of Yankee engineers had deliberately crashed their trains to block the rails.

Through the early morning hours of Sunday, July twenty-first, General McDowell was pushing up thirty thousand men toward a waiting force of some twenty-six thousand Confederates. At the same hour, Johnston was attempting to launch a plan of attack conceived by Beauregard—a slash from his right flank.

With morning, the largest American armies ever assembled made ready for the first great bloodletting of the war. The day was ideal for the purpose, clear and warm. The Confederates began by bungling, for General Ewell, who was to lead the attack, did not get his orders and did not move as he should. Soon the Yankees advanced, and the two raw armies, little more than mobs, fell upon each other.

It did not begin as a day of significance for Jackson. He lay back in reserve on a hot hillside as the opening scenes rolled before him. In the distance, through heat waves, rose a dust cloud, and the young Confederate gunners used the cloud as a target, firing steadily.

At nine forty-five, bluecoats emerged from dust opposite the stream, and the first of the Federal charges came. The enemy crossed at a place called Sudley Ford and soon struck the Louisiana Tigers, the spirited men of Major Rob Wheat. The enemy was at first driven off, but Wheat was wounded, and a South Carolina regiment was roughly handled. The Federals finally drove off the Tigers and South Carolinians. Up and down Bull Run a string of terrible little battles exploded, as if they had no relation one to the other; in each, green troops fought as if for the lives of all.

As noon approached, General Johnston, who had left the assault to Beauregard, finally became restless and rode into the field. Johnston told Beauregard to throw his reserves into action, and shouted, "The battle is there. I am going." Beauregard followed him.

Johnston, guided by an accurate ear, came to the key terrain of the day, a place called the Henry House Hill, owned by a widow, Judith Henry. Near by was the home of a free Negro, one Robinson. The Generals studied the field.

Numbers of Confederate troops were at hand. On the face of the hill was a shrunken, but stubborn, South Carolina brigade. Behind the crest of the hill, just out of the fire and superbly placed, were troops in good order, most of them lying at ease. A six-gun battery in their center joined fire on the enemy. Officers were trying to rally broken regiments on the hill and to stop a stream of frightened men through the woodlands. No orders were needed for the resting brigade. It was found to be Jackson's, waiting as calmly as if it had been through a thousand such searing battles. Two South Carolina brigades, under General Bee and Colonel N. G. Evans, were now falling back to the slope, lashed by blue waves of infantry. The surge of battle came nearer Jackson's men.

Captain Imboden, who was near Jackson, had already been upbraided by the General for cursing in battle. Old Jack was slightly wounded. Imboden recorded it:

"The contest that ensued was terrific. Jackson ordered me to go from battery to battery and see that the guns were properly aimed and the fuses cut the right length. This was the work of but a few minutes. . . . I stopped to ask Jackson's permission to rejoin my battery. The fight was just then hot enough to make him feel well. His eyes fairly blazed. He had a way of throwing up his left hand with the open palm toward the person he was addressing. And, as he told me to go, he made this gesture. The air was full of flying missiles, and as he spoke he jerked down his hand, and I saw that blood was streaming from it. I exclaimed, 'General, you are wounded.' 'Only a scratch, a mere scratch,' he replied, and binding it hastily with a handkerchief, he galloped away along his line."

Shells were falling about the Henry House, where the eighty-year-old widow lay with her two sons, all of them invalids. The sons, one of them recalled, were "shocked when we saw the Union troops coming from Sudley Ford," and they tried to move their mother, who refused adamantly, until shells had plunged into the house. The hobbling men took her on a mattress toward the home of a neighbor, but soon Mrs. Henry, frightened, "begged so hard to be taken back that we returned to the house, and had just replaced her in bed when she was instantly killed by a shell." The house began to flame almost in the center of Jackson's line.

The enemy appeared on the crest of the hill, infantrymen in blue outlined clearly against the sky in the sights of Jackson's prone marksmen. When his brigade fired, the Yankees were literally blown into oblivion; artillery drove survivors of that attack down the hill. The fight pressed in once more, into an ever smaller space.

The Federal commanders, Heintzelman, Hunter and Tyler, threw their regiments against the position—all told, twenty-five thousand Union troops. The hill was being defended for the moment with ninety-eight hundred men, in the brigades of Jackson, Bee, Bartow and Wade Hampton. The affair could not last long. More dark files advanced in the distance, bound for this hill.

The Federals pushed over a rise called Matthews Hill, and now passed the Henry House. Into this melee Stuart came at the head of his reckless riders. They emerged on the smoky flank near men in red uniforms; Stuart thought these were Alabama troops he had seen earlier. He shouted, "Don't run boys. We're here!" It was an error. The men were the Zouaves of Heintzelman; and Stuart, with no other course left to him, rode into their midst at top speed. He lost a few men, but the New York troops scattered and were no longer in the battle.

Then came one of those unfathomable moments of battle which turn the tide. It swept the Federals from a field won, thus far, at great sacrifice. Almost as Stuart spread panic among the Zouaves, one of Jackson's infantry regiments, the Thirty-third Virginia, stormed from its pine brush cover. It charged a battery of Union guns, but these guns, strangely, did not fire on the Southern attack. Officers evidently were uncertain as to whether the Virginians were friends or foes. The delay was fatal. At seventy yards the graycoats fired, wiping out the gunners. Jackson had to fight for the guns even longer, for a band of Maine men seized them, and waves of battle plunged back and forth in the full heat of the afternoon.

Near three o'clock, the combined weight of Stuart's charge and Jackson's move began to tell. More Confederates rallied about the guns, and from Manassas Junction the last of Johnston's reinforcements came up. The Federal troops moved back under the weight of numbers, and a few companies, already having fought beyond their limits of endurance, gave way. Regiments turned to the rear, taking others with them. From the Confederate front rose the first Rebel Yell of the war, and Colonel Arnold Elzey, at the head of his Marylanders, led pursuit of the Federals.

Jackson had already won the sobriquet which was to become more famous than he and to obscure for history most other events of his life.

In the heaviest of the fighting, when the Southerners were being driven from the hill, General Bee yelled to his South Carolinians, pointing to Jackson's men, who steadily awaited the next attack:

"Look, there stands Jackson like a stone wall. Rally behind the Virginians, men!"

Bee was soon fatally wounded, but his shout had helped to hold his men from flight, and a number of them remembered his words. The name spread: Stonewall. And the silent officer who had commanded on Henry House Hill became overnight a legend in the army.

Jackson came down the hill as the Federal tide ebbed, while bullets still flew. As he galloped toward a bridge below him, he held aloft one hand and looked upward. Some thought he was praying, others that he beckoned his men, or favored the wounded hand; and some, like Maury, thought he might be about the curious business of balancing his weight.

McDowell had lost three thousand men, nearly half of them as prisoners; the Confederate loss was just under two thousand—only a dozen prisoners—and when the Federal retreat became flight, it seemed that each man fled from certain death.

Warren Lee Goss saw Jackson's men snatch the Federal guns in the turning point of the day, and the first moments of panic:

"The batteries were in an open field next to us. We were watching to see what they'd do next, when a terrible volley was poured into them. It was like a pack of Fourth of July firecrackers under a barrel, magnified a thousand times. The Rebels had crept upon them unawares, and the men at the batteries were about all killed or wounded.

"The dead cannoneers lay with the rammers of their guns and sponges and lanyards still in their hands. . . . Those who could get away didn't wait. . . . It must have been four o'clock in the afternoon, at a time when our fire had become scattered and feeble, that the rumor passed from one to another that the Rebels had got reinforcements. Where are ours? we asked. There was no confusion or panic then, but discouragement . . . Our men began to feel it was no use to fight, cursing their generals because no reinforcements were sent to them. The men had now . . . been marching and fighting thirteen hours. The enemy were pressing up, and we fell back. We didn't run."

Confederates saw it, however, as "one dense mass of fugitives . . . the whole of the Federal army . . . rushing madly in the direction of Washington."

President Davis came up through chaos at the rear of his army, among skulkers and wounded, thinking that the day had brought

THE MEN AROUND JACKSON

Military amateurs, most of them young, chosen for gifts in their fields, worked with Jackson through his Civil War career of 21 months. They ranged from the stern and unpopular chief of staff, The Rev. Dabney, to the gay young lawyer-biographer Kyd Douglas, and from the transplanted Yankee map-maker Hotchkiss to McGuire, who became a nationally famous physician. Some important photos are missing from this post-war composite, chief among them those of John Harman, whose wagons moved Jackson's troops, and Stapleton Crutchfield, a fine young gunner.

The West Point Graduate

The Veteran Turned Teacher

The open, sensitive countenance of Jackson in his twenties became almost unrecognizable in the bearded portraits of 1861-63. Here, upper left, is the Jackson newly graduated from West Point, probably in 1846, when he was 22; upper right, the face becoming firmer, is a photograph of 1851, when Jackson, a veteran of the Mexican War and long months of barracks life, reported to Virginia Military Institute.

The photograph below is of Jackson's second wife, Mary Anna Morrison, taken near the end of the war, when she was a young widow.

Anna Jackson

"THE BEAMING SUNLIGHT OF HIS *HOME-LOOK*"

Jackson's wife (Anna) thought this the best likeness of him. It shows him in a Winchester, Virginia, camera studio—either in the winter of 1861-62 or the following year. He had just played seamstress himself, sewing on the third button from the top on his left breast, while the photographer waited. There is minor controversy over this picture, which is one of the only two made during the Civil War. The weight of evidence seems to be that it was made prior to the Valley Campaign, in early 1862, but Kyd Douglas and other witnesses place it a year later, not long before Fredericksburg and Chancellorsville. In any event, only the strongest persuasion led Jackson to sit for the portrait, which was made by Lupton or Routzahn of Winchester—probably the latter.

Above, Federal work parties clear the wreckage of Manassas Junction where, in August, 1862, Jackson's slashing march to the rear of Pope's army imperilled Union forces, destroyed $1,000,000 in supplies, and crippled Pope.

Below, helpless Union sick and wounded, abandoned in the swamps below Richmond on June 30, 1862. Jackson swept them up, capturing 2,500 on the edge of White Oak Swamp, incidentally contributing to the chief failure of his military career.

dcfeat. But when he and Johnston and Beauregard met in sight of the enemy retreat, Davis almost lost control of himself. He rushed to Colonel Elzey, who had now halted the chase, and cried, "General Elzey, you are the Blücher of the day!"

Davis wrote Lee: "We have won a glorious though dear-bought victory. Night closed on the enemy in full flight and closely pursued."

Lee replied in a message to Johnston: "I almost wept for joy at the glorious victory achieved by our brave troops."

While Confederates celebrated, the Federals tore on as if the devil were at their heels. William Howard Russell wrote for his readers in the *London Times:*

"On the hill beside me there was a crowd of civilians . . . in all sorts of vehicles, with a few of the fairer sex . . . a lady with an opera glass . . . was quite beside herself when an unusually heavy discharge roused the current of her blood—'That is splendid. Oh, my! Is that not first-rate? I guess we will be in Richmond tomorrow.'

"An officer . . . galloped along the front, waving his cap and shouting . . . 'We've whipped them on all points. . . . We have taken all their batteries. They are retreating as fast as they can, and we are after them.' The Congressmen shook hands with each other and cried out: 'Bully for us! Bravo! Didn't I tell you so?' . . .

"I had ridden three or four miles . . . every moment the crowd increased; drivers and men cried out . . . 'Turn back! Turn back! We are whipped!' They seized the heads of the horses and swore at opposing drivers. . . .

"The uproar and the dust were beyond description . . . some cavalry soldiers, flourishing their sabers, and preceded by an officer, who cried out, 'Make way there—make way for the General,' attempted to force a covered wagon, in which there was seated a man with a bloody handkerchief round his head, through the press. . . .

"The scene on the road had now assumed an aspect which had not a parallel in any description I have ever read. Infantry soldiers on mules and draft horses with the harness clinging to their heels . . . ambulances crowded . . . wagons swarming with men

who threw out the contents in the road to make room, grinding
through a shouting, screaming mass of men on foot who were
. . . yelling with rage at every halt and shrieking out: 'Here are
the cavalry! Will you get on?'

"A fresh outburst of artillery . . . in an instant the mass of
vehicles and retreating soldiers, teamsters, and civilians, as if
agonized by an electric shock, quivered throughout the tortuous
line . . . drivers lashed their maddened horses and, leaping
from the carts, left them to their fate, and ran. . . ."

It went on through the night, and the next day, in a rainstorm,
remnants of the undefeated, but terrified, Union army, streamed
through the streets of Washington.

It had not been Jackson's fight; but in the night when burial
parties were out, men everywhere about Manassas were remembering him. He had said things in battle which men now magnified.

Once to an officer who had dashed up to him when things
looked worst, shouting, "General, the day is going against us,"
Jackson had replied calmly, "If you think so, sir, don't say anything about it." And he had held his troops so coolly, until the
enemy was once within fifty yards, saying, "Hold your fire until
they're on you, then fire and give them the bayonet. And when
you charge, yell like furies."

Jackson's brigade had lost as heavily as any other: 488 of its
3,000 men were dead or wounded, and many of them were on
the Henry House Hill tonight, where surgeons with their saws
made huge piles of amputated limbs.

Jackson went to a surgeon for treatment of his finger that night,
and said, "Give me 10,000 men, and I would be in Washington
tomorrow." He would not be able to forget the lost opportunity
for the chase. General Johnston was even now assembling reasons for his failure to press for victory, to show that his army
was more disorganized in victory than McDowell's in defeat;
but Jackson was never to accept it. For weeks he growled about
the dissipated chance to bring the North to its knees and end the
war.

The next morning he wrote Anna:

My precious pet—Yesterday we fought a great battle
and gained a glorious victory, for which all the glory is
due to God alone. Although under heavy fire for several . . . hours, I received only one wound, the breaking
of the longest finger of my left hand; but the doctor says the
finger can be saved. It was broken about midway between
the hand and the knuckle, the ball passing on the side next
the forefinger. . . .

Whilst great credit is due to other parts of our gallant
army, God made my brigade more instrumental than any
other in repulsing the main attack. This is for your information only—say nothing about it. Let others speak praise, not
myself.

A few days later he added:

And so you think the papers ought to say more about
your husband! My brigade is not a brigade of newspaper
correspondents. I know that the First Brigade was the first
to meet and pass our retreating forces—to push on with
no other aid than the smiles of God . . . to arrest the
victorious foe in his onward progress—to hold him in check
until reinforcements arrived—and finally to charge bayonets
and thus advancing, pierce the enemy's center. I am well
satisfied with what it did, and so are my generals. . . .

As you think the papers do not notice me enough, I
send a specimen, which you will see from the upper part of
the paper is a leader. My darling, you must never distrust
our God. . . . In due time He will manifest His pleasure.

You must not be concerned at seeing other parts of the
army lauded, and my brigade not mentioned. "Truth is
mighty, and will prevail."

Jackson caused a brief sensation back in Lexington with a
letter to Dr. White, his pastor. A day or so after Bull Run, the
minister anxiously opened an envelope with Jackson's well-
known scrawl over it, and a small crowd gathered, expecting
news of the great battle. The letter read:

My dear pastor—In my tent last night, after a fatiguing
day's service, I remembered that I had failed to send you
my contribution for our colored Sunday school. Enclosed
you will find my check . . .

About this time he made a mortal enemy, an officer who got word that his wife was on her death bed. When the officer asked Jackson for leave, so that he could be with his wife in her last hours, Old Jack stared at him, saying only, "Man, man, do you love your wife more than your country?" The officer could not understand the emotion which had seized his commander; the wife died and the officer never forgave.

Jackson was consistent, however. When Anna wrote, asking him to take a furlough and visit her in the Morrison home in North Carolina, he declined firmly, saying that he could not set a bad example for others.

Bull Run gave the Confederacy a false view of the months ahead, of the worth of Federal troops, and the sagacity of its own commanders. But Beauregard, though his glory was soon to dim, correctly assayed the contributions of his officers. He gave high praise to Jackson who, with the remnants of three other brigades, had almost incredibly held the center of his line. If Jackson had need of reassurance, he found it plentiful in the army's attentions after the battle.

Old Jack knew, too, from the action along Bull Run, the work of men who were to become his lieutenants in the Shenandoah.

Arnold Elzey, who had taken over the reinforcements when a superior was shot down, was soon promoted to brigadier general; he was a man after Jackson's heart. He had charged his men before they went into battle: "Here's the signal, men," with hand before his face, "And the watchword is Sumter." When he had studied the field, seeing flags in the breeze, he led the men forward, yelling, "Stars and Stripes! Stars and Stripes! Give it to 'em boys!" Elzey was out of the old army, and had served in Mexico; a man of long experience.

He had a failing which had not come to Jackson's attention: he could not dispense with his evening toddy. One night, in a gay mood, he served officers with drinks and even called in the sentries on duty. Early in the morning, when Elzey was sound asleep, a sentry tugged at him in the headquarters tent, with, "General, General, ain't it about time for us to take another drink?" The furious Elzey had his drinking companion arrested, but the incident improved his reputation among the men. Elzey was to fight with Jackson in famous campaigns.

Another who was to do so was Major Roberdeau Wheat, the soldier of fortune whose career had begun in the Mexican War and continued around the world, wherever there was fighting. He was said to be the only man in the army who would, or could, command the Louisiana Tigers, whose ranks were reputed to be filled with felons from New Orleans prisons.

Wheat, son of an Episcopal rector of Alexandria, Virginia, was seriously wounded at Bull Run, shot through both lungs. A surgeon examined him. "There is no instance on record of recovery from such a wound," the doctor said. "I don't feel like dying yet," Wheat replied. "I will put my case on record." He did so. The six-foot lawyer recovered in a short time and was ready for fight once more.

Jackson already had, too, the man who was to become invaluable—his chief surgeon, Dr. Hunter McGuire. The young physician was just twenty-six, but had been trained at Winchester Medical College, in his home town, and at the University of Pennsylvania. Of great ability, he was to become a professor of surgery and president of the American Medical Association.

At Jackson's urging, Anna came north by train to his camp near Manassas, riding the last few miles in a jouncing car filled with soldiers. Even years later, in writing of the trip, Anna sounded frightened at memory of passing through the army: "A lady seemed to be a great curiosity to the soldiers, scores of whom filed through the car to take a look." And, when she was forced to wait in a hospital for her husband: "There was no lock on the door, and the tramp of men's feet, as they passed continually to and fro and threatened entrance, was not conducive to a peaceful frame of mind." Anna also had a grim view from her window: squads of soldiers making coffins for their companions who had fallen.

Jackson arrived in an ambulance to rescue her, and took her to his tent in the yard of a family of the neighborhood. They passed a brief holiday. She sang "Dixie" for him several times; he had not heard the song before and insisted on so many repetitions that they ended by giggling like children over the tune.

Anna met the officers of the army and seemed impressed by General Johnston. Many spoke to her of Jackson's part in the victory at Bull Run, but, Anna said, "he, with his characteristic modesty, gave all the credit to his noble men."

He took her over the field of Bull Run, which she found of little interest; Bull Run itself was "a small, insignificant stream," but as she rode in the jolting ambulance with Jackson and General Pendleton, she saw unforgettable sights: the carcasses of horses and bones of men.

When Anna had returned home, Jackson wrote of a visit from Jefferson Davis, who had come to inspect the army:

> He looked quite thin. . . . His voice and manners are very mild. I saw no exhibition of that fire which I had supposed him to possess. The President introduced the subject of the condition of my section of the state (he meant Western Virginia) but did not so much as intimate that he designed sending me there. I told him, when he spoke of my native region, that I felt a very deep interest in it. He spoke hopefully of that section.

Jackson wrote a joking letter: "If I get into winter quarters, will little ex-Anna Morrison come and keep house for me? . . . Now, remember, I don't want to change housekeepers."

In the same letter, with studied calm, he gave her important news: "I am very thankful to God who withholds no good thing from me (though I am utterly unworthy and ungrateful) for making me a major general. . . . The commission dates from the 7th of October."

The Reverend White visited the camp; and on one evening when Jackson prayed at supper, the minister was deeply impressed with his eloquence. Then, White wrote: "With that calm dignity of mien . . . for which he was so remarkable, he said, 'Doctor, I would be glad to learn more fully than I have yet done what your views are of the prayers of faith.' " The two spent long hours in the night, probing their faith.

Dr. White was in camp when Jackson got orders to command in Western Virginia, a move which was to mean so much to him. He said to White: "Such a degree of public confidence . . .

should be prized; but, apart from that, promotion among men is only a temptation and a trouble. Had this communication not come as an order, I should instantly have declined it, and continued in command of my old brigade."

Old Jack worked night and day to prepare for his new post on the frontier, until there was but one last chore—to say farewell to the Stonewall Brigade. He had the men drawn up in ranks:

"Officers and men of the First Brigade, I am not here to make a speech, but simply to say farewell. I first met you at Harpers Ferry in the commencement of the war. . . . You have already gained a brilliant and deservedly high reputation . . . and I trust in the future . . . you will gain more victories. . . . You have already gained a proud position in the history of this, our second War of Independence. I shall look with great anxiety to your future movements, and I trust whenever I hear of the First Brigade on the field of battle it will be of still nobler deeds. . . ."

Then, as if he sensed that neither he nor the men had been quite satisfied with this rhetoric, he stood in his stirrups and called in the screeching voice:

"In the Army of the Shenandoah you were the First Brigade; in the Army of the Potomac you were the First Brigade; in the second corps of this army you are the First Brigade; you are the First Brigade in the affections of your general; and I hope by your future deeds and bearing you will be handed down as the First Brigade in our second War of Independence. Farewell!"

He spurred off amid a deafening yell from the troops and disappeared, waving his disreputable old cap over his head.

The speech, despite its gaudy Napoleonic roll, was detected as one of importance by Kyd Douglas and another young officer, who wrote it down from their memories and sent it to the Richmond *Dispatch*, which published it to cheer the populace.

10

Old Jack took over his command in Winchester, where he found three sleepy little brigades and a handful of militia, some of whom were armed with flintlocks. But in mid-November, when he called for reinforcements for the Valley, he was sent the old Stonewall Brigade, which he had recently departed. He worked with his troops under little danger from the enemy.

The most promising of Union commanders had now been removed from Western Virginia, where he had won a small victory, and he was made commander in chief of the United States armies: George B. McClellan. Old Fuss and Feathers Scott had been deposed in Washington, sunk like McDowell in the bog of misery after Bull Run. Scott had shouted: "I am the greatest coward in America. I have fought this battle, sir, against my judgment; I think the President of the United States ought to remove me today for doing it." Lincoln was not slow to act.

Jackson was not affected by the larger strategy in these weeks. He drilled men and tried to develop a staff. His first attempt at discipline of officers brought mutiny; men accustomed to the informal life of an isolated post were outraged at Jackson's order that they were not to go in or out of Winchester without passes from headquarters. Some wrote impassioned protests at this "un-

158

warranted assumption of authority" which "disparaged their dignity." Jackson's reply was calm, but unrelenting; he accused the officers of neglect of duty, incompetence and subversion. They submitted to his strict discipline.

In the first brisk weather of coming winter, he drove his men on what seemed a foolish errand: to destroy a canal dam and locks beside the Potomac, where men chopped away at the wooden cribs while standing in waist-deep water and suffering under rifle fire from the enemy. He was only partially successful and lost a few men on the outing; survivors grumbled and added to the stories that he was insane.

More troops came in, some of them under the command of General W. W. Loring; these were in a notable state of indiscipline.

One cold day when the little army was trailing through the hill country, Jackson halted his staff and climbed a persimmon tree which was heavy with the tart fruit. He clambered far into the crown of the rugged tree and was caught so that he could not move. He was obliged to call his officers for help, and they, howling with laughter, fetched rails to rescue him. He returned to earth with an air of wounded dignity and added an unconvincing note to the chorus of laughter.

Jackson wrote Anna as if he were unsure of himself: "The rank of major general does not appear to be recognized by the laws of the Confederate States, so far as I have seen." He then became more cheerful:

> But I expect to have two aides, and at least an adjutant general. I am making up my staff slowly. . . . I don't think that a major general will be paid more than $301 a month, but as commander of an army my additional pay is $100, making in all $401 a month. I send you a check for $1,000, which I wish invested in Confederate bonds. . . . You had better not sell your coupons from the bonds . . . but let the Confederacy keep the gold. Citizens should not receive a cent of gold from the government when it is so scarce.

Major J. T. L. Preston of his staff was writing home at this time: "We have a merry table, but . . . Jackson as grave as a signpost, until something chances to overcome him, and then he breaks out into a laugh so awkward that it is manifest he has never laughed enough to learn how. He is a most simple-hearted man."

Anna was soon on her way to her husband. She reached Winchester on a frozen December night, and was told that Jackson was off on a raid. She walked from the stagecoach to the hotel with an elderly minister as an escort:

"I noticed a small group of soldiers standing on the sidewalk, but they remained as silent spectators . . . my escort led me up the long stairway. . . . I turned to look back, for one figure among that group looked startlingly familiar, but as he had not come forward, I felt that I must be mistaken.

"An officer muffled up in a military coat, and cap drawn over his eyes, followed us in rapid pursuit, and by the time we were upon the top step a pair of strong arms caught me in the rear; the captive's head was thrown back, and she was kissed again and again by her husband, before she could realize the delightful surprise he had given her. The good old minister chuckled gleefully."

Anna lived in the General's cottage of four rooms, whose floor matting, piano and "beautiful papering and five paintings" seemed elegant to him. They boarded with the Reverend James Graham and his family, ardent and friendly Presbyterians. Winchester, Anna found, was "rich in happy homes . . . social refinement and elegant hospitality . . . lovely Christian characters . . . true specimens of patrician blood." She confessed that she saw everything "through a rose-colored light" that winter.

Jackson opened his first campaign on January first, with Turner Ashby's improving cavalry in his front to lead an attack on Bath and Romney, enemy outposts in the mountains. His men were sure he had gone mad with this drive over mountain roads in midwinter. The weather at the start was unusual, bright and mild; by night chill winds blew once more.

Jackson was cold in the saddle. He had been given an unaccustomed gift by an old man of the region; Jackson was under the impression that it was wine, but it was in fact a bottle of liquor. When he became chilled, the General turned up the bottle and drank freely. When he had consumed about half of it, he passed the bottle among his staff. These officers, not yet familiar with Jackson's idiosyncrasies, did not properly value this miracle; they simply drank the remainder of the liquor. Within a few moments, as they rode toward the enemy, Jackson began a most unnatural chattering. Sweat appeared on his face, and despite the cold air, he unfastened his coat, garrulously discussing a variety of subjects. Jackson was, for the only recorded time in his life, half drunk.

The army moved on Bath in the morning, and the Federal garrison fled toward Hancock, Maryland. There was scarcely a skirmish at the village, but the troops feasted on stores left by the enemy—coffee and canned fruits and condensed milk. Men slept in the empty resort hotel by the village springs, bedded down in the ballroom and wrapped in lace curtains and other spoils. Jackson gave them brief rest.

The General's aims were not modest on this expedition. He proposed through Alec Boteler, now in Congress, that he be allowed to recruit twenty thousand mountain men and sweep down on Pittsburgh and Harrisburg. The army of Johnston was to cross the Potomac and meet him in the North. Boteler found in Richmond no support for such a daring assault; at this time there was nothing to hint that the politicians might be rejecting a plan which would conquer the Federal armies. It was only a wild scheme by an officer with an unimpressive reputation.

Through cold fields Jackson's men moved on Hancock, a village strung along a slope. Ashby was sent in under a flag of truce and, blindfolded, was led to Federal headquarters, where he delivered Jackson's demand for a surrender. He returned with a refusal, and Jackson's guns fired a few rounds into the town; the enemy fell back. Ashby returned with the story that Yankees had whispered as he passed: "That's the famous Ashby." It appeared that Jackson's command was drawing attention.

Old Jack pushed on to Romney, where he left General Loring and his troops. He was aware that Loring's rebellious men

had opposed this campaign and were in a state of "demoraliza-
tion." But he was not prepared for the storm that followed.

Loring and his officers appealed to Richmond for relief from
the orders of this madman. They were dangerously exposed to
the enemy, they wrote, and were to be sacrified to no purpose.
They should be withdrawn.

Unaware of this, Jackson was making angry protests of his
own. He denounced the atrocities of Federal commanders in the
district, complaining of houses and mills burned, saying, "The
track from Romney to Hanging Rock, a distance of fifteen miles,
was one of desolation. The number of dead animals lying along
the roadside, where they had been shot by the enemy, exem-
plified the spirit of that part of the Northern army."

His report claimed that he had, within four days, saved Western Virginia for the South. He was to receive a shock soon after,
when the people of this region voted overwhelmingly for separation from Virginia, and created the loyal state of West Virginia.

There was another jolt nearer at hand, a telegram from Secretary of War Judah P. Benjamin. Jackson read with "astonishment":

> Our news indicates that a movement is being made to cut
> off General Loring's command. Order him back to Win-
> chester immediately.

It was one moment of war for which Jackson was unprepared;
he had not dreamed that his authority might be challenged by
the civilians of Richmond. His reaction was immediate. He recalled Loring, though that move wasted the brief campaign he
had just concluded. He wrote to Benjamin on January 31, 1862:

> Sir,—Your order requiring me to direct General Loring
> to return . . . has been received and promptly complied
> with.
> With such interference in my command, I cannot expect
> to be of much service in the field, and I accordingly request
> to be ordered to report for duty to the Superintendent of
> the Virginia Military Institute at Lexington, as has been done
> in the case of other professors.
> Should this application not be granted, I respectfully re-

quest that the President will accept my resignation from the army.

I am, sir, very respectfully, your obedient servant.

Virginia rocked with the news.

General Johnston, to whom the letter was forwarded, recognized the talent at stake. He wrote on the back of the dispatch:

Respectfully forwarded with great regret. I don't know how the loss of this officer can be supplied. General officers are much wanted in this department.

Even so, vexed as he was by difficult men, Benjamin might well have let Jackson depart the service, had it not been for the furore breaking over him.

Johnston chided Benjamin for his order to Jackson:

The discipline of the army cannot be maintained under such circumstances. The direct tendency of the orders is to insulate the commanding general from his troops . . . and to harass him with the constant fear that his most matured plans may be marred by orders from his government.

Jackson overlooked no source of help. He wrote Governor Letcher, denouncing Benjamin's "attempt to control military operations in detail from the Secretary's desk at a distance," and added:

As a single order like that . . . may destroy the entire fruits of a campaign, I cannot reasonably expect, if my operations are thus interfered with, to be of much service in the field. A sense of duty brought me into the field, and has thus far kept me. It now appears to be my duty to return to the Institute, and I hope that you will leave no stone unturned to get me there.

I desire to say nothing against the Secretary of War. I take it for granted that he has done what he believes to be best, but I regard such a policy as ruinous.

Letcher wrote Jackson, urging that he withdraw his resignation, but he challenged Benjamin, too. The Secretary was inclined to back down and make no issue of the matter with the aroused Stonewall.

General Johnston in the meantime wrote Jackson urging coolheadedness in dealing with Richmond politicians:

My Dear Friend—I have just read, and with profound regret, your letter . . . asking to be relieved from your present command. . . . Let me beg you to reconsider . . .

The danger in which our very existence . . . lies, requires sacrifices from us all who have been educated as soldiers.

Let us dispassionately reason with the government on this subject of command, and if we fail . . . then ask to be relieved. . . .

I have taken the liberty to detain your letter to make this appeal to your patriotism, not merely from warm feelings of personal regard, but from the official opinion which makes me regard you as necessary to the service of the country in your present position.

Friends, thunderstruck at thought of his retirement, pressed Jackson in Winchester. One man emotionally declared that the name of Stonewall alone was a great force in the war, cheering the South, terrorizing the North. Jackson made a modest protest: "No, no. You greatly overestimate my capacity for usefulness. A better man will soon be sent to take my place. The government have no confidence in my capacity, or they wouldn't countermand my orders like this, and throw away the fruits of victory. No, sir. I must resign, and give my place to someone in whom they have more confidence."

Anna overheard men beseeching Jackson to change his mind. When one told Jackson he should be willing to make sacrifices, Stonewall shouted:

"Sacrifices! Have I not made them? What is my life here— a daily sacrifice! Never will I withhold sacrifices for my country, if they avail anything. I will serve anywhere—even if as a private soldier. But if this way of making war is to prevail, the country is ruined. My duty requires me to protest with all my power, and that way is to resign."

Jackson at last surrendered, however. He wrote Letcher:

Governor,—If my retiring from the army would produce that effect which you have named in your letter, I, of course, would not desire to leave the service . . . you are authorized to withdraw my resignation. . . . My reasons for resigning were set forth in my letter, and my views remain unchanged; and if the Secretary persists in the ruinous policy . . . I feel that no officer can serve his country better than by making his strongest possible protest. . . .

Letcher sent Jackson an assurance that he would no longer feel interference from Richmond.

In this episode, as in many to come, the Confederacy had yeoman service from the unheralded Alec Boteler, the link between the Valley commander and official Richmond. Boteler delivered Letcher's final letter to Jackson, and argued with the General for hours, until he convinced him that he must remain in the army.

Jackson rendered invaluable service, too, in protecting field commanders from interference. He also revealed a grim singleness of purpose. He had not hesitated to use every weapon at hand. Within a day or so after his challenge to Benjamin, almost every man of influence in Virginia had been made aware of the struggle and had taken sides, most of them with Jackson.

Stonewall thought Loring "should be cashiered" for his part in the affair, for starting trouble over danger which "does not exist." Richmond, however, transferred Loring within a few days—and promoted him to major general.

None of these vexations seemed to touch Jackson's life with Anna in Winchester. She described the winter as one of the happiest times of their lives, and recalled Jackson as engaging, even jolly. There are stories of his running up and down stairs with a small boy clinging to his back, and of his saying, when he found some officers and young women playing "artillery" with overturned parlor chairs: "Captain, when this engagement is over, make a full report to me."

Old Jack had been eager enough to reach Anna after his expedition. He rode so fast that an officer joked, "Well, General, I'm not so anxious to see Mrs. Jackson as to break my neck keeping up with you, and with your permission I shall fall back and take it more leisurely." Jackson pushed Sorrel forty miles that day. Anna wrote: "He bounded into the sitting room as

joyous and as fresh as a schoolboy," then sat by the fire, exclaiming, "Oh, this is the very essence of comfort."

About this time, amid the controversy between Jackson and
Benjamin and his officers, Anna conceived a child. In March,
after two months that had passed like a honeymoon, Jackson
turned to war once more.

Old Jack had some four thousand men, and the greatly superior armies of General Banks and General Shields lay north of
him, near the Potomac. Richmond took its eye from Jackson
now, to watch in horror the coils of Union strength gathering
near its own walls. For a vast Federal army under General Mc-
Clellan was pushing up the Peninsula between the York and
the James, intending to strike Richmond by the shortest route
from the sea and choke the Confederacy.

In these times, robbed of reserves and facing what promised
to become disaster, General Johnston could tell Jackson only:
Remain in the Valley if possible; hold the enemy, but expose
yourself little, and take no chance of defeat; stay near enough
to the enemy to prevent reinforcement of McClellan by those
Federal troops in the Valley. In short, threaten, but do not fight.

Jackson was to give these orders the most liberal interpreta-
tion. They were the foundation of the Valley campaign, which
now loomed before him.

In early March he deserted Winchester. He loaded his sick
and wounded on a train, and put Anna aboard as well. She recalled: "He told me that when his 'sunshine' was gone out of
the room which had been to us the holy of holies on earth that
winter, he never wanted to enter it again . . . to the last moment he lingered at the door of the coach . . . with bright
smiles."

When they met again, thirteen months later, he was to be a
changed man: architect of a dozen victories, a lieutenant general
with a peerless reputation on either side of the Potomac—and a
doting father, as well.

Jackson began a series of moves against the enemy whose
brilliant consequences could not have been foretold. General
Banks was stumbling down the Valley toward Winchester, in

such force that he could not long be halted. His regiments were scattered, however, and according to Jackson's spies, a quick blow was possible. Jackson had no lack of informants. He wrote: "I have taken especial pains to obtain information respecting General Banks. . . . I will see what can be effected through the Catholic priests at Martinsburg."

In leaving Winchester, he had ordered his wagons left just outside the town so that in the morning he could feed and supply his troops, and then strike the Union advance. His orders given, he went to the home of the Reverend Graham, which was filled with gloom at the prospect of Federal occupation of the town. Jackson seemed inexplicably cheerful to the Grahams.

His mood changed rapidly. After supper he went to a meeting of his officers and found that the wagons, contrary to his plan, had been dragged many miles away, and that his cleverly planned attack was impossible. He gave his officers no sign of wrath, but an hour or so later, watching the evacuation of Winchester from a hilltop, he growled to Dr. Hunter McGuire, "That's the last council of war I will ever hold."

Jackson's men fell southward, to camp about forty miles below Winchester. On March twenty-first, Jackson had word that the enemy was moving in his direction. Old Jack abruptly sought an opportunity for attack. He sent out Ashby, who was prone to see such chances everywhere. The cavalryman was told by natives that the enemy was straggling. Ashby called for Jackson and the infantry. The commander replied with a long, hard march by the little corps which was to acquire legendary legs; some regiments made twenty-seven miles the first day and sixteen the next.

Early on Sunday afternoon, March twenty-third, Jackson came to the village of Kernstown, just four miles south of the Winchester he had so recently occupied. He had little choice as to whether he should give battle, for his column was within sight of the enemy, who might call up reinforcements. And Ashby's guns were already engaged. Stonewall's strict observance of the Sabbath was broken. He flung out a skirmish line.

It was a vital moment for him, the opening of the first battle of his career as an independent commander. He was poorly prepared. The roads behind were filled with his stragglers, men who could not keep the pace he had set; he had no more than three thousand men for the battle.

He had able lieutenants. Brigadier General Richard Garnett led Jackson's old brigade; and vigorous colonels, Sam Fulkerson and Jesse Burks, were with the other brigades. Jackson ordered Burks to help Ashby hold the turnpike, sent a few cavalrymen to the left flank, and pushed Garnett and Fulkerson's brigades to the right. The men were quickly in position and went forward toward a wooded ridge. No one knew how many Federals awaited them, though Ashby's report led Jackson to believe that he had flushed an isolated segment of the Union army, and would soon cut it to pieces.

Enemy troops moved into the open and fired at the Confederate flank, but were beaten off. Jackson watched with mounting excitement. He had his thirty guns in action, and a flank attack, delivered in force, seemed likely to drive the Federals from the town. But the roar of battle seemed to grow; he threw in reserves, but the enemy line did not waver. Some of his men began to stumble backward from one sheltered position to another. Jackson could not understand. Officers shouted at the men, momentarily halting the rearward flow. Someone returned to Jackson: "Ammunition giving out."

Jackson stared at the officer as if he had gone mad, and anger came into his face.

Dr. Hunter McGuire passed, and Jackson ordered him to send the wounded to the rear.

"But that requires time, General," McGuire said. "Can you stay here to protect us?"

"Make yourself easy about that. This army stays here until the last wounded man is removed."

McGuire looked over the field where the Yankees were coming out of the woodlands in overpowering force.

"Before I will leave them to the enemy I will lose many more men," Jackson said.

He went to the front and, from a ridge near old Opequon Church, looked down on the massing enemy troops. They were stout regiments from Ohio, Indiana, Illinois and Pennsylvania.

A private trotted past Jackson, bound for the rear. Old Jack reined Sorrel. "Where are you going, man?"

"All my ca'tridges are gone, General. I don't know where to get 'em."

"Then go back and give 'em the bayonet, man!" Old Jack shouted. But the man ran rearward, and others joined him. Jackson could not stop the retreat.

One end of the wedge-shaped Confederate line had curled its flank on the crest of the ridge; it was now being broken by Union troops. Jackson's guns tried valiantly, but could not stem the enemy rush. And far below, through a toll gate on the main road, the bluecoat infantry was still pouring. They seemed numberless. General Garnett watched his men falling as long as he could bear it, then ordered them back out of the deadly fire. They deserted a stone fence on the ridge and moved out of the battle.

Jackson saw the retreating men and galloped to Garnett. He ordered a halt to the withdrawal and, yanking a drummer boy to a knoll, commanded him to beat a rally. Soldiers swarmed past them as if they did not exist. Jackson shouted at Garnett, saying that the reserves could have saved the day if he had held his position. But the rear regiments were already spread out in a thin line ready to cover the retreat. Jackson could do no more. He had to watch as about two hundred men of his rearguard and a couple of guns were captured by the enemy. The line of retreat fell back slowly, morosely, as officers remembered it, until after dark. The army went to the provision trains at Newtown, some five or six miles in the rear. The Federals did not follow, for their losses had been more severe than Jackson's, and they did not welcome the prospect of a running battle at night. Jackson had 80 dead and 342 wounded. But though he had been driven from the field, none of his regiments had suffered the fate of the Federal 110th Pennsylvania, which had been scattered and did not return until after the battle.

Ashby had led Jackson into the repulse, for he had been seriously misinformed as to Federal strength; the cavalryman was misled by a stratagem of Shields, who had hidden his main body of troops. Reprimand for Ashby was pointless; he had fought like a demon all day, and his troopers had saved Jackson in the final moments. It was Garnett who, in the grim view of the commander, had behaved in an unsoldierly fashion. Jackson's anger fixed on this officer; it seemed to grow in the gloomy night.

Colonel William Allan, who had just a year ago left his study of mathematics at the University of Virginia, and was now Jackson's ordnance officer, recorded a few moments of this night:

"Weary and dispirited . . . the little army which had marched fourteen miles in the morning . . . attacked a force more than double its own, and for three hours had wrestled for victory . . . sank to rest. In the fence corners, under trees, and around the wagons they threw themselves down, many too weary to eat. . . .

"Jackson shared the open-air bivouac with his men . . . his staff, overcome by weariness, dropped away one by one, until only Maj. W. J. Hawks, the chief commissary officer, remained with the General. . . .

"Knowing the General had fasted all day, the Major soon obtained some bread and meat from the nearest squad of soldiers, and after they had satisfied their hunger, they slept soundly on the rail-bed in a fence-corner."

Jackson may have had strangely mixed dreams in his sleep of exhaustion. After supper one of his unabashed cavalry privates had sought to beard the General.

"The Yanks don't seem willing to leave Winchester, sir," the soldier said.

"Winchester is a very pleasant place to stay."

"I heard they were retreating," the boy said. "I guess they were retreating after us, General."

Jackson stood. "I think I may say I'm satisfied, sir." And he strode off, leaving the grinning boy at a campfire.

Or the General might have turned in his head an astounding letter from Boteler, in which his agent had jokingly suggested that, since people in Richmond were prominently mentioning Stonewall for President, to succeed Jefferson Davis, he had best conduct himself accordingly. The General had been disturbed; his discomfort at the suggestion was obvious, though some of his shrewder officers noted that the report had circulated rather freely through the official family for so intimate a secret. The General must have allowed the picture to flicker through his disciplined mind: President T. J. Jackson, commander in chief —clearly it would be his duty to command the troops of the Confederacy in the field. But the vision had been fleeting.

The next morning found the army hurrying toward the village of Mount Jackson and its old camp. The enemy did not follow. Jackson wrote Anna:

> Yesterday important considerations, in my opinion, rendered it necessary to attack the enemy near Winchester. . . . Our men fought bravely but the superior numbers of the enemy repulsed me. Many valuable lives were lost. Our God has been my shield. . . ."

Jackson began to understand, if he had not on the field of Kernstown, that his defeat had nonetheless been a blow to the Federals, who were now obliged to regard Jackson's force as a potential offensive army and not a mere observation party in the distant mountains. Washington could not consider removing Federal troops from the Valley to aid in the siege of Richmond. Instead, reinforcements were now sent to General Shields. The Rebel Jackson appeared to be dangerous.

Old Jack's thoughts would not leave Garnett. At the end of the month he accused this officer of a long list of failures at Kernstown, removed him from command, and put him under arrest. The army was stunned, and officers were almost openly in rebellion. Garnett was known as a brave and aggressive officer who could not have deserved Jackson's charges, which were almost brutal in tone. Garnett, he said, had failed to move his brigade promptly into place, to provide proper support, to keep his regiments intact, to remain with his command—and to hold his ground.

Jackson placed General Charles Winder in Garnett's post. His men did not conceal their resentment. General Taylor wrote: "I have never met officer or soldier, present at Kernstown, who failed to condemn the harsh treatment of Garnett after that action."

It was almost as if Jackson, unable to bear the thought of defeat, sought a victim on whom to fasten the blame.

Richmond evidently agreed with the troops, for Jackson was ordered to release Garnett from arrest and assign him to duty. Jackson's reply was uncompromising: "I have only to say that I have no desire to see the case pressed any further; but that I regard General Garnett as so incompetent . . . that, instead of building up a brigade, a good one, if turned over to him, would actually deteriorate under his command."

Jackson also wrestled further with his conscience over whether he had properly attacked the enemy on Sunday. He wrote to Anna:

> You appear much concerned at my attacking on Sunday. I was greatly concerned, too; but I felt it my duty to do it, in consideration of the ruinous effects that might result from postponing the battle until the morning. So far as I can see, my course was a wise one; the best that I could do under the circumstances, though very distasteful to my feelings; and I hope and pray to our Heavenly Father that I may never again be circumstanced as on that day.

That might have seemed sufficient, but he could not dismiss the subject:

> I believed that so far as our troops were concerned, necessity and mercy both called for the battle. I do hope the war will soon be over, and that I will never again have to take the field.
>
> Arms is a profession that . . . requires an officer to do what he fears may be wrong, and yet . . . must be done, if success is to be attained. And this fact of its being necessary to success, and being accompanied with success, and that a departure from it is accompanied with disaster, suggests that it must be right.

Having led Anna through those dizzy rounds of reasoning, he went to the heart of the matter:

> Had I fought the battle on Monday instead of Sunday, I fear our cause would have suffered; whereas, as things turned out, I consider our cause gained much from the engagement.

Jackson was also carrying on a steady correspondence with Richmond, especially with Porcher Miles of South Carolina, chairman of the military committee of Congress. He furnished the politician with many of his most profound military opinions, chief among them arguments in favor of the Conscription Act, which did so much to swell the ranks of the armies, Jackson's included. Even Turner Ashby found himself at the head of a large force—larger, in fact, than he yet quite knew how to handle.

Jackson asked Richmond for five thousand more men, but got instead only the tiny command of General Edward Johnson, lying near Staunton. Old Jack tried to impress members of rebellious religious sects into the army, and once arrested a number of conscientious objectors who tried to escape to the North. He made teamsters of several hundred of these men whose religious faith forbade them to fight.

Jackson continued to lie in camp, with Ashby's horsemen screening him. The Federal command now thought it must have been mistaken as to the threat of Stonewall.

On April first, General McClellan wired General Banks: "I doubt whether Johnston will now reinforce Jackson with a view to offensive operations. The time has probably passed when he could gain anything by so doing . . . in regard to your movements, the most important thing is to throw Jackson well back."

Banks in turn wired President Lincoln: "The Rebel Jackson has abandoned the Valley of Virginia permanently, and is en route to Gordonsville by way of the mountains."

Retreat was far from Jackson's mind; he spent his days in ceaseless effort to prepare for attack. Now, at last, he had maps, one of the necessities of a swift campaign. He found a young topographical engineer on the staff of a militia colonel and saw that his talents were being wasted. Jackson snatched him for his staff: Jed Hotchkiss, who was to become an indispensable aide to Jackson. Hotchkiss recalled that the General called him in without warning, saying only, "I want you to make me a map of the Valley from Harpers Ferry to Lexington, showing all the points of offense and defense between those points. Mr. Pendleton will give you orders for whatever outfit you want.

Good morning, sir." The promise of the coming campaign was in the brief interview.

Hotchkiss went to work, and Jackson followed suit; it was now that he began to memorize the charts of distances in the Valley, figures to become so useful to him.

He did not forget the spiritual needs of the troops. The Reverend Dabney described him making devout appearances at worship services and once handing out religious pamphlets to his privates in their camp; he carried saddlebags filled with the tracts.

There was trouble with his officers. Some swore they would not serve under Jackson, and when a reorganization came, with elections of new officers, Colonel A. C. Cummings of the Thirty-third Virginia refused his post and resigned. Richmond, in Jackson's view, sent the wrong men to replace lost officers. A newcomer was General William B. Taliaferro, who had won Jackson's contempt in the winter for allowing his brigade "to become so demoralized that I had to abandon an important enterprise in consequence." He complained of the reappearance of this officer only in Richmond dispatches, however, and put up an appearance of satisfaction with his command.

There was now a surprising bit of good news: Richmond wanted General Banks held off so that he could not menace supply lines to the capital. Jackson was to get reinforcements—the seven thousand fine troops of General Ewell.

While the Valley army waited, Turner Ashby performed one of the feats of daring that made him the hero of the countryside. As the army watched from a hillside on an April day, the dust of a Federal advance appeared, with Union cavalry driving at top speed. Just a few yards in front of them, on a white horse, was the figure of Ashby, firing at his pursuers, and himself under fire. It was clear that he would not have time to burn the covered bridge in front of him, as he had been ordered to do in case of an enemy advance. Nevertheless he reined at the bridge as if to set fire to the brush piled against its timbers. The Yankees were upon him. One of the enemy fired, narrowly missing Ashby, striking his stallion in the side. Ashby cut the Federal from the saddle with his saber and disappeared into the bridge. Confederate officers thought he would never reappear; but he dashed out and, joining his troops, he got to the ground and stood over his dying horse, oblivious to the scattered fire of the engagement he had brought to the camp.

That was not enough to save Ashby from a collision with Jackson. The cavalry companies, now grown to twenty-one, were scattered over the countryside and were wilder than ever. Near Woodstock, the enemy had surprised a body of them while they were making merry on native applejack, had captured many and driven others into the hills. Jackson chose this time to impose discipline on Ashby. He divided the cavalry into regiments, for the purpose of training. Ashby was to command only the advance regiments, which were to guard the army.

Ashby and his next in command, Major O. R. Funsten, so camp gossip said, offered their resignations in an instant. The army buzzed with the clash, for though the troops knew well enough that Ashby maintained no discipline, they understood his worth just as Jackson did; Old Jack, his privates knew, had a hard choice. He could bring Ashby to heel, but he might well lose him in the doing.

Nothing in Jackson's career hinted that he would compromise in this crisis, but he did just that. General Winder, a close friend to Ashby, became a mediator. He went to Jackson, probably with Ashby's resignation in his pocket, and tried to placate the commander. Jackson agreed to talk with the cavalryman.

The army craned necks after Ashby as he trotted through camp and disappeared into Old Jack's headquarters. He was inside for more than two hours. No word of their talk came from the room, but the trouble passed. An order went out detaching all cavalry to Ashby's command, as before; and though the dashing horseman was only technically in charge, the army understood that he had won and would fight the troopers almost as he chose.

Old John Harman, the quartermaster, who had thought "the army is in great danger from our crackbrained General," now wrote that "the difficulty has been settled for the present by General Jackson backing square down."

Jackson explained to Lee in a tone he seldom used: "Such was Colonel Ashby's influence over his command that I became well satisfied that if I persisted in my attempt to increase the efficiency of the cavalry it would produce the contrary effect, as Colonel Ashby's influence, who is very popular with his men, would be thrown against me."

In short, Jackson saw that he was whipped, and he saved face as best he could, though his behavior was in the best interest of the service, too.

Now Kyd Douglas joined the staff; he was a young lawyer, raised at Shepherdstown on the Potomac, who had been to college in Pennsylvania, at Franklin and Marshall, and had come home from his new career in St. Louis when Virginia seceded from the Union. He was a friend of Sandie Pendleton's, and for that reason was called to headquarters duty. A courier found him chopping at the company woodpile and took him to meet the strange commander. His introduction was typical:

"At midnight came a quiet message, 'The General wishes to see Lieutenant Boswell.'—his engineer officer. Lieutenant James K. Boswell, expecting to ride, dressed himself for it and departed. . . . In a few minutes he returned with the information that the General only wanted to know the distance from Gordonsville to Orange Court House. Fifteen minutes later, the General sent to him again to get the same information in writing. I learned afterward that occasionally his staff officers were subject to petty ills of that kind. . . ."

Douglas had more to learn. On a rainy night near Harrisonburg, Jackson casually handed Douglas a dispatch for General Ewell, who was across the Massanuttons and the Blue Ridge, near Culpeper. Douglas was to deliver the paper by daylight, and the paper was too precious to be entrusted to an ordinary courier. Douglas had never seen the country he was to ride, but he left at a gallop to the laconic farewell of Old Jack: "A successful and pleasant ride."

Goading and leading a series of weary horses some 105 miles in the storm, Douglas found Ewell, and fell, almost fainting, as he delivered the message. He spent a day in bed, and rode, through rain once more, to rejoin the army. Then, after his delivery of the vital message which set the Valley campaign in motion:

"I went into the General's room to report. It was empty of furniture and on the hearth were some dying coals of a wood fire. He was lying on the floor upon a thin mattress, wrapped in a blanket and asleep. I awoke him and made my report. He listened politely and then with, 'Very good. You did get there in time. Good night.', he turned over to sleep and I left the room. I will not attempt to describe my surprise and indignation at this cool reception."

In the morning, however, Jackson sent for Douglas and without warning offered him a permanent place on his staff, as assistant inspector general. Old Jack thus acquired one of the most faithful and discerning observers of his campaigns.

Almost the same day, Jackson began the secret moves of the campaign which was to win him renown.

Leaving Banks mystified behind him, and his own General Ewell in almost the same state, Jackson disappeared with his little command on the road toward Staunton.

The army was two and a half days in going sixteen miles, for Jackson persisted in taking a river road incredibly deep in mud and sinkholes which sapped the strength of his men and patience of his officers. Jackson himself got into the mud and tugged at wagons and guns which were held fast in the mire. There was further danger that Federal sentries would fire across the river at any moment. When the men, soaked in mud, reached high ground, they soundly cursed the commander who had scorned a good road for one more remote—and bottomless. The army then climbed the Blue Ridge and passed Brown's Gap. Trains took them into Staunton, where they were joined by two hundred cadets of the Virginia Military Institute.

Jackson wrote Anna of the grim march only: "The road up the river was so treacherous that I could only advance about six miles per day, and to leave the road was at the risk of sinking yet deeper in the quicksands, in which that locality abounds. The country is one of the loveliest I have ever seen."

He made one more apology for being forced to violate the

Sabbath by marching. He added: "Dr. Dabney is here, and I am thankful to God for it. He comes up to my highest expectations as a staff officer."

Jackson now turned to the first stroke in clearing the enemy from his Valley. General Frémont, with his force divided into three segments, was moving to the west of him. General R. H. Milroy and General Robert C. Schenck commanded his divisions. Jackson thought that by moving quickly he could prevent the junction of these men. He marched westward from Staunton on May seventh to make an attempt.

He met General Edward Johnson with his men and turned him about as his vanguard. General Winder had vexations on the march. As Jackson had instructed him, he had forbidden his men to bring their knapsacks, and as he rode past the ranks, men hooted at him, "More baggage! More baggage!" Winder was enraged but could not find the offenders, though he halted the column to search for them.

Just eighteen miles out of Staunton, hungry and in ill humor, the army ran into the first Federal outposts. The men were in a fighting mood. The Reverend Dabney overheard a Georgia private: "We never come all this way to run before Yankees."

General Milroy was camped before them with thirty-seven hundred troops at the foot of Bull Pasture Mountain, in strong position, though reinforcements were some distance away. He had no inkling of Jackson's coming.

Banks had spread assurances that all was well: "A Negro employed in Jackson's tent came in . . . and reports preparation for retreat of Jackson . . . you need have no apprehensions for our safety.

"Jackson is bound for Richmond . . . is on half-rations, his supplies having been cut off by our advance. There is nothing to be done in this valley."

General Milroy discovered, with the sight of swarming gray figures on Sitlington Hill on the morning of May eighth, the gravity of the error of Banks. Already Jackson commanded the Federal position, but there was hot and bloody work ahead. While Milroy sent out frantic messages for help, Jackson advanced his men.

Stonewall was at first cautious, for the Federals filled the village; at about 10 A.M. they got reinforcements when Schenck's troops arrived after a day-and-night march of thirty-four miles. There was light skirmishing during the early afternoon. Confederates lay on their hillside, contemplating the ugly task of storming over this landscape cut by hills and ravines, with a bridge dominated by Union cannon. Scouts reported to Jackson a track over the mountain by which the enemy might be taken in the rear. Jackson was giving orders, perhaps dreaming of the victories he had seen won in Mexico by such a ruse, when the Federals astounded him by charging his front.

The so-called battle of McDowell was an affair of limited slaughter on the slope in front of Jackson's lines, for the Yankee infantry stormed the precipitous hill like veterans accustomed to heavy fire, and they did not pause. Jackson's three thousand banged away at the twenty five hundred attacking Federals. Old Jack was almost driven from his position. He had earlier warned Richmond that the Western troops of the Federals would be troublesome, and he now saw their mettle. The Ohio and West Virginia boys pulled themselves up the slope, which in places was almost sheer rock face. They drove back the Twelfth Georgia regiment in some quarters but could not hold the ground. The Georgians were today the only regiment in Jackson's army which insisted upon remaining on the exposed side of the ridge—and they stayed there, suffering heavy casualties, despite several orders from Jackson that they return to a more protected spot.

Even Jackson's superior numbers and fine position did not suffice, and the Rebel line needed reserves. One regiment did not wait to be called: the Forty-fourth Virginia charged without orders when the fire swelled. Jackson had to call up others before driving off the enemy. After fighting with skill and vigor for four hours, the Federals retired in good order. They built numerous fires around the village of McDowell; in the morning they had disappeared.

Jackson had struck at an exposed portion of the invading army but had by no means crippled it; his officers counted 500 dead and wounded, including the serious toll of 54 officers; Union losses were about 175.

The General went to bed early; and when his servant, Jim, approached with food, Jackson refused, though he had not eaten since morning. "I want none," he said. "Nothing but sleep."

He rose to find Milroy gone and sent a brief message to Richmond: "God blessed our arms with victory at McDowell yesterday." He tried to follow the Federals, with but little success. His wagon train was in poor condition, and forest fires set by Milroy made pursuit difficult and dangerous.

He turned back from the chase, now with other thoughts in mind. He wrote Anna:

> How I do desire to see our country free and at peace! It appears to me that I would appreciate home more than I have ever done before. . . . Yesterday Dr. Dabney preached an excellent sermon from the text, "Come unto me, all ye that labor and are heavy laden, and I will give you rest." It is a great privilege to have him with me.

Jackson had one failure here. He had called the cadet corps of the Institute, hoping to make the child soldiers a permanent part of his army. He had them a few days; but on May seventeenth, they were recalled by the Board of Visitors of the school, which abruptly canceled Old Jack's plans. He surrendered without comment.

He now moved near New Market, where he had called Ewell to meet him; and he pored over maps in the nights and muttered over his memory charts. He cast about for means of using the great parallelogram of roads in the Valley which surrounded the Massanutton range. He did not lose sight of the vast strategic value of the lone road crossing the Massanuttons, near the center of the parallelogram. He puzzled over the country, and heard constant reports of scouts and spies.

He was then ready for the campaign which was to free his Valley and build his reputation as a singular commander. Already he had firmly in his mind the small outlying towns which he was to make famous in the month ahead: Front Royal, Winchester, Cross Keys, Port Republic.

Book Two:

☆☆☆ *All things work together for my good.*

—JACKSON

Prologue:

★★★ SMILE, MR. DAVIS

A smoky spring dawn came to Richmond, with a hint of hot weather in the swamp-scented breeze that crept among the Seven Hills. In the east a Federal observation balloon hung over the verdant tangle, like a monstrous new planet in the April sunshine. The James rolled beneath the ranks of its bridges, but its familiar voice was unheard.

The city had not slept, was full of the passage of soldiers, and caught in the frenzy of preparation for a siege.

Bitter odors rose from the ruins of a cartridge factory, where last night an explosion had killed ten women and girls.

A squad of workmen shambled through paling shadows to dig up the Revolutionary cannon from their honored places as curbstones to provide metal for the shells of the army. The groaning wagons went downhill to the Tredegar Iron Works, where the night shift was dragging out, and the low plumes of smoke drifted about the heads of the aristocrats of the city's laborers—sixteen dollars a day.

A shop window held a wry cartoon this morning. It depicted the flight of Confederate Congressmen from the Yankees by canalboat, for they feared the railroads; an escort of women gave protection from frogs and snakes on the bank.

183

The views were lovely, for it was a city of long white bridges, wooded islands in its river, and with charming hills: Shockoe, Union, Church, Council Chamber, Gamble's, French Garden, Navy. From the heights could be seen the oldest part of the city, all but filling the mile-long plain which swept from the river up the tree-covered terraces to the Capitol.

The day's papers had little news of the armies, and almost all the rest was unpleasant:

The *Dispatch* complained of a new bordello in front of the soldier's hospital of the Young Men's Christian Association, from which women beckoned to the wounded. The paper was incensed over the prostitutes "of both sexes" swarming in the city: "They have been disporting themselves extensively on the sidewalks and in hacks and open carriages . . . [indulging in] smirks and smiles, winks and remarks not of a choice kind in loud voices."

Last week there had been a Thanksgiving Day, but feasts were skimpy, except in the hotels, where rich officers and profiteers lived extravagantly. The Secretary of War had a letter from General Lee, and it had not been kept a secret:

> The troops . . . have for some time past been confined to reduced rations consisting of 18 ounces of flour, four ounces of bacon of indifferent quality, with occasional supplies of rice, sugar or molasses [this for each 100 men, every third day].
> The men are cheerful, and I receive but few complaints. . . . Symtoms of scurvy are appearing among them, and . . . each regiment is directed to send a daily detail to gather sassafras buds, wild onions and garlic, lambs quarters and poke sprouts, but for so large an army the supply obtained is very small.

Early on this morning, a remarkable mob began to assemble inside the wrought-iron fence in Capitol Square before the venerable building which was a replica of Jefferson's love, the Maison Carée of Nîmes. The guards paid little attention as the people gathered on the steps of the Capitol, for most of them were young women and girls, with a sprinkling of old men and adolescent boys. They had clearly met by concert, drifting in by twos and threes, quietly, nodding to friends, sitting, talking in hushed voices. The guards were aware that something unusual was astir, but there was yet no hint of violence; in fact, the square bore a singularly peaceful look, as if these people had gathered for a Sunday service of some sort, for most were dressed in their simple best. They clustered under the linden trees, milling patiently, as if in expectation. A number stared at the surrounding buildings as if these bore some special significance, at the roughly stuccoed brickwork of the Capitol which was, close at hand, a rather ignoble edition of its famed ancestor.

Some women harangued their neighbors at the fringes of the crowd:

"I took out $800 of their damned money yesterday, and all it bought was two pounds of tea, and a sack of coffee and 60 pounds of sugar! Do they think we'll stand it forever?"

Another shouted, and for the first time the guards turned to watch: "Yes, by God—and milk for our babies is just $4 the quart! That's all. And who's to pay?"

Other voices: "And the damned planters lying up drunk at the Spotswood Hotel, drinking $10 likker and eating up $3 venison."

"And they pay their army substitutes $5,000—to go and get killed for them."

Some women shouted now at the guards, as if they were to blame for the troubles of the city.

"Damn your kind! You let the rich out of the army on habeas corpus, or whatever in God's name it is, and you run down the poor by night! You're worse than the Yankees!"

Abruptly, the mob had a leader. As if she had been in hiding, a huge woman appeared in the crowd, shouldering into the open before a guard, heedless of the cocked musket in his hands. She wore an old army jacket cut off at the shoulders and exposing huge reddened arms. Flecks of blood laced the yellow butcher's apron which strained about her body. She turned to the crowd, holding up a dirty palm.

A few wails burst from the throng:

"Bread! Bread!"

"The Union! Give us the Union!"

"Feed our babies!"

The woman glared over the crowd as if judging whether she could quiet it; and then, astonishingly, she leapt to the rim of a fountain, and standing with the sparkling water over her ankles, and grimacing hugely, she flung one hand in a silent, eloquent gesture, pointing out of the square. For an instant she was like some grotesque figure cast on the fountain. The crowd, with undertones of guttural excitement, began to stream away.

The guards assumed poses of nonchalance until the last of the people had left the square, and then they ran. Within a few moments the bell in the city alarm tower began to toll.

The mob flowed westward, hurrying and almost noiseless, going down Ninth Street, past the offices of the War Department and across Main Street, growing larger at each step, with curiosity-seekers coming to join.

A faithful diarist stood on the street—J. B. Jones, a clerk in the War Office: "The mob . . . preserving silence, and so far, good order. Not knowing the meaning of such a procession I asked a pale boy where they were going. A young woman, seemingly emaciated, but yet with a smile, answered that they were going to find something to eat. I could not for the life of me restrain from expressing the hope that they might be successful, and I remarked that they were going in the right direction to find plenty in the hands of extortioners. I did not follow to see what they did."

The mob poured into Cary Street, still in its deadly silence, and approached the stores of the speculators, men who had become rich since war began. Windows began to smash. The women now ran and, in smaller mobs, rushed into doorways and drove out the merchants; some of these men howled in fear as they ran. The women, aided by a handful of men, seized all the drays and wagons in the street and sent out raiding parties for more; they commandeered drivers, and set groups to guard them. They loaded stores into wagons: flour, meal, shoes, cotton goods, jugs of molasses, baskets of eggs, jars of milk.

Others swarmed around the corner into Main Street, where shops had begun to close as word of the riot spread. The mob was now about four thousand strong and had a new set of leaders. Dozens of plate-glass windows were smashed; and in the clatter, people broke into the stores to drag out bolts of silk, arms full of jewelry, liquors, senseless luxuries from pharmacies, manikins from the windows, huge fashionable women's hats, armloads of cigars.

In the midst of this, a company of the home guard wheeled into the street, advancing with bayonets; some of the mob ran. Governor Letcher appeared, shouting in an effort to get attention. There was a steady chorus of cries, and in the background looting continued. A bugle was blown. It became quieter. The governor beckoned to the mayor, who stood on the curb waving for silence. He had a clerk read the city's Riot Act in a loud, contemptuous voice.

"I will fire on you in five minutes," the governor yelled. "If you have not dispersed I will fire on you. In five minutes." His face was red and sweating profusely, and he looked as if he would give the order with glee.

A buzzing at the rear announced the coming of Jefferson Davis. He stepped from his carriage at the moment a woman was screaming epithets at Governor Letcher, daring him to violence, and threatening him with lynching. Davis went past her fearlessly, a slight erect figure with a flushed face, its lantern jaws flexed in anger. The President mounted a dray piled with loot, breathing hard, looking down on the people.

"Bread! Bread!" the women chanted, lifting their hands.

"Citizens! Hear me!"

They hooted him down. "Our children are starving! We want bread and the Union!"

"You're disgraceful!" the Mississippi soldier said to the mob. "This is worse than a Yankee victory. Go to your homes!"

"Bread! Bread or no soldiers. Throwing our sons to them damned butchers of yours—and the lapdog generals lie around your house!"

"Go home, people. So these bayonets can be sent against our common enemy!"

Laughter swept the street.

"This will bring famine on you! It is the sure way to prevent food coming to the city—the farmers will be afraid. Don't you understand me?"

There were further catcalls and screams of derision. "Money! Bread! Union!"

"If any are in want . . ." the President began.

A fury of cries drowned him out.

"If you are in need, I will provide for you as I can from my own purse."

A pandemonium of insults.

"I will share my last loaf with you. I hope you will bear our privations as our brave army does."

A command unheard by the mob passed among the soldiers, who advanced to surround the President; the mob began to fall back, and to quiet. The people now seemed willing to listen.

"Bear privation with fortitude and continue united against the Northern invaders, who are the authors of all our sufferings. Hear me, people of the Confederacy!"

The cold-faced man was obviously sincere and, as he stepped down from the dray, seemed aware that he had not reached the people. There was something in his manner to indicate that he found the necessity of speaking to them unpleasant. He went back into his carriage, as stern and forthright as he had come. The crowd straggled away, ahead of the bayonets of the guard. There were few arrests.

The commander of the city guard asked the President for troops from near-by camps to teach the mob stern lessons, but Davis declined.

The President, however, took steps to close the incident, and to keep it from the ears of the enemy. He had an order sent to the newspapers:

> To the Richmond Press,
> Gentlemen:
> The unfortunate disturbance which occurred today . . . is liable to misconstruction and misinterpretation abroad.
> I . . . make a special appeal to the editors and reporters of the press at Richmond, and earnestly request them to avoid all reference directly or indirectly to the affair. . . .

There was a more direct order to the telegraph company to "permit nothing relative to the unfortunate disturbance . . . to be sent over the telegraph lines in any direction for any purpose."

At three in the afternoon, when things were quiet, the Government opened its first free public commissary. Without previous announcement, rice was distributed to all who came; but the place was not open for long.

Two days later the *Enquirer* violated the order of censorship, but in this language:

> A handful of prostitutes, professional thieves, Irish and Yankee hags, gallows birds from all lands but our own, congregated in Richmond with a woman huckster at their head, who buys veal at the toll gate for 100 and sells the same for 250 in the morning market, undertook the other day to put into private practice the principles of the commissary department.
>
> Swearing that they would have goods at Government prices they broke open half a dozen shoe stores, hat stores and tobacco houses and robbed them of everything but bread, which was just the thing they wanted least.

That week, too, General Longstreet asked for more troops, but was refused because of the threat of riots in the city.

Squads of Yankee prisoners swung through the Richmond streets, defiantly shouting, "They'll hang Jeff Davis on a sour apple tree!" Urchins ran behind them, enchanted by strange uniforms, learning the new song.

Sporadically, throughout the city, army bands appeared, as if on schedule. They played "Dixie," and "Bonnie Blue Flag." There was a good deal in the papers about Confederate victories and the sufferings of the faithful soldiers.

11

★★★ THE DASH TO RICHMOND

Far out in Western Virginia, at the village of Port Republic, it was June ninth—and for Jackson a fitting day to mark the end of a triumphant campaign which was to become his chief fame.

The Federal flight from Port Republic had left him in a rare state. He had his victory before noon, and cantered among Taylor's brigade of Louisianans, smiling in pride, passing congratulations. He found Taylor and seized his hand, promising him the big guns his men had taken. The guns were now hot, still firing at the retreating Federals, whom Jackson's corps had now seen in retreat the length of the Valley from Front Royal to Winchester and back to the south of the Massanuttons.

Ewell was at one of the cannon himself, helping fire final salutes at the enemy.

For the first time in his career, Jackson saw his men go mad; cheering broke from every file as they caught sight of him, and the Irish regiment broke into actual tumult. A gunner rode cock-horse on a cannon, near the generals, shouting to Taylor, "We told ye to bet on our boys!"

In the celebration, Jackson did not forget the enemy. The

190

guns rolled until almost dark. He went into the defile, seeing far below the army of Shields, a dark current on the road to Luray. The Federals moved swiftly, not in a rout, precisely, but in full, undisguised retreat. Jackson's men chased them for eight miles. Jackson returned to the battlefield where booty was being gathered: six big guns, eight hundred muskets, dozens of wagons, 450 prisoners.

Jackson and Ewell were together, watching. Old Jack put his hand on his lieutenant's arm. "He who does not see the hand of God in this is blind, sir, blind!"

Ewell wagged his bald head, grinning, knowing that the tone of slight levity was only for him, and that Jackson was literally speaking his mind. Ewell thought, perhaps, of his own timely arrival on the scene, when his men had clawed the Federals from Jackson's flank and saved him from disaster.

The battlefield, they noted, was more thickly covered with dead than any they had seen. Jackson's men had paid heavily. Taylor's fine Seventh Regiment was cut to bits, and others were shrunken.

Numbers of the men, including General Taylor, got their noon meal from the haversacks of Federal dead.

Jackson and Ewell rode over the field. Jackson hailed a medical officer.

"Did you bring off all the wounded?"

"All of ours, sir. Not the enemy's."

"Why not, Captain?"

"They shelled us from across the river."

"You had your hospital flag on the field?"

"Yes, sir. In plain sight."

"And they shelled that?"

"Yes."

"Take your men to their quarters. I would rather let them all die than have one of my men shot intentionally under the yellow flag, trying to save their wounded."

The anger was passing and did not mar his mood of triumph, but it endured until he had written a stern note to Shields, protesting Frémont's shelling of medical parties. The anger flashed like fire as he spoke to Ewell of an incident in the battle.

Jackson had heard the story: A Federal officer on a white horse had galloped boldly under fire, in clear sight of Confederate riflemen, urging his men to the fight. And Ewell, taken with the show of gallantry, went down his own lines, ordering his men not to fire on the Federal and his horse. Finally, however, the brave enemy officer had fallen.

Jackson asked Ewell if the story were true. Ewell admitted that it was and commented on the stirring picture made by the officer. Jackson cut him short with a new show of wrath, of a sort he was to display more than once. "Never do such a thing again, General Ewell. This is no ordinary war. The brave Federal officers are the very kind that must be killed. Shoot the brave officers and the cowards will run away and take the men with them."

Inexplicably, the army was hurried up the steep mountain road to the east. The troops could not know that they had seen the last of their Valley enemies and were bound for Richmond. Old Jack only pushed them on through a cold rain. The men dragged slowly. They did not recount their victories as they climbed the slope. They straggled, and men were out of ranks, though not so badly as at Winchester, when Jackson had complained to Ewell, "The evil of straggling has become enormous." Jackson himself did not look backward through the spring fighting.

The Valley campaign was over. Its fruits were not yet visible to all, but it was plain that Jackson had immobilized many Federal divisions on the Potomac, had struck fear into Lincoln and his Cabinet, and had prevented the strong reinforcement of McClellan before Richmond.

Jackson had, in fact, saved Richmond. He had kept a potential force of 175,000 Federals from joining in the encirclement of the city which might have taken place, that spring. His campaign had made such demands on his troops as fighting men had seldom known. On many days his divisions had marched thirty-five miles. Between May thirtieth and June fifth, in the retreat southward to Port Republic, the army had made 15 miles a day, 104 miles in all.

In one month the army had freed Staunton, checkmating the

armies of Milroy and Schenck; had chased Banks from Virginia for a time; and had kept McDowell and his thirty-five thousand from their march to Richmond. The trio of great dangers—Banks, Frémont and Shields—had not only failed to crush him but had been battered in turn.

Critics, turning to classic standards, were to find flaws in Jackson's handling of troops, cavalry, guns; but he had performed miracles of a sort and made his name known everywhere. He had made such intimate use of his knowledge of Valley terrain that it became his particular locale in history and was to be studied by soldiers of many nations. All had been accomplished with men who were largely inexperienced; almost without exception his staff, his regimental officers, his troops, were green at the start.

He had begun on March twenty-second. Since then, it was just forty-eight marching days; the troops had slogged 676 miles, an average of 14 miles a day. They had fought six formal skirmishing actions, had brushed with the enemy almost daily for the past month. There had been five pitched battles. Nowhere had Jackson commanded more than seventeen thousand men; but with few exceptions, he had managed to concentrate superior numbers and outnumber the Federals at each point of attack. Yet he had not hesitated to assault forces twice the size of his own. From start to finish he had faced about sixty-two thousand Federal troops in the region, any and all of them available to fall upon him at the whim of the Washington high command.

He had taken thirty-five hundred prisoners, counted thirty-five hundred Federal dead, captured over ten thousand muskets and rifles, seized or burned stores of incalculable value. He had captured nine precious cannon. Against this his losses seemed slight: twenty-five hundred dead and wounded, six hundred prisoners, three guns.

He could look back to errors and oversights on the part of the staff, artillery, cavalry and himself. But he had attempted to build on the errors. And on the western battlefields which he was preparing to leave, he had struck the war's hardest blows against Federal morale: first, against Lincoln and his Washington advisers; second, against the Federal field commanders in the Valley; third, against the fine regiments of Union soldiers which, so poorly led as to be cut to pieces by superior tactics, often lost heart and gave way to panic. Jackson's very name was now worth many Confederate divisions. In his presence, the Federal anxieties had steadily increased, and Union strategy had been seriously altered. In the praise falling upon the leader and the Valley army from all sides, it could be seen that the Confederacy recognized its most accomplished soldiers.

Jackson could now speak to Imboden of his methods, so often demonstrated in the Valley:

> Always mystify. Mislead and surprise the enemy if possible. And when you strike and overcome him, never let up in pursuit so long as your men have strength to follow, for an army routed, if hotly pursued, becomes panic-stricken, and can then be destroyed by half their number.
>
> Another rule—never fight against heavy odds, if by any possible maneuvering you can hurl your own forces on only a part, and that the weakest part, of your enemy and crush it. Such tactics will win every time, and a small army may thus destroy a large one in detail, and repeated victory will make it invincible.

Struggling up the mountain this night, the army felt little of the spirit of invincibility. The rain continued; and when they camped in Brown's Gap, the wind reached the men. The darkness was intense. One corporal, Edward Moore of the Rockbridge Artillery, recalled dolefully that he made his way up the hill by following a grisly caisson. A soldier of the Second Virginia, his head blown off by a cannon shot and a white handkerchief tied over his shoulders, had been strapped to the carriage. Moore and his companions trudged along, with eyes on the bobbing white blur. The night was uncomfortable, but morning saw the army moving down into a pleasant valley and warming weather. There was no sign of the enemy.

Before Jackson left the scene of his last battle in the Valley, he had clashed with his quartermaster, John Harman. He had told Harman to glean the field of muskets and all else of value, but muskets in particular. Harman reported that he had completed the task. Many of the guns, he said, looked like those of his own men. Jackson shouted with an anger revealing this as a sore subject with him.

"The enemy has thousands of weapons like them," he said. "I want to hear no more such talk—and never from an officer!"

"I won't be talked to like that," Harman said. "I will give you my resignation this instant."

The quartermaster stalked out angrily, despite Jackson's call. The General was finally able to explain that he had for months been vexed by stories that Confederate soldiers were throwing away their arms, and that he had lost his temper upon hearing the tale from Harman. He refused to accept the resignation and Harman, his wrath still smoldering, agreed to remain in the service.

Jackson's mind turned to Richmond, where Lee's dispatches beckoned him. From afar, even to the conqueror of the Valley, the scene was dazzling. The scale of battle would be much vaster than he had known in the Shenandoah, thus the opportunity for glory would be greater. He knew well the chief of the enemy forces, McClellan, his West Point classmate. And he had troops keen for fight. They had struck hard in the Valley, and they could, of course, perform equally well in the east.

McClellan's huge army lay below Richmond after weeks of fighting its way up the Peninsula from Yorktown. Lee could hardly hope to drive it back without the aid of Jackson, and he must conceal Jackson's coming as long as possible. To that end, he sent reinforcements to the Valley commander. These were the troops of General Whiting, which marched across the state to meet Stonewall just as he was moving eastward. There were rumors set afloat that a big offensive was planned for the Valley. Even General Whiting was left in the dark. When Lee called for secrecy, Jackson responded wholeheartedly.

Whiting had reported to Jackson at Port Republic, in ignorance of the developing plan. There was a pleasant enough greeting for the commander of fresh and veteran brigades, but the strangest and most perfunctory conversation: the weather, springtime, roads from Richmond, the absence of the enemy. Whiting returned to his troops at Staunton in a flaming temper.

"Jackson treated me like a dog. It's an outrage!"

Surely the commander was polite, John Imboden suggested, for Jackson was never less than civil to officers.

"Oh, hang him! He was polite enough. But not one word—not after marching all this way, hurrying to him. Not a whisper of an order, or a word about his plans. Not even to me, after all this!

"Do you know what I got out of him, in the end? Why, he simply told me to come back here to Staunton, and he would send orders. I hadn't the slightest notion what they would be. He treated me like a child, I tell you. I believe he hasn't more sense than my horse!"

By breakfast time the hot-tempered Whiting was confirmed in his opinion. He had a brief order from Jackson: he was to board the train and move to Gordonsville, at once. Whiting roared once more.

"I told you he was a fool, didn't I? Why, I just came through Gordonsville day before yesterday, and now he sends me back east."

Old Jack passed a strict order that no soldier was even to mention the plans of the army, and this air of mystery in a state of ignorance afforded the troops several days of raucous jests. They trapped Jackson himself.

He rode among the men one morning and saw one of Hood's soldiers who had wandered into an orchard, where he had climbed a cherry tree and was gobbling ripe fruit. Old Jack rode to him.

"Where are you going, soldier?"

"I don't know."

"What command are you in?"

"I don't know."

"Well, what state are you from?"

"I don't know."

Jackson called to another soldier. "What's the meaning of this?"

"Well, Old Jack and Old Hood passed orders yesterday that we didn't know a durned thing till after the next fight, and we're keeping our mouths shut."

Jackson laughed and trotted away.

On June thirteenth, Jackson declared a day of rest for the troops and posted a proclamation:

The fortitude of the troops under fatigue and their valor in action have again, under the blessing of divine Providence, placed it in the power of the commanding general to congratulate them on the victories of June 8 and 9.

While beset on both flanks by two boastful armies, you have escaped their toils, inflicting successively crushing blows upon each of your pursuers. Let a few more such efforts be made, and you may confidently hope that our beautiful valley will be cleansed from the pollution of the invader's presence.

He called for a period of thanksgiving and "divine service in all regiments."

On the same day, he called the tireless Colonel Boteler into headquarters, and once more sent him to Richmond to ask for reinforcements so that Jackson could invade the North. Boteler was to deliver the message verbally to Lee, assuring him that Jackson was ready to move to Richmond, but suggesting that the Valley army, turned loose above the Potomac, would bring the North up howling, demanding that McClellan's grand army be brought home to defend native soil.

"If they will only give me 60,000 men," he said in his squeaky voice. "I will go right on to Pennsylvania. I will not go down the Valley; I don't want the people there to be harassed. I will go with 40,000 if the President will give them to me.

"My route will be along the east of the Blue Ridge—I ought not to have told you even that. But in two weeks I could be at Harrisburg."

He was afire with the plan, but did not lose sight of Lee's primary interest in the trenches about Richmond. He had written: "Circumstances greatly favor my moving to Richmond in accordance with your plan. I will remain if practicable in this neighborhood until I hear from you, and rest the troops who are greatly fatigued."

Only Boteler knew of Jackson's reincarnated scheme of invasion. The staff officers could do more than guess at their destination. For five days, in any event, few thought of movement, and the regiments lay content in the meadows of the limestone valley. Jackson wrote Anna of the place, which was familiar to her, and of Weyer's Cave near by, where she had once been sight-seeing. He asked, "Wouldn't you like to get home again?"

Lee now sent Jackson insistent dispatches: He must hurry to Richmond. McClellan was becoming stronger, and there was danger that he might creep forward behind his trenches until the city was enveloped. Lee put the order gently: "If you agree"; but the compelling haste was clear in every line. Jackson was to conceal his movements and come as swiftly as possible to the capital. It was an order to delight Jackson; he might have written it himself. Lee had not even commented on Jackson's plan of invading the North; he would send private word by Colonel Boteler.

Jackson had already closed the roads about him with his cavalry and taken trouble to confuse the enemy. At almost the same moment Jackson read Lee's order, General Nathaniel P. Banks was telegraphing Washington that Old Jack was advancing on him in overwhelming force.

Jackson began to spin his veil of secrecy in earnest. The army began to tell this story of him, though it was of dubious accuracy:

One night he rode out in the rain to play his mysterious game. He had written Colonel T. T. Munford, his new cavalry chief, ordering a meeting at the village of Mount Crawford, ten miles away on the Valley turnpike. They were to meet at the head of the single street, and Munford was warned "not to ask for me or anybody."

Munford reached the village at the proper hour. Dim light revealed a motionless figure in the road. Munford approached, and the figure saluted.

"Ah, Colonel, here you are. Any news from the front?"

"All quiet, General."

"Good. Now, Munford, I want you to produce on the enemy the impression that I am going to advance."

"Yes, sir."

Jackson sat for two or three minutes telling his cavalryman how the dismounted riflemen should be pressed close against the enemy lines, and pickets kept there, alert; how to keep plentiful fires burning and to spread false reports. Abruptly, the General called farewell and rode off, Sorrel going into a slow gallop in the resounding darkness. Munford stared after him.

Jackson sent for Jed Hotchkiss, and the engineer went in with his maps. The General put him through a catechism on roads and streams and the points of strength in the Valley. Hotchkiss, when dismissed, had the idea that the coming offensive would be in the direction of Lexington.

Within half an hour, Hotchkiss was puzzled by a second call from Jackson. Casually, close-mouthed, like a horse trader's opening to his intended victim, Jackson said, "Major, there's been some fighting down about Richmond, there at Seven Pines, I believe. Will you let me see maps of that country?"

Hotchkiss fetched maps of lowland Virginia—poor ones— and for most of the afternoon the two studied the roads, woodlands, streams, fords, heights, swamps, and all eminences and obstructions. When it was done: "Thank you, Major. That will be all."

Hotchkiss went to his tent with the suspicion that the army was to sweep eastward and join the fight for Richmond.

Even Ewell knew nothing; he blithely gave leave to some of his staff officers, telling them in confidence that reinforcements were coming and that the Valley army would soon fall upon Banks again. The good-humored Ewell did not resent secrecy now. When some of Jackson's staff, left behind, reported to Ewell for duty, the bald Indian fighter said with heavy sarcasm, "I ain't commanding but a division, and am only marching under orders. I don't know where, of course. I've not got much staff left, but that's more than I've any use for, the way it is now. I have a little suspicion about Richmond, but I can't say."

And Jackson's staff, without instructions, set out in pursuit of their commander, who had disappeared.

Now and again officers bearded Jackson about his overpowering love of secrecy. Old Jack would smile patiently: "If my coat knew my plans, as Frederick the Great once said, I would take it off and burn it. And if I can deceive my friends, I can make certain of deceiving my enemies."

On June seventeenth, the troops had begun the eastward swing. Jackson met one of his brigade commanders near headquarters.

"Colonel, have you received the order?"

"No, sir."

"I want you to march."

"When, sir."

"Now."

"Which way?"

"Get in the cars—go with Lawton."

"How must I send my wagons and battery?"

"By the road."

"Well, General, I hate to keep asking fool questions, but I can't send my men off without knowing which road to send them."

Jackson laughed, but only briefly. "Send them by the road the others take." And he rode on.

The next day he had most of his troops in Staunton, moving along the Virginia Central Railroad. Still his officers did not know that Lee had called in the Valley troops, nor that Boteler had returned, bringing verbal refusal of Jackson's offensive into the North. The prospect of a blow into Pennsylvania appealed to Lee, but the straits in which the capital found itself made invasion an impossibility. First things first; the investing of Richmond must be foiled without delay.

Jackson was out of Staunton and into Waynesboro within a few hours. In the dusk the General, riding with Major Hotchkiss, a courier and another officer, had a spectacular view of the army, which lay in camp over the Blue Ridge, for miles. Campfires blazed on either side of the climbing road, from the base to the summit. Hotchkiss went ahead to find quarters for the General. He once failed and returned to report.

"General, I fear we will not find our wagons tonight."

Jackson, more earnestly than the occasion called for, Hotchkiss thought, replied, "Never take counsel of your fears, Major. See if you can find us a place to sleep, and something to eat if you can."

The four finally rode through the gap and down the eastern slope, to a farmhouse owned by one James McCue. They ate well there, and retired to a single large room with three beds.

When the lamp had been blown out, Hotchkiss and the General lay for a time talking. The Major idly reviewed for Jackson the gossip of the day, about the destination of the army. Jackson laughed at each guess Hotchkiss made. Just before they fell silent, the General piped, "Do any of them say I'm going to Washington?" He laughed as if this were the greatest joke of all.

Hotchkiss saw Jackson kneel by his bed for more than five minutes. He thought of what Jim had told the staff somewhere back on the route of the Valley campaign:

"Gentlemen, when my General goes to getting up in the night to pray, you better watch out. There's going to be hell to pay. He prays all the time, but when I see him up at night, I never asks no questions. I pack the haversack, because he's sure to call for it next morning."

The next day Jackson reached Mechum's River. He met the Reverend Dabney there and beckoned him into a little hotel room, locking the door.

"I am going to Richmond ahead of the troops. To see General Lee. On the train. The corps is going to join in an attack on McClellan—but I will be back to you before you reach Richmond.

"Dabney, I want you to march the troops to Richmond, following the rail line as much as you can. I want you to march at the head of Ewell's division."

He gave Dabney orders to preserve secrecy, and shook hands. He went out to board an express train for the east. Kyd Douglas thought he looked like a passenger bound for Europe, shaking hands with everyone in sight. Old Jack clambered into the mail car, but even there could hardly break off a conversation with an elderly man who had hung around the station, clumsily trying to discover Jackson's destination. Just before the train moved, the old man surrendered subtlety and shouted, "General, where are you going?"

"Can you keep a secret?"

"Oh, yes."

"Ah, so can I."

The train left the old man grinning after it.

Jackson had scarcely disappeared when Ewell beseiged Dabney, "Dammit, now, excuse me, Major. Reverend. But Jackson is driving us mad. He don't say a word to so much as move a horse. And here, now, he's gone off on the railroad without trusting me—his senior Major General—with a single solitary word. No order, no hint of where we're going.

"But that quartermaster of his, that Old John Harman, he knows it all, I suppose. He's been telling the troops we're heading for Richmond to fight McClellan."

Dabney offered consoling words, assuring Ewell that he ranked high in Jackson's esteem, and that Harman, if he knew anything, had only guessed it. Ewell continued to protest. This time, Jackson had gone too far; it was an additional insult to Ewell because he had so lately recanted from his original opinion that Jackson was insane. He had said as much to Colonel Munford:

"I take it all back, and will never prejudge another man. Old Jackson is no fool; he knows how to keep his own counsel, and does curious things; but he has method in his madness; he has disappointed me entirely."

Today it appeared that this might not be a mature judgment, after all. This season of secrecy seemed more irrational than any other Jackson had yet displayed.

General Winder, too, was still smarting from a hurt Jackson had given him. As the swing to Richmond began, Winder, the able West Point-trained brigade commander who led the Stonewall Brigade, had asked Jackson for a brief leave. He wanted, innocently, to go to Richmond itself. He was as ignorant of the developing movement as anyone else, and was incensed when Jackson refused him, bluntly and without reason given. Winder was already tender where Jackson was concerned, for he felt that Stonewall interfered unnecessarily in the command of his old brigade. Today he bristled. He had no means of knowing Jackson's distracted mind was far away, already in the moist trenches of the Peninsula, facing McClellan. Winder offered his resignation. Jackson accepted it.

General Taylor saved the day. Winder went to the Louisiana camp with his news, and Taylor became unusually excited, for he admired the ability of this effective field commander. Taylor went to Jackson, begging that he reconsider and persuade Winder to remain. The crafty young officer first described the glory Old

Jack had won in the Valley, and pictured his honors as enduring to late ages. He saw something in Jackson's face like pleasure. He wrote:

"Observing him closely, I caught a glimpse of the man's inner nature. It was but a glimpse. The curtain closed, and he was absorbed in prayer. Yet in that moment I saw an ambition as boundless as Cromwell's, and as merciless."

Jackson remained speechless. He gave no promise to make amends with Winder; but as Taylor left, Old Jack rose. "I think I'll ride out with you, General," he said.

Later in the night, Taylor learned Jackson had visited Winder, that the resignation was withdrawn, and the service had saved a fine officer.

The army moved rapidly eastward, despite all handicaps. Raiding Federal cavalry had burned a railroad bridge of the South Anna River near the village of Frederickshall, and Jackson's officers were obliged to move the troops and supplies over a broken rail line, using fewer than two hundred small cars. They used an ingenious "riding and tying plan," loading the cars with supplies at the western terminus near Charlottesville, unloading them at the South Anna, then shuttling the cars back again to pick up troops along the route. The corps thus moved toward Richmond, but in considerable disorder.

The Reverend Dabney was outraged at the lack of discipline. He found one officer who had allowed his wagons to roll far ahead of his mounted guard, but when Dabney upbraided him, the officer said blandly, "I just come along. I had no orders from nobody."

It was an eloquent statement of the confusion inherent in a movement by an army whose commander could not bring himself to reveal the destination. When Dabney complained to Jackson of the lack of discipline, he was assured that there was a more pressing problem at hand: however it could be done, the corps must be pushed into place in front of Richmond before the enemy collected his wits and came out of the trenches to end the war.

On Saturday, June twenty-first, Jackson and Dabney took an

enforced rest in Gordonsville, while Jackson sent out scouts to investigate a rumor that a Federal raid was reaching toward his line of march, with Union infantry only sixteen miles away, on the Rapidan. The rumor proved to be false, and the army moved on.

Until this moment, the gossips had a wide range of choice as objectives for the army, for it could still have moved toward Washington. But Jackson ended that possibility, going on to the east, so that the army could now be aiming only for Fredericksburg or Richmond. Jackson preserved his secrecy.

He muttered to Dabney, "Will you take a railroad ride with me? We will leave our horses with the staff." The two boarded a train after dark. Jackson fell asleep in the bunk of the mail clerk almost at once. Sidings were so infrequent, and traffic so heavy, that it was dawn before they reached Frederickshall, only twenty-six miles away. Jackson went to the home of Nathaniel Harris, where General Hood and General Whiting already had quarters. He went out to hear Dabney preach during the day, and talked with a guide Dabney had found, who was to show them the roads to Richmond.

In the afternoon, Jackson said cautious farewells to his generals in the Harris house. Late at night, Jackson had Whiting aroused to write out a pass and an impressment order so that he might get relays of fresh horses on the route to Richmond. Quartermaster Harman was to ride with Jackson from Frederickshall. He got firm orders to address Old Jack only as "Colonel," so that no chance remark might identify him. Mrs. Harris asked Jackson what time he would like his breakfast tomorrow, but the General could not bring himself to divulge his plans, even then. He said he would eat at the usual hour.

It was not an easy ride, fifty-two miles in about fourteen hours. They were forced into a late start by Jackson's insistence that they wait until 1 A.M., so that he would not break the Sabbath. They avoided crowds and took the most covert route through the city, after entering on Three Chopt Road; few people saw them, and those who recognized the General were so certain that he was still in the Valley that they did not believe their eyes.

Jackson came to Lee's headquarters in the Dabbs's farmhouse

near Nine Mile Bridge in the midafternoon, confident that his
week-long efforts to baffle the enemy had been successful, and
that he had taken every precaution to screen the move of the
corps. The enemy, he thought, could not dream that he was near.
He was wrong.

A Confederate deserter had left Gordonsville at about the time
Jackson rode to the east, having divined that Stonewall was heading for Richmond. This man was picked up by Union horsemen
on June twenty-fourth at Hanover Court House, and he—name-
less in the official records—provided McClellan with the news.
The deserter reported Jackson near Richmond with his entire
army from the Valley, ready to strike the Union flank. He estimated Jackson's strength at fifteen brigades. A telegram to Washington brought a flurry of new orders, and the Federals attempted
to prepare a reception. Jackson was to find that all things, including military security, were different here in the east.

Jackson was badly worn by the ride and dismounted stiffly,
dust-covered, sore and sleepy. He found that Lee was at work and
waited for him in the yard, resting against the picket fence, head
down. He was slumped there when General D. H. Hill rode up.
The grizzled little South Carolinian had been called from his
camp near Seven Pines for a conference with Lee. He was surprised to see his newly famous brother-in-law. Jackson, he was
positive, had only yesterday been far down the Valley, confront-
ing Banks and Shields; heavy reinforcements had gone to him.
Yet here he was. The two had not met since Jackson had earned
his exalted reputation in the Valley. They passed warm greetings.

Things were bad in these parts, the barbed-tongued Hill told
Jackson. His men had been falling back before McClellan's army,
which was all but numberless. There was little food; for the last
three days his men had been issued nothing but corn in the shuck.
Several thousand soldiers had fled to Richmond on pretext of
sickness. And the very cannon were untrustworthy; the scoundrels
of the ordnance department used brittle metal in gun barrels, and
shells often burst in the mouths of artillery pieces.

Jackson made little reply to his outspoken friend, whom he had
known so well for so many years. Hill was in some ways like
Jackson—a schoolteacher who had married one of the Morrison

girls; a man of strong religious bent; a firm warrior for temperance who had ordered liquor poured out when found in his camps. He was now fresh from the bloody holding action against McClellan, which had ceased only when the Federals, within sight of the spires of Richmond, had dug in to gather strength for the kill.

Hill and Jackson went in to Lee. The commander in chief, gravely courteous, greeted them and offered refreshments. Jackson took only a glass of milk and downed it in a few gulps. Lee began to explain the plan of assault on the Yankees, though in general terms. It was a bold plan, born of desperation in an effort to stave off a siege of Richmond. Lee offered it calmly, clothed with assurance, as if it were an everyday affair to abandon the capital city by stripping it of troops and, with a force of 85,000 men, to march against the trenches of an enemy of 105,000. But there was none too much daring here for Jackson, who had more than once pressed bolder schemes upon Lee. Old Jack considered with a cold mind.

The other general officers entered, and Lee began to explain in detail. He now faced Jackson, D. H. Hill, Longstreet, and A. P. Hill.

But for A. P. Hill, a year younger at thirty-seven, Jackson was the junior officer in the council; yet he brought to the conference room a prestige the others lacked, even Lee.

The conqueror from the western battlefields was surely not a presence: an inexpressive face, almost hostile with indifference, a beard yellowed with dust; the uniform wrinkled from the road. Yet about him clung his Valley reputation, and there was a delicate note of deference in the air. Jackson wore the greenest laurels of the Confederacy, though as if utterly unaware of them. He was, to this day, the South's lone invincible general.

Old Jack watched Lee closely. He had not seen the commander for months, though they had exchanged messages almost daily. His admiration of the older man was sincere; he had not joined the gossip about the ascent of the staff officer, the paper-shuffler, the engineer.

Lee was fifty-five. He had held command for just three weeks, and had fought no battle beyond direction of the final hours of the inconclusive action at Seven Pines. He was, Jackson knew, intimately influential with President Davis; a man of ability and charm who would have little difficulty with his officers. There was a gentle authority in his voice. His manner of offering his plan of battle bordered on humility, but Jackson was quick to see its daring of conception. Here was true Virginia aristocracy, too, if a man believed in that: The commander was a son of Washington's great cavalryman of the Revolution, who had left as an echo behind him, "First in war, first in peace . . ."

Lee had overcome family shame and bankruptcy, had led a distinguished career in the United States Army, and at last had left the fine ancestral home of his wife to the enemy and come to Richmond to follow his destiny with Virginia. Jackson trusted Lee. If the role of lieutenant was uncomfortable to him, Old Jack did not reveal it.

Jackson had no fear of Lee's background, either as aristocrat or Old Army engineer. He had marked the vision of the commander during the Valley campaign, as well as his lack of that false pride which had already overcome many a Confederate dandy.

Lee had once shown himself to the troops of the army he had begun to call, somewhat grandly, the Army of Northern Virginia. One sharp-eyed cannoneer had recorded his debut:

"General Lee first appeared before us in citizens' dress, in white duck with a bob tail coat; jogging along without our suspecting who he was. We thought at first he was a jolly easy going miller or distiller on a visit as a civilian to the front, and perhaps carrying out a canteen of whisky for the boys. He showed himself good-natured . . . stopping once to reprove, though very gently, the drivers for unmercifully beating their horses when they stalled; and walking about and laughing at one of Artemus Ward's stories; and kept in a good humor about it the rest of the day."

Lee spoke as became the man who had lately written, on taking command from the wounded Johnston: "I wish that his mantle had fallen on an abler man, or that I were able to drive our enemies back to their homes. I have no ambition and no desire but the attainment of this object, and therefore only wish for its accomplishment by him that can do it most speedily and thoroughly."

Jackson listened to Lee, perhaps surprised by the candor with which the commander laid his problem before subordinates, a course Jackson could not have taken. The Valley conqueror was perhaps less attentive than he might have been to the other lieutenants present. All were West Pointers, able soldiers, evidently in high favor with Lee. Longstreet, a captain and Union paymaster when war came; squat, domineering, stubborn, becoming deaf at the age of forty-one. Jackson had known him slightly in Mexico. Red-haired A. P. Hill, hot-tempered and brilliant, had been with Jackson at West Point; he was yet untested in field command. Jackson knew D. H. Hill thoroughly from Lexington friendship. Hill had a tongue noted for its asperity, was nearsighted, wore thick spectacles, and was prone to be intolerant of others, though a thorough soldier.

The other men were aware of the details of Lee's plan and its development in days of conversation with President Davis. Lee explained for Jackson's benefit that McClellan's forces lay roughly along a north-south line, across the Chickahominy River. The northern flank seemed to invite attack. Victory there would pinch off the enemy's rail transport and force his troops to the south to retreat, or to come from their trenches and fight.

Only details of the plan remained, for the proposal had been argued freely by the generals before Jackson's arrival. Lee spoke briefly, saying that Jackson's command was near by and would take part in the attack. He showed Jackson how his Valley troops would push the attack north of the river, coming down from Totopotomoy Creek to the southward, thereby opening the Chickahominy bridges to other units of the army, which would not have to cross in face of enemy fire. He said little more. Lee left the room to attend to other business and left the officers to confer. Longstreet led the discussion.

Jackson did not challenge the decision that his corps should take the longest road (his men now lay at Beaver Dam Station, fifteen miles northwest of Richmond) and assume the most difficult objective. He was to march through strange country to Ashland, a railroad station just north of Richmond, and then move southward, advising General Branch of A. P. Hill's division, which would be the unit on his right. The word would be passed in turn to the other divisions, lying still farther south and east. The divisions were to move eastward in echelon, on roughly parallel roads, and strike the enemy simultaneously, or almost so. Jackson's objective lay near the village of Mechanicsville, where the council anticipated little resistance. Hill and Jackson, united, would push from there toward Cold Harbor and Mc-Clellan's exposed line of supply. That would enable Longstreet to move up, over a bridge made safe by Jackson's advance.

Jackson frowned in concentration, for though he had pored over the maps of this region with Hotchkiss, he was not familiar with the details; and Hotchkiss was gone, sent back to the Valley to more map making. Jackson was by no means at home with the terrain of which the others spoke so familiarly, but he made no protest.

When could he move? How soon could the Jackson troops pass Ashland, ready to march down against Mechanicsville? Perhaps in memory of the open Valley country, confident of the ability of the Foot Cavalry, Jackson said, "Tomorrow."

That meant that battle could be given on the following day, which would be June twenty-fifth. But Longstreet demurred. He knew well the kinds of roads Jackson was to meet: narrow, screened with jungles of luxuriant swamp growth, cut by sluggish streams, meandering and confusing. He proposed that Jackson allow two days for the movement. Jackson agreed.

Lee returned to hear Longstreet's summary of their decision and nodded approval. He promised a set of written orders covering the movement of the four big divisions. It was almost dark when the officers left the Dabbs's farmhouse, and Jackson began the long ride back to meet his men.

On his way, he ran afoul one of his well-trained pickets, who refused to let him pass and engaged in a terse exchange with Old Jack, the soldier admitting only that he belonged to "Company D, Southern army." The soldier scolded Jackson for his inquisitiveness, until a companion recognized the General and allowed him to go by.

Jackson reached his troops at Beaver Dam Station in a downpour of rain. Things were in a state. Major Dabney had fallen ill of some intestinal complaint, and even before his illness had been unable to cope with the scattered troops. The column was strung out almost halfway to the Valley; twenty miles and more separated the lead and rear brigades, and the wagons were everywhere. His other officers were weary for lack of sleep, and Old Jack himself, all but sleepless for two nights, was on the verge of collapse. If he saw anything dangerous in the condition of his division, however, he said nothing. He gave no orders for furious haste.

Jackson fell into bed, leaving his mud-soaked uniform and boots at the fireside. He had been a bit feverish, but it did not seem serious, and this was known only to Jim. His miserable columns pulled themselves together in the rain as he slept, but made little progress in preparation for the first big assault of the combined armies. The eastern rivers rose, the swamps filled, and a few miles away waited the massive lines of the enemy.

12

☆★★ STRANGE FAILURES

The boggy country below Richmond swarmed with the 105,000 Federals and their hangers-on. It was the most grandly equipped army of history, and there was scarcely room for it between the York and the James. With the army was an exotic party: the Prince de Joinville, of the house of Orleans and pretender to the French throne; and his nephews, the Duc de Chartres and the Comte de Paris. They were on McClellan's personal staff, and serious soldiers they were.

The prince was astonished that the amateur soldiers of the United States were paid the handsome sum of thirteen dollars a month and would one day draw pensions of about forty francs monthly, this for soldiers who by European standards were capricious and undependable, and so well fed that they usually threw away most of their rations. It did not look like war to the prince.

It was like a gay fete, he thought, with the observation balloons in the air, bands playing, signal flags flapping from the flowering trees. In the soft nights the ceaseless songs of mockingbirds literally wore out the Frenchman. And he marveled at New York newspapers sold on the battlefields, and at the signs of embalmers advertising their grim work.

211

The army shocked an American, as well, for some Federal officers lived like emperors. George A. Townsend, a gifted reporter with the invaders, wrote of one who "furnished one of the deserted mansions, and brought a lady from the North to keep it in order. He drove a span that rivalled anything in Broadway, and his wines were luscious. His establishment reminded me of that of Napoleon III, in the late Italian war, and yet, this man was receiving merely a colonel's pay. My impression was that everybody at White House robbed the government, and in the end, to cover their delinquencies, these scoundrels set fire to an immense quantity of stores and squared their accounts thus: "Burned on the Pamunkey, June 28, commissary, quartermaster's and hospital stores, one million dollars."

Over this country, a few days earlier, Jeb Stuart and his troopers had dashed in their most spectacular exploit, a ride completely around McClellan's army. They had discovered the Federal flank in the air north of the Chickahominy, where an exposed segment of the army was commanded by the dandy of the Federal forces, General Fitz John Porter.

Now, in the last days of June, the renowned aeronaut of the Union army, Professor S. T. C. Lowe, a veteran of seven thousand ascensions, floated in his balloon, *Constitution,* over the swamps, sending down by wire descriptions of the terrain and the enemy. Townsend rode with him in the swaying car:

"The Chickahominy was visible beyond us, winding like a ribbon of silver through the ridgy landscape. Far and wide stretched the Federal camps. . . . As we climbed higher . . . Richmond lay only a little way off . . . with the James stretching white and sinuous from its feet to the horizon. We could see the streets, the suburbs, the bridges, the outlying roads, nay, the moving masses of people. The Capitol sat white and colossal on Shockoe Hill. . . . The fortifications were revealed in part only, for they took the hue of the soil, and blended with it. . . . The Confederates were seen running to the cover of the woods . . . but we knew the location of their camp fires by the smoke. . . .

"A panorama so beautiful would have been rare at any time, but this was thrice interesting. . . . Across these plains the hordes at our feet were either to advance victoriously, or be driven eastward with dusty banners and dripping hands. Those white farmhouses were to be the receptacles for the groaning and the mangled; thousands were to be received beneath the turf of those pasture fields; and no rod of ground, on any side, should not smoke with the blood of the slain."

Confederate cannon fire drove the balloon from the sky. This was one of the final enemy glimpses of Richmond until the dark months near the end of the war.

The entangled woodland over which the Federal balloonists gazed concealed the first moves in Lee's huge effort to drive the enemy from Richmond's gates. To the south of his line before the city, Lee was leaving General Magruder with little more than a token force, to hoodwink McClellan and hold him from the city—while the bulk of Confederate strength, in the divisions of A. P. Hill, Longstreet and D. H. Hill, were passed to the northward, where, at the appearance of Jackson, they would be ready to join the attack from the left flank.

The morning of June twenty-fourth brought little movement by the conquerors from the Valley. Jackson slept through several rainy hours, for he had got less than ten hours' sleep in the past four days and nights. His command advanced a short distance, but in the front were enemy pickets, and creeks where men had to be put over on logs.

In the thronging of the army getting under way, no one seemed to think it singular that Jackson, worn by unusual service, should be responsible for the pivotal movement which was to launch the attack, though he had the longest route to cover and was, of all Lee's lieutenants, the least familiar with the country.

On this Tuesday, Jackson had to place his trust in new guides, one of whom was Captain C. W. Dabney, brother of the ailing reverend; another was Lincoln Sydnor, a native of the region, who rode with Ewell's portion of the Jackson column. Jackson was to miss Hotchkiss nonetheless, for despite the intensive training of his mind over the years, he had never been able to envision the full possibilities of a military landscape until he had seen it himself. And all Confederates had reason to complain of their maps this week. D. H. Hill remembered bitterly: "The map furnished me (and I suppose the six other major generals had no better) was very full in regard to everything in our own lines; but a red line on the east side of the Chickahominy and nearly parallel to it, without any points marked on it, was our only guide to the route."

General Taylor, though he was to make most of the coming marches in an ambulance, could complain as well: "Confederate commanders knew no more about the topography of the country, the whole of it within a day's march of the city of Richmond, than they did about Central Africa . . . we were profoundly ignorant . . . without maps, and . . . nearly . . . helpless."

When Jackson got out of bed on June twenty-fourth, his men were leaving Beaver Dam Station, with almost forty miles to go before reaching their objective on the Federal flank—this a precise spot on the map, Hundley's Corner, a village south of Totopotomoy Creek. The men were already learning in the rain-swept morning that the Valley marches had not held such terrors after all. They went through blind thickets at the roadside, with soft soil sucking at their boots; there were Yankees, insects, and, despite the rain, exhausting heat. Even Lincoln Sydnor was at a loss, for the enemy had cut so many new roads in the tangle that he lost his landmarks and led the column out of its way.

General Ewell cursed Sydnor so vehemently that Jackson, riding up, was forced to calm him. Ewell had threatened hanging for the guide because the heavy guns had to be wheeled about into the proper path, with long, hard labor. During the day, perhaps at the home of Henry Carter, where he stopped with some staff officers, Jackson read a memorandum of Lee's order describing how the forces of Jackson, the Hills and Longstreet would move toward the enemy. He had this reduction, in writing, of the decision of the council of war:

> Maj Gen Jackson to be in position on Wednesday night on the Hanover Ct. Ho. Road, or near that road, about half way between Half Sink Bridge, and Hanover Ct. Ho. . . .
>
> Gen Jackson will commence his movement, precisely at 3 o'clock Thursday morning, and the moment he moves, send messengers to Gen Branch, who will immediately move himself. . . .

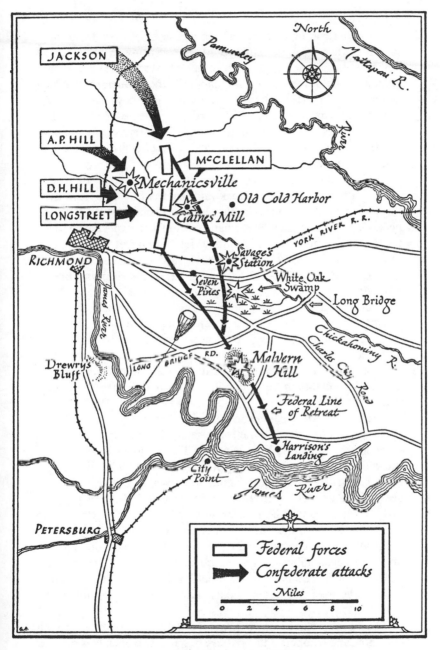

THE SEVEN DAYS

The order continued to specify how passage of word from Jackson to Branch to A. P. Hill would set the army in motion, and how the units, joining in the vicinity of Mechanicsville, would make the line of the enemy untenable. In the council of war, and in Lee's headquarters, these precautions must have seemed substantial safeguards against failure of the scheme of attack. But by now Jackson, far out in the jungle country, could see that the timetable would be difficult to meet. Lee brought a slight complication with an order to Jackson during the night which gave him a somewhat longer route. Old Jack was still depended upon to turn Beaver Dam Creek and pry the Federals from their forbidding rifle pits so that a bloody frontal assault would not be necessary. No one knew just when Jackson was expected to reach the creek. Despite mounting difficulties, it was yet impossible to foresee that the army, split into awkward divisions, would fail its first great test in co-ordination, and that the resulting breakdown in command would exact heavy penalties.

General Taylor, riding near Jackson, was complaining of swamp fever: "I suffered from severe pains in the head and loins, and . . . found it impossible to mount my horse; so the brigade marched under the senior colonel. . . . I had scarce consciousness to comprehend messages." But if Jackson felt any such illness as was claiming hundreds in each army, he made no complaint.

The next morning, Jackson looked out into more rain, though by now just a drizzle, and the roads seemed to be better. The men were sleepy and slow, however. The Reverend Dabney thought the officers incompetent slugabeds, dulled by "julep-drinking." He recalled: "The brigade commanders would not or could not get rations cooked, their own breakfasts and their men under order earlier than an hour after sunrise." Yet Jackson's column somehow made more than twenty miles on this day, and by nightfall, weary and wet, camped at Ashland. Jackson was late and had seven miles to go before crossing the Virginia Central Railroad, but he saw he could not push farther tonight and let the men fall out of ranks. At sunset, he was joined by Stuart.

The cavalry chief was to cover the flank of the advance with two thousand troopers and a battery of guns. Old Jack was pleased

to see Stuart, and as the two consulted at the roadside, the passing
Valley troops cheered. The picture of the unkempt Jackson con-
versing with the knightly Stuart was striking to several observers;
and the contrast between Sorrel and his dusty rider and the cava-
liers of cavalry officers in gray, with cocked hats, black plumes
and high boots, made an impression to outlast battle memories.

There had been faint uneasiness at Lee's headquarters during
the day, which passed without word from Jackson. All else was
well. The Hills and Longstreet were nearing their objectives,
having stolen away from the front lines with elaborate ruses to
lull McClellan.

McClellan's position of this day was not due to his carelessness
alone. He had as many troops as seemed likely to perform well
in such country, but he had been complaining to Washington
that Secretary of War Stanton had willfully withheld the troops
of General McDowell from him. McClellan thus thought that
he lacked the proper reinforcements. Tonight the Federal general sent out a command instructing his officers that the "true
field of battle" was the Union trenches. In short, he had no idea
of attacking the Confederates, though this possibility was a matter of some concern at Lee's headquarters on this day. The day
passed without alarm on the part of the enemy.

At Ashland, Jackson was in a testy mood by the end of the
day. Union cavalrymen had driven in Stuart's pickets; telegraph
lines from the town had been cut; the corps was still short of its
objective. General Winder got the full benefit of Jackson's temper
when he came with other brigadiers to report.

"You must have your men cook and be ready to start at dawn,"
Old Jack said.

"Impossible," Winder said. "My baggage train is far back."

"General Winder, it must be done," Jackson barked, and even
the Reverend Dabney thought the commander "scarcely courteous."

Jackson sought to help make up lost time by changing the
hour of start from 3 A.M. to 2:30 A.M., and told his brigadiers to
have rations cooked overnight. He sent Lee a note on his planned
time of departure and added that high streams and burned bridges
had delayed him. He had hardly sent this message when he had

one from Lee, suggesting that Jackson divide his forces for tomorrow's march so that one of his columns might more quickly
join General Branch.

Late at night, generals Ewell and Whiting went to Jackson's
quarters, asking permission to change their routes for the march.

"Let me think over it," Jackson said, and as he compared their
suggestion with the latest order from Lee, the officers left him.
Outside, Ewell squealed:

"Don't you know why Old Jackson wouldn't tell us right off?
He's going to pray over it first."

A few moments later, when he returned for a forgotten sword,
Ewell saw his prophecy borne out. He opened the door to find
Jackson on his knees at the bedside.

Prayers failed to bring an early start for the army; long after
sunrise on Thursday, Jackson's men were still in lines about the
wells of Ashland, where water was scarce. The sun already blazed
on the steaming countryside.

At eight o'clock the column was in motion on the Ashcake
Road, and an hour and a half later—some six hours behind
schedule—Jackson crossed the Virginia Central Railroad. He
obeyed orders by sending a note to Branch, far down on the right
flank, advising him of the crossing. Enemy scouts now appeared
in the front, a portent of heavy resistance.

There was no frenzy of haste. Men marched under a cloudless
sky, straggling to roadside springs and wells. Jackson, riding with
Kyd Douglas, passed the birthplace of Henry Clay, and made
some brief admiring comments on the statesman of the Old South.
The next stop was in the home of a Dr. Shelton, on the route,
where Jackson and Stuart talked over the country ahead.

In the middle of the day, their exact positions and progress unknown to Jackson, the big divisions to the south neared their
assigned positions. In their order of proximity to Jackson they
were: Branch, then A. P. Hill's main force, D. H. Hill and Longstreet.

A. P. Hill, at this hour still cautious, had warned Branch:
"Wait for Jackson's notification before you move unless I send
you further orders."

From heights near Mechanicsville, some five miles to the southwest of Jackson's goal, Lee had set up headquarters. Here the commander in chief waited for the far-flung and intricate operation to move to its climax.

At 3 P.M., Jackson crossed Totopotomoy Creek, drove off enemy cavalry, put out flames on a burning bridge and engaged a Federal battery. Jackson strove to keep the Union guns quiet, evidently to avoid launching the other divisions into premature attack. He found Bradley Johnson of the Marylanders near the stream.

"What's that firing, Colonel?"

"It's the enemy, with guns and skirmishers in the thicket."

"Why don't you stop them?"

"We can't do it, without charging or shelling."

"Well, sir, you must stop that firing. Make them keep quiet."

Johnson brought up the Baltimore Artillery, or a couple of its guns, and drove off the Federals.

It was from this moment, which seemed so inconsequential, that the "fog of war" was to roll over the day's fighting, obscuring the exact sequence of events and making impossible the assignment of blame for the lack of precision in Confederate movements.

Jackson and Branch came into contact without Stonewall's knowledge. Ewell's advance saw the North Carolina troops of Branch approach in new uniforms, so well-dressed that they appeared to be Yankees, and almost fired on them. But when the regiments joined, sadly for Lee's plan of assault, neither Branch nor Ewell reported the fact, and thus headquarters was not informed.

Perhaps in this moment of midafternoon, the attack on the Federal line was already blighted. Perhaps Lee's plan was too unwieldy; perhaps Jackson had been given more than he could accomplish; perhaps poor maps and ignorance of terrain was fatal; perhaps Jackson was just now slow-witted from a touch of fever or lack of sleep.

There was no such conjecture this day. There was fighting on a widely separated front. Ewell sent men toward Beaver Dam

Creek in a skirmish line, and they engaged the enemy. Jackson's column had come to its objective.

At three o'clock, while Jackson was dealing with Federal guns at Totopotomoy, A. P. Hill's patience snapped. He ordered his men over the Chickahominy, which they passed with ease, and into Mechanicsville. His men trotted into zones of Federal fire in violation of Lee's orders, for Hill was to move only when he heard Jackson's guns. Hill later said blandly that he had rushed forward "rather than hazard the failure of the whole plan by longer deferring it." In recriminations to come, the youthful red-head, notoriously impatient, was to draw bitter criticism for this afternoon's work.

McClellan was fully prepared to meet Hill's attack, coming as it did with no flank support, and the scene at Mechanicsville became confused, with many Confederates falling. The men of D. H. Hill and Longstreet now crowded in. No one could tell, in the growing thunder of musketry and cannon fire, just what had gone astray. Lee rode into the front but could make out little. There was no sign of Jackson. And it was about 6 P.M. before Branch, the connecting link, fought his way into Mechanicsville.

Lee could do little to mend affairs on the front. He sent T. W. Sydnor, a cavalry lieutenant, to A. P. Hill, to direct Hill not to launch another forward movement. Hill evidently thought Lee's order left to his discretion the wisdom of a flank attack. And now, in the twilight, into veritable walls of flame, went the brigades of General Ripley and General Dorsey Pender. Their moments in the open seemed hours, for the lines of rifle pits took a heavy toll.

D. H. Hill saw "a bloody and disastrous repulse . . . we were lavish of blood in those days." Nearly every officer in the storming units went down; one Georgia regiment was all but annihilated. Almost two thousand men fell here; a Union officer thought they lay "like flies in a bowl of sugar" on the exposed slope. The butchery was over at nine o'clock.

The enemy had not been shaken along the line of Beaver Dam Creek, and the Army of Northern Virginia had passed its first day of offensive without the aid of Jackson, who was to have led the way. If Old Jack had turned the northern end of the Union line, the Federals could not have held the stream. Perhaps more to the point—if A. P. Hill had obeyed orders, the great losses would not have been incurred.

Lee tried to discover the flaws, and questioned A. P. Hill and Sydnor and other officers, but there was little time, and much to be done for tomorrow. The ranks were torn, but the strength of the army was intact. While wagons groaned into Richmond with the cargoes of wounded, the army prepared for battle once more.

Jackson had reached his designated position at the height of the Mechanicsville storm, and he heard clearly the guns of Hill. It is likely that he thought they signaled nothing more daring than a crossing of the Chickahominy. Old Jack had waited, in any event. It was late, and in his position, with darkness approaching, he could have done little or nothing to save the casualties of A. P. Hill.

D. H. Hill, somewhat petulantly defending Jackson's role of the day, was to say that "the hooded falcon cannot strike the quarry," intimating that the Valley chieftain could fight only when independent of superiors. Jackson was to refute that in the coming campaigns. Tonight, the best that could be determined in Lee's headquarters was that the Valley troops, for some reason, had not accomplished the miracles they had made so commonplace in the western fighting, and that the Federal flank yet held firm.

At daylight on June twenty-seventh, Lee hurled forward his whole army, intending to crush the twenty-five-thousand-odd of Fitz John Porter's Fifth Corps; there were lingering hopes that McClellan might yet be destroyed.

A. P. Hill's skirmishers discovered the enemy had gone from Beaver Dam Creek. The Federals had stealthily removed most of the big guns and marched to the rear. The enemy had undoubtedly found Old Jack on their flank in the night—as perhaps Jackson had foreseen—and had abandoned a position thus made useless. Lee pursued into the heavily wooded swamplands. His plan for the chase was to use roads running roughly parallel to the Chickahominy, with Longstreet nearest the river, A. P. Hill next, then D. H. Hill. In the rear of the latter, Jackson was to follow.

Near noon, Jackson's column collided with that of D. H. Hill; and in the confusion of a sudden meeting, there was firing, with a few casualties.

Stuart and his troopers soon met the Pennsylvania Lancers, a well-tailored enemy regiment known as "the finest body of troops in the world." Captain William W. Blackford, one of Stuart's captains, would not forget the clash:

"I felt a little creeping of the flesh when I saw this splendid looking body of men, about seven hundred strong, drawn up in line of battle in a large open field . . . armed with long poles with glittering steel points . . . a tall forest of lances held erect and at the end of each, just below the head, a red pennant fluttering in the breeze.

"Stuart quickly threw a regiment into line . . . and down upon them we swept with a yell, at full speed. They lowered their lances to a level and started in fine style to meet us midway, but long before we reached them the gay lancers' hearts failed them and they turned to fly. For miles the exciting chase was kept up, the road was strewn with lances."

The lancers returned to fight later in the afternoon when General Porter, as Townsend saw it, "hurled lancers and cavalry upon the masses of Stonewall Jackson and the Hills, but the butternut infantry formed impenetrable squares, hemmed in with rods of steel, and as the horsemen galloped around them, searching for pervious points, they were swept from their saddles with volleys of musketry."

Lee and Jackson met for the first time on the field of battle at 1 P.M., near a church east of Beaver Dam Creek. Curious Alabamans of Trimble's brigade watched them. Jackson saluted, reined short and dismounted. Lee's grandly dressed staff stared at the strange figure of the army's most famous field officer, as Stonewall took instructions from the commander. Lee sat on a cedar stump at the roadside, himself looking so undistinguished that the Reverend Dabney had to be told who he was. Jackson listened with his disreputable cap in hand, and soon mounted to ride away. The Alabamans remained to stare at the gold-braided brilliance of the young men who rode with Lee.

By two o'clock, the battle raged in A. P. Hill's front toward the river, in a wilderness of thickets. Few Federals were in Jackson's front at this hour. A cultured South Carolina fire-eater, Maxcy Gregg, found himself in the van of Lee's army, and his men stormed through undergrowth to the site of Gaines' Mill, where Lee had thought McClellan might make a stand. Gregg found the place unoccupied, and since strong hills lay there, he spread his men along them and waited for the enemy. Gregg began the fighting on the spot which was to give its name to the battle of the day.

When the Confederates finally reached the main strength of McClellan, there was no mistaking it, for a very hurricane of firing tore the woodlands. The Union troops had been waiting in thick cover, a position almost unassailable, in front of which the Rebel divisions were cruelly bled in the early afternoon. While this fighting raged, all but beyond control, nothing had been heard from Jackson on the far left of Lee's position. Old Jack had not reported since he had left Lee at their private conference. And he now had marching with him a potent force, fourteen brigades, including those of D. H. Hill, his brother-in-law.

In the lengthening hours, Lee watched the troops of Longstreet and A. P. Hill take punishment; still Jackson did not appear. Men in the ranks openly doubted that Stonewall had come down from the Valley. At headquarters there was anxiety even deeper than yesterday's. Where could Jackson be now?

Not even the lengthy report he would write in the winter to come would answer that question fully. He had been busy since leaving Lee, orienting his troops in the green maze. At three o'clock, it was known, he had been at the Cold Harbor Cross roads with his brigadiers, Ewell, Elzey, Lawton and Whiting. D. H. Hill was ahead of him, waiting near the menacing Federal position at a place known as Boatswain Swamp. Harvey Hill had halted because the enemy guns covered the only road over which he could bring up artillery. Jackson was needed there. That he was delayed could be blamed on nothing but his old habit of secretiveness, which was to him a cardinal military virtue.

Jackson had found a native guide and told him no more than he thought essential—that the army wanted to march to Old Cold Harbor (there was also a Cold Harbor near by). The guide had taken the column four miles astray southward in the swampland, down the shortest road to Jackson's announced destination. Jackson discovered the error only when he came within sound of guns. They were in the wrong quarter.

"Where is that firing?"

"About Gaines' Mill," the guide said.

"Does this road lead by there?"

"Yes. By there to Cold Harbor."

"But I do not want to go to Gaines' Mill, I want to go to Cold Harbor, coming in so that the Mill is on the right."

The guide, becoming vexed, explained that the column should have long ago taken an eastbound road to make a longer circuit —which it could have done with ease if Jackson had not been so close-mouthed. Jackson held his temper. A few moments later, when an officer suggested that the delay of an hour or more might be disastrous to the waiting army, Jackson was able to reply, "No, let us trust that the providence of God will so over-rule that no mischief will result."

Lee was not so trusting. He had sent his aide, Major Walter Taylor, to locate Jackson, and Taylor came upon Ewell in the narrow road at the head of the Valley column. Jackson was to-ward the rear, but if Lee must have help, Ewell could offer three brigades. After a brief conference, Ewell led the troops of Richard Taylor, Isaac Trimble and Arnold Elzey off the road into con-fusing woodlands. The men had no idea in what direction they moved; they came in on the flank of A. P. Hill's desperate men, who shouted to them that certain death waited if they charged ahead. The Valley veterans gave derisive replies and went on toward the enemy. It was impossible for any single regiment to make out the situation, which in general was that the Federals lay along a ridge in this wilderness, between the Confederates and the Chickahominy, and it appeared that nothing could move them.

Ewell seemed everywhere in the strange fighting. When the Fifteenth Alabama ran out of ammunition, Ewell himself went to see more brought up, and sent in support the Fourth Texas, men who came in at a crouching run through the swamp, like turkey hunters. When it seemed that Ewell's men must fall back, one regiment after another being torn and unable to move forward in one continuous line, reinforcements came. Lawton's brigade of Georgians—men with new rifles from home, three thousand strong, not yet blooded—struck hard. There was a good deal of shouting at sight of them. Some Marylanders plunged forward at about the same time, though in one corner a curious diversion caught hundreds: a soldier waved aloft bundles of mail from home, and men crowded about him while charging infantry passed.

Ewell's columns charged through a ghostly dust cloud in a field of stubble, and hundreds more died there as the sickly sun began to set. It was all but dark when Ewell led the final charge against the Federal line. Here at last the Confederate line was straightened out and drove the enemy. Before the guns had ceased, the lanterns of doctors and burial parties bobbed in the thickets.

Jackson had begun to work swiftly as Ewell attacked. He sent a message to Lee by Captain Boswell, reporting that the Valley men had closed on the enemy flank; this was soon apparent to all by the swelling of fire. Kyd Douglas said that he never again heard such a heavy volume of musketry. At sound of it, officers rode down the lines of other divisions, yelling that Jackson had struck. There were cheers in the storm of sound.

Jackson conferred with A. P. Hill and then D. H. Hill and was aware of the situation on their fronts. As Ewell's battle raged, Douglas noted, Jackson went to the region of heavy fighting: "At that moment someone handed him a lemon . . . immediately a small piece was bitten out of it and slowly and unsparingly he began to extract its flavor and juice. From that moment until darkness ended the battle, that lemon scarcely left his lips except to be used . . . to emphasize an order. He listened to Yankee shout or Rebel Yell, to the sound of musketry . . . to all the signs of promise or apprehension, but he never for an instant lost his interest in that lemon."

Once Jackson paused, his face as calm as ever. "I think I never had a better lemon." He held the fruit until Sandie Pendleton came up to explain that a vast yell carrying through the forest came from the Stonewall Brigade, which Winder had taken into the swamp on a pell-mell charge. Jackson then tossed away the lemon.

"We soon shall have good news from that charge," he said. "Yes. They are driving the enemy."

The day had already cost fearfully in both officers and men. The Louisiana Tigers, for the first time, had been driven back and broken. And Major Rob Wheat was dead.

To the last, Wheat had asked for Jackson at each passage of a staff officer and sent a blessing to "The Old General." That day Douglas had seen Wheat's last meeting with Jackson.

"General, we are about to get into a hot fight," Wheat said. "It's likely many of us may be killed. I want to ask you for myself and my men not to expose yourself. . . . Just let me tell them that you promised not to expose yourself and then they'll fight like—er—ah—Tigers!"

Jackson shook hands with Wheat, thanking him. "Just like Wheat," he said to a staff officer. "He thinks of the safety of others. Too brave ever to think of himself."

Wheat was soon dead under Union fire, and officers reported that as he died he asked if Jackson had escaped harm and said a prayer for the General.

One of the day's delays under Jackson grew from a shortage of staff officers. In the instant that Old Jack found Ewell was engaged, he had to send simultaneous messages to Whiting and Winder that they must move up in echelon and come between Ewell and D. H. Hill into the developing line of battle. He sent his quartermaster, John Harman, with the message. Harman was a wagoner and not a scholar, and in passing the order to Whiting, he became confused and managed to give the impression that Whiting was to remain just where he was. Whiting's understanding was not improved by his feelings toward Jackson at the moment. It was Whiting who had felt Old Jack's wrath after the collision with D. H. Hill's men in the morning.

At any rate, Whiting did not move, and thus Winder could not, for the road was barred by troops, and Ewell suffered alone. The troops must soon get into line if the day was to be won. The Reverend Dabney stepped into the breach. He had overheard the conversation between Jackson and Harman, and he shrewdly suspected that Harman needed an interpreter for the phrase "in echelon." Dabney went to Whiting as soon as he could finish his own errand and asked if the instructions had come through. Whiting growled, "Yes. That man has been here with a farrago of which I could understand nothing." Dabney urged Whiting to attack at once and save Ewell's men. Whiting's brigade moved. It was now that the big advance began.

Jackson met Lee in a roadway. The commander in chief had no rebuke for Jackson's tardy attack. Instead:

"Ah, General. I am very glad to see you. I had hoped to be with you before now."

Jackson mumbled something that could not be heard and jerked his head.

"That fire is very heavy," Lee said. "Do you think your men can stand it?"

"They can stand almost anything. They can stand that."

Lee talked of his plan for battle in the short remaining daylight, and Jackson went into the perplexing area of fields and pine groves and swamp thickets to watch over the vital left flank.

After five hours of heavy fighting, at a cost it could ill afford to pay, the Army of Northern Virginia had at last concentrated and was moving forward as a unit. All the divisions now surged ahead. Jackson sent his brigadiers a dramatic order: "This affair has hung in the balance long enough; sweep the field with the bayonet."

The Federals broke, first where Hood had swept in with his Texans (the First Texas lost about six hundred of its eight hundred men; the Fourth Texas lost all field officers, and ended under command of a captain). As darkness closed in, Lee held most of the field.

The reporter Townsend saw the retreat: "An immense throng of panic-stricken people came surging down the slippery bridge. A few carried muskets, but I saw several wantonly throw their pieces into the flood. . . . Fear, anguish, cowardice, despair, disgust were the predominant expressions. . . . A horseman rode past me, with blood streaming from his mouth and hanging in gouts from his saturated beard . . . black boys were besetting the wounded with buckets of cool lemonade. It was a common occurrence for the couples that carried the wounded on stretchers to stop on the way, purchase a glass of the beverage, and drink it."

In the Confederate rear, a group of fifteen or twenty prisoners moved, almost jauntily. One called to bystanders, "Gentlemen, we had the honor of being captured by Stonewall Jackson himself." The General, exposed during the bewildering engagement of the two huge armed mobs, had come upon these men in a road and impetuously charged them, ordering their surrender.

At night, having played a major, if belated, role in the concentration of the army for its first major thrust, Jackson visited Stuart. He ordered the cavalryman to go forward at daylight and to try to reach the White House, the home of W. H. F. Lee, now used as McClellan's headquarters. The two daring commanders schemed to capture the Union general and all his staff.

Jackson then went to Selwyn, the home of the Hogan family, where he met Lee and Longstreet. Lee sent a victory message to President Davis, giving credit to the Lord for the saving of Richmond, in a phrase Jackson might have used: "Profoundly grateful to Almighty God."

The generals talked over the terrible day, whose casualties were not fully known to them. Longstreet thought there had been more brave deeds on this field than on any other of the war. Lee had made general plans for the next day: He would pursue McClellan wherever the trail led.

Jackson left for his own headquarters. He found many of his ablest officers among the thirty-seven hundred casualties of his division. Among the dead were colonels Isaac Seymour of the Louisianans, Sam Fulkerson of the Third Brigade, and J. W. Allen of the Second Virginia. General Elzey had a painful head wound. In all, the army had lost eight thousand; ten colonels were dead, and many others wounded.

Deep among the Chickahominy swamps tonight, General McClellan sat in the White House, his small frame tense with anger. He wrote to Secretary Stanton, now in disregard for the consequences:

I now know the full history of the day. Our men did all that men could do, but they were overwhelmed by vastly superior numbers.

I again repeat that I am not responsible for this, and I say it with the earnestness of a general who feels in his heart the loss of every brave man who has been needlessly sacrificed today.

If I save this army now, I tell you plainly that I owe no thanks to you or to any other persons in Washington.

You have done your best to sacrifice this army.

A grave misconception had heightened McClellan's anger. His spies, led by the far-famed Allan Pinkerton, had convinced him that Lee's army outnumbered him, almost two to one.

In the uncertain lantern light the Federal general saw that it was twenty minutes after midnight, and he signed the message which contained all the defiance and contempt of a military man for civilian meddlers, and sent it on to Washington, where it was to play a part in changing his destiny and that of the Union.

On Saturday morning, June twenty-eighth, Lee allowed the army to stand on the line of battle; and while men attended the wounded and buried the dead, he attempted to puzzle out the intentions of McClellan. At 10 A.M., he had Jackson send Ewell's division along the river, pushing as far as Bottom's Bridge, to see what had happened in the front. The news from there was exciting. The enemy had burned the Chickahominy bridges they had built with such patience and everywhere had abandoned rich stores. Ewell's men were feasting on desiccated vegetables and fresh Java from Union supply dumps. The smoke of burning magazines lay over the swamps.

Jackson gave part of the morning to riding over the field of last night's fighting. One officer thought he looked "brisk enough" today. When Old Jack came to the littered spot where the Texans of Hood had hit the enemy, he spoke as he seldom did: "The men who carried this position were soldiers indeed."

The roads were dry, and dust clouds hung over the lowlands. It was clear that McClellan was on the move, but Lee could not yet know just where. The problem was fairly simple, but needed time to unravel:

Lee could not afford to uncover Richmond to give chase; yet he must soon strike, or permit McClellan to escape altogether. The Federals might be moving down the Peninsula toward York-town, whence they had come; they might also be moving south-ward to the James, to make a major change in the line of assault upon Richmond. Lee had shrewdly concluded that McClellan would take the latter course long before reports of scouts made that clear. In the evening, Lee went to bed in the home of a Dr. Gaines, where Longstreet was already sleeping. Orders were ready to open the pursuit in the morning.

Early on Sunday, the divisions of Longstreet and A. P. Hill crossed the Chickahominy, moving southward, hurrying after the enemy. Lee's plan was now to strike McClellan as he moved, for the enemy had to cross a vast bog known as White Oak Swamp, on the fringes of the river, which made a large bend in the area. The Federals must take their endless trains over the narrow swamp roads and cross the river once more. Lee reasoned that he might fall upon the retreating column today if he could drive down the riverside.

Two of Longstreet's engineers had found Federal trenches on the Chickahominy empty, even the big fortifications at Golding's Farm, which was the keystone of the enemy line. It was clear that McClellan had given up hopes of taking Richmond in this campaign, or at least over this route. Lee made hurried plans to trap The Little Napoleon in or near White Oak Swamp.

Jackson's column, near the ruined Grapevine Bridge, was ordered to repair the structure, cross the river, drive down the right bank and give support to General John Magruder. There might be battle at the swamp.

There were diversions today. The Federals, bent upon destroy-ing what they could not salvage, plunged many locomotives over a broken bridge into the Chickahominy, most of them loaded with ammunition, which exploded the boilers in the sluggish stream and sent vast echoes over the bottom lands. Stuart and his riders found unusual loot.

Cavalrymen made lemonade by the barrel and pawed among

cases of fine wines and liquors. Some eggs, packed in barrels of salt, had been roasted in the fires, and men broke open the kegs, picking out the tasty eggs. Colonel W. H. F. Lee, who went in with Stuart, had trouble with his riders; before he was aware of it, scores of them were roaring drunk. Lee cannily spread the rumor that the liquor was poisoned by the enemy. Blackford saw "bottles of champagne and beer and whisky . . . sailing through the air, exploding as they fell like little bomb-shells; while the expression of agony on the tipsy faces of those who had indulged too freely, as they held their hands to their stomachs, was ludicrous in the extreme."

The troopers were busy all day. Among their chores was destroying a few surviving locomotives, which they did by firing cannon into the boilers at short range. They also came upon Yankee newspapers which commented sagely on McClellan's strategy of "changing base," and the cavalrymen joked over that. A dog fight, when one of the combatants ran, drew cries of, "Look at him changing his base!"

At the Grapevine Bridge, Jackson was about the more mundane task of repairing his bridge so that he might cross the river. The Reverend Dabney was charged with repairs, but his party of soldiers moved so slowly that Jackson impatiently called in Major Claibourne R. Mason, one of the group of civilian specialists the General had gathered about him. And Mason, though he was not an engineer, quickly raised a stout bridge. Still, it was midafternoon when Jackson himself crossed the incompleted structure and rode to the abandoned headquarters of McClellan in the Trent House. He was here in the late afternoon when General Magruder, after some confusing hours, attacked the Federal rear guard at Savage's Station. This action took place not far from Jackson, but he made no effort to join it since his troops had not yet come over the bridge.

Magruder's attack, limited as it was, stood as the only substantial action of the day. The army had advanced only five miles, giving the enemy another day of grace to cross the dangerous swamp.

Lee did not hide his chagrin in a dispatch to Magruder, who

had been in the position of attack and thus drew the commander's blame: "I regret very much that you have made so little progress today in the pursuit of the enemy. . . . We must lose no more time or he will escape us entirely."

Lee also sent Major Walter Taylor to talk with Magruder. Handsome John told Taylor with some vehemence the curious story of Jackson's behavior during the day:

General D. R. Jones, one of Magruder's officers, had expected Jackson's aid in the attack on Savage's Station, since their troops held adjoining positions. Before the attack, Jones sent to Jackson for assurance of his co-operation, and got the reply: "I have other important duty to perform." It went into the official records, and some were to hazard the guess that Jackson could not fight at this moment, since he had to say his prayers. There was a more logical explanation.

When the messenger from Jones approached him, Jackson was making an effort to get troops over the river, and making little progress. He saw that he was three miles from the scene of skirmishing and could not move his brigades in time. Therefore, in his customary mood of reticence, he probably told the messenger of his "other important work"—meaning the essential river crossing.

Whatever the explanation, it remained that Jackson had not spent a profitable day. His orders had been simple and clear, and his task did not appear too difficult; once more the Valley army had failed to shine. Lee might have justly asked himself if Stonewall seemed still in the grip of the inexplicable malady which had slowed him at Gaines' Mill and immobilized him at Mechanicsville. From headquarters, it seemed that Old Jack had been a long time at repairing his bridge, and that once he crossed the river, he was in superb position to pounce on Savage's Station, a short distance away.

The entire army had achieved little; there was no brilliance to report. Longstreet and A. P. Hill had waited in reserve for developments which had not been forthcoming.

Jackson spent an uncomfortable night. He went to sleep in the open soon after dark, having issued orders to march before dawn. Near midnight, a torrential rain burst over the Peninsula, ruining Jackson's sleep. He rose and prepared to work through the night.

At 3:30 A.M. he appeared at Magruder's headquarters, and "Prince John," Jackson's old commander of the Mexican War, seemed pathetically happy to see him. Jackson gave assurances that the Valley troops would be moving at daylight, and Magruder could now bring himself to rest. His report read: "I then slept an hour—the first in forty-eight."

The enemy retreated in the night and the last dark hours found Lee working, determined on a course of action. He would seek to get between McClellan and the James and strike him heavily. Then, perhaps, not only would Richmond be saved. Perhaps the war hung in the balance, as well.

13

★★★ THE LONGEST OF ALL DAYS

When the first gray light of Monday, June thirtieth, crept through the swamps of the Chickahominy country, Jackson was astir and working with great energy. His staff, aware of the wearing effects of this week, conspired to leave him late abed, but he was up soon after his usual hour. Dr. Hunter McGuire, who had intimate knowledge of the General's physical condition, was struck by his unusual vigor this morning.

Others, including John Gill, a headquarters courier, thought Jackson in "a bad humor," and noted that both commander and command were wearied by constant fighting, marching, and lack of sleep and proper food. The Reverend Dabney later recalled the Jackson of this important day as exhausted by "the wear of gigantic cares."

Old Jack's sleep last night, after being interrupted by the storm, was limited to a few uncomfortable moments in the damp bedclothes of a wagon. He stood by a campfire at dawn to dry his clothes, and soon rode in the direction of White Oak Swamp Bridge, already anxious about the moving of his column. Last night he had asked Colonel Munford to have his cavalrymen on the move just at the hour of sunrise. Munford, like the

234

rest of the army, had been caught in the night storm, and his troopers were scattered. Of this morning, Munford wrote:

"When I arrived, to my horror, there sat Jackson waiting for me. He was in a bad humor, and said, 'Colonel, my orders to you were to be here at sunrise.' I explained my situation, telling him we had no provisions, and that the storm and dark night had conspired against me. When I got through he replied, 'Yes, sir. But Colonel, I ordered you to be here at sunrise. Move on with your regiment. If you meet the enemy drive in his pickets, and if you want artillery, Colonel Crutchfield will furnish you.'

"I started on with my little handful of men. As others came straggling on to join me, Jackson noticed it, and sent two couriers to inform me that 'my men were straggling badly.' I rode back and went over the same story, hoping that he would be impressed with my difficulties. He listened to me, but replied as before, 'Yes, sir. But I ordered you to be here at sunrise, and I have been waiting for you a quarter of an hour.'

"Seeing that he was in a peculiar mood, I determined to make the best of my trouble, sent my adjutant back, and made him halt the stragglers as they came up. . . . When we came upon the enemy's picket we charged, and pushed the picket every step of the way into their camp."

With the cavalry launched, Old Jack turned to his infantry. His orders today were of increased importance, and his haste indicated that he understood their urgency; he worked as if aware that yesterday's slow pace had cost Lee the opportunity to destroy McClellan's army.

Jackson and Lee met early today. One soldier who watched them was Robert Stiles, to whom the scene appeared thus, forty years later:

"Jackson began talking in a jerky, impetuous way, meanwhile drawing . . . on the ground with the toe of his right boot. He traced two sides of a triangle with promptness and precision; then starting at the end of the second line, began to draw a third projected toward the first.

"This third line he traced slowly and with hesitation, alternately looking up at Lee's face and down at his diagram, meanwhile talking earnestly; and when at last the . . . triangle was complete, he raised his foot, and stamped it down with emphasis, saying, 'We've got him.'; then signaled for his horse . . . vaulted into the saddle and was off."

In his effort to trap McClellan, Lee was throwing four columns after the enemy. Jackson was to enter White Oak Swamp from the north. He had been given the place of greatest responsibility despite the lack of agressiveness on the part of the Valley army this week. Magruder had fumbled, and Lee had pulled him back to support A. P. Hill and Longstreet. The latter divisions would move eastward on parallel roads and strike McClellan on the south side of White Oak Swamp. Lee intended to engage the enemy in the vicinity known variously as Glendale, Riddell's Shop and Frayser's Farm.

Jackson, whose twenty thousand were now alone in the Federal rear, was to strike to the south and roll the enemy into the path of the columns of Longstreet and A. P. Hill. Haste was essential to this battle plan, for McClellan was nearing the James, where the huge cannon of the gunboats would give him protection.

As the men from the Valley neared the swamp, the very landscape seemed in league against their progress—for now they rode through unmistakable signs of Union rout. Near Savage's Station they took many prisoners and the sick of a hospital "remarkable for the extent and convenience of its accommodations." Jackson's men spent some of the morning gathering spoils and sending to the rear skulkers and walking wounded of the enemy.

An officer riding near Jackson commented that the prisoners were too numerous and were surrendering all too willingly. Jackson replied, "It's cheaper to feed them than to fight them." He was impressed by the prisoners, however. "They really appear gratified at the idea of being taken. I have never seen prisoners so contented."

The commander seems not to have noticed the spoils which struck the Reverend Dabney; among them, "mounds of grain and rice and hillocks of mess beef smoldering; tens of thousands of axes, picks and shovels." John Casler, a private of the Thirty-third Virginia, saw "molasses knee deep in a railroad ditch, and great piles of burnt coffee. Some of it was burnt too much for use, but some was scorched just enough to be good." This slowed the men, for such spoils were too precious to be passed by. Jackson galloped endlessly during the morning, trying to speed the march.

As noon approached, with D. H. Hill charged with sweeping up prisoners and collecting loot, Jackson paused, probably at the side of a sandy swamp road, and wrote to Anna:

> Near White Oak Swamp Bridge
> An ever-kind Providence has greatly blessed our efforts and given us great reason for thankfulness in having defended Richmond. Today the enemy is retreating. . . . Many prisoners are falling into our hands. . . . I had a wet bed last night, as the rain fell in torrents, and haven't seen much rest since. . . .
> You must give fifty dollars for church purposes, and more should you be disposed. Keep an account of the amount, as we must give at least one tenth of our income. I would like very much to see my darling, but hope that God will enable me to remain at the post of duty until, in His own good time, He blesses us with independence. This going home has injured the army immensely.

Jackson then went toward the front, and began to examine the borders of White Oak Swamp, a forbidding scene. The bog seemed impenetrable in most places. It was an ill-shaped crescent whose dark waters sprawled through thick hardwood growth for some ten miles before draining into the Chickahominy. Today, as Jackson gazed over it, the swamp was like a vast stagnant river, high from recent rains. His infantry might break through the growth of briars, bamboo and vines under the great trees, but could not pass the endless pools and marshy depths. There appeared to be no openings in the thickets.

The White Oak Swamp Bridge, where Jackson had appeared, was the safest and best means of passing the swamp. The Federals had crossed a few hours earlier and were still in evidence. Occasional shots from sharpshooters felled men in the growing Confederate column at this spot, leaving wisps of dim smoke in the far trees. D. H. Hill and Jackson studied the ground with field glasses. A few bluecoats were in the open, on high ground across the stream.

A battery of enemy artillery was in sight, backed by what appeared to be a regiment of infantry whose men were asleep in an abandoned field. It was now a bit after noon, but Jackson did not hurry his reconnaissance. The bridge, he saw, was broken and could hardly be repaired in face of the enemy fire. There were other means of crossing the swamp—by fords lying to the right and left. But these had not been mentioned in Jackson's orders.

Old Jack's humor was improved by now. Munford recalled: "When Jackson came up he was smiling, and he at once ordered Colonel Crutchfield to bring up his artillery, and very soon the batteries were at work."

It was not quite so simple, however. Jackson's position overlooking the ruined bridge was a low bluff, most of it exposed to the enemy, so that guns must be brought up with care. Engineers and sweating soldiers worked for an hour or more to cut a road in a ravine; the guns came up while the cavalry paraded in front to screen them. Crutchfield placed twenty-eight big guns in a row, and the instant the cavalrymen galloped off, this battery fired in almost perfect unison upon Federal infantry in the wooded swamp.

Captain Thomas Livermore, a young New Hampshire soldier, was in the Union ranks:

"Hell seemed to have opened upon us . . . teams of six mules which belonged to a pontoon train . . . fled up the hill . . . stragglers and non-combatants fled in all directions, while the air was filled with clouds of dust and wreaths of smoke which spread out from the fierce clouds, breathing fire of bursting shells, and the ear was dimmed with explosions. . . .

". . . New York volunteers . . . attempted to escape . . . and retreated right down toward us. General Caldwell . . . galloped to our rear and cried out, 'Fifth New Hampshire, rise up!' and we rose, leveled our bayonets, and received the ―― at their points . . . after a little confusion they went back and behaved themselves.

"The shot hit some of our men and scattered their vitals and brains upon the ground. . . . I saw a shot strike in the 2nd Delaware . . . which threw a man's head perhaps twenty feet into the air, and the bleeding trunk fell over toward us. . . . I do not know that I have ever feared artillery as I did then. . . ."

It was 1:45 P.M. when this salvo burst upon the enemy, and though it was accurate and devastating, it did not drive the Federals from the position. Jackson watched the enemy fire three or four rounds in reply and pull back most of their guns from the field, leaving three in the open. Jackson sent for Munford.

"Colonel, move your regiment over the creek and secure those guns."

Hill and Jackson rode with Munford as the troopers approached the stream. The cavalryman glanced at the broken bridge, a "tangled mass which seemed to prevent a crossing," and told Jackson it could not be used. Jackson waved an impatient hand.

"Yes, Colonel. Try it."

Munford led the first squadron among the sprawling timbers in the water, and a few men "floundered over." Before he could form up his men on the south bank, Jackson was barking.

"Move on those guns, Colonel!"

Munford got two squadrons across, and had a battery in the road challenge the Federal guns in an effort to drive the enemy from the vicinity of the bridge. Hill, Jackson and Munford were with the troopers when they reached the abandoned Union guns, but the rifle fire was so heavy that the officers turned off. Jackson went back swiftly over the route he had come, with Hill following. Munford disappeared, using a track into the heart of the swamp.

Old Jack seemed suddenly weary as he returned from inspection of the enemy position, and though the ground about him stirred with action, he sat under a tree, heavy-eyed. His first visitor found him unresponsive.

General A. R. Wright came from General Huger's column, which was the nearest force to Jackson in the scheme of attack. Wright explained that he had been sent to make sure the area north of the swamp was free of the enemy, and that he had scouted along New Road, seeing no trace of the Federals. Wright then asked Jackson for orders.

In a tone strange for him, Jackson said that he had no orders. Federals were in such strength in the swamp, Old Jack added, that Wright should retrace the safe route to Huger.

Wright left Jackson. There was no suggestion that a staff officer accompany him or establish contact with Huger. Jackson simply remained under his tree. He fell asleep, and no one moved to disturb him. He seemed exhausted.

Within a short time the departed General Wright, driven off at one ford, had gone some three or four miles from Jackson's position and found a crossing of the swamp. He moved through without opposition. But there was no officer to bring word to Jackson; and no indication from Jackson that he desired this information.

D. H. Hill busied himself around the damaged bridge as Jackson slept. Hill was told by troops who had been trying to repair the bridge that the fire was too heavy for them. The brusque little general sent out a brigade on his own initiative, and this force crossed the creek and settled in a strip of woodland from which it drove the Federals. Hill had less success in finding men to work on the bridge. Survivors of earlier parties refused to return and remained adamant under a tongue-lashing from Hill. Another party tried the task, but was driven off, and Hill could find no more volunteers. Jackson slept on.

Hill had discovered that General Franklin's corps was the Federal force in front, and now, impatient to be at the enemy, Hill sent a messenger to General Huger. The messenger was to ask if Huger could not attack from his near-by road and drive the enemy from their position near the bridge.

Precious time was passing. Already General Lee and President Davis, waiting to the southwest with Longstreet's division, were wondering anew at Jackson's immobility. They had expected to hear Stonewall's attack earlier in the day, and to hear Huger's men join the pursuit. Huger had not yet reported to headquarters that his road was blocked by felled trees, miles of them; he was even now cutting a new road through the forest to pass his guns.

Jackson's artillery still rolled, but it was becoming clear that the guns could not force a decision at this crossing; the enemy hung on stubbornly in the depths of the swamp. It appeared that Jackson, for the first time in his career, had literally given up the field. He still made no effort to examine fords above or below him, though at all other times he was keenly sensitive about his flanks and methodically sought chances for turning attacks. When Old Jack woke up, he sat on his log for a time, staring before him as if he had no interest in the fighting.

A messenger from Longstreet intruded upon Jackson's rest. He was Captain J. W. Fairfax, who talked with the commander beyond earshot of the diarists of the staff. Longstreet had been put on the alert by cannon fire and wanted to know the exact state of affairs. Records were to omit Jackson's reply to Fairfax, but it was likely a simple statement that the heavy force of the enemy had halted him at the bridge.

Sometime during the early afternoon, Jackson got a message from Colonel Munford, accompanied by some captured newspapers. It was news that on any other day would have electrified Jackson: Munford was deep in the swamp. He had located a trail leading to the south side of the swamp and had already tested it. He now awaited orders.

Jackson made no reply to this, nor did he stir from the afternoon's lethargy to send an officer to inspect the crossing proposed by Munford. He simply took the newspapers.

That was not the only message to be deflected by Jackson's inertia. General Wade Hampton, a fiery and capable South Carolina cavalry leader, came on the scene. Hampton said that he had been far into the swamp with a couple of his officers. In the pines to the left of the roadway, he had found a narrow, firm crossing of the stream. It was no more than ten or fifteen feet wide. Beyond it, unsuspecting, some Federal troops lay in a ravine. It was another opening by which the enemy might be struck and perhaps routed.

Jackson appeared interested. He asked Hampton if the hidden

crossing could be bridged and sent the South Carolinian into the swamp to superintend the effort. Hampton was soon back at Jackson's side.

Old Jack sat stolidly on his log, his cap far down on his nose, eyes shut. He was motionless until Hampton completed his report, which was to the effect that the crossing was ready, a bridge was built, and guns could be passed over it. Further, the enemy did not seem to suspect the immediate presence of a Confederate assault column.

Jackson then astonished Hampton. He rose and walked away. There was no word of thanks, commendation or approval, and no orders. Hampton was left to wonder at the unusual behavior of the Valley conqueror.

From the south, across the swamp, now came a heavy volume of cannon fire. Jackson could not know it, but these were the guns of Longstreet and A. P. Hill, whose divisions fought McClellan's army alone. Lee had been forced to throw them into an unequal fight to prevent the enemy's unchallenged parade to the safety of the James. The furious firing was the herald of great slaughter, for the outnumbered Confederate brigades were dashing in gallant, futile charges against Federal cannon at Frayser's Farm. Jackson's was but one of the missing parts of the un-co-ordinated army this afternoon; about fifty thousand Confederate troops lay idle in the swamplands while the deadly little battle wore on.

Jackson's guns now began to slow. There was no sign that they were effective with their fire blasting into the deep woods, and they were drawing furious replies. The men who had been attempting to repair the bridge now gave up once and for all, announcing that they would no longer face the sniping from the timber. Jackson gave no orders, and the command remained in its place. The scene here quieted, and in the lengthening shadows supper fires began to smoke. From this bluff, the day of opportunity seemed to have been wasted, many officers thought. A number of men noted Jackson's curious inactivity.

Douglas, though he could not recall "a moment when he rested," wrote that Jackson "does not seem to have been his very self. If he had been up to the Stonewall standard that he

had established in the Valley . . . he would have found the
way to do more effective service that bloody day, and it would
have been a sad one for the Army of the Potomac."

D. H. Hill, who was near by during these hours later discovered to be so vital, wrote: "An important factor in this inaction was Jackson's pity for his own corps, worn out by long
and exhausting marches and reduced in numbers by its numerous sanguinary battles. He thought that the garrison of Richmond ought to now bear the brunt of the fighting."

There was camp gossip, dating from this afternoon, that
Jackson had expressed himself in this vein, saying that he did
not intend that his men should do all the fighting; but there
was no more than gossip, and the attitude was by no means
characteristic in Jackson.

Colonel William Allan, chief of Jackson's ordnance, though
he defended his chief, thought Old Jack might have done more
today: "Jackson, ignorant of the country, had in the swamp
and Franklin's veterans substantial causes of delay, but they
were not such obstacles as usually held Jackson in check.
Vigorous demonstrations at the fords, above and below, as well
as at White Oak Swamp Bridge, would probably have secured
a crossing at one point or another, and the tremendous prize
at stake was such to justify any efforts."

In any event, Jackson failed to storm the position, or even
to try with his usual vigor; he had scouted conditions in the
area, but not thoroughly; he had been in touch with near-by
commanders but did not respond to the opportunities they presented. He had, as Hampton and others were to report, been
asleep, or nearly so, in crucial hours of the afternoon.

A long furore was to rage over the Jackson of these hot,
cannon-shaken hours at the edge of the White Oak Swamp, and
critics were to become virtual scholars in the lore and gossip
of Jackson's command. The day was to be known as the low
point in Jackson's military career, though no one was to be
able to present a thorough and authentic explanation of the
General's behavior during these hours. It was to be said that he
was insane, that he was engaged in fanatic prayer, that he was
sulking under Lee's command, that he was husbanding the lives

of his men, and that he was simply exhausted. There were bountiful physical factors to account for the performance, in the combination of lost sleep, poor food, possible fever, all at a time when Jackson was expected to direct the largest force he had ever commanded in a strange and difficult country. This week, moreover, saw the army fail in one test of command after another, with errors on the part of officers from Lee downward. Jackson's role of today could have become of overwhelming importance only to veterans of a beaten army who looked back on lost chances of victory.

Eight months later, Stonewall was to write a calm report of the action and his role, in words giving no hint of regret or failure. He seemed to feel that no detailed explanation was necessary, considering the skill and tenacity of the enemy: "A heavy cannonading in front announced the engagement of General Longstreet at Frazier's Farm, and made me eager to press forward; but the marshy character of the soil, the destruction of the bridge over the marsh and creek, and the strong position of the enemy for defending the passage, prevented my advancing until the following morning."

As darkness closed in, Jackson sat with some of his staff at a campfire. The Reverend Dabney watched him closely as he ate. Jackson fell asleep with a bit of biscuit between his teeth.

He suddenly roused and looked about. "Gentlemen, let us get to bed, and rise early, and see if tomorrow we can't do something."

As if he were conscious that the day had been a failure, but that the blame lay with someone else, and not with him. On that note the sound of cannon fire died across the swamp, and Jackson's camp fell silent amid the rising sounds of frogs and insects in the watery wilderness. Jackson slept.

14

★★★ SEVEN BLOODY DAYS AT AN END

Jackson was once more out early, on July first, moving with such alacrity as to suggest that yesterday had been only a nightmare. He ordered stragglers rounded up and put into action. Ewell's troops, who had joined late yesterday, now became the rear guard. The enemy had left the bridge crossing of the swamp, and the Valley army pushed on.

It was not an easy march. Water was scarce, for one thing; the retreating enemy had thrown medicines into the wells and springs to save them from Confederate hands, and the water could not be drunk. There were plentiful spoils to be gathered, however.

Jackson's division went into the front of the entire army, once it had crossed the swamp. Before daybreak it made contact with the main force of Lee's army, Magruder's troops, who had come up late last night to relieve the worn regiments of Longstreet and A. P. Hill. The army pulled together in the early morning. Even General Huger advanced, finding his road now clear. The general officers sought Lee. On the Long Bridge Road, Lee met with Magruder, Longstreet and A. P. Hill. Some thought the commander had a wan look, and that the bitter disappointment of yesterday was in his face. Lee was calm and deferential in manner, however, as he spoke of the battle at Frayser's Farm, and gave his orders for the day.

While these officers conferred, Jackson arrived at Willis Church, not far away. He had been active. Lee talked with a prisoner sent by Old Jack, a Federal surgeon taken at the Savage's Station hospital, Dr. N. F. Marsh. This doctor asked for medicines and care for his wounded men. Lee offered all the help possible and began his efforts to have the wounded prisoners exchanged, a policy which was to endure for most of the war. Longstreet seized the occasion for espionage. He questioned Marsh as to the identity of Federal regiments the army had faced, but the doctor said he knew only General McCall's division, to which he belonged. This general had been captured, and Longstreet, in his usual heavy fashion, bespoke his confidence for the day with:

"McCall is safe in Richmond; but if his division had not fought so stubbornly on this road, we would have captured your whole army. Never mind—we will do it yet."

No other officers expressed such optimism. Lee, in fact, was dubious that he would be able even to direct affairs that day, because he was so weary that he could scarcely ride. He asked Longstreet to remain at his side so that the latter might take command of the army if the need arose. Lee and Longstreet now rode to Willis Church, where they met D. H. Hill, who was pessimistic indeed.

Hill told them that a chaplain from his division, the Reverend L. W. Allen, a native of this neighborhood, had given a doleful warning of the low bluff known as Malvern Hill, which rose, a mile and a half long and half a mile wide, in the swamp country near the banks of the James.

"If McClellan is there in strength, we had better let him alone," Hill said.

Longstreet made another of his weighty jokes. "Don't get scared, now that we have got him whipped."

Lee did not enter this discussion, but he gave orders for an immediate push forward. Jackson, since his column was already in the road near the church, was to lead the chase of the enemy. Lee already had evidence that Stonewall was in an active mood today. Magruder had talked with Jackson and had offered to put his own men in front. Jackson had refused, saying that the Valley troops were fresher.

At about noon, D. H. Hill saw Jackson at hard labor: "Some time was spent in reconnoitering. . . . I saw Jackson helping with his own hands to push Reilly's North Carolina battery farther forward. It was soon disabled, the woods around us being filled with shrieking and exploding shells."

Lee was in an unusually tense mood. When General Jubal A. Early asked the commander for orders and expressed his anxiety that McClellan might escape, Lee snapped, "Yes! He will get away because I cannot have my orders carried out!"

Lee followed Jackson's path to the front, where he found confusion once more threatening his plans. His position before Malvern Hill was by no means ideal; it had to lie along a marshy, jungle-grown creek called Western Run, which crossed the road and wound into deep woodlands. There was one map in the army with a reasonably accurate representation of this neighborhood, and Lee had that. General Magruder was already lost and out of position, and it took time to move him into his proper place. Meanwhile the enemy casually shelled the gathering Confederate horde.

Jackson had a close call from a shell, which he treated with indifference. Kyd Douglas watched him: "Nearly a mile in the rear of his line . . . sitting on the roadside with his back against a tree, writing a note . . . a shell from a Parrott gun struck the column in front of us and exploded. Five or six men were killed or wounded, and dust was thrown over the General and his paper. Without raising his head he shook the paper to relieve it and proceeded with his note. . . . When the message was finished and folded he rose, gave explicit instructions that the dead be carried out of sight and the wounded cared for, and rode off to the front."

Jackson soon met Lee and Ewell, and the generals talked, with their staffs about them, as firing increased. An officer galloped up to report artillery being ruined by Federal fire. Jackson turned to ride away, but Lee protested.

"Colonel Crutchfield is there. He will know what to do."

Jackson rode off as if he heard nothing, Pendleton and Douglas at his side, directly into the path of Union cannon fire. One shell bounced near by and howled over their heads, another whizzed between Jackson and Pendleton, and a third burst so near as to scatter dirt over Jackson and Sorrel. The horse went to his haunches in fright, and Jackson impatiently lifted him. At that moment a staff officer arrived from Lee with an order: "General Lee presents his compliments and directs that you return at once." Jackson galloped from the exposed position.

Officers studied the Federal lines with care; they seemed all but unassailable. The crest of the hill was some 150 feet above the lowlands, and here McClellan had ranged his artillery in masses. Skirmishers held the foot of the slope, with the winding stream and thick woodlands adding protection. The Union infantry lay near the guns, regiment on regiment. Storming up the hill would be murderous, since men would be forced to climb slowly through fields of wheat, in sight of the guns. A millpond covered the right flank, and the artillery the left, from a position over a broad meadow. The enemy had seldom chosen so superb a position.

Lee sent Longstreet to examine the left, with an eye to developing an attack from that direction. Old Pete returned with the suggestion that Lee bring up all available guns—at least one hundred—and drive off the enemy artillery by firing at it from slight angles. An infantry assault could follow. Jackson disagreed with Longstreet. A frontal assault would be too costly, even with such precautions, he said. Why not a flank attack by the right?

Lee rode toward the ground Jackson indicated, but for some reason did not trouble to make a close study of it. The commander took a brief look and reached a decision: He would follow Longstreet's suggestion. The orders went out. Guns were to be brought up quickly to the highest available ground, so that they could reach the enemy batteries. This meant cutting roads through woods, and that work was begun. Few guns appeared, however. D. H. Hill's artillerymen had run out of ammunition, and their guns had been left behind White Oak

Swamp. Lee's chief of heavy ordnance, General W. N. Pendleton, was expected to bring up the reserve guns, but he was astray today, aimlessly searching for Lee. And Jackson's artilleryman, Colonel Crutchfield, was ill; this was unknown at headquarters.

Three Confederate guns soon opened on the enemy—and were broken to pieces by the blazing Union line. Lee's guns were opened one or two at a time before others were ready to support; McClellan's gunners thus blasted them almost at their leisure. Lee had to watch much of this in futile wrath, for thick growth on the front prevented instant control. Once, in midafternoon, he counted a scant twenty guns challenging the entire line of the enemy. He fumed, for he had already sent this order: "Batteries have been established to rake the enemy's line. If it is broken, as is probable, Armistead, who can witness the effect of the fire, has been ordered to charge with a yell."

It was as clear to Lee as to the apprehensive infantrymen in the waiting lines that the cannonade might not last the afternoon, much less break the Federal line. There was little hope that the brigade led by Armistead would show the way to victory.

Lee made an effort to improve things. He once more turned to thoughts of flank attack, and at about three o'clock rode far out to Jackson's left with Longstreet. He found a way to strike the enemy in this quarter, and was debating how he could best bring up the reserve troops, when he had messages from the front which canceled those plans. The messages later proved to be confused and erroneous. They indicated that the enemy was falling back, and that the leading brigade under Armistead was pushing forward. Magruder, in particular, was now in a position to smash the enemy line. On strength of this news, Lee gave orders to carry out the original plan of attack.

Magruder's men trotted into the open. Their nervous general had planned to launch fifteen thousand in this attack, but only one thousand came forth. Even these men were delayed by Magruder's insistence upon making a speech to them. They went into close musket range of the Federals, just four hundred yards from the big guns. The lines were badly mangled. Reinforcements came up, but no more than five thousand were in the attack in this sector, attempting to storm a farmhouse on the forbidding hill. The attack was not a success. There was worse to come.

D. H. Hill, from his post near the center, had watched developments on either hand and had concluded that the day would pass without an attack. There would be the six or eight hours of lying under artillery fire, but nothing more punishing, for he believed that the slope could not be stormed.

When he heard Magruder's firing, however, Hill assumed that this was the signal Lee had provided, and ordered his officers, "That must be the general advance! Bring up your brigades as soon as possible and join it."

This was the beginning of wholesale slaughter. For though it was already nearing 7 P.M., and shadows were on the slope, there was yet time on this terrible hillside to wreck a division.

Most of the storming regiments were North Carolinians who went upward without hesitation. Hill was to write: "The courage of the soldiers was sublime." On the open hill, however, there was only death. The enemy gunners redoubled their fire. In the storm of shell the finest regiments fell apart. One brigade, under General Garland, went halfway up the hill and was forced to lie down and await support. Colonel J. B. Gordon took a brigade to within two hundred yards of the crest. All over the hill were halted troops; hundreds were falling, especially officers and color-bearers. There was little artillery support. In the confusion of this massacre, and the drifting of other regiments over the field, Hill called on Jackson for reinforcements.

Jackson's division had rested beyond this fury, suffering no more than occasional bursts of artillery. When Jackson attempted to send some of Ewell's men to the aid of Hill, they could hardly push through the confusion of the roadway. General Early, trying to get through the press, saw "a large number of men retreating from the battlefield," and "a very deep ditch filled with skulkers." The streaming to the rear was so powerful that Early became separated from his command.

It was now too late, much too late for Lee. He had failed, and Jackson had failed, to give Hill and Magruder assistance in the last hour of slaughter; but the confusions of the field, the pressure of the enemy's deadly guns, and the handicap of the forested plain with its narrow roads, all prevented instant action. The exposed brigades were forced to take their terrible losses before recoiling into the woodlands at the foot of the hill.

Lee was to write: "D. H. Hill pressed forward across the open field and engaged the enemy gallantly, breaking and driving back his first line; but a simultaneous advance of other troops not taking place, he found himself unable to maintain the ground. . . . Jackson sent to support his own division, and that part of Ewell's which was in reserve; but owing to the increasing darkness, and the intricacy of the forest and swamp, they did not arrive in time. . . ."

Men remembered that there was no end to the roar of enemy field guns, from midafternoon until night fell, and over them were the fantastic crashes of the long cannon of the hidden gunboats on the James, throwing in the shells which the Rebels called "lamp posts."

Ewell's division went up at dusk, under a moonless sky lit like midday with the artillery. They passed Jackson, who sat his horse in perfect calm, trying to read during the hottest of the fire. The troops pressed on, with Colonel Bradley Johnson leading them. In the darkness some of them heard Ewell's squeaky lisp: "Whose troops are these?" When some Marylander replied, Ewell shouted, "Thank God! You Maryland boys are the only ones I can find faced in the right direction."

One of Ewell's men remembered:

"Then commenced a night of horrors. It appears we were holding ground fought over in the day by D. H. Hill's North Carolina troops, and the ground was covered with their dead and wounded. There would be a long drawn-out scream, and then the wounded would yell out: 'Fourteenth North Carolina!' . . . 'Fourth North Carolina!' on all sides."

D. H. Hill was aghast at the fate of his troops:

"I never saw anything more grandly heroic than the advance after sunset of the nine brigades. Unfortunately, they did not move together, and were beaten in detail. As each brigade emerged from the woods, from fifty to one hundred guns opened upon it, tearing great gaps in its ranks; but the heroes reeled on and were shot down by the reserves at the guns. . . . It was not war—it was murder.

"Our loss was double that of the Federals. . . . The artillery practice was kept up till nine o'clock at night. . . . I estimate that my division in that battle was 6,500 strong, and that the loss was 2,000."

Once more Jackson's own casualties had been light, though this day, because of the nature of the field, there was to be little criticism of his inaction. The delay at White Oak Swamp, army strategists were suggesting, had brought on the fearful day at Malvern Hill. But some of Lee's generals were also saying that a competent reconnaissance would have prevented any attack at all on that day's position.

Captain Blackford of Stuart's cavalry, who passed through dark woods in search of Jackson, was struck by the ghastly spectacle under the trees: the lights, the groans, the work of surgeons, the lines of ambulances and the countless wounded. Blackford found Old Jack, reported that Stuart would join him soon, and explained what had happened to McClellan at the White House. Jackson laughed at Blackford's description of the Union strategy.

"That's good! That's good!" Jackson cried. "Changing his base, is he? Ha! Ha!"

And after his first laugh of the day, Jackson invited Blackford to spend the night at his headquarters.

Jackson went to the rear at about ten o'clock, weary despite his failure to get into the front-line attack. He slept on the ground, where Jim made him a pallet, just out of the path of stragglers and wounded; he was almost immediately asleep after eating a light supper. His rest was short, for in the rainy night his brigade commanders became anxious and at 1 A.M. aroused him for instructions.

The officers told Jackson that the enemy was likely to attack in the morning, and they were concerned about their exposed positions. Jackson heard them out as if he had little interest in the discussion, and after he had asked one or two casual questions said, "No. I think he will clear out in the morning."

Jackson's prediction was borne out in the fog and sifting rain of dawn. Along their road Ewell's men found the enemy gone, and saw this scene:

A wandering rail fence covered with thick growth of sassafras, dogwood and blackberry, where charging North Carolinians had yesterday ripped down rails to get at the enemy; bodies lay piled along the fence, some sitting gruesomely erect on the rails. On the open ground beyond lay complete files of men, each on his face, with musket grasped before him. Within ten feet of a ruined Union battery were windrows of dead men.

Colonel Moxley Sorrel, riding this road, went to a shanty in the woods, where he found General Ewell asleep. Ewell stirred, raised his head and stared. "Mithther Thorrel, can you tell me why we had 500 of our men killed on thith field yethterday?" Sorrel did not answer. Ewell covered his head.

Blackford rode into the field at daybreak with Jackson and saw details of men collecting and covering the dead. Jackson gave this an attention which surprised Blackford, who wrote:

"There was another peculiarity about this field . . . that greatly added to its horrors. It is a fact well-known among medical men . . . that under certain circumstances . . . when death comes suddenly from a wound the muscles become, instantly, perfectly rigid, and so remain. Owing probably to the extreme fatigue and excitement Jackson's troops had been through . . . many of the bodies presented instances of this phenomenon.

"One man lay on his back with his legs raised in the air, one hand clutching a handful of grass on the ground, the other holding aloft at arm's length . . . a bunch of turf torn up by the roots, at which he was glaring with his eyes wide open. . . . Quite a number held their muskets with one or both hands, and one poor fellow died in the act of loading."

For hours the army gathered the dead; and to Blackford's amazement, Jackson stood over the working men as they laid out rows, with up to fifty bodies in each, and spread blankets or oilcloths over them. Jackson sent others to hide equipment of the dead in ravines. He looked about the field, sending men to pick up every scrap of cloth or grisly debris. Jackson was stranger even than his reputation, Blackford thought. But he saw at the end that the scene was much less depressing and that the numbers of casualties appeared much less.

"Why did you have the field cleaned like this?" the cavalryman asked Jackson.

"Because I am going to attack here presently, as soon as the fog rises, and it won't do to march troops over their own dead, you know. That's what I'm doing it for."

The attack was not to be. Jackson and Lee soon entered another council of war. President Davis had once more come out to the battlefield, this time without previous notice.

Jackson was first to arrive at headquarters, which was in the home of a family named Poindexter. Old Jack stood with Lee at a fireside, reporting his observations of the morning. The enemy was fleeing in disorder, he said. He had fallen silent, and Lee was dictating to his aide, Walter Taylor (who was now a colonel), when Longstreet blustered in, shouting that he must send a message to his wife in Richmond announcing his survival of battle. Lee calmed him with a soft reply and asked Old Pete's opinion on last night's engagement.

"General," Longstreet said soberly, "I think you hurt them about as much as they hurt you."

This was a doleful note for Lee, though it was perhaps a bit more optimistic than was warranted. At this moment President Davis stepped into the room unannounced. Lee was revealed in one of his rare moments of uncertainty, for he said quickly, "President, I am glad to see you."

Watching officers noted the unusual address, and with even greater interest watched the meeting of Davis and Jackson. Old Jack's figure had stiffened at the moment the President entered.

After Lee and Davis had exchanged greetings, Lee presented Jackson, whom the President had seen only briefly, after Bull Run. The staffs enjoyed the scene. Jackson, who had long resented the role of Davis in the incident of Loring and the expedition to Romney, in Western Virginia, now refused to offer his hand. He stood at attention, looking beyond Davis.

Lee turned to Davis. "Why, don't you know General Jackson? This is our Stonewall Jackson."

Davis bowed, but did not bring forth his hand. Jackson gave a brisk salute and remained silent.

Lee and Davis talked of the military situation, and gaping young staff officers heard the two leaders of the Confederacy in an unrestrained discussion. Davis proposed an attack on McClellan, immediately. Lee gave him a patient explanation as to why it could not be done. They talked as the rain poured in torrents over the swamp country. Jackson did not speak until the two had reached the decision that the Federals could not be attacked today. When asked for his opinion, Old Jack spoke quietly: "They have not all got away if we go immediately after them."

The council ended with the decision to remain in the neighborhood with the army. Jackson did not protest, or repeat his opinion. The President, who had been seeking liquor for his drenched party, was glad to see the doors opened and other officers crowding in, one of them Major Charles Marshall of Lee's staff, who had a silver flask of "excellent old whisky" given him by the captured Federal, General George A. McCall.

Douglas noted that the President "touched it very lightly; General Lee declined, saying that he would not deprive some young officer of a drink which he would better appreciate. General Longstreet took a good, soldierly swig of it. General Jackson declined, and also General Stuart." Stuart's suggestion that McCall must have poisoned the liquor did not affect the thirst of the staff, and the flask was soon empty.

There was little to be done that day. The army was moved forward painfully; and A. P. Hill and Longstreet, whose divisions were the best marchers of the campaign, could make but two miles in the rain.

On this dreary day, General Richard Taylor left the army, leaving a gap in Jackson's command. Taylor, who had been in an ambulance for more than a week, was now ordered to the western theater of the war, but paralysis of the legs was to prevent his active soldiering for a time. On Jackson's recommendation, Taylor had been made a major general.

In the afternoon, Stuart and a handful of troopers found the enemy on the James River, and though a horse battery and a Congrieve "Rocket Battery" shelled the enemy, the cavalrymen seemed to do more harm than good. First, the experimental rockets, throwing "liquid damnation," came howling back like boomerangs to scatter the Confederates. Further, Stuart had stirred and educated the enemy, for the Federals soon saw that the ridge from which Stuart was firing should be seized as a bit of commanding ground, and the bluecoats occupied it.

The next morning, July third, Jackson followed Stuart's lead over the poor road to the river, but the force made little progress in the mud, and Jackson went into camp at sunset with only three miles covered. He gave orders to move before dawn and told his staff officers they should breakfast and be in the saddle when the army moved. He also ordered that guides be sent to General Ewell, just at dawn.

In the early morning, Jim shook awake the young staff officers in a farmhouse room; the General was asking for them, and breakfast was ready. Douglas, first up, met the General as he emerged from his room. When Jackson learned that the guides had not been sent to Ewell, but were still asleep, he sent them off without breakfast. His temper was not improved when he found his own staff tardy. He could not conceal his anger.

Only Jim had eaten breakfast, but Jackson ordered the meal dispensed with and told the servant to pack his equipment and have the wagon rolling within ten minutes. As Douglas mourned and other officers arrived cursing, Jim poured fresh coffee on the ground and stored away the rest of the food. Even the Reverend Dabney, appearing sleepy-eyed and half-dressed, did not manage a bite to eat for all his skill, for Jim had determined that if his favorites went hungry, all would do so. The caravan got underway with tempers short.

The sport was only beginning, for Jackson, moving rapidly, also found General Ewell abed, and before staff officers he gave Ewell a tongue-lashing, and sent Douglas to put Ewell's troops in motion. Douglas used the visit to beg a breakfast, and when he returned, had the poor grace to tell his fellows of the meal in detail. The staff at large did not eat until one o'clock in the afternoon.

On this day, the common soldiers of Confederacy and Union made their own brief truce; and in defiance of officers, the nation was reunited in a blackberry patch. Private Casler was there:

"The next day, the 4th of July, we lay in line of battle all day, my regiment being on picket; but not a shot was fired. The post I was on was in the woods, and in front of us was an open field; beyond the field were woods, and the enemy was on picket there. This field was full of blackberries; so our boys and the Yanks made a bargain not to fire at each other, and went out in the field, leaving one man on each post with the arms, and gathered berries together and talked over the fight, traded tobacco and coffee and exchanged newspapers as peacefully and kindly as if they had not been engaged for the last seven days in butchering one another."

The line of battle lay beneath Evelington Hill, the heights held by the Federals near the James River. Jackson was insistent that he could not join an attack here today, for his men were in no condition to fight. Lee arrived, and Longstreet urged an assault. Lee was skeptical. He took Jackson and rode along every foot of the front, at many points dismounting to study the terrain through glasses. The two could find no means of attacking, for McClellan had covered well the flanks on the ridge so obligingly pointed out to him by Stuart. And behind this ridge lay the entire Federal army, confident as it waited beneath the gunboats. The enemy had crowded about Harrison's Landing, near the historic Westover, home of the Byrd family. There was little to be done beyond the expression of bitter regret in Lee's report on the Seven Days: "Under ordinary circumstances the Federal army should have been destroyed."

Such regret had a strange sound, perhaps, coming from a commander who in one week had sent a vastly superior invading army reeling back from Richmond's gates to this beachhead on the river. But Lee, like the jealous, bickering officers who now raised a jackal's chorus, saw beyond this temporary victory over McClellan; for they had glimpsed the dazzling opportunity to crush the military effort of the North, an opportunity dashed by human failures and unwieldly command.

The week, of course, had been far from a failure. Richmond's delivery was hailed by the Confederacy as a triumph. After all, the enemy was now only a disheartened fraction of the host of a week ago, cowering on the river bank in such fear that Lee dared to withdraw his infantry and post a cavalry watch on the invaders. In this week, to be sure, the Army of Northern Virginia had paid a fearful cost, more than twenty thousand casualties. There was reason to believe the enemy loss much greater, but the Confederacy could not bear such exchanges. Lee had taken some ten thousand prisoners, and seized fifty-two precious cannon and more than thirty thousand muskets.

Of these grievous losses Jackson had borne few. His Valley army of three brigades had lost only 208 dead and wounded; and the total force he commanded before Richmond, though it was almost a quarter of the entire army, had suffered only twelve hundred casualties, or about 6 per cent of the total loss.

Criticism was plentiful, and some of it did not spare Jackson, though Lee placed no blame on him for his part in the campaign. Longstreet, D. H. Hill and others were critical of Jackson in varying degree, and a lesser officer, Robert Toombs of Georgia, scored both Lee and Jackson. This hotheaded officer, a prewar Senator, wrote after the Seven Days: "Stonewall Jackson and his troops did little or nothing in these battles of the Chickahominy, and Lee was far below the occasion."

There were now changes in command, and in light of the failures in the Seven Days, they seemed fortunate. General Magruder had his wish and was transferred to the West, though not until President Davis had consulted with him over army gossip that Magruder had been drunk in battle and had hidden from enemy fire. General Huger, at his request, was sent to South Carolina. D. H. Hill, though he had behaved bravely and well, was needed in North Carolina, and was moved there. The transfers of Magruder and Huger were accomplished with a great flurry of written reports by the generals, which stirred controversy in their wake.

General Pendleton, the artillery chief, made a curious report as to the failure of the big guns at Malvern Hill: he had been slightly ill and had wandered over the field, unable first to find Lee, and then to find suitable spots for his guns. There was a tacit admission of his inability to handle the army's ordnance in the field, though he had shown initiative in concentrating command of the artillery, and in making voluminous reports.

Jackson did not, now or later, give a hint in official reports that his role in the Chickahominy country had been less effective than usual, but he hinted that his thoughts were on the subject in a letter to Anna:

"During the past week I have not been well, have suffered from fever and debility, but through the blessing of an ever-kind Providence I am much better today."

This was his first and only written mention of his condition in these days.

Jackson, oblivious to critics, had some small adventures this week. He and Douglas, riding the lines one day, halted to pick berries on a hillside, though the young officer protested that enemy rifle fire was becoming dangerously warm. Jackson calmly sat his horse, eating berries, and then, Douglas wrote:

"He paused, and turning to me, with a large, shining berry poised between his thumb and finger, enquired maladroitly in what part of the body I would prefer being shot. I replied that primarily I'd prefer being hit in the clothes but if it was made a question of body, I'd prefer any place to my face or joints. . . .

"He said he had the old-fashioned horror of being shot in the back, and so great was his prejudice on the subject that he had often found himself turning his face in the direction from which the bullets came."

The Yankee bullets drove Jackson away only when the horses became nervous. On this ride with Douglas, Jackson came upon General Toombs in an awkward position. Jackson saw that the picket lines of Toombs were not connected to flanking brigades, and were thus dangerously "in the air," inviting attack. Jackson went to the headquarters of Toombs, whom he found stretched in a small tent, having a siesta. When aroused, Toombs said he had left the detail of placing pickets to a staff officer, who had turned it over to a field officer. Toombs said he thought the situation must be satisfactory. Jackson snapped at him and ordered him to go in person to rectify his front line. Toombs went off obediently, giving Douglas memories of past contrasts between this Georgian he had once heard in eloquent speech in the United States Senate, and his commanding general who had so recently been only a quaint and derided professor in Lexington.

On a hot afternoon of this week, Jackson did his only nonmilitary, nonreligious reading of the war, a sensational paper-backed novel, bound in garish yellow, and illustrated with fetching woodcuts. The General had halted beneath a tree for a noon nap, as he often did. When he awoke, he astonished his staff by asking if there was a novel about headquarters. It had been long before the war when he last read one, he said. A headquarters clerk, Hugh McGuire, passed a cheap book to Douglas, who handed it to Jackson. As the young officers watched, Jackson read through the short volume with the air of a man performing an essential duty. Now and then the staff saw the grim face smile. When he was done, Jackson returned the book, thanking McGuire and Douglas. "It's been a long time since I read a novel," he said. "And it will be a long time until I read another."

The staff began to enjoy itself. At the end of a letter to Anna, Jackson had written: "Last week I received a present of a beautiful summer hat from a lady in Cumberland. Our Heavenly Father gives me friends wherever I go. . . . It would be delightful to see my darling, but we know that all things are ordered for the best."

When the hat arrived, there was diversion at headquarters, for in a rare mood Jackson had tried on the hat before his mirror, and the comic appearance of the commander peering forth from beneath the broad straw brim set the officers to howling at the "caricature" he became. The General only glanced at his image, and passed the hat to Jim, who with ironic dignity bore it away on his finger tips; the hat was never seen again.

Jackson twice had encounters on the roads below Richmond. One night as he rode with his staff, he fell asleep in the saddle. Dr. McGuire often had to keep him on the horse by holding the

General's coattail, and despite a pact between them to recipro-
cate, McGuire never got such service from Jackson. On this night,
going toward headquarters, Jackson was swaying in his saddle
as the group passed the campfire of some stragglers who were
cooking corn. One of these men came into the road and, failing
to recognize the entourage, shouted to Jackson, "Hello! I say, old
fellow, where the devil did you get your likker?"

The General started awake. "Dr. McGuire, did you speak to
me? Captain Pendleton, did you? Somebody did." He halted.

The soldier gaped. "Good God, it's Old Jack!" He fled into
the dark. The staff roared its laughter, and when the incident was
explained to Jackson, he joined them. He quickly dismounted,
however, tied Sorrel to a fence, and lay by the road for half an
hour's nap. It was almost 1 A.M. when he stirred.

Jackson also clashed with a neighboring farmer, who, cursing
in a loud voice, charged the General with a cane when he rode
into a grainfield. The farmer was finally made to understand
Jackson's identity; but in Douglas's version, he was not abashed
and continued to scold Jackson for his bad example to his men.
In the version given by Mrs. Jackson, who wrote from a distance,
and always with a penchant for the inspiring story, the farmer
simpered when told who Jackson was: "What! Stonewall Jackson? General, ride over my whole field; do whatever you like
with it, sir!"

A day later Jackson, passing the place, pointed it out as the
scene of the "severest lecture" he had ever had, adding that it had
made him careful of private property.

On July eighth, as Lee began the full-scale movement back to
Richmond, Jackson came near to insubordination. He once more
advanced his favorite scheme: give him forty thousand men and
he would invade the North. Now, with General John Pope in
Federal command in Western Virginia, and McClellan cowed on
the James, a blow into enemy country would be the best possible
defense for the Confederacy. He pressed the plan upon Lee at
some length. The commander gave no answer, asking time to
think it over. Jackson determined to go over Lee's head—impetuously, considering the tenor of the last meeting of President Davis
and Jackson. Old Jack called the useful Botelei.

Colonel Boteler found the General excited.

"Do you know we are losing valuable time here?" Jackson asked. "We are repeating the blunder after the battle of Manassas—giving the enemy leisure to recover from his defeat while we suffer from inaction." The thin voice rose. "Yes—we are wasting precious time in this malarial place, when we should be elsewhere. I want to talk with you about it."

Jackson once more outlined his plan, saying that since McClellan was whipped, Richmond was safe—and that the time had come to launch the offensive Old Jack had proposed in May, while he was still in the Valley. He would follow any leader Davis would appoint, Jackson told Boteler; he asked his agent to go to the President and ask permission for the project. Jackson offered assurance that he sought no personal gain. Boteler was cautious. Why should the problem be taken to Davis, when the President would merely refer it to Lee? Why did Jackson not talk with Lee?

"I have already done so."

"What does he say?"

"Nothing. Don't think I complain of his silence; he doubtless has a good reason for it."

"Then don't you think General Lee is slow making up his mind?"

"Slow? By no means, Colonel. On the contrary, his perception is as quick and unerring as his judgment is infallible. But with the vast responsibilities resting on him, he is perfectly right in withholding a hasty expression of his opinions and purposes."

Boteler recalled his outburst at a much later date, and it bears marks of cautious reflection. But there was even more. Boteler said this did not satisfy Jackson, who, far from being trapped into criticism of his commander, added:

"So great is my confidence in General Lee that I am willing to follow him blindfolded. But I fear he is unable to give me a definite answer now because of influences at Richmond."

Boteler went to Davis with Jackson's argument, but aroused no enthusiasm in the President, who thought decision should be delayed. Davis was already thinking of dealing with Pope in the northwest section of the state, and he was ready to send Jackson after the Union general.

On July tenth, Jackson's corps arrived in the neighborhood of Richmond, and here the Reverend Dabney left the service. The staff did not seem unhappy to see him go. Douglas thought Dabney "too old, too reverend, . . . with no previous training . . . no experience."

Jackson wrote: "It was with tearful eyes that I consented to our separation." But Dabney, after three months' service on the staff, was ill, and insisted that he must go. There were perhaps other reasons for his departure, for Dabney, who was to become an early Jackson biographer, wrote of his troubles at the opening of the Seven Days:

"Here we had a disastrous illustration of the lack of an organized and intelligent general staff. . . . As chief of Jackson's staff, I had two assistant adjutant generals, two men of the engineer department, and two clerks. . . . For orderlies and couriers? A detail from some cavalry company which happened to bivouac near. The men were sent to me without any reference to their local knowledge, their intelligence, or their courage; most probably they were selected by their captain on account of their lack of these qualities. Next to the Commander in Chief, the chief of the general staff should be the best man in the country."

Now, for good or evil, Dabney was gone. Sandie Pendleton became acting chief, and Jackson revealed another stern phase of his nature in a letter to Anna. His wife was seeking to get her brother, Lieutenant Joseph Morrison, a place on Jackson's staff. The General declared: "If you will vouch for Joseph's being an early riser during the remainder of the war, I will give him an aide-ship. I do not want to make an appointment on my staff except of such as are early risers; but if you will vouch for him to rise regularly at dawn, I will offer him the position."

Joseph, fresh from Virginia Military Institute, was soon appointed, and within a few weeks joined the staff.

Jackson now made headquarters in a tent in the yard of a farmhouse some two miles from Richmond, on the Mechanicsville Road. He had declined a room in the house, saying that he would not interfere with the farm family. He was to remain here for about a week, with only two visits to Richmond. He went into the city for a brief talk with Lee one night. On Sunday, July thirteenth, he went in to church.

Early Sunday morning, Jackson rode into Richmond, accompanied by McGuire, Pendleton and Douglas. He led them to a Presbyterian church whose pastor was the Reverend Moses D. Hoge, where he took a side pew, as if endeavoring to avoid notice. At the end of the service, however, the congregation had recognized him as the hero of the Valley, and people crowded about him, pushing his staff officers into a corner. The young men finally got the General into the open, but no sooner had he reached the sidewalk than a lady ran up and led Jackson away with her. He returned in about fifteen minutes. (Mrs. Jackson wrote that this woman was the mother of a boy killed in the General's ranks.)

The staff had numerous concerns in these days, in addition to the charms of the city. The army was alive with rumors and gossip, and feuds were growing. One had begun in a Richmond newspaper, which published an article praising General A. P. Hill—the reporter was with Hill's staff—and criticizing Longstreet. This had reached the point of exchanged insults between the two generals. Longstreet had placed Hill under arrest.

The Valley soldiers took no part in this controversy, but another now rose in their midst. An officer of Ewell's division, without the knowledge of Ewell, had gone to the War Department saying that the officers and men were dissatisfied under Jackson's command. They wished to be transferred to some other general. The report spread through the city, and Ewell went immediately to General Samuel Cooper, the Adjutant General, to disclaim the report and request that the division be left under Jackson. Cooper assured him that no change was contemplated.

On the night of July thirteenth, just before they prepared to leave the Richmond area for a new theater of war, Jackson's officers discovered the unspoken state of mind of their commander, who inadvertently revealed that he was looking backward.

McGuire, Crutchfield and Pendleton were in a room discussing the recent battles when Jackson passed through. One of the officers wondered aloud if it would not have been better for Jackson to have moved to the aid of Longstreet at the battle of Frayser's Farm, and Jackson's quick voice broke in: "If General Lee had wanted me, he could have sent for me."

He could hardly have said with greater eloquence that his memories were yet in the humid swampland, and that the roaring jungles of the Chickahominy haunted him—though he was never to admit a failure, here or elsewhere.

15

★★★ THE DEBUT OF GENERAL POPE

On July twelfth, Lee had learned that a new Federal offensive was under way in northern Virginia, for General John Pope had taken Culpeper, introducing a grim method of waging war. Pope intended to live off the countryside and to scourge it; there were already tales of depredations in his wake. Lee moved with a swiftness indicating that the high command had long since reached a decision. He told Jackson to march immediately to the northwest.

Jackson was to take his men, including Ewell's division, and go as far as Gordonsville, if possible. Lee expected a blow at the enemy but he left that to Jackson's discretion. The orders were delivered on July thirteenth, and the following day found Jackson on the move. The Valley troops left behind many of their comrades, as well as the problem of defending Richmond against McClellan.

The first day's march ended abruptly in a rainstorm, from which Jackson took shelter in a hospitable farmhouse. The morning found him in Ashland, where he chose one of a number of breakfast invitations and sat for a time in the parlor of a roadside home, bouncing a little girl on his knee and listening as an

266

older girl played the piano. He puzzled the young lady and his officers, asking, "Won't you play a piece of music they call 'Dixie'? I heard it a few days ago and thought it was beautiful."

The girl protested that she had just sung "Dixie," the oldest and most popular Southern war song.

"Ah, indeed," Jackson said. "I didn't know it."

At a cottage on the dusty road, Jackson and his staff halted. A middle-aged woman emerged and, at the General's request for water, brought him a big stone pitcher, without glass or dipper. Old Jack turned it up and drank for a long time. The woman, noting the air of respect the men had for this unprepossessing drinker, asked a cavalryman who he was.

The woman, evidently stricken to find herself in Stonewall's presence, took the pitcher as in a daze, and to the surprise of the waiting thirsty, poured the water on the ground and disappeared into the house. She returned with a pail and dipper for the others, telling officers that no one else should ever drink from that pitcher; it was to be saved for her children and their heirs forever.

There were days of marching and waiting, with spies and scouts in advance to watch the invaders. One of the scouts was Captain John Mosby, who was sent to Jackson by Jeb Stuart. He was a handsome boy just out of a Federal prison, with a recommendation as "bold, intelligent, discreet." And Stuart sent a question by Mosby: Had Jackson received the copy of Napoleon's *Maxims* Stuart had sent earlier? Old Jack had indeed, but had not opened it, and at his death would leave unread these writings of his military model.

Jackson's men approached Gordonsville, entertaining themselves with jests about the new enemy commander. Pope had arrived from the Western theater in gusts of oratory, reported to have said, "My headquarters are in the saddle." Pope denied authorship of the striking phrase but did not halt its circulation. There was a report that Jackson, in reply to Pope, had shouted, "I can whip any man who doesn't know his headquarters from his hindquarters." But Kyd Douglas vowed Jackson had said no such thing; Old Jack, instead, had given only a grim smile upon hearing Pope's declarations, hinting at bloody work ahead.

Pope had in fact, begun pompously. He had addressed his new regiments:

"Let us understand each other. I have come to you from the West, where we have always seen the backs of our enemies. . . . I presume I have been called here to pursue the same system. . . . I hear constantly of 'taking strong positions and holding them,' of 'lines of retreat.' . . . Let us discard such ideas. The strongest position a soldier should desire to occupy is one from which he can most easily advance against the enemy."

The army laughed over Dick Ewell's reported reply: "By God, he'll never see the backs of my men. Their pants are out at the rear and the sight would paralyze this Western bully."

Jackson now had to deal with a bullying officer in his own ranks. Officers and men complained to him that General Winder was torturing his troops for the least infraction of discipline. Many men had been "bucked and gagged," with arms tied beneath their knees and held by stakes, and with naked bayonets placed in their mouths. Jackson ordered an end to the practice, but Winder found other punishments, and Private Casler wrote in anger:

"General Winder would often have some of the men tied up by the thumbs at his headquarters all day for some small offense.

"He was a good general and a brave man, and knew how to handle troops in battle, but he was very severe, and very tyrannical, so much so that he was 'spotted' by some of the brigade; and we could hear it remarked by some that the very next fight we got into would be the last for Winder."

The next fight was not far away.

As they marched farther from Richmond, the troops seemed to improve in morale and to forget the terrible fields of the Chickahominy. Jackson drilled them frequently, and officers were writing home that the army had not been in such fighting trim for many months.

On July twentieth, General Ewell revealed that his spirits were returning to normal, after describing to his sister, Lizzie, the horrors of the Peninsula, where it was "impossible for twenty miles below Richmond to get out of sight and smell of dead horses." He then wrote of the enemy near by:

"The Yankees are now in Culpeper, and, I learn, are systematically destroying all the growing crops and everything the people have to live on. Sometime they ride into the fields and swing their sabers to cut down the growing corn. They seem bent on starving out the women and children left by the war. It is astonishing to me that our people do not pass laws to form regiments of blacks. The Yankees are fighting low foreigners against the best of our people, whereas were we to fight our Negroes they would be a fair offset. We would not as now be fighting kings against men, to use a comparison from chequers."

And on a hot day, as Ewell trotted by his troops in a roadway, he gave testimony that Jackson, too, was experiencing a return of the spirit which had moved him in the Valley, and that his mood was one of readiness to meet the enemy.

Ewell passed an army chaplain and asked, "Doctor, can you tell me where we're going?"

"That question I should like to ask you, General, if it is a proper one."

"I pledge you my word, Doctor, that I do not know whether we march north, south, east or west, or whether we will march at all. General Jackson simply ordered me to have the division ready to move at dawn. I have been ready ever since, and have no further intimation of his plans. That is almost all I ever know of his designs."

Jackson was anxious for battle, but for a few days the details of preparation all but overwhelmed him. He did not become less devout, however. A Presbyterian minister, a Reverend Ewing, who took Jackson into his house for a few days, was more impressed with Old Jack's piety than his military bearing: "There was something very striking in his prayers. He did not pray to men, but to God. His tones were deep, solemn, tremulous. . . . I never heard anyone pray who seemed to be pervaded more fully by a spirit of self-abnegation." The army could sense no such spirit in its chief.

This week Jackson got heavy reinforcements. Lee sent him the twelve thousand tough veterans of A. P. Hill, spared from Richmond, though their departure left Lee only fifty-six thousand to face McClellan. Hill came gladly, for Lee had removed him from arrest by Longstreet, saying that it was for the good of the service to halt the quarrel. The young redhead must have been relieved to escape the stern discipline of Old Pete. He could not know that he was approaching an even more uncomfortable squabble.

The coming of Hill was accompanied by a warning from Lee to Jackson which illustrated the extreme candor of the commander's relation with the Valley conqueror. In a remarkable order, Lee wrote:

> A. P. Hill you will, I think, find a good officer with whom you can consult, and by advising with your division commanders as to their movements much trouble can be saved you in arranging details, as they can act more intelligently. I wish to save you trouble from increasing your command.

This scolding was undoubtedly plain to Jackson, though somewhat veiled. Lee was willing to entrust the safety of Virginia's northwestern border to Old Jack and to give him some twenty-five thousand men for the defense, but found it necessary at this date to instruct Jackson, as if he were a young cadet, in his first lessons of command. Lee was introducing to him an officer he had known since West Point, and recommending him. More, he was warning Jackson that he must not keep secrets from Hill and urging him to abandon his customary reticence and reveal plans to his division commanders. At this order, somehow, Jackson's ill will seemed to turn toward Powell Hill, as if he were to blame for the lecture delivered by Lee.

The week was a busy one, too, because of a court-martial. Jackson had never given up the affair of General Garnett, whom he had charged with neglect of duty on that cold March Sunday at Kernstown. Through postponements caused by battle, Old Jack had pursued the cause, and Lee had regretfully sent a traveling court with Jackson's army. It was sitting this week in Ewell's headquarters. Jackson was also trying, with less success, to push to a conclusion the trial of Colonel Z. T. Conner, who had run from his troops at Front Royal in the Valley campaign.

But Jackson could not give full time even to these matters of such compelling interest to him. The cavalry still plagued him.

Since the death of Ashby, and Jackson's transfer to the Richmond front, the Valley cavalrymen had been more or less independent, and had elected their own officers, as was the practice in other regiments. But now Jefferson Davis intervened. Without consulting Jackson, and spurning the suggestions of Lee, the President named Beverly Robertson, an old West Pointer with a bald head and a flowing mustache, as chief of Jackson's cavalry. Robertson had seen little active fighting, and he brought with him a taste for the most severe discipline. There was an immediate reaction from the troopers, long accustomed to free and easy ways which not even Jackson had been able to mend in the days of Ashby. There were complaints. The problem was the more difficult for Jackson because he disapproved of Robertson, perhaps because the cavalryman had been thrust upon him.

But now matters reached a climax. On Robertson's orders, Colonel W. E. ("Grumble") Jones had taken his Seventh Virginia troopers toward the Rapidan River and had run into Federal cavalry at the village of Orange. Jones was wounded and his men were roughly handled, with ten dead and fifty captured. Robertson had offered no support. Jackson asked Lee to remove Robertson from his command and to replace him with Jones. The patient reply from Lee was couched in firm paternal tones:

That subject is not so easily arranged, and without knowing any of the circumstances attending it except as related by you, I fear the judgment passed [on Robertson] may be hasty. Neither am I sufficiently informed of the qualifications of Col. W. E. Jones, though having for him high esteem, to say whether he is better qualified.

In short, it was a rebuke, and an ultimatum scarcely concealed. Jackson was to attend to the affairs of his army and leave at rest such problems of command. Even so, Lee had not allowed all of his feeling to creep into the dispatch to Jackson, for he had lately written President Davis an explanation of the affair: "Probably Jackson may expect too much, and Robertson may be preparing his men for service, which I have understood they much needed. With uninstructed officers, an undisciplined brigade of cavalry is no trifling undertaking and requires time to regulate."

It was an impressive demonstration that Lee, busy as he was

with the watching of McClellan on the James and the army of
General Burnside at Fortress Monroe, had still a complete understanding of Jackson, his problems, needs and moods; and though
he could be inflexibly firm with him, yet gave full rein to the
talents of his lieutenant. Lee was in almost constant touch with
Gordonsville.

Amid these concerns, Jackson wrote Anna a letter reflecting
no difficult moments, but which instead was aglow with confidence and religious joy.

> My darling wife, I am just overburdened with work, and
> I hope you will not think hard at receiving only short letters
> from your loving husband. A number of officers are with
> me, but people keep coming to my tent—though let me
> say no more. A Christian should never complain. The
> apostle Paul said, "I glory in tribulations!" What a bright
> example for others!

One affair which he did not appear to bear as a tribulation was
the court-martial of Garnett, where he appeared as a stern-faced
accuser and took the witness stand, submitting to cross-examina-
tion by Garnett.

"What was your plan of battle at Kernstown?" Garnett asked.

"First to defeat the enemy by gaining heights on his right,
which commanded his position, pressing on toward Winchester,
then turning his right and getting in his rear."

Garnett, waiting through the reply with the air of a man conscious of his advantage, asked, "Did you communicate this plan
to me before or during the action?"

"I did not to my recollection." Jackson's voice and face were
uncompromising, and by his air he was unconscious of the fact
that he was defending one of his unique military principles. The
spectacle was enjoyable to listening officers, though Jackson's
stand was scarcely a surprise to them.

For some hours the trial went on, with the generals clashing
over details of that battleground of March twenty-third, so intent that they might well have been on the scene this day. The
versions of Garnett and Jackson were incompatible, just as were
the long written reports each had filed. Garnett had written that
Jackson had kept him "entirely ignorant," as profoundly igno-

rant "as the humblest private." Jackson was vindictive, Garnett said, and had treacherously filed secret charges against him, seeking to drive him out of the army. He challenged Jackson's "motives and truthfulness." Across the face of Jackson's charges Garnett wrote the single word "Lie."

The court was destined to adjourn without a decision, and just now war interrupted. Spies came to Jackson with news from the front, and news of a sort he could not disregard: The enemy was vulnerable. Pope had scattered his force, and though it occupied Culpeper, only a fraction had arrived there. With haste, the Confederates had an opportunity for attack. Jackson suspended the court-martial and issued orders that sent men streaming from the three big camps about Gordonsville. There were a few inconsequential delays.

The army moved in a heat wave; and the baked air soughed in one room where there was genuine consternation at news of the march. There lay General Winder, so ill for the past few days that Dr. McGuire forbade him to go into the field. Winder suffered today, for if Jackson went into battle, he felt that he must rejoin his brigade, whatever McGuire's orders; on the other hand, if the army was simply changing positions, Winder would be content to lie obediently in bed. In this dilemma he sent young Mc-Henry Howard, a staff officer, to try and find out from Jackson the plans of the army. Howard was reluctant, knowing the fierce defense of privacy which was habitual with Jackson. He went only on Winder's direct order.

Howard found Jackson kneeling in his room as he packed a carpetbag for the road.

"General Winder sent me to say that he is too sick to go with the command."

"General Winder sick? I'm sorry for that."

"Yes, sir, and the medical director has told him he must not go with the brigade. But he sent me to ask you if there will be a battle, and if so, when, and he would be up, and which way the army is going."

After this nervous utterance, Howard stood as if expecting a lightning bolt. Jackson remained on his knees in deep thought, and smiled at the uncertain boy.

"Say to General Winder that I am truly sorry that he is sick."
He paused. "That there will be a battle, but not tomorrow, and
I hope he will be up; tell him the army will march to Barnett's
Ford, and he can learn its further direction from there."

Howard went from the headquarters as if from the presence of
a miracle.

Even as he emerged, troops were moving.

Jackson had sent Captain Blackford of Stuart's command to
scout the enemy, and the horseman returned with a full report
of Pope's strength. Jackson called for him to appear in person.
Blackford wrote:

"I found the General in a tent with nothing but a roll of blankets . . . and two stools and a table. He was seated on one stool
and motioned me to the other, asking . . . me to tell what I had
seen. After . . . a few minutes I perceived he was fast asleep.
I stopped and waited for several minutes. He woke up and said:
'Proceed.' I did so for a few minutes when I noted he was asleep
again so I stopped. He slept longer this time and when he awoke
he said . . . 'You may proceed to your quarters.' "

On the afternoon of August seventh, two regiments of Federal
cavalry were driven from the fords of the Rapidan and fled into
Culpeper, reporting a huge Confederate advance. General Pope,
thinking this a Rebel feint, placed an entire regiment under arrest
for cowardice.

That night, Jackson's army camped around Orange Court
House. When the commander arrived in the village, not finding
a house at his immediate disposal, he sat on a stile in a street and
soon fell asleep. He was taken to the home of the Willis family
near by. Before retiring, Jackson gave marching orders. The army
would move at dawn, with Ewell leading, Powell Hill following,
and Jackson's old brigade, now under Winder, as a rear guard.
Jackson made changes in the orders, deciding after a further
study of his maps to send Ewell on a different road from the other
divisions. The army was to reunite at Barnett's Ford.

The change of plan was a refinement Jackson added to give
more protection to his wagon trains. General Hill knew nothing
of the change—or later said so. The result was a traffic snarl

among marching troops that opened a long feud between Hill and Jackson.

Early August eighth, Hill rose, alert and ready for work. He followed Jackson's orders, going to the road to which his troops had been assigned. He assumed that troops passing him there belonged to Ewell's division, as the original orders had specified. After thousands of these men had passed, Hill found that they were Winder's men instead, and that Ewell was on some other route.

Hill decided that, rather than break into the marching column to take his place, he would await its passage and then put his men behind. Jackson rode up to him in the roadway, and in short tones asked why Hill's men were not marching. Hill tried to explain. An argument began which lasted most of the day.

Orders went awry. Hill claimed that Jackson sent him word to halt the comedy of errors and return to Orange Court House. Jackson recalled nothing of the sort and said he had twice urged Hill to press forward. In any event, Ewell moved but eight miles, and Hill but one, though their troops were legendary marchers. And while the command fretted, men suffered. Private Casler reported that eight men in ranks dropped dead from sunstroke.

Whatever was to blame for the failure of the army today, Jackson had not given heed to the strong advice of Lee; he had refused to give his confidence to Powell Hill, as he had refused it to others. His inability to share his plans had cost him a long march against the enemy.

Saturday, August ninth, began with few signs of looming battle. At 4 A.M. Jackson had given the insistent Winder formal command of his division, and though this officer remained in an ambulance, he clung to his post.

Caution was in order today, for Jackson knew little of the situation ahead. He did not know to what extent Pope's command was separated. He was by no means optimistic over his own affairs. Before leaving headquarters, he wrote to Lee:

> I am not making much progress. The enemy's cavalry yesterday and last night also threatened my train. . . . Today I do not expect much more than to close up and clear the country around the train of the enemy's cavalry. I fear

that the expedition will, in consequence of my tardy movements, be productive of but little good. . . . The enemy's
infantry, from reports brought in last night, is about 5
miles in front; his cavalry near ours.

The day continued unpromising as Jackson rode through the
moving army toward the Robertson River. For once the Federal
cavalry was being fought with skill and daring, and Pope had
flung the shifting screen of blue riders for as much as twenty
miles before him—it was a handicap to which Jackson was not
accustomed.

An amusing incident at a ford entertained several officers. Jackson had come up while Old John Harman was empurpling the
air with his oaths, trying to push over the wagons by the very
power of profanity.

"Don't you think you could do as well without such cursing?"
Jackson asked.

Harman roared. "You think anybody can make a damned set
of mules pull without swearing, you just try it, General! Go ahead,
I'll stand by."

Harman stepped back and Jackson presided over the ford as
a lightly loaded wagon splashed across with no difficulty. "You
see how easy it is, Major?" he called.

"Wait till one of them damned ordnance wagons comes along!"

At that moment, a huge ammunition wagon jolted into the
stream and stuck. Harman shouted, "Better let me damn 'em,
General. Nothing else will do."

Jackson left when another wagon became stuck in the place,
saying mildly, "Well, Major. I guess you will have to have your
way."

As he rode from earshot, Harman blasted forth with such torrents of profanity that mules and Negro drivers yanked their
wagons from the ford and shortly passed Jackson.

Jackson sent impatient messages to Beverly Robertson, urging
him to get information on the enemy. Invariably, he got the surprising reply that Robertson was helpless, since so many of his
men were straggling. Jackson became uneasy, and ten miles south
of Culpeper, when he had crossed the river, he left his twelve
hundred loaded wagons, or most of them, guarded by two brigades

under Maxcy Gregg and A. R. Lawton. The rest of the column pushed northward.

Jackson had placed the troops of General Jubal Early in the front; Early had lately recovered from a wound of the Peninsula campaign, and now had General Elzey's old brigade. Behind him were some of the Louisiana troops, and then Winder's. Despite the heat of the day, Winder had emerged from his ambulance and now rode with his troops, daring the sun. At the rear, with discipline tense, came the division of A. P. Hill, who seemed determined to give Jackson no opportunity to repeat yesterday's critical scowls.

Thus the army, twenty-four thousand strong, waded the river and hurried on. Just before noon it was halted. Robertson's cavalry found Federal cavalry massed on a hilltop. Early's infantry came up and fired a few cannon at the enemy. This drew an ominous reply—heavy artillery fire from the rear of the bluecoats. The Federals were on hand in some force.

Early halted at a fork of the road on a pleasant landscape, and Ewell soon came up. They saw heavy woods marking a fork of the road, the right turn of which led to Culpeper; the left, to Madison Court House. Small streams ran on either side of the road, crossing the Culpeper fork. On every quarter except the front, cleared land rolled away in meadows and, on the right, extended to the bluff slopes of Cedar Mountain, known locally as Slaughter's Mountain.

After about an hour of reconnaissance by Early and Ewell, Jackson arrived. This was about 11:30 A.M. He found his two generals at a farmhouse and interrupted Ewell's play on the porch, where the latter romped with some children.

Jackson spread a map on the porch floor and leaned over it with Ewell. This was a brief scene, for Jackson found the terrain uninvolved. The General was almost casual. He and Ewell saw instantly the importance of Cedar Mountain, the key to this field, from which guns could sweep most of the open space. Jackson wasted no time with orders: Ewell was to send forward two brigades to the right, over the slopes of the mountain toward the Federal flank. Early was to push along the Culpeper road, with Winder's brigade to his left and rear. Hill's men were not put into line. These plans were made almost contemptuously, for Jackson did not go up to study the Federal position, nor did he send officers to do so.

As he finished with his map, Jackson lay down on the porch, his old cap over his eyes, and slept for a few moments while the infantry went into position. And, at this example, Ewell found a shady spot and napped himself. It was as if, in the bustle of preparing for battle, Jackson felt a supreme confidence, an absolute disregard for his adversary; as if, having survived the massive battles of the eastern swamps, he would fight in his familiar open country without a thought for the outcome.

As Jackson slept, there was an unusual stir among the enemy in the neighborhood of Culpeper. The reporter, Alfred Townsend, admired the scene as the Union soldiers went out to meet Stonewall:

"Regiments were pouring by all the roads and lanes . . . thousands of bayonets, extending as far as the eye could reach . . . enhanced by the music of a score of bands, throbbing all at the same moment with wild music . . . volunteers roared their national ballads. 'St. Patrick's Day' . . . 'Bonnie Dundee' . . . snatches of German sword-songs were drowned by the thrilling chorus of the 'Star-Spangled Banner' . . . a stave of 'John Brown's Body,' and the wild, mournful music would be caught up by all—Germans, Celts, Saxons, till the little town rang with the thunder. . . . Suddenly, as if by rehearsal, all hats would go up, all bayonets toss and glisten, and huzzas would deafen the winds, while the horses reared . . . the masses passed eastward, while the prisoners in the court house cupola looked down, and the citizens peeped in fear through crevices of windows."

The Federals who approached Slaughter's Mountain in such martial fashion saw a chilling view: High on a cedar-studded mountainside ahead of them, with cannon smoke dappling the woodland, the Rebels were shelling skirmishers. Thick woods, a small stream, wheat and cornfields lay in front. The line of waiting Federal ambulances was no more depressing than this landscape. A wicked little engagement was under way, with losses mounting. The Confederate guns commanded the open ground in the front.

Jackson had prepared for the arrival of the enemy with his customary reticence. Only Ewell knew his entire battle plan; and some general officers, including Powell Hill, were told almost nothing. General Taliaferro, next in command to Winder, had the most limited orders. One result was that the left wing of the army went forward with Early, near the Culpeper road, and was insecurely placed by Winder, without protection, at the edge of a dense woodland. Perhaps because he was ill, Winder was slow in moving. It was four o'clock before his men were settled, and by then Early, commanding in the center, had his guns firing on the enemy.

One detail which had escaped Jackson because of his failure to study the ground was an extension of the enemy line, which made it impossible for Winder to carry out a contemplated attack from his flank. The officer on the far end of the line here, under Winder, was Lieutenant Colonel T. S. Garnett, of limited field experience. It was in his sector that the army was most vulnerable, though that had not yet become obvious.

An artillery duel rumbled in the hills, and though it seemed a minor skirmish to veterans of the Seven Days, men were killed and guns put out of action. General Winder, who had stripped off his coat in the heat, stood by one of his batteries and was shouting directions when a shell tore through his arm and chest. He fell stiffly to the ground; and as he lay quivering and unconscious, an officer arrived from General Early with the warning that a Federal infantry column was creeping in on the position. The enemy was concentrating in the woods to the left, beyond the wheat field.

Winder soon left the field on a stretcher. His aide, McHenry Howard, leaned over him. "General, do you know me?"

"Oh, yes." Winder spoke a few wandering words about his wife and children, and a chaplain approached.

"General, lift up your head to God."

"I do. I do lift it up to him."

Howard was with Winder when he died at sunset in a roadside grove; Winder's hand in Howard's grew colder soon after he had seen the Stonewall Brigade going in to fight; and Winder asked how the battle was going, then died. Jackson and others were to write feelingly of his passing, but Private Casler, who saw Winder on his stretcher, wrote:

"His death was not much lamented by the brigade, for it probably saved some of them the trouble of carrying out their threats to kill him."

Word of Winder's fate went quickly to Taliaferro, who realized his own ignorance of a front suddenly entrusted to him. Taliaferro went far to the left, exploring, and found the last of his regiment in the deep woods, exposed to attack. He returned to direct artillery fire upon the gathering Federals as the only feasible means of defense.

Jackson soon learned of the loss of Winder and rode to the spot where Colonel Garnett held the flank. Old Jack had but the briefest of warnings: "Look well to the left flank." Garnett would be sent reinforcements, Jackson said. These came, and the afternoon wore on in cannon fire, a concentration of wagons and men on the road in the Confederate center, and a spreading confusion. It was late, nearing six o'clock, when the artillery duel ceased at last. A Federal infantry attack broke upon Jackson's left.

The enemy had never attacked more savagely. It was but a few minutes until the remnants of the far-left Confederate brigades came tumbling in retreat across the lines to the rear, their guns gone. Cheers of the enemy drowned even the heavy musketry on the front, and now the bluecoats came hurtling about the rear of Taliaferro's men. Three brigades broke, following the example of the frightened men of the left. Reinforcements from Hill's division were coming up, but if they were not hurried the lines would fall to pieces before Jackson could halt the rout.

Everywhere, in the cornfield, at the edge of the wheat, and along the woodlands of the stream, Federals and Confederates fought hand to hand, with musket butts and bayonets. Jackson saw his big guns endangered by the reckless enemy charge, and had them taken to the rear, a sight which spurred the enemy to even fiercer charges. Whole companies on either side were captured and recaptured within moments. Every commander in Garnett's brigade was down, dead or wounded. Not even on the Chickahominy had the Valley troops been so near to ruin.

Jackson appeared at the edge of the woods amid his struggling men. A staff officer's memory was that he shouted these dramatic words: "Rally, brave men, and press forward! Your general will lead you! Jackson will lead you! Follow me!"

He was not to go forward, however, for as he yelled, General Taliaferro insisted that he go to the rear. Jackson stared for a moment at the turmoil of the fight, and then went back, muttering his curious, familiar "Good, good."

A few men rallied around Jackson, and a semblance of a line gathered to face the enemy. More important, the rapid, almost intuitive, orders he had given at the moment of the Federal onslaught were being carried out with magical effect. The Stonewall Brigade came up from reserve, cutting through the mass. Its heavy fire began to drive off the enemy, and though the new line was short and exposed to counterattack, the Federals retreated toward their ridge. As a new moment of danger arrived, Jackson left the field, galloping back to find some of Hill's men. He discovered the leading brigade near the front in a woodland, halted as their commander, General L. O'B. Branch, an oratorical North Carolinian, shouted to them a speech of encouragement. Jackson smiled, but there was no humor in his quick, "Push forward, General. Push forward." This brigade charged and Jackson's line was joined again. He now watched it advance at a swift trot, and was so pleased that he rode up and down behind the men of Branch, doffing his hat to the troops.

In a twinkling, Jackson had won his victory, and just at the moment of darkness. His day was assured when Ewell, escaping cross fire which had halted him on the left, came across and joined the center. The Federals were on the point of a rout when they crossed the stream. In a last effort to save his infantry, the Union commander threw a handful of cavalry into the open—174 men who dashed down the road against the Confederate mass. There was a flurry of firing, and only seventy-one of the brave bluecoats went back to their lines.

The little battle of Cedar Mountain was over (it was also to be known as Cedar Run and Slaughter's Mountain). Jackson pushed Hill's division forward in the road; but except for a moonlight artillery duel, there was little action. A prisoner said that a new Federal corps had been brought up; Jackson called a halt. His army filled the countryside, and there was no house for him, though the staff searched up and down the roads. Wounded occupied every shelter.

Jackson took a cloak from one of his staff and was soon asleep in grass at the roadside. He was offered food but turned away. "No. I want rest. Nothing but rest."

He had lost about twelve hundred, and had been badly hurt, despite his great advantage in numbers. Only 229 of his casualties were dead, however; half of the losses were in the ranks of Garnett and Taliaferro. The Federal advantage had come from a combination of careless reconnaissance by Jackson, uninformed officers, and the accidents of the field, particularly the death of Winder. The Federals, paying heavily for their rash charge over the open into superior forces, had lost almost a third of their force, some twenty-four hundred casualties.

It had been a near thing for Jackson, despite the foolhardiness of the enemy. Perhaps he had been too casual, even insolent, in launching his own movement before Hill's men were at hand; perhaps he had not taken precautions on his flanks which were to be expected of a veteran field commander.

Yet in the thick of the fighting, when the enemy had been on the verge of victory, Jackson's decisions had come like lightning, fashioning a series of orders: Bring up fresh troops. Extend the lines. Launch Ewell's wing.

Jackson was to say that this battle was the most successful he fought, but in his report to Lee he offered the usual, modest "God blessed our arms with another victory."

His troops spent August tenth gathering and burying the dead and picking up spoils of the field. Stuart arrived on a tour of inspection of his cavalry. For a few days, at least, Jackson would be assured of keen eyes on the surrounding countryside, and Robertson's fumbling would not vex him.

There was a truce the next day, to continue burial of the dead, and that night Jackson took his troops back southward over the Rapidan, where the enemy did not follow.

He wrote to Anna August twelfth:

> On last Saturday our God again crowned our arms with victory. . . . I can hardly think of the fall of Brigadier-General C. S. Winder without tearful eyes. Let us all unite more earnestly in imploring God's aid in fighting our battles for us. . . . If God be for us, who can be against us? That He will still be with us and give us victory until our independence shall be established . . . is my earnest and oft-repeated prayer. While we attach so much importance to being free from temporal bondage, we must attach far more to being free from the bondage of sin.

He added to his official report to Richmond:

> In order to render thanks to Almighty God for the victory at Cedar Run, and other victories, and to implore His continued favor in the future, divine service was held in the army on the 14th of August.

The battle had shown Old Jack a stern taskmaster toward young Joe Morrison, Anna's brother, who had recently joined the staff. Morrison had ridden into the most dangerous part of the field and when his horse was shot in the head, the lieutenant was covered with blood. When staff officers warned Jackson that the boy should be sent toward the rear, the General remarked, "His behavior will be an example to the troops—and he will learn discretion after one or two battles."

16

★★★ THE FOOT CAVALRY AT A GALLOP

From Richmond, as Jackson pulled back from his little
battle, Lee saw the opening of an irresistible opportunity to upset the Federal grand strategy.

McClellan was leaving his base on the James and moving up
the Potomac to reinforce Pope. The combined forces would then
attempt to slash toward Richmond from the north. Union strategists feared that Pope might now be overwhelmed before Mc-
Clellan could reach him; and though Lee could not know it,
McClellan was telegraphing Washington of an uneasiness felt
throughout the North: "I don't like Jackson's movements. He
will appear suddenly when least expected." This was soon to be
recognized as prophecy.

Lee acted with characteristic daring. He sent to Jackson the
ten tough brigades of Longstreet, so that it would indeed be
possible to defeat Pope. And then, as the Union strategy became
more clear, Lee himself left Richmond, bound for Gordonsville
to assume command of the combined forces. Richmond was left
with a dwindled force of defense, but Lee convinced the anxious
Jefferson Davis of the security of the city and the soundness of
his developing strategy.

284

When Longstreet reached Gordonsville, he had an immediate call from Jackson, who sought to transfer command to Old Pete, as senior general officer. Longstreet declined, since Lee would arrive so shortly.

The coming of Lee brought anguish to the secretive Jackson. Stonewall met the commander as he stepped from the train in Gordonsville, which was crawling with troops; but he went tight-lipped to his own headquarters and said nothing of the arrival of Lee. One of his younger aides had accompanied him, and at the evening meal with the staff, the young man casually mentioned Lee's presence in the town. Jackson gave him a public scolding:

"It is not necessary for servants, couriers and soldiers to know this. Staff officers must make it a point to keep such things to themselves."

Scouts now found Pope's army awkwardly placed between the arms of the Rappahannock and Rapidan rivers, and Lee sent Stuart forward to strike the enemy in this position where he would be all but helpless. Stuart rode swiftly, but his troopers went astray. Under the command of Colonel Fitz Lee, they did not report as ordered, and Stuart himself was almost captured, far outside the lines. He escaped Yankee horsemen by seconds, and in the doing lost one of his gaily plumed hats, laying the basis for an army joke at his expense.

Pope's army took alarm and moved north of the Rappahannock, and there were investigations as to Fitz Lee's tardiness. He had not got his orders in time, for one thing; for another, Union cavalry had dashed into a road whose ford was allegedly guarded by Longstreet. The latter omission was traced to General Toombs, who withdrew the road guard on his own initiative, despite orders to the contrary. Toombs was put under arrest, but the next day went about wearing his saber in violation of orders, and in addition made an indignant, rebellious speech to his cheering troops. Lee ordered him to Gordonsville and kept him there.

More quarrels threatened Jackson. He avoided a clash with Ewell, who challenged the accuracy of Old Jack's report on Cedar Mountain, saying that Jackson unduly praised Winder without mention of the fine work of Early. Jackson replied that

he had not intended to discuss the roles of "our surviving officers," and with a calm, reasoned letter quieted both Ewell and
Early.

Ewell, whose fighting spirit was outwardly as fiery as ever, was
hardly the optimist in writing to his sister Lizzie this week:

"I fully condole with you over the gloomy prospect in regard
to the war. Some 100,000 human beings have been massacred
in every conceivable form of horror, with three times as many
wounded, all because a set of fanatical abolitionists and unprin-
cipled politicians backed by women in petticoats and pants and
children . . ."

A. P. Hill drew Jackson's wrathful attention once more. Lee
held a council with his generals on August fifteenth, and three
days later Jackson turned his corps up the Rappahannock. As
he prepared to cross the Rapidan on August twentieth, en route
to the Rappahannock, Jackson had given Hill insistent orders, in
memory of the slow start of his men for Cedar Mountain. Hill
must be moving at "moonrise," with three days' rations cooked;
but much later Jackson found the regiments in camp, still with
no orders to move, and he ordered them on peremptorily, convinced anew that Powell Hill might require stern discipline before he became a true soldier.

This expedition ended fruitlessly for Jackson, resulting in no
more than confused skirmishing and crossing and recrossing of
the Rappahannock, once leaving an isolated segment of the
army in some danger. There followed a time of jockeying for
position with the enemy along the line of the river, during which
Stuart took Pope's eye from Lee's main force with a bold raid
against the Federal commander's headquarters at Catlett's Station, some fifteen miles northeast, and though they missed the
Union general, the cavalrymen brought home one of his fine coats,
in exchange for Stuart's lost hat. Stuart thought this so rollicking
a joke that he could hardly wait to show the coat to Jackson.

He found Old Jack in a grim mood, for the Valley commander's sweep upriver had ended as he stood hip-deep in water for
some hours, helping rebuild a burned bridge; this in a rainstorm,
leaving Jackson wringing wet and muddy. The work had led to
nothing more stirring than an artillery duel.

Jackson reclined on a rail fence as Stuart approached. The cavalryman displayed the fine blue broadcloth coat, glittering with brass buttons, bearing its label: "John Pope, Major General." Stuart gave a humorous account of the earlier loss of his hat and said he had a proposition for Pope. Jackson gave vent to the rare laughter Stuart alone seemed able to inspire, while the cavalry chief wrote a dispatch for Pope:

"General, You have my hat and plume. I have your blue coat. I have the honor to propose a cartel for a fair exchange of the prisoners."

Stuart left a chuckling Jackson—and went off to send the coat to Richmond for safekeeping. It ended in a museum.

Jackson soon went to supervise a grim task. Three deserters from his ranks had been caught, and now he was ready to hang them. He marched his entire division to watch the execution, and then, to spare none from the moral lesson, marched the files close by the bodies, where the death wounds could be seen by every man in every company. He then joined another council of war.

Douglas recalled the conference:

"It was a curious scene. A table was placed almost in the middle of a field, with not even a tree within hearing. General Lee sat at the table on which was spread a map. General Longstreet sat on his right, General Stuart on his left, and General Jackson stood opposite him; these four and no more. A group of staff officers were lounging on the grass of an adjacent knoll. The consultation was a very brief one. As it closed I was called by General Jackson and I heard the only sentence of that consultation I ever heard reported. It was uttered by the secretive Jackson and it was—'I will be moving within an hour.' "

Other officers recalled a different scene: of Lee and Jackson meeting for a few quiet moments in the village of Jeffersonton for the passing of important orders. Whatever the means, Jackson was soon off with his wing of the army.

Lee had discovered that Pope was being reinforced by the troops of General Burnside, out of Fredericksburg, implying a concentration of Union strength in the northern area of Virginia. Pope must be attacked immediately, before he became too strong. The first move was to swing far behind him with a force of fearless, hard-fighting troops which could move swiftly, live off the country, and fight off the Federals once they were discovered. Lee chose Jackson's men without hesitation.

Since Jackson could not cross the Rappahannock here, a new means of assault must be conceived. The solution was the most daring yet devised between Lee and Jackson.

Jackson was to swing far up the river, unknown to the enemy, choose his crossing and hit Pope's line of supply far in the enemy rear, along the Orange and Alexandria Railroad. There was real danger of discovery. If the Federals were at all alert, they could well cut off Jackson's force in the ridge of hills near Manassas Junction; for Jackson must almost inevitably pass Thoroughfare Gap in his assault.

Lee would remain in his present position long enough to divert the enemy's attention, keeping the remainder of the force. This would place Jackson between Pope and Washington. Lee hoped this would force a Federal retreat, which would lengthen the route of reinforcement for Pope from Fredericksburg. Lee also planned to go to Jackson's side with Longstreet's men long before the enemy could fall upon Jackson.

It was an assignment more promising than any of the Valley operations, and just to Jackson's taste. There was no hesitation over the dangers of division, or of Jackson's vulnerability if attacked in force. One evening the troops of Old Jack cooked rations, put aside knapsacks, gathered cattle herds, and were soon on the road. There was some grumbling and confusion, and thousands of men left with no more than a bit of half-cooked beef. But they were off on what was to become Jackson's most celebrated march.

Dr. McGuire afterward thought that Jackson had conceived this blow, for he saw Lee and Jackson conferring just before the march. "Jackson—for him—was very much excited, drawing with the toe of his boot a map in the sand, and gesticulating in a much more earnest way than he was in the habit of doing. General Lee was simply listening, and after Jackson got through, he nodded his head."

The columns were never leaner, nor the men hungrier, and the cornfields along the route suffered, and the beef herd dimin-

ished. Jackson moved seven miles upriver, waded one of the
headwaters of the Rappahannock, and behind Virginia cavalry
pushed on toward Manassas Junction. Captain Boswell rode in
front as a guide. There was one moment of unscheduled inspira-
tion as the men reached the village of Salem, where they arrived
near sunset, at the end of one day's relentless drive. Jackson had

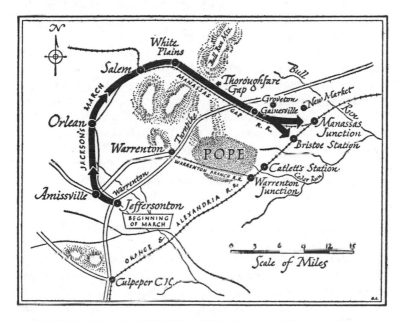

ROUTE OF JACKSON'S SWEEP AROUND POPE—
AUGUST 1862

paused at the roadside and mopped his brow, staring at the sunset in the mountains. A passing regiment began to cheer, but he
signaled them to remain quiet, and these troops went by with
silently raised hats. When the Stonewall Brigade passed, some
officers recalled, the men would not be silenced, and Jackson
turned to a staff officer, evidently deeply moved. "Who could
not win with such troops as these?" he asked.

He passed unusual praise that night for the brisk march. The
adventure was well started. If the mountain pass were not held in

great strength by the Federals, there was hope of success. The next day was as long as the first, and the going harder.

At midmorning, the good news came racing down the column, and the pace thereafter seemed faster: The Bull Run Mountains were undefended. Thoroughfare Gap hadn't even a picket in it. Jackson's men could pass behind the hills and fall upon the vast piles of stores at the railroad junction, if the Federals did not suddenly spring to life.

Captain Blackford, trying to get through to Jackson with a message from Stuart, spent many hours in an effort to pass the infantry—for the men were allowed great freedom and were not required to close ranks, so that rapid marchers were not hindered. Blackford saw hundreds limping, carrying shoes in hand, and saw many who fainted; but the rear guard was lenient and told laggards to follow when they could. The walking mob would not let him through, and when he barked orders from the saddle, the privates would pretend deafness, and allow their muskets to cross, barring his way. Blackford took to the fields and raced the regiments to Bristoe Station, on the railroad near Pope's supply center.

He found Jackson in a house near the station, fast asleep in a rocking chair. Sandie Pendleton was asleep at the doorway of Jackson's room. He was shaken awake and given a message. Pendleton aroused Jackson, shouting to him that a general had disobeyed an order. "General, he failed to put a picket at the crossroads, and the following brigade took the wrong road."

Jackson rolled his eyes at Pendleton and said, "Put him under arrest and prefer charges." He was sleeping in an instant.

To this moment the enemy had no idea of Jackson's arrival in their rear, nor even of his march; cavalrymen had gobbled up the only Yankees seen on the march, and now, though Ewell's men were but a few hundred yards from the Federal sentries at Bristoe Station, the thrust was still a secret. Jackson had kept it so with orders unusual even for him. Taliaferro recalled: "The orders to his division chiefs were like this: 'March to a crossroad; a staff officer there will inform you which fork to take; and so to the next fork, where you will find a courier with a sealed direction pointing out the road.' "

The Confederates knew almost as little as Pope of this thrust in his rear.

The word now spread, for eager troops rushed the station; and after one train escaped in a hail of futile bullets, two others were derailed; and an engineer who followed, seeing the disaster, backed off and gave the alarm. Jackson had the bridge burned at this point, and rails torn up. The army also had a laugh at Old Jack's expense.

In the wreck of a train was a middle-aged Washington politician who injured a leg in the crash. Captain William Oates of an Alabama regiment was near by to write: "He was laid upon the ground near a fire. He inquired who we were, and when informed he expressed a desire to see Stonewall Jackson. I pointed out Jackson to him, who just then stood on the opposite side of the fire. . . . He requested to be raised, which was done. He surveyed the great Confederate general in his dingy gray uniform, with his cap pulled down on his nose, for half a minute, and then in a tone of disappointment and disgust exclaimed, 'O my God! Lay me down!' " It was a cry which echoed through the army for the next few days.

The tired troops slept in the road, worn from the march which had taken some of them fifty-four miles. When Jackson learned that vast Yankee stores were piled temptingly at Manassas Junction, only seven miles up the tracks, he sent General Ike Trimble's brigade to seize them. Trimble was happy enough, as the file went slowly ahead in the darkness, but the men were footsore, stiff and resentful. At about midnight, with the aid of Stuart's cavalrymen, Trimble's men seized the station. There was little resistance. A holiday began.

Private Casler and others in the ranks found a means to circumvent the order that the fancy sutler's stores were only for officers: "We would form in a solid mass around the tents and commence pushing one another toward the center until the guard, who was not very particular about it, would give way, and then we would make the good things fly for a short time, until some officer would ride up with more guards and disperse us." The men in ranks managed to break into buildings and get coffee, sugar, whisky, molasses and other luxuries, and literally tore up one railroad car of medicines because it also happened to contain brandy; the men tossed about the precious morphine and chloroform, over protests of surgeons, to get at the precious potables.

Jackson tried to stop the wild plunder, and his officers poured out the plentiful supplies of whisky; all over the area soldiers fell to earth, scooping and lapping the liquid before it drained away. They were still at it when there appeared a bold and badly informed New Jersey brigade of Federal troops, which ran straight into Jackson's arms.

Old Jack waited for the enemy at the head of a full division in battle order, expecting the newcomers to turn back at sight of his lines. For the only time in his career, he seemed anxious to save the enemy from annihilation. His cannon battered the Federal line, but the Jerseymen would not halt, and came on rapidly toward their certain destruction.

Jackson rode into the open, exposed himself and waved a white handkerchief. The artillery quieted. He shouted a demand that the Federals surrender, but got only a defiant answer from a bluecoat in a front rank who knelt and aimed carefully at the General, the bullet coming so near its mark that artillerymen with Jackson heard its whine.

Jackson reopened the fire; but even when the enemy broke and fled in disorder over a railroad bridge, the General did not throw his men into the chase. He brought in three hundred prisoners. And when he returned, having discovered Federals creeping in on his position, he countermanded his orders concerning the spoils of the depot. The men were told to take what they wished, without restraint.

Men long near starvation, plagued with dysentery from a green corn diet, now gobbled delicacies of which most of them had never heard: canned lobster salad, pickled oysters, wines from Europe, fine brandies. There was coffee by the barrel. Douglas saw one man "bending beneath the weight of a score of boxes of cigars." Another had coffee to last through the winter, and many wore shoes tied in great bunches around their necks.

It was a moment of paradise to the tattered troops, and though Jackson was likely unaware of the stimulus to morale in this glimpse of life as led by the enemy, it was to help in future engagements. When the ragged butternut files charged over battlefields with such verve, it was not always Native Southern Courage which drove them. They were often simply scampering to be first among the fallen foe, to seize shoes, clothing and food, and to loot the knapsacks filled as their own had never been. The enemy brought today's revelry to an abrupt end.

General Pope, now thoroughly alarmed, sent troops toward his rear to protect the road to Alexandria, at first uncertain where Jackson lay, or in what strength he had come. Hooker's regiments fell on those of Ewell, and outnumbered them, but Ewell and Early withdrew from their position with such skill that they suffered almost no loss. They got back to Manassas Junction, Early so careful as to leave not one scrap of debris behind to suggest haste; he had the very harnesses taken from fallen horses.

A. P. Hill captured dispatches which showed Pope to be concentrating around Manassas Junction in order to attack Jackson. Stonewall had moved his troops into an open, exposed position, a little over a mile from the scene of last year's triumph at Bull Run, within sight of the Henry House Hill. He had determined to block Pope here and to wait for the arrival of General Lee with Longstreet's troops, when the army would be able to give battle to the growing Union invasion force.

Jackson waited for the Federals while his troops settled into place along a ridge in the vicinity called Groveton, in the heat of the blazing sun of August twenty-eighth. Men poured into a dusty woodland on the hillside. Captain Blackford rode to the spot:

"The men were packed like herring in a barrel in the woods behind the old railroad; there was scarce room enough to ride between the long rows of stacked arms, with the men stretched out on the ground between them, laughing and playing cards. . . . No music or shouting was allowed, but the men had no restrictions as to laughing and talking . . . and the woods sounded like the hum of a beehive in the warm sunshine."

The approach of enemy columns had made Jackson anxious

for the arrival of Lee, whose march over the route Old Jack had used was tense and dramatic. Jackson's couriers had been passing freely through Thoroughfare Gap to send news to Lee; but now, as the commander came to the Bull Run Mountains, the pass was found to be blocked and held by Federals. Longstreet's troops fought a brief evening battle before clearing the pass, and Lee had an anxious moment. While he had his supper, the big Federal guns boomed in the mountain pass; and beyond, far to the east, he could hear the roll of musketry, as Jackson was engaged. Perhaps his army was being torn apart while its strength was divided.

Lee, as he approached Thoroughfare Gap, had sent a courier to Jackson, and the man got through, pounding the last nineteen miles at top speed. In the late afternoon, he galloped up the hillside to Jackson. Old Jack grinned at the dispatch, which told him only that Lee and Longstreet were at the Gap, and that reinforcements would arrive by morning. Stonewall betrayed his relief.

"Where is the man who brought this dispatch?" Jackson asked. "I must shake hands with him."

He solemnly took the hand of the young dispatch rider. He took from Captain Blackford "a long deep draught" of buttermilk from a near-by farm. General Ewell, who came up belatedly, cried, "For God's sake, give me some." But the supply was gone.

Jackson turned his attention to the Federal troops, thousands of whom swarmed within sight. The enemy marched as if they knew little of the Confederate strength or position. Regiments of bluecoats passed quite near to Jackson, who rode alone in the open, watching. Blackford wrote:

"General Jackson rode all day in a restless way, mostly alone. When he was uneasy he was cross as a bear, and neither his generals nor his staff liked to come near him. . . . The expression of his face . . . reminded you of an explosive missile, an unlucky spark applied to which would blow you sky high. . . .

"We could almost tell his thoughts by his movements. Sometimes he would halt, then trot on rapidly, halt again, wheel his horse . . . About a quarter of a mile off, troops were now opposite us. All felt sure Jackson could never resist the temptation, and that the order to attack would come soon, even if Longstreet was behind the mountain."

Jackson whirled his horse and galloped back to his officers. "Here he comes, by God," someone shouted. The General's manner struck the officers as unusually calm, even for him, as he gave a little salute.

"Bring out your men, gentlemen," he said to the brigade commanders.

Blackford recalled that the troops roared like "cages of wild beasts at the scent of blood" when the orders went into the ranks. And, he wrote: "In an incredibly short time long columns of glittering brigades, like huge serpents, glided out upon the open field, to be as quickly deployed into lines of battle."

Like soldiers on parade Jackson's men went out, with guns dashing up into position on the flanks, and the battle flags catching the last of the sunlight. The Union troops wheeled to face them, and the fury of fire broke, covering the plain with smoke. The brief, fierce engagement of Groveton was on.

The Federals opened with an effort to storm cannon which were punishing them, but as the blue wave fanned over the slight rise, it was broken by a waiting Confederate line, which lay on the ground to deliver its fire. There were infantry charges, and sharp fighting through an orchard and farmyard. The long opposing lines came within a hundred yards of each other in the open, and appalling musketry left the field strewn with bodies. Two brigades from Wisconsin and another from Indiana, men of General John Gibbon, fought the Valley veterans to a standstill.

Long after dark, until about 9 P.M., the furious struggle went on. It was only then that Jackson began to discover the serious cost of fighting alone. Ewell was badly wounded. Dr. McGuire and his helpers worked over the profane veteran who was Jackson's most effective lieutenant, and came reluctantly to the conclusion that a leg must be amputated. Thus passed from the service Dick Ewell, to return no more until after Jackson's death.

There was much more to be reported. General Taliaferro was wounded, though not seriously. Two fine Virginia colonels were dead: John F. Neff and Lawson Botts. Many a fighting unit was no longer recognizable. The Stonewall Brigade had lost about 200 men this short evening, and now had but 435 in its ranks. The twenty-first Georgia regiment was all but gone. It came out of the fight with but 69 of its 242 men unhurt.

Though it was painful, the affair had been fought by mere fractions of the armies and had served Jackson's purpose of halting Pope's vanguard—by drawing forward the entire Federal army so that it might be assailed when Longstreet arrived. There seemed some doubt, tonight, that he might come in time. Jackson saw no immediate danger, but he was anxious.

The Federals withdrew from the Groveton field after midnight. Back at his headquarters, in ignorance of the approach of Lee with reinforcements, Pope wrote that his men had "intercepted the retreat of the enemy . . . and I see no possibility of his escape."

As August twenty-ninth dawned, Jackson's line waited, running from Bull Run on the north, along a commanding ridge, through the cut of the unfinished railroad, with its steep banks. It was a strong position from which to greet the enemy, but there were about fifty thousand Federals within striking distance. If Longstreet did not come soon, Jackson might be trapped at last.

17

★★★ SECOND MANASSAS

At daylight on August twenty-ninth, when Old Jack looked across to the familiar terrain of the old battlefield of Bull Run, big Federal regiments were shifting their serpentine blue lines. Jackson puzzled over the intentions of General Pope; for some hours it was not clear what the Union command had in mind for the day.

Jackson pulled back his troops from the ground of last night's fighting, where the bodies lay in such straight rows that they seemed to be regiments at rest, waiting for the command to rise and charge. The Confederates now squeezed into a narrow front, some three thousand yards across; the guns were hauled into place and grinned down from a slight elevation behind the line, which lay along the old railroad cut. Men waited for the Yankees in this strong position.

Now, after the brilliant march of fifty-four miles in two days— a feat now being hailed throughout the Confederacy—the time of peril had come for Jackson.

The Union command was moving to crush his force between two wings of its big army, and, with fifty thousand men to throw against Jackson's worn twenty-three thousand, seemed in a

297

position to do just that, before Lee could bring up reinforcements.

Jackson's command was changed today. In the absence of Taliaferro, General William E. Starke, a newcomer, had taken over one division. In Ewell's place was General A. R. Lawton. The position of the army seemed good, except that the enemy would have the cover of woods when attacking the left; and A. P. Hill, whose six brigades were on this end of the line, drew up his men in double files as a safeguard. Half of Ewell's troops were in the center, the others far out to the right, guarding the flank beyond Starke and his men. For most of its length the line looked down a sloping pasture to a small stream called Young's Brook, a perfect field of fire. Jackson could do no more.

Hundreds of Federal wounded lay before Jackson, many crying for attention. The Yankees, according to Captain Blackford, made no effort to help their wounded, "with their usual neglect"; and Blackford, with permission from Jackson, sent medical officers to the Union boys after Confederates had been cared for. The bluecoats were grateful to Stonewall, Blackford remembered, especially those who had suffered for want of water.

Near nine o'clock, when the dew was still on the undergrowth, Jackson called Stuart. The cavalryman was to take a regiment of troopers to the rear, back toward the blue bulk of the Bull Run Mountains, where the Warrenton road should contain the hurrying divisions of Longstreet—five of them. Jackson ordered Stuart to open communications with them and make way for their safe arrival on his flank, alongside the men of General Early on the far right.

The morning passed in quiet, for the most part. There were a few nervous rattles of musketry and rare growls of the big guns. The Confederates, becoming more anxious each hour, turned from watching the Federal lines to stare rearward, searching for a reassuring dust cloud along the Warrenton road. The men of the thinned ranks could only wait.

Stuart and his men soon saw signs of the approaching reinforcements as they went to the southwest, and they drove on until the red pillar in the sky over the Warrenton road was unmistakable. Longstreet was at hand.

The troopers found Lee and his staff in advance of the column. Stuart, Longstreet and Lee rode together as Stuart explained Jackson's position and the threatening moves of the enemy. Within a mile or so, the generals dismounted and squatted at the roadside as Stuart pointed out the details on his map. While the trio conferred, Longstreet's veterans padded in the road, Blackford said, "at a swinging step, covered with dust so thick that all looked as if they had been painted one color." The men neared Jackson's flank and turned off the highway, filing into position at a wide angle to the line of battle. The second march to Manassas was complete, as remarkable in its way as Jackson's own, for Longstreet had been equally swift, though he had been forced to fight for a time at Thoroughfare Gap.

At about ten thirty, the approach of the relief column was plain to General Starke, who could not be sure whether the troops coming in so confidently were the men under Longstreet, or an assault force of the enemy. A courier was hurried to identify them. From the strong positions along the railroad cut, Jackson's men rose to peer at the newcomers, violating orders to expose themselves, for they were already under fire from the Federals.

The first Yankee attacks were light. One small party came, inexplicably, at the Confederate center, lonely in the open when other Federal units had fallen back. This forlorn charge was led by a mounted major who was soon shot down. Jackson was to overhear an Alabama captain censure his men for killing the brave officer, and the commander could not refrain from snapping, as he had at Ewell at Port Republic, "No, Captain. The men are right. Kill the brave ones. They lead on the others."

The enemy increased the attacks, and in waves the bluecoats came on over the open and into the woods as well. Fighting was hottest in the woods on A. P. Hill's front. From his distance, Jackson could not see the cause of it. A gap of more than one hundred yards had been left in the line here. This was made

serious by the presence of a deep embankment of the railroad
in front of the gap, a spot offering cover to the enemy. The
protected ditch was now filled with a mass of Federal troops,
which ran out during the next assault and all but broke Hill's
line. Confederate reserves were called up and the storm became
intense. It was bloody, close work, for in the thick cover Hill
could not aid his troops with artillery. The attacks rose and
waned, until the Federal generals seemed to weary of it. By
noon there was a lull.

This was short-lived, for a Federal thrust against Hill was
launched from the troublesome railroad cut and had to be
thrown back with a costly counterattack. The men who fought
for Jackson here were chiefly Georgians, who were described by
one of General Toombs's officers: "I carried into the fight over
100 men who were barefoot, many of whom left bloody foot-
prints among the thorns and briars through which they rushed
with . . . really jubilant impetuosity, upon the serried ranks
of the foe."

With the Georgians fought North Carolinians under Maxcy
Gregg, an officer who was almost defiant when General Hill
asked if he could hold his ground. He would hold on through
everything, Gregg replied. Ammunition was almost gone, to be
sure. But there was still the bayonet.

Perhaps this spurred Hill to send his report to Jackson at this
point. He saw Confederates dashing into the open under fire,
stripping the enemy dead and wounded of their cartridge boxes,
so that they might continue the fight.

Kyd Douglas came to Hill and took a doleful message for
Jackson: The next attack would crumble Hill's line, despite
all he could do. This was grim news, for though Longstreet's
advance was filing into position, the divisions of reinforcements
were by no means ready for fight. Jackson must hold off the
enemy himself.

Jackson's somber face depressed officers about him as he
received Hill's message, but his voice was quick and firm.

"Tell him if they attack he must beat them."

Old Jack did not leave the chore to Douglas, but rode to Hill.

"General, your men have done nobly," Jackson said. "If you

are attacked again you will beat back the enemy." Hill rode down his lines with Jackson shouting after him, "I'll expect you to beat them."

A rousing yell from the woods which drowned the sound of firing announced Hill's success, and soon a courier found Jackson, bringing Hill's compliments, and word of the repulse.

Jackson gave a curious smile. "Tell him I knew he would do it," he said.

The line was not safe, however. In some quarters, men fought with stones against the enemy, which would not be driven away. On the left, Federal troops under General Phil Kearny pushed back the Rebels and held the ground under fierce counterattacks. The line had now retreated to the ridge, and General Gregg had drawn his sword, crying in hoarse dramatic tones, "Let us die here, my men, let us die here!" Reserves coming up passed this scene; and Gregg's weary men, who had faced the enemy for seven hours, lay in the hot grass, with orders to thrust up their bayonets if the enemy drove back the front line and walked over them.

Jackson rode behind the hard-pressed lines. For a time he yelled to the men, "Can you stand it for just two hours? Two hours, men."

At last, soldiers were to recall: "Just half an hour, men. We can bear it as long as that."

The fierce fighting wavered up and down the field, except where General Fitz John Porter had halted on one flank, an act for which he would later face trial. It seemed to the Confederates an afternoon without end. "The sun went down so slowly!" wrote Ham Chamberlayne, a Virginia soldier. Douglas had the same feeling: "For the first time in my life I understood what was meant by 'Joshua's sun standing still on Gideon,' for it would not go down."

The red light shone on endless piles of Union dead along the railroad cut, particularly in Hill's front. In this quarter, when the fighting was at its peak, Jackson seemed to invite death. One of Hill's colonels watched fearfully: "The Federal sharpshooters at this time held possession of the wood, and kept up a deadly fire of single shots when any one of us was exposed.

Every lieutenant who had to change position did so at the risk
of his life. What was my horror, during an interval in the attack, to see General Jackson himself walking quickly down the
railroad cut, examining our position, and calmly looking into
the wood that concealed the enemy! Strange to say, he was not
molested."

The day ended on an ominous note. Jackson had to resist the
enemy alone. From his post on a commanding hill, General
Lee had been urging a reluctant Longstreet to send forward his
divisions in an attack. Longstreet argued with the commander.
The ground was too forbidding, he said, and he declined to
obey Lee's orders, at last: "I suggested that, the day being far
spent, it might be well to advance before night on a forced
reconnaissance, get our troops into the most favorable positions,
and have all things ready for battle the next morning."

This limited forward move set off the day's last firing, for the
Federal commanders, quite by chance, gave their men the same
order. The flashing guns were stilled only after midnight.

Night brought glum scenes to Confederate headquarters, for
casualties had once more been heavy, and the loss of officers
was appalling. Old Ike Trimble was wounded, Gregg had lost
forty of his officers; Field and Forno, brigade commanders,
were shot. General Dorsey Pender had narrowly escaped death
from a bursting shell. All parts of Jackson's force had suffered,
but Gregg had lost six hundred men. One South Carolina regiment, the Thirteenth, had lost half its troops.

Hunter McGuire had a strange moment with Old Jack after
the battle. Willy Preston, a boy from Lexington, and the son
of Jackson's friends and neighbors, had recently joined the
army; he was a great favorite with the General. McGuire, calling the roll of the wounded as Jackson sat by a fire and Jim
prepared coffee, said that Willy was mortally wounded. Mc-
Guire wrote:

"Jim . . . rolled on the ground groaning, in his agony of
grief, but the General's face was a study. The muscles in his face
were twitching convulsively, and his eyes were all aglow. He
gripped me by the shoulder until it hurt me, and in a savage,

threatening manner asked why I had left the boy. In a few seconds he recovered himself and turned and walked into the woods alone.

"He soon came back. . . . We were still sitting by the fire, drinking coffee out of our tin cups, when I said, 'We have won this battle by the hardest kind of fighting.'

"And he answered me very gently and softly, 'No. No, we have won it by the blessing of Almighty God.' "

In the night, Longstreet's men, still unidentified by Pope, settled in their position, the line running at a wide angle to that of Jackson on his right flank. By dawn all was quiet, and day broke in still heat, the plain of Manassas so dry that random shells set afire the grass, which sent boiling white flumes of smoke over the fields. The Confederates waited in supreme confidence despite the thinned ranks of Jackson; if Pope dared throw his attacks within the outspread arms of this force, he might be destroyed. The Rebel line had now spread enormously: some fifty-five thousand men, on a front of about four miles.

The morning passed with rare shots fired by skirmishers, and the far marching of Union troops, who raised dust in the background. At noon, planning to cut off what he imagined to be a Rebel retreat, Pope sent two columns along the Warrenton road. When these had come near the Confederate line, General Porter advised Pope's headquarters that Longstreet had arrived. Pope disregarded this report, and in the memory of one of his privates, Warren Lee Goss, the Union commander thought the news "an invention of Porter's."

On the Warrenton road, Pope had installed General McDowell, an officer Goss heard freely discussed in the ranks: "Nothing was more common than to hear him denounced. 'Sergeant,' said a gray-haired officer, 'how does the battle go?' 'We are holding our own,' replied a noncommissioned officer, 'but McDowell has charge of the left.' 'Then God save the left!' growled the officer. 'I'd rather shoot McDowell than Jackson.' It was a common remark that Pope had his headquarters in the saddle, and McDowell his head in a basket."

Jackson watched the limited Federal movements and spoke

to a brigade commander in his line, Colonel W. H. S. Baylor: "Well, it looks as if there will be no fight today, but keep your men in line and ready."

The General then went rearward and talked with Lee, Longstreet and Stuart. Together they puzzled over the intentions of the enemy. Jackson soon went back to his own lines, sucking on one of the lemons from the treasure house of Manassas Junction. He soon disturbed the noon silence by sending a battery of the Rockbridge Artillery to break up a concentration of Union guns in the distance. This was so quickly done that Jackson was moved to praise of the gunners: "That was handsomely done, very handsomely done."

The afternoon droned away, and the sound of the armies, some 128,000 men, was a faint, peaceful humming. At three o'clock, Jackson was in the rear of his line scratching off a note to Lee. There was the report of one gun as he wrote, a shot that throbbed in the still air. Jackson got to his feet and handed Douglas the unfinished and forgotten note. "That's the signal for a general attack," Jackson said. He mounted.

Douglas glanced at the note, which read: "Notwithstanding the threatening movements of the enemy, I am still of the opinion expressed this morning that he does not intend to attack us." Douglas heard the rising crackle of musketry on the front. Before they reached the scene of action, the General had trouble with his horse; he was not riding Sorrel, but a small bay taken from the Federals yesterday. The horse stood stubbornly and refused to go forward, even under Jackson's impatient spurring. The General dismounted and exchanged horses with Douglas, whom he sent to General Longstreet asking for reinforcements.

Federals ran forward in triple lines across the open, and they seemed much more dangerous than yesterday. The attacks were heavier on the right, but were threatening everywhere, for the Yankee infantry drove beyond its advance of the day before.

When Douglas gave Longstreet Jackson's message, asking for help, Old Pete replied, "Certainly, but before the division can reach him, that attack will be broken by artillery."

Viewed from Jackson's position, the situation gave no such promise. A. P. Hill's line had been pierced, and reinforcements were hurriedly mending it. A captain rode to Jackson with the report that Colonel Baylor had been shot. Jackson could not hear in the tumult.

"What brigade, sir?"

"The Stonewall Brigade."

"Go back, give my compliments to them, and tell the Stonewall Brigade to maintain her reputation."

The captain returned, with Jackson shouting after him to hold his position until help came.

At the moment when it appeared Jackson must give way, Longstreet opened a fearful artillery barrage from the ridge. His batteries stood on high ground, from which they fired almost straight down the flanks of the charging enemy lines; there had seldom been such targets. From the first rounds, Longstreet's gunners began to tear apart Pope's attack.

J. B. Polley, a private who went out with Jackson's counterattack, wrote of what he saw from the ranks of Hood's Texas Brigade: "A ghastly spectacle met our eyes. An acre of ground was literally covered with dead, dying and wounded Zouaves, the variegated colors of whose peculiar uniforms gave the scene the appearance of a Texas hillside in spring, painted with wild flowers of every hue and color. Not fifty of the Zouaves escaped whole. . . . Then, as General Hood said, the 5th Texas 'slipped its bridle and went wild.' Had not they been recalled, they would have gone right on to the Potomac."

Jackson's surge, timed perfectly with the murderous fire of Longstreet, rolled Pope's army back. As this wing advanced, Longstreet hurled his own divisions upon the Union files, and there was a vast, mad scramble over last year's battleground of Bull Run. Much of the interior of the swirling storm was seen by Alexander Hunter, a private in a Virginia regiment:

"How the shells rained upon us . . . but the living wall kept on. It seemed as if we were walking on torpedoes. They crackled, split and exploded all around, throwing dirt and ejecting little spirts of smoke that for a moment dimmed the sky. . . .

"On came the Yankees in splendid style, and some of us forgot to fire our muskets while watching them. . . . It was high time to be leaving, we thought, when right behind us there came with a rush a fresh Rebel brigade. . . . A tremendous sheet of flame burst from our line . . . and with a wild yell the gray swept on toward the 6-gun battery that had been sending forth a stream of death. . . . We could see the sullen black mouths pointing at us, and behind them the gunners. It was for a second only, like the rising of a curtain for a moment on a hideous tableau . . . a noise as if an earthquake had riven the place. . . . The appalling sound of iron grapeshot was heard tearing its way through space and through bodies. . . . Mercifully for us . . . the guns were elevated too high. . . . Of course the execution was fearful . . . the ground was covered with victims, and the screams of the wounded rose high. . . .

"At last the enemy staggered, wavered, broke and fled. . . . It was unutterably grand. Jackson could be seen swinging his left on his right as a pivot, and Longstreet with his entire corps in the reverse method. The whole Yankee army was in retreat, and certainly nothing but darkness prevented it from becoming *une affair flambee.*"

Near the climax of the Confederate rush, Longstreet sent a message to Jackson, offering congratulations and more troops. Jackson could now grin. "Tell General Longstreet that I am obliged to him, but I don't need them now; if he gets hard pressed I'll send him reinforcements." This seemed sheer bravado to listening officers, for the only troops under Jackson's command were those in the front, caught up in the fiery duel with the Federals.

Longstreet viewed the battle with a fond eye for his own men, saw no cowards or skulkers, but, amid the rather grand phrases of his description, paused to criticize Jackson:

"The heavy fumes of gunpowder hanging about our ranks, as stimulating as sparkling wine, charged the atmosphere with the light and splendor of battle. The noble horses took the spirit of the riders. As orders were given, the staff pressed their spurs, and 25,000 braves moved in line as by a single impulse.

"Leaving the broken ranks for Jackson to deal with, our fight was made against the lines near my front. Jackson failed to pull up even on the left, which gave opportunity for some of the enemy's batteries to turn their fire across the right wing as we advanced. . . . It was severely threatening upon General Lee . . . who would ride under it, notwithstanding appeals to avoid it.

"When the last guns were fired, the thickening twilight concealed the lines of friend and foe . . . and a gentle rain closely following, the plateau was shut off from view. . . . As long as the enemy held the plateau, he covered the line of retreat by the turnpike and the bridge at Young's Branch. As he retired, heavy darkness gave safe conduct to such of his columns as could find their way through the weird mists."

Jackson rode along the old line of battle in the fading light of day, passing dead and wounded by the hundreds. A young soldier from the ranks which had fought so fiercely here was feebly, painfully, trying to climb the earthen bank of the railroad cut. Jackson rode to him.

"Have you been wounded?"

"Yes, General. But have we whipped 'em?"

Jackson nodded and dismounted. "What is your regiment?"

"The Fourth Virginia, General. Your old brigade. I've been wounded four times, but never as bad as this. I hope I'll soon be able to follow you again."

Jackson walked to the soldier, picking his way among piles of round stones which his men had used to beat off the enemy. He put a hand on the wounded boy's head, and to the listening Kyd Douglas the General's voice seemed lower and huskier than usual.

"You are worthy of the Old Brigade, and I hope with God's blessing, you soon will be well enough to return to it."

Officers were sent for an ambulance and doctors. The soldier lay sobbing, attempting to voice his gratitude, but he could only weep and shake his head, as tears streamed on his cheeks.

The Federal troops had fled across Bull Run, and the leading Confederates were along the old Henry House Hill, which would always live in Jackson's memory.

General Pope wired to Washington another claim of victory:

> The battle was most furious for hours without cessation, and the losses on both sides very heavy. The enemy is badly whipped, and we shall do well enough. Do not be uneasy. We will hold our own here.

It was one of the last of Pope's outrageously inaccurate estimates of his enemy in northern Virginia.

As he wrote his dispatch, many of his finest units were in full retreat. John M. Gould, one of Pope's author-soldiers, described the experience of his Maine regiment: "Our turn came to retreat, and we marched steadily, profoundly thankful for the prospect of having our regular rations and a full pipe again. These things were more prominent in our minds than the sadness and humiliation of our position—but war will destroy all that is noble in man's nature.

"We marched from nine till twelve, pulling one foot after the other. . . . We had been starved till we were sick and brutish; we were chafed and raw from lice and rough clothing; we were footsore and lame, there was hardly a man of us who was not afflicted with diarrhea; we had filled our clothes with dust and perspiration till they were all but rotten; our blood was thin and heated, and now this fierce north wind searched our very marrow. . . .

"At midnight we were halted on heights somewhere near Alexandria. We were groaning with pain, numb and shivering. . . . One o'clock, and we still went on . . . our regiment had now dwindled to a few officers and a color guard. . . . Two o'clock, and a staff officer rode up saying, 'The General directs you to stack arms and rest for the night.' The men dropped as if they had been shot.

"It was the darkest day and the darkest hour in our regimental history."

Even now Lee planned to force the attack so that Pope might be destroyed. Through the night, he conferred with Jackson, Longstreet and Stuart. He gave Jackson orders to cross Bull

Run at Sudley's Ford, and down a road known as the Little River turnpike, whence he might cut off the retreat. Jackson left muttering, "Good, good." By daylight he was ready to follow Stuart's troopers on the chase. The day opened with a driving rain, and roads soon melted into ditches of mud. The army lurched ahead.

Soldiers looked in fascinated horror at the field they passed. E. A. Moore of the artillery wrote of "the striking difference between the Federals and Confederates who remained unburied for twenty-four hours or more. . . . While the Confederates underwent no perceptible change in color or otherwise, the Federals became much swollen and discolored. This was, of course, attributable to the difference in their food and drink. . . .

"Where Jackson's old division had been attacked, at least three-fourths of the men who made the charge had been killed and lay in a line as they had fallen.

"I could have walked a quarter of a mile in almost a straight line on their dead bodies without putting a foot to the ground. By such evidences as this, our minds had been entirely disabused of the idea, 'The Northerners would not fight.' "

Jackson was busy all day, trying to hurry his march in the face of cruel obstacles. Not only were the roads mere bogs; the men were nearing starvation, for the captured rations from the depot were long since gone. In the most sternly disciplined regiments, veterans dropped out and fell upon the cornfields. Jed Hotchkiss wrote: "The soldiers were very bad, stealing everything eatable they could lay their hands on, after trying to buy it. They were nearly famished."

Jackson and Lee met in the morning for a look at the enemy, and then Stonewall took time for a tour of Federal hospitals on the field. At each tent men stirred, crawling, hobbling and climbing to have a look at the celebrated Confederate conqueror.

At about this time, General Lee had a painful accident. He was standing in a grove during the rain, dry enough in his rubber cloak and coveralls, when someone raised the alarm that Federal cavalry was coming. The shout startled Lee's big gray, Traveler, who plunged, and Lee dived for his reins. The commander fell on his hands; a doctor found a small bone broken in one wrist and a severe strain in the other. Lee went into an ambulance, where he was to travel for several days.

The chase was becoming ineffectual. The roads could not be overcome, and Jackson, when he reached his objective on the Federal flank tomorrow, could hardly deal with Pope's entire army. Longstreet remained behind to clear the battlefield, later to follow the route of Jackson. In addition, D. H. Hill was coming up from the south with reinforcements, though these were not likely to arrive in time to destroy the Union army. And the problem of feeding the men grew more serious each day. Stragglers were everywhere.

The next day was the first of September. Jackson pushed slowly toward the enemy, collided with a Federal wing in the midst of a thunderstorm and fought a brief battle. This sharp encounter was known as Chantilly, from a ruined mansion near by, or Ox Hill, from a neighborhood eminence. It soon died away.

General Branch led the assault of Jackson's troops, charging his men across wet fields and through woodlands, until halted by fierce resistance. Here his ammunition ran low, and Branch sent a message that one of his regiments must retire because the ammunition was wet from the rain. Jackson heard this complaint and drawled, "My compliments to the Colonel, and tell him the enemy's ammunition is just as wet as his."

The bootless fight went on in charge and countercharge, with the line of Jackson turned until it crossed a loop of the Little River turnpike. It sputtered out when darkness came. Among the dead was General Phil Kearny, one of the most able of the Federal high command; the Union ranks lost some thousand men, and Jackson about five hundred.

As the guns died away under the rumbling thunder at Chantilly, a campaign had ended. At the end of June, when Lee had so recently assumed command, a vast Federal army had crouched just outside Richmond. That was just two months ago.

Today, at the beginning of September, Pope was retreating across the Potomac, and Virginia was all but free of the invaders.

TWO WEEKS TO LIVE

"As he never presented a finer appearance in health and dress (wearing the handsome suit given him by General Stuart), I persuaded him to sit for his picture. After arranging his hair myself, which was unusually long for him, and curled in large ringlets, he sat in the hall of the house, where a strong wind blew in his face, causing him to frown, and giving a sternness to his countenance that was not natural."

   —Anna Jackson, recalling this photo of her husband by Minis of Richmond, taken at Hamilton's Crossing, Va., two weeks before Chancellorsville.

A. P. Hill

Valentine Museum, Richmond, Va.

John Imboden

Southern Historical Collectic

JACKSON'S COMRADES IN BATTLE

A. P. Hill, proud, sensitive, able, squabbled with Jackson in the last ten months of Stonewall's life; their quarrel cost the Confederacy dearly. John Imboden, artillerist, who was close to Jackson from the battle at Bull Run, witnessed his wounding there and advanced his experiments in battle. Dick Ewell began thinking Jackson insane, and ended his loyal and most able lieutenant. D. H. Hill, Jackson's brother-in-law, ambitious, thin-skinned, but a capable fighter.

Richard Ewell

Valentine Museum, Richmond, Va.

D. H. Hill

Confederate Museum, Richmond,

BLOODIEST DAY OF THE WAR

Fateful Antietam, or Sharpsburg, where loss of a general order cost the Confederates a chance to strike the heart of the North. Above, a rare action scene, looking into the haze of Union guns raining upon Southern lines (far right), as artillery horses wait, a quarter mile below the watchful Federal soldier.

Below, next day's scene at the Dunkard Church, where Jackson's 19,000 held against a Federal corps, and where Old Jack calmly collected his remnants for counter-attack. An important engagement in Jackson's development, Antietam cost 23,500 casualties in the two armies.

Jackson's death mask, made in Richmond by the sculptor, Frederick Volck, two days after the general succumbed to pneumonia.

Below, part of the cost of the terrible engagement at Chancellorsville, whose greatest loss to the Confederate cause was Jackson, but where many hundreds of wounded men, on both sides, were burned in the blazing thickets at night in the wilderness.

Valentine Museum, Richmond, Va.

Courtesy of The New York Historical Society, N.Y.C.

Jackson had not been able, alone, to halt Pope, nor even to destroy his wagon train; perhaps Lee might have thrown forward Longstreet as well, though the roads had been discouraging and the army severely bled. In any event, there had been nothing since Jackson had left Richmond except victory after victory. The last of these was the most breath-taking of all. Throughout the Confederacy men now began to talk of the exposed Yankee border—and of a thrust into Northern territory, an invasion which could end the war.

In his councils, Lee began to make just such bold plans.

18

★★★ INVASION!

Jackson wrote his usual Monday letter to Anna on September first, almost casually enumerating the battles of the past week, "in all of which God gave us the victory." He still found an intimate relation between the Lord and Confederate triumph, as in the closing of this letter:

> It greatly encourages me to feel that so many of God's people are praying for that part of our force under my command. The Lord has answered their prayers; He has again placed us across Bull Run; and I pray that He will make our arms entirely successful, and that all the glory will be given to His holy name, and none of it to man. God has blessed me through his great mercy.

In that mood, Jackson had fought through the thunderstorm at Chantilly. By the next morning, with the assent of Jefferson Davis, Lee began the move of which Jackson had dreamed since leaving Lexington. Stonewall at last had orders to lead the army across the Potomac into Maryland. They would carry the war to the enemy's country at last, as Jackson had urged since the first battle of Bull Run. While Pope's whipped army crowded

312

in the Washington defenses, the war would suddenly shift its scenes. Pennsylvania. New York, perhaps.

Lee was not blind to the condition of his army. The ranks were thin, even with the arrival of the division of D. H. Hill and the additional brigades of Lafayette McLaws and John Walker. The survivors of the bitter campaign against Pope were also worn and hungry, and straggling in such numbers that the commander put officers throughout the region to direct laggards to Winchester, where they were gathered to avoid their capture.

Lee wrote to Davis: "The army is not properly equipped for an invasion. . . . It lacks much of the material of war, is feeble in transportation, the animals being much reduced, and the men are poorly provided with clothes and in thousands of instances are destitute of shoes. . . . What concerns me most is the fear of getting out of ammunition."

The stakes were so large, however, as to make any risk seem paltry. The army's rolls would show about sixty-five thousand men in ranks, but the commander knew that the total was swiftly dwindling as the tattered, hungry men sought food, or slipped away homeward. The word that the army was to invade the North had the curious effect of hastening desertion and straggling. By the thousands men protested that they had not enlisted to invade Yankee territory; they would fight only to defend their homes.

At Jackson's headquarters, there was such excitement over the march that these matters got scant attention. Richmond would now be freed from the threat of attack; the Federal army would be chased all over the North, seeking to find Lee; the thousands of loyal Southerners in Maryland would flock to join the ranks.

There were changes in command which seemed of little importance just now. General Garnett went out of the division, since Jackson would not consider giving him a brigade. Of Jackson's fourteen brigades, many were only fragments; eight were now under command of colonels; field officers of experience were suddenly rare, and general officers almost extinct.

Jackson took the road. Along the route, people who gathered to gawk at the troops particularly sought Stonewall, whose fame had spread widely. At times, crowds pressed all about him, as he glared with vexation and embarrassment, and many threw their arms about the neck of his horse. (Sorrel was still missing, having strayed or been stolen the week before. He was soon to return.)

As the army went through the village of Leesburg, a woman in a doorway recognized Jackson, dashed into the road and tossed her scarf before his horse. Jackson halted, at a loss to understand; he stared at the young woman on the sidewalk, and then at the scarf, until a staff officer advised him, "She means you to ride over it, General."

Jackson turned with a smile, doffed his cap, and, in Anna's words, "gallantly rode over the scarf."

At about this time Jackson was also dealing sternly with stragglers, and with the marching problems of A. P. Hill. He gave brief orders that men leaving the ranks were to be shot on sight. And on September fourth, he put Hill under arrest, for the latest in a series of failures to get his men under way according to Jackson's orders.

The night before, as usual, Jackson had planned an early start; and when he rode out at dawn, he found most of Powell Hill's brigades were not only out of line; they had not yet broken camp. Jackson found Maxcy Gregg, whose men showed no sign of readiness, and asked him shortly why he had not obeyed orders. Gregg replied heatedly that the men must fill canteens, and the two bristling generals, in a brief argument in a roadway, laid the basis for future enmity.

Jackson rode with an eye on A. P. Hill, who did not take proper steps to halt straggling. After most of an hour had passed, Jackson expected the men to pause for their customary ten-minute rest, but Hill ordered no halt. Jackson, in an obvious temper, gave orders for the leading brigade to halt. Hill rode back to the commander of this brigade, Ed. Thomas, and demanded to know why he had stopped.

"By whose orders did you stop?"

"By General Jackson's," Thomas said.

Jackson was sitting his horse at the side of Thomas.

Hill turned to Old Jack. "If you are going to give orders, you have no need of me." Hill unbuckled his sword and handed it to Jackson.

"Consider yourself under arrest for neglect of duty," Jackson said.

"You're not fit to be a general," Hill snapped, and turned away.

Jackson placed Branch in command of Hill's men, and the column wound on northward toward the river of the border.

The army looked more like a world congress of chicken thieves than a band of liberators as it began to ford the Potomac into enemy country. They were four days crossing at White's Ford. The first of them waded the broad stream on September fourth, rolling their trousers to splash along on the firm, pebbly bottom, going no more than hip-deep; miles of men, with bands blaring away as they moved. When Jackson appeared on horseback and took off his cap in salute, cheering broke out. The curious from the Maryland and Virginia sides of the river gathered to watch. The passage of the cavalry was a thrilling spectacle to Heros von Borcke, the flamboyant "Major Bandbox" who was in Stuart's coterie:

"A magnificent sight as the long column of many thousand horsemen stretched across this beautiful Potomac. The evening sun slanted upon its clear placid waters, and burnished them with gold, while the arms of the soldiers glittered and blazed in its radiance. There were few moments . . . of the war, of excitement more intense, or exhilaration more delightful, than when we ascended the opposite bank to the familiar but now strangely thrilling music of 'Maryland, My Maryland.' "

But the army was lamentably ragged and hungry, and from a close inspection was by no means impressive—a stream of scarecrows limping up out of the water, their wagons and guns on leaning, creaking wheels, men wizened by sun and exposure and the long strain of battles, bedeviled by itch and vermin. On the Maryland bank a young boy who watched them go by— Leighton Parks—had this recollection:

"They were the dirtiest men I ever saw, a most ragged, lean and hungry set of wolves. Yet there was a dash about them that the Northern men lacked. They rode like circus riders. Many of them were from the far South and spoke a dialect I could scarcely understand. They were profane beyond belief and talked incessantly."

Many apprehensive Marylanders expected this noisy horde to fall like a plague upon the fat countryside, but though Lee had resigned himself to feeding the men from cornfields, he imposed a rigid discipline about the town of Frederick, which lay eight miles from the site of the crossing; guards were posted at the town limits, and soldiers forbidden to enter without passes.

Lee had brought only fifty-three thousand across the river, so that at least eleven thousand stragglers fell off behind him. A Charleston newspaper reported that forty thousand pairs of shoes were needed in the army, and the barefoot condition of the troops was to exact penalties in the days ahead. The army settled down near Frederick.

As the regiments rested, there came news that the Federal Government had unhorsed Pope and replaced him with General McClellan. Despite the victories won before Richmond in the spring, the Confederate command received this as sobering news. McClellan was not bold, but he was able. Lee had respect for him.

Jackson found admirers in Maryland. He was brought many gifts, among them a big, bony, powerful gray mare, which was to substitute for the still-missing Sorrel. When he mounted the mare, Old Jack found her slow and stubborn, and touched her flanks with spurs. She reared and fell, and flung Jackson to the ground with violence. He was unconscious for a time, and for half an hour was unable to move. There was a searing pain in his back, and doctors placed him in an ambulance, fearing a crippling injury to his spine. He rapidly improved, but was to be in pain for days; temporarily, he gave command of his troops to D. H. Hill. Thus Lee and Jackson, both handicapped, remained close by their tents at Best's Grove, near Frederick. The Marylanders saw little of them.

On September sixth, however, Jackson was trapped. Douglas witnessed his discomfort: "In the afternoon the General was called to General Lee's tent. En route he met an open carriage containing two bright Baltimore girls, who at sight of him sprang from the carriage, rushed up to him, one took his hand, the other threw her arms about him, and talked with the wildest enthusiasm, both at the same time, until he seemed simply miserable. In a minute or two . . . they were driven away happy and delighted; he stood for a moment cap in hand, bowing, speechless, paralyzed."

Jackson had missed church attendance of late, and on Sunday night, September seventh, he asked Douglas and young Joe Morrison to go into Frederick with him for worship. The General would not leave until he had gone through the formality of having a pass issued for them. Jackson rode in his ambulance, and the young officers on horseback. They went to the German Reformed Church, in the absence of a Presbyterian service.

Jackson sat quietly, and before the minister, a Reverend Zacharias, had more than opened his sermon, the General was fast asleep, chin on chest, and his cap fallen to the floor. He slept through most of the service, even while the pastor offered a daring prayer for the President of the United States, and members of the congregation stole looks at Stonewall. He roused only at the sound of the organ and the raising of a hymn.

Back in his camp, Jackson was obliged to carry on army business despite the Sabbath. He replied to Powell Hill, who had asked for a copy of the charges to be placed against him. Jackson gave him no satisfaction, saying that a copy would be sent to him if his case became the subject of a court-martial. In the meantime, the fretting General Hill was to remain with his men, uncertain as to when, where, or whether he might be given a trial; or on what charges he would be tried.

On Monday morning, disappointed at the absence of Enoch L. Lowe, a former Governor of Maryland who was expected to come and urge his people to join the Confederates, Lee released a proclamation to the people of the state. After damning the Federals for "suppression" of Maryland, the document explained that the Confederate army had come to free the state from domination and to restore its rights. The paper ended:

This, citizens of Maryland, is our mission, so far as you are concerned. No constraint upon your free will is intended; no intimidation will be allowed within the limits of this army, at least. Marylanders shall once more enjoy their ancient freedom of thought and speech. We know no enemies among you, and will protect all, of every opinion. It is for you to decide your destiny freely and without constraint. This army will respect your choice, whatever it may be; and while the Southern people will rejoice to welcome you to your natural position among them, they will only welcome you when you come of your own free will.

Many men of the army abandoned themselves to a holiday about Frederick, with resulting incidents that were to live long in memories. Stuart and von Borcke and the young officers of the cavalry staged a ball at the village of Urbana, outside Frederick, decorating their hall with the shell-torn regimental colors, dancing to music from a battle-tested regimental band. This occasion was interrupted by a raid from Federal cavalry, and the young women of the neighborhood who had gathered were forced to wait for an hour or so until, after midnight, the warriors returned.

One affair in Frederick brought Jackson a bit of anxiety. He had a report that some of his "foreign" troops, while in a store of the town, had insulted some Maryland women. Jackson instantly thought that the culprits must be men from Louisiana, and he ordered General Starke to parade his entire command through the Frederick streets, so that the guilty men might be identified. Starke rebelled. He had not only kept his men under rigid discipline, he said, but he had also arrested some officers for failure to enforce it. Starke would march his men through the town only if all other troops which might be guilty were ordered to do likewise. Jackson put him under arrest.

The crisis was passed with the discovery that the men involved came from another command. Starke's men enjoyed the report that they were soldiers of Jackson's own old brigade.

Here Jackson added to his staff a corporal who had lately been a Presbyterian ministerial student: James Power Smith, an aide who was to remain with him to the end. Smith, astonished at his call from Jackson, blushingly withstood inspection by civilian visitors to Jackson's tent, and entered, expecting to be disciplined for some indiscretion:

"In a few minutes the General came in, and seating himself on the wooden stool brought from the mess hall of the Virginia Military Institute, he leaned his elbow on the little camp table with his face in his hands. . . . 'I have merely sent for you to ask whether you would accept the position of aide-de-camp on my staff.' It was like a clap of thunder from a clear sky. If he had said that I . . . was to be a major general, I could not have been more surprised."

Smith soon reported for duty with a fine new mare, who, in high spirits, promptly kicked Jackson on the foot. "To the end of our life together," Smith recalled, "he thought I rode a kicking horse, and invariably pulled away from me when I rode up to him."

Smith's mates of the Rockbridge Artillery scoffed when he told his news, but when they were convinced, he was carried around camp on their shoulders until a captain threatened "the whole lot, aide-de-camp and all, would be sent to the guard house."

These diversions came to an end on September ninth, for then Lee called Jackson into his tent and began to unfold further plans of the invasion. There was one last precaution Lee must take before sweeping farther north. He must make the rear secure by wiping out the Federal garrisons at Harpers Ferry and Martinsburg, along the Potomac. Lee would take the main army west of Hagerstown, Maryland, and wait for the outposts to be taken.

Lee told Jackson that the outposts should be captured, as well as the towns seized, and that made the problem delicate and complex. He meant that three forces should be sent against Harpers Ferry: Jackson with his whole division would come against the town from the south. Lafayette McLaws and R. H. Anderson, with brigades from Longstreet's division, would work over rough Maryland countryside to take Maryland Heights, which overlooked Harpers Ferry from the north bank of the Potomac. And General John G. Walker, whose troops were fresh from Richmond, would seize Loudoun Heights, also a commanding position over the town. All these moves were essential to take both town and garrison.

It meant a serious division of Lee's strength in the face of the enemy, a course Longstreet had opposed with all his stubborn will during the week's discussions. The plan offered dizzying possibilities, however. If McClellan remained quiet, as Lee was positive he would, then the army could divide for this maneuver, clear the Virginia border and concentrate once more about Hagerstown. That would place Harrisburg, the Pennsylvania capital, about seventy miles away. Even the greatest Northern cities would be in striking distance. Lee could interrupt the flow of men and supplies from the great Midwest.

While Lee and Jackson talked in the commander's tent, Longstreet approached. He was on the point of leaving when he found Lee in consultation, but his heavy voice was recognized, and he was invited to join the conversation. He was unalterably opposed to the plan, and when Lee continued to expound it, Longstreet sat sulkily. He argued for the dispatch of the entire army to Harpers Ferry, a more laborious course, but one which would not involve the classic blunder of dividing force in the front of the enemy.

Lee was in no mood to heed Longstreet's advice of caution. He outlined the orders and promised written copies for the general officers. Longstreet and Jackson left and other officers involved were called by aides. General Walker soon sat before Lee; and as the plan was explained, with the aid of a map, Walker sat open-mouthed. Lee traced the proposed route down to the Potomac, and smiled at Walker's stare.

"You doubtless regard it hazardous to leave McClellan on my line of communication, and to march into the heart of the enemy's country?"

Walker nodded.

"Are you acquainted with General McClellan? He is an able general, but a very cautious one. His enemies among his own people think him too much so. His army is in a very demoralized and chaotic condition, and will not be ready for offensive operations—or he will not think it so—for three or four weeks. Before that time I hope to be on the Susquehanna."

The orders were soon prepared. Colonel R. H. Chilton, a West Pointer on Lee's staff, was entrusted with the handling of the papers. He made a copy for each of the general officers involved. The orders were complete and concise, outlining the entire plan of operation, and including routes to be followed by each segment of the divided army. The move was to begin in the morning.

Jackson got his copy of the order during the evening, marked "Confidential. Special Order 191." He read it carefully. Jackson determined to send D. H. Hill a copy of this order since Hill had briefly, and technically, come under Jackson's command as the army crossed the river. Under this order, Hill was to march with Longstreet.

Jackson copied the order in his own remarkable handwriting. It went to Hill's headquarters, where it was read. Some officer on Hill's staff—it could not be determined just which officer—concluded that the copy of this order previously received from Lee was now of no value, and could be thrown away. He wrapped it about three cigars, and thoughtlessly thrust the package into his pocket.

Unaware of the adventures of the two flimsy sheets of paper which were to play so fateful a role in this campaign of invasion, Jackson began the movement as scheduled, on Wednesday, September tenth. He made a rather amateurish effort at deceiving the enemy as he trotted through the Frederick streets. In the hearing of a number of townspeople, he asked in a loud voice for a map of Chambersburg, Pennsylvania. He also stopped passers-by to ask information on roads leading northward—whereas his route lay along the Potomac, crossing to the southern side, approaching Martinsburg, and then taking Harpers Ferry from the rear.

One last visit was made by Jackson in Frederick, at the home of a Dr. Ross, the Presbyterian minister. Jackson found the pastor still abed and left a note with a servant, refusing to disturb the minister. The command then trailed out of town.

Kyd Douglas noted with emphasis that the route did not pass the house of elderly Barbara Frietchie, who was an invalid of ninety-six, and in no condition to be justly included in a Whittier poem.

The road lay west through Middletown, a farm village lying in a broad valley of unsurpassed beauty, and here Jackson found the Union spirit untrammeled. Two pretty girls decked in red, white and blue ribbons stood at the roadside, waving United States flags. The girls laughed at the General, and as he lifted his cap to them, they flapped their colors under his nose. "We evidently have no friends in this town," Old Jack said to his staff. Douglas recorded that the girls blushed and retreated.

On September eleventh, hurrying on, Jackson made a thrust at Martinsburg, but the garrison escaped to Harpers Ferry. Old Jack stopped at the Everett House, a hotel in Martinsburg, and the public besieged him. A crowd gathered, but Jackson, pleading the call of duty, fell back before them. He said he must get off dispatches to General Lee. He went to work behind locked doors and shuttered windows.

Men, women and children pecked at the windows, shouting for Jackson. Some hung about his horse, which they thought to be Sorrel and not simply a temporary mount; before a sentinel intervened, the crowd had plucked handfuls of hair from the animal's mane and tail, for the making of bracelets and other souvenirs.

Someone soon forced a window open. Roses were flung in at Jackson. The General gave up with a gruff, pleased, "Now admit the ladies."

They came in a rush, taking his hands, chattering happily at him. Small boys asked to join his ranks, little girls asked furloughs for their fathers. One girl asked for a button from his coat, and he cut off one for her. As if that were a signal to dismember him, the crowd lunged forward. Buttons disappeared from his coat, even at the rear, where boys stripped them from his coattails. Jackson smiled and stammered, at a complete loss, "Thank you, thank you." He went through a few moments of autographing when the buttons were gone. He signed a book for a young girl and then, since the besiegers lacked paper, he had foolscap brought, and scrawled over and over the all-but-illegible "T. J. Jackson." A woman begged for a lock of hair, and the General, passing a quick hand over his thin locks, took alarm. He brought the interview to an end, and officers moved the crowd from the building.

At noon he disappeared for an hour or so, and his staff could not find him. The officers thought he was visiting on a back street of the town, eating lunch with a "plain old man and his wife" who had a son marching in his old brigade.

Early on the next day, September thirteenth, destined to be a day of misfortune for Lee and the army, Jackson moved toward Harpers Ferry. Before noon his vanguard looked down on the town. There was no sign of McLaws or Walker across the river. Jackson went into camp.

On this day, too, Powell Hill saw the approach of battle and could no longer contain himself. Impatient to be removed from arrest, he asked Douglas to intercede for him with Jackson. Hill said only that he wanted no other man to command his troops in action; he offered no apologies.

It was surprisingly simple. Jackson listened as Douglas spoke of Hill's desire to fight and sent him instantly to order Hill to active command. General Branch was notified of the change; and the red-haired Hill, stubborn and able in battle, and Jackson's lone experienced division commander, was once more ready for action. Jackson's righteous anger at a breach of discipline could not overcome his respect for a sturdy fighter. The commander had succumbed to Hill's plea without even a comment.

Jackson was not ready to storm Harpers Ferry, for all the forces were late. The surrounding hills were bare of troops, and old Jack's signal officers got no response to their insistent flagging. The General spread his men and took precautions to prevent the garrison's escape. He waited.

Back in Frederick, on this day, the slow advance of the Federal army arrived, skirmishers leading the vast force of almost ninety thousand men. McClellan was creeping now, precisely as Lee had calculated when he dared to order the division of the Confederate army. The Federals were concentrating, drawing in more supplies, asking reinforcements, taking measured steps of caution.

At noon, the men of the Twelfth Army Corps appeared in Frederick, among them the Twenty-seventh Indiana Volunteers. The soldiers halted in a grove near the village, broke ranks and stacked their arms. On this site, so recently, the Confederate troops of D. H. Hill had camped. There was still the gamy odor of their rags and their crude facilities.

In Company F of the Twenty-seventh Indiana, Private B. W. Mitchell stacked his gun with others and stooped to take from the ground three cigars, encased in a wrapper of heavy paper. He was attracted by the writing on this paper: "Confidential." It was addressed from the Headquarters, Army of Northern Virginia, and dated September ninth. It seemed to be an order for marching, and was undoubtedly Rebel.

Mitchell called to his sergeant, John M. Bloss. The sergeant read the names of Longstreet, Jackson, McLaws and Walker, and the signature itself: "By command of Gen'l. R. E. Lee, R. H. Chilton, A. A. Gen'l." Perhaps Bloss appropriated the cigars; he took Mitchell and his paper to their commander, General Silas Cosgrove. The General in turn sent it to his commander, General A. S. Williams.

In the headquarters of Williams was Colonel Samuel Pittman, an Old Army man who had served with Chilton of Lee's staff. Pittman instantly recognized the handwriting. The document was genuine. It went upward to McClellan's headquarters.

The small man who found pleasure in likening himself to Napoleon must have reached the climax of his career as he grinned over the lost order. He accepted it as authentic, for within an hour his military personality was transformed. He had the army driving forward, as if he knew precisely what moves should be made and would brook no delay. It was a new McClellan who moved to the chase.

The order spared none of Lee's secrets. It read, in part:

The army will resume its march tomorrow, taking the Hagerstown Road. Gen'l. Jackson's command will form the advance, and after passing Middletown with such portions as he may select, take the route toward Sharpsburg, cross the

Potomac at the most convenient point, and by Friday morning take possession of the B.&O.R.R., capture such of the enemy as may be at Martinsburg and intercept such as may attempt to escape from Harpers Ferry.

Gen'l Longstreet's command will pursue the main road as far as Boonsboro, where it will halt with reserve supply and baggage wagons of this army.

The order was even more specific about the moves of General McLaws, General Anderson and General Walker. McClellan, tracing the marching order of the Confederates on his map, could envision the supreme opportunity to destroy Lee. The Confederates could not conceivably pull together the isolated columns before he was among them. McClellan wrote to Lincoln:

"Here is a paper with which, if I cannot whip Bobbie Lee I will be willing to go home."

He was to have in answer to his trumpeting of confidence only the sober reply from Lincoln:

"Destroy the Rebel army if possible."

It appeared that McClellan would do just that. His cavalry bobbed up where Lee had least expected it. And to the west, where D. H. Hill's troops lay along South Mountain, anticipating nothing more adventurous than skirmishing, there rolled a crashing prelude to battle. From Turner's Gap, Hill's men saw thousands of campfires and knew that they faced the Federal army, and not simply a couple of cavalry brigades.

Lee puzzled over the new aggressiveness and the startlingly perceptive moves of McClellan, but did not allow this to deter action to save his army. Hill was ordered to hold South Mountain as long as possible, with the aid of Stuart, who was covering the passes. More than that, Lee sent backward the heavy column of Longstreet for rear-guard action. Until the three columns of assault returned from Harpers Ferry, McClellan must be held off.

Lee was becoming concerned for the regiments he had sent to the east. There was a report in the army that a Southern sympathizer had come through the lines during the night, bringing word that McClellan had found the "Lost Order." Whether Lee learned of this is uncertain, but he could not have remained long in doubt that the enemy had gained rare insight into his plans. While Jackson waited at Harpers Ferry for McLaws and Walker to close in from the north, and Lee watched the threatening developments from near Hagerstown, Harvey Hill was forced to fight a strange battle at South Mountain.

Hill was unfamiliar with the peaks he was to defend and was slow in getting his men to the heights. When he had moved but three thousand of them into place, he could look eastward to a sight which moved him, the oncoming Federal army: "The marching columns extended back as far as eye could see in the distance; but many of the troops had already arrived and were in double lines of battle, and those advancing were taking up positions as soon as they arrived. It was a grand and glorious spectacle, and it was impossible to look at it without admiration. I had never seen so tremendous an army before, and I did not see one like it afterward."

Hill fought poorly on his little mountain, even considering the meagerness of his strength. Though his men met the enemy with courage, their commander seemed at a loss, and in an unconscious moment he confessed his discomfort in a role of independent command. "I do not remember ever to have experienced a feeling of greater loneliness. It seemed as though we were deserted 'by all the world and the rest of mankind.' "

Hill was saved by the timidity or stupidity of McClellan's field officers, for the Yankee skirmishers, after they had rolled the few Rebels off the commanding ridge of South Mountain, were halted in their tracks, as if their officers could not conceive of their having been successful on this height. Hill's men took a welcome two-hour rest from fighting, and when the enemy resumed attacks, reinforcements had come up. By nightfall, the arrival of Longstreet's vanguard gave Hill security. After lunging toward the exposed army of Lee, McClellan had paused, hesitated, and now his momentum was lost.

Jackson, across the Potomac at Harpers Ferry, had no reassurance of Federal difficulties as September fourteenth dawned. He had troubles of his own.

His signalmen were in touch with General Walker, across the river, but could not reach McLaws. Walker's big guns were in place and ready to join the cannonade upon Harpers Ferry. He was anxious to begin.

Jackson soon learned the cause of the delay in McLaws's arrival. His column had been attacked from the rear. A brief, savage battle was fought by McLaws, who ended in confusion as did Harvey Hill, higher on the mountain. But here, too, the Federals halted just when they had victory in their grasp.

Jackson could do little but stare over the broad river at its junction with the Shenandoah. The day dragged on with Stonewall complaining of the slow progress of signals and the failure of McLaws to appear. In the afternoon, he advanced one brigade slightly, toward Harpers Ferry, and this simple move seemed to panic the enemy, who fell back from a strong position at the mere sight of the gray files. With limited artillery fire, Jackson closed the ring tighter about the town. At dark he wrote Lee:

> Through God's blessing, the advance which commenced this evening, has been successful thus far, and I look to Him for complete success tomorrow. The advance has been directed to resume at dawn tomorrow morning. I am thankful that our loss has been small.

When Lee read that, he felt relief for the first time since his adventure had begun to escape his control. The commander had been on the point of sending D. H. Hill's hard-pressed men south of the Potomac, and retreating with his entire army, thus bringing the invasion to an end. Now, with the reassuring news that Jackson would soon be free of his task, Lee returned to his original plan. The army could concentrate to the westward and receive the enemy.

Jackson prepared the final blow at Harpers Ferry during the night, and through the hours of darkness men and animals strained to lift the guns into position. In the first light, a circle of guns began to flame, and after an hour of this fire the garrison was overcome. Answering fire, never heavy, dwindled and ceased, and almost before the infantry attack could get into the open, the Union men emerged with a white flag.

Jackson received General Julius White from the garrison, and staff officers noted the contrast between the immaculate Union victim and the dusty, wrinkled conqueror. White asked for terms. Jackson refused, saying that surrender must be unconditional. White was turned over to A. P. Hill and was soon delighted to learn that Jackson, overcome by a fit of generosity—or puzzled as to how to care for prisoners—had paroled the eleven thousand captive officers and men and allowed them to keep their small arms. The Federal property was seized, excepting a supply of rations, which he allowed the garrison to eat.

Jackson wrote Lee that he was coming to his aid, leaving only A. P. Hill on the scene at Harpers Ferry. He promised to move when he had fed his troops. Hill would have to care for most of the seventy-three big guns and thirteen thousand muskets captured in the town.

Old Jack soon tore his men away from captured food and put his column in motion. He found time to speak with Stuart's strutting von Borcke at the time of departure: "Ah, this is all very well, Major, but we have yet much hard work ahead of us."

Douglas overheard a well-fed captive call as Jackson passed, "Boys, he ain't much for looks, but if we'd had him we wouldn't have got caught in this trap." The Union ranks shouted at sight of Jackson, and he exchanged salutes with them. A Northern reporter found Old Jack unimpressive and "seedy," and "in general appearance was in no respect to be distinguished from the mongrel, barefooted crew who follow his fortunes. I had heard much of the decayed appearance of the rebel soldiers, but such a looking crowd! Ireland in her worst straits could present no parallel, and yet they glory in their shame."

By midafternoon, the ragged men were already on their way to the rescue of Lee—who had asked Jackson to meet him at Sharpsburg, Maryland.

Jackson pushed them all night, for the situation at Sharpsburg had become threatening. McClellan was advancing as if ready to attack. Old Jack's men rejoined the army early on September sixteenth, after a march of sixteen miles that even their commander found "severe." With Jackson and Longstreet at hand, Lee now had twenty-two brigades to face the enemy and could make a stout fight. If McClellan did not attack at once, perhaps McLaws and Walker would arrive with their men, perhaps A. P.

Hill would complete the paroling of prisoners at Harpers Ferry and take his place in the line. If all the troops could be assembled, Lee would be ready for a major battle. McClellan gave him one more day's respite.

General Walker arrived at Sharpsburg in the afternoon, increasing Lee's strength; but it was still just twenty-five thousand. Three divisions were missing, and if they came up before the blue masses across Antietam Creek surged forward, the Confederates would have but forty thousand troops, as against the eighty-seven thousand of McClellan.

Walker found Lee curiously calm: "If he had had a well-equipped army of 100,000 veterans at his back he could not have appeared more composed and confident." The day before, Lee had ventured the opinion that McClellan would not attack despite his vast strength. But tonight he revealed his anxiety by sending riders splashing over the Potomac with urgent messages for A. P. Hill: He must hurry. The life of the army was at stake.

There were a few vicious stabs by the enemy as night drew on. Artillery banged away, and in some spots the skirmish lines tangled. The enemy appeared in great numbers. There was promise of early slaughter tomorrow.

Jackson seemed apprehensive of what lay ahead. At about ten o'clock, General Hood asked Old Jack to allow his Texans to retire from the front line so that they could cook. His men were near starvation, Hood said. He had already asked Lee for help, but the commander had no replacements. Jackson agreed to spread his thin line, if Hood would return tomorrow in case of need. In a soft rain, with pickets fretful and firing at shadows, two brigades from Ewell's old division went into the line and the Texans moved to the rear.

The Confederate line lay in a crude arc, on knolls between the village of Sharpsburg and Antietam Creek, facing the rolling country which looked toward South Mountain in the east. Both right and left the flanks came near the Potomac, which coiled about the town. From north to south, the divisions were placed: Jackson (with the troops of D. H. Hill included) along the Hagerstown Road; Longstreet, spraddling the Boonsboro Road and shielding the village; and last, General Walker, on the lower flank overlooking the Antietam.

There were striking landmarks, soon to become famous in the history of these armies: Burnside's Bridge, to earn its name on the flank of Longstreet; a Dunker Church on Hagerstown Road, with groves near by known as East Wood and West Wood; and, not far from the church, a farm road to be known as Bloody Lane.

Jackson, holding the upper part of this position, felt the first Union thrust in the darkness before dawn. At the first light, artillery began. McClellan had long delayed, for reasons which were to remain obscure. The Federal commander realized that some of Lee's divisions had been south of the Potomac. Perhaps the mere presence of Lee had deepened his instinct of caution. His discovery of the Lost Order had brought him to Sharpsburg, but for one long day had not overcome his timidity.

This morning, however, he was fully awake. At six thirty, a crushing attack by Hooker's corps caved a huge gap in Lee's line between Jackson and Hill. This drive routed the brigade of Lawton and brushed aside the heavy reinforcements of three brigades as if they were nothing. Federals were streaming along the Hagerstown Road and taking strong positions in the wood about the Dunker Church.

Jackson called up Hood's men, but they could do little more than join the stubborn retreat. Already the army was in danger of annihilation. A scramble ensued at Lee's headquarters, as the commander sought every available man in an effort to stem the tide until the troops of McLaws and Anderson could arrive from the south. They were near by in Sharpsburg, resting after an exhausting march, but Lee hurried them into the breach.

Lee was improvising a perilous concentration, pulling men from the right and center to help Jackson in his effort to repair the left. The Confederate line was now defended weakly by seven brigades along a front of a mile and a half, where McClellan might attack at any moment. But Lee had little choice. He must halt the enemy on the north, or the war might well end for him today. Nor was Jackson's plight his only concern. At some distance from the furious fighting at the Dunker Church, D. H. Hill's three thousand men were caught in such intense action that they

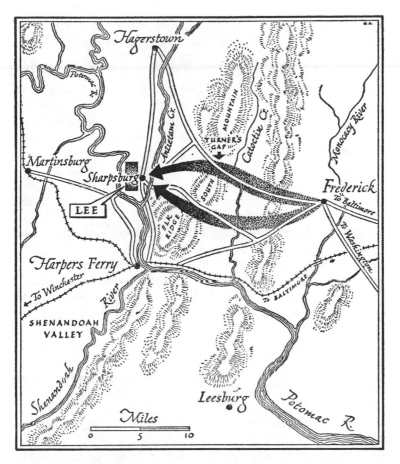

McCLELLAN LEAPS AT LEE AT SHARPSBURG

had long ago forgotten their flanks and fought for their lives. General Anderson's brigade now moved into the line.

The army was without reserves. Until A. P. Hill came marching up from the river, there was nothing to be done but fight with the outnumbered men already so heavily engaged.

After he had withstood the enemy fire for more than an hour, General Hood sent a message: "Tell General Jackson unless I get reinforcements I must be forced back, but I am going on while I can." Hood's men were running out of ammunition and giving ground. To a fellow officer who asked where Hood's division was, the Texan replied, "Dead on the field."

Not far from this scene was the big cornfield where so many men were to die. Major Rufus Dawes of the Federal army, who came in with his Wisconsin boys, wrote:

"As we appeared at the edge of the corn, a long line of men in butternut and gray rose up from the ground. Simultaneously, the hostile battle lines opened a tremendous fire upon each other. Men, I can not say fell; they were knocked out of the ranks by the dozens. But we jumped over the fence and pushed on, loading, firing, and shouting. . . . There was . . . great . . . excitement . . . reckless disregard of life . . .

"Everybody tears cartridges, loads, passes guns, or shoots. . . . The men are loading and firing with demoniacal fury and shouting and laughing hysterically, and the whole field before us is covered with rebels fleeing for life, into the woods. Great numbers of them are shot while climbing over the high post and rail fences along the turnpike. We push on over the open fields half way to the little church. The powder is bad, and the guns have become very dirty. It takes hard pounding to get the bullets down, and our firing is becoming slow. A long and steady line of rebel gray . . . comes sweeping down through the woods around the church. They raise the yell and fire. It is like a scythe running through our line. 'Now save, who can.' It is a race for life that each man runs for the cornfield . . . the headlong flight continues . . . Of 280 men who were at the cornfield and pike, 150 were killed or wounded. This was the most dreadful slaughter to which our regiment was subjected in the war."

This and near-by fighting had all but wrecked the Confederate army. More than half of two brigades—Lawton's and Hays's—had been killed or wounded at the first attack. General Lawton was wounded, as were two other commanders, John R. Jones and Starke, the latter mortally. The First Texas had lost eight successive color bearers; the Tenth Georgia lost 57 per cent of its men.

But somehow, though the most courageous officers were becoming desperate, the front began to reform. Strangely, McClellan had not flung his fresh and heavy corps into the breach won by Hooker's assault. There was, however, scarcely time to take notice of this tactical error on the fighting line. General Hood had called, "For God's sake, more troops."

In the sunken road becoming known as Bloody Lane broke out fighting that was to be celebrated as the most terrible of the war. Some of it was seen by the Federal, Thomas Livermore, of New Hampshire:

"I heard old General Richardson cry out . . . and saw that gallant old fellow advancing . . . almost alone, afoot and with his bare sword in his hand, and his face as black as a thunder cloud . . . and he roared out, 'God damn the field officers!' . . .

"We swept over the road into the cornfield . . . and down into a ravine . . . all the time being pelted with canister. . . . We opened a withering, literally withering, fire on the rebels. . . .

"On looking around me I found that we were in the old, sunken road . . . In this road there lay so many dead rebels that they formed a line which one might have walked upon as far as I could see, many . . . killed by the most horrible wounds of shot and shell, and they lay just as they had been killed apparently, amid the blood which was soaking the earth. It was on this ghastly flooring that we kneeled for the last struggle."

The Federals next swung their piecemeal attack to the Confederate center. Here Colonel John B. Gordon of Lee's front line was cut down with five wounds. Gordon had taken his place with ringing oratory: "These men are going to stay here, General, till the sun goes down or victory is ours!"

General R. H. Anderson had fallen in this area, and, like other units robbed of their officers, his brigade began to wander. The situation deteriorated to the point where General D. H. Hill dismounted and led a futile charge of some two hundred infantrymen against Federal guns. Longstreet joined a battery, held the horses and helped call the results of the fire as the cannon held off the enemy from a gap in his line.

Just as it seemed that the center must cave in, taking the entire army to ruin, there came a lull. For the second time, with a great body of fresh troops at hand, the enemy failed to press the advantage. The battle droned away to an artillery duel in the hot hour after noon.

It appeared that Jackson's wing had passed its fiery crisis. For more than six hours, Stonewall had struggled to prevent the battle being snatched from his hands. Despite the furious charge and countercharge of the morning, he had played a major role in saving the army this morning.

In the face of ruin, he could not forget his compulsion for attack. Once, during the morning, he saw the Thirty-third North Carolina of Colonel Matt Ransom charge Federal guns but come running back. He ordered Ransom to try once more. Ransom said the guns were too heavily supported. Jackson scoffed. He called for a volunteer to climb a tall tree, and Private William Hood was soon high in the limbs. Jackson looked up.

"How many troops can you see over there?"

"Oceans of them."

"Count the flags, sir!"

"One, two, three." Federal sharpshooters sent bullets winging through the tree, clipping foliage. Jackson took no notice, and the private continued to count under the fire until he had reached "Thirty-nine!"

Even for Jackson, there were too many regiments to permit a charge by Ransom, and he fell then to arguing with the North Carolinian as to why he had dared to attack so heavy a formation.

Stonewall remained with his staff in the West Wood near the Dunker Church in the fury of the first Union attack, and even as he saw his line overwhelmed by numbers, he made plans for attack. While men went mad in the cornfield and Bloody Lane, and Hood's Texans were disintegrating, and all commanders called for reinforcements, the cool, detached mind of Jackson turned to attack.

He displayed no excitement when he sent an aide to General Walker at the heaviest of the fighting: Support Hood, clear the enemy from West Wood, put men between the church and the nearest artillery battery. And as Walker thus held the line and for a moment stabilized the front, Jackson rode to find General McLaws, and told him to strike at the right of the enemy's attack. He rode swiftly for several minutes, giving the orders himself.

It was the result of that work which sent the "long and steady line of rebel gray" sweeping into the cornfield, and in an instant put General Sedgwick's big Federal division in such straits that an officer wrote: "Change of front was impossible. In less time than it takes to tell it the ground was strewn with the bodies of the dead and wounded. . . . Nearly 2,000 men were disabled in a moment."

At the climax of this, Jackson, sitting his horse near McLaws, was moved by the yelping of the Rebel Yell over the fields, and he said, "God has been very kind to us this day."

He was to see nothing so incredible as victory, however, even on his limited front. The Federals soon had heavy reinforcements and support from their fine artillery, and they turned to break Jackson's attack with great slaughter. He had once more confused the enemy and canceled other planned attacks, but Jackson had done little more than survive.

The Confederate army was fearfully torn, yet the enemy had paid even more dearly. Six hours of fighting had cost the combatants some thirteen thousand men, sixteen of them general officers.

It was Lee, in his decision to remain north of the Potomac and his further choice of the unfortunate terrain, who had set the day's price for survival. For his part, Jackson had fought with about nineteen thousand troops and with them had flung off thirty thousand. The enemy had outnumbered him in cannon, by one hundred to forty.

Officers found Jackson calm, almost serene, in the morning's action. Dr. McGuire, who sought removal of field hospitals to the safety of the south bank of the Potomac, found Stonewall apparently little concerned over the outcome of the battle. He accepted some peaches brought by McGuire, and was eating them as the medical director, expressing fear for the afternoon, reported on the casualties. Jackson pointed to the enemy. "Dr. McGuire, they have done their worst."

So far as Jackson's wing was concerned, the Federals bore out his prediction. At 2 P.M., having failed at both left and center, McClellan struck at Lee's right, where the withdrawal of men had left only the command of General D. R. Jones, with a front of a mile and a half defended by a mere two thousand men.

The Antietam wandered through this front; and there was a

stone bridge just below the position of the tiny band of General Toombs. Federals had half-heartedly rushed the bridge in the morning but had been badly defeated as they came up over an exposed route. Now, abruptly, as Jones and Toombs arrayed their survivors on the hillside, two Federal regiments ran to the crossing and were pouring over before cannon could be brought to bear on them. The enemy line fanned upward.

Lee had been given a few moments to save himself, not long enough to bring up support from other segments of the line, but enough to crowd more guns on this front. The artillerymen brought in loads of canister, and when the Federals broke into a run on the slope, a barrage fell upon them. The guns made the fighting equal for a time, but it could not last, even with the cheering news that A. P. Hill was coming up, finally. The right began to sag; Union troops stole in on the flank. One brigade after another was forced from the heights and pushed back, with heavy casualties, into the village of Sharpsburg, and fighting rolled into the dusty streets. Officers went down, among them General L. O'B. Branch. The Union troops were within a mile and a half of cutting the only Confederate line of retreat. Resistance was becoming scattered on this flank, and Lee seemed near the end of his resources.

Two hopes remained. A. P. Hill was not far away with his troops. And Jackson was attempting a flank movement against the enemy's right, seeking to circle to McClellan's rear.

General Walker described how, when enemy attacks ceased on Jackson's front, he had found Stonewall:

"Under an apple tree, sitting on his horse, with one leg thrown carelessly over the pommel of his saddle, plucking and eating the fruit. Without making any reply to my report, he asked me abruptly, 'Can you spare me a regiment and a battery?' "

Walker offered him the strong Forty-ninth North Carolina.

"Jackson said that he wished to make up, from the different commands on our left, a force of four or five thousand men, and give them to Stuart, with orders to turn the enemy's right and attack him in the rear; that I must give orders to my division to . . . attack the enemy as soon as I should hear Stuart's guns—and that our whole left wing would move to the attack at the same time. Then, replacing his foot in the stirrup, he said with great emphasis: 'We'll drive McClellan into the Potomac.' "

Years later Walker marveled at Jackson's audacity in plotting this assault, in the face of disaster, as imperturbably as if putting his cadets through maneuvers on the Lexington parade ground.

The army waited hours for Jackson. When, at three thirty, the guns had not been heard, Longstreet ordered a charge. Walker explained Jackson's plan, and Longstreet withdrew his order. Walker recalled:

"While we were discussing this subject, Jackson himself joined us with the information of Stuart's failure to turn the Federal right, for the reason that he had found it securely posted on the Potomac. Upon my expressing surprise at this statement, Jackson replied that he had also been surprised, as he supposed the Potomac much farther away. . . . He added: 'It is a great pity—we should have driven McClellan into the Potomac.' "

At that moment, on the right of the line, McClellan was very near to driving Lee against the river himself. The Confederates fell back through Sharpsburg. And then, at an instant which seemed miraculous, Hill's men came trotting through the village, going straight at the enemy. Hill rode past in his fiery red battle shirt. Those men turned back the enemy on this flank. Help had come at a moment when all seemed lost.

David Thompson, in the ranks of General Burnside as the Federals stormed the bridge and mounted the hill, saw things with a remarkable clarity as his comrades began to break:

"I remember . . . seeing an officer riding diagonally across the field, a most inviting target, instinctively bending his head down over his horse's neck, as though he were riding through a driving rain. While my eye was on him I saw, between me and him, a rolled overcoat with its straps on bound into the air and fall among the furrows. One of the enemy's grapeshot had plowed a groove in the skull of a young fellow and had cut his overcoat from his shoulders. He never stirred from his position, but lay there face downward—a dreadful spectacle. A moment after, I heard a man cursing a comrade for lying on him heavily. He was cursing a dying man. . . .

"Human nature was on the rack, and there burst forth from

it the most vehement, terrible swearing I have ever heard. . . . Whether the regiment was thrown into disorder or not, I never knew. I only remember that as we rose and started all the fire that had been held back so long was loosed. In a second the air was full of the hiss of bullets. . . . The mental strain was so great that I saw at that moment the singular effect mentioned, I think, in the life of Goethe in a similar occasion—the whole landscape for an instant turned slightly red."

As night came down, the victorious Rebel Yell announced the retreat of Burnside; and among the ten thousand of the Confederate dead and wounded, Lee settled down to wait. His general officers evidently expected him to withdraw in the night, but he stayed on the ground. With daylight it was clear that the enemy had not moved, and that McClellan had posted his big guns as if anticipating attack. Almost incredibly, the Yankees did not come forward. The grateful Confederates cooked and ate almost all day, for rations were more plentiful than they had been since before Second Manassas.

The battle of Sharpsburg was over, the bloodiest single day of the war. The horrors were not over for women of the neighborhood who looked after the wounded. One of the nurses, aghast at the sight of so much suffering, finally cried, "Oh, I hope if I faint some one will kick me into a corner and let me lie there!"

Another nurse, Mary Bedinger Mitchell, wrote:

"We would catch our breath and listen, and try not to sob, and turn back to the forlorn hospitals. . . . On our side of the river there were noise, confusion, dust; throngs of stragglers, horsemen galloping about; wagons blocking each other, and teamsters wrangling; and a continued din of shouting, swearing and rumbling, in the midst of which men were dying, fresh wounded arriving, surgeons amputating limbs and dressing wounds . . . The wounded filled every building and overflowed into the country around, into farm houses, barns, corn-cribs, cabins . . . There were six churches, and they were all full; the Odd Fellows' Hall, the Freemasons' . . . every inch of space, and yet the cry was for more room . . ."

There was a lull through the day on the battlefield, as both armies cared for the wounded and buried the dead. In one ravine, men remembered in horror, bodies were piled fifteen feet deep. McClellan could now count the grim toll of twenty-seven thousand casualties for the Maryland campaign, including the captives of Harpers Ferry. Lee found more than a third of his army on the bloody rolls today.

Lee had won his daring gamble that McClellan would not attack on the second day at Sharpsburg; but it was clear that he could not himself attack, with all those blue masses within sight and his own line dangerously near the river banks.

The lone gay spirit of the day was an unidentified North Carolinian who had been captured by the Federals. He ambled along toward a Union prison, a ragged, drawling man who afforded his captors much amusement.

"To what command do you belong?"

"To old Stonewall, more'n anybody else."

The marching prisoners passed a park of artillery, and the Tarheel stopped to admire it. He read aloud the mark on each big barrel: "U.S."

"Well, what now, Johnny Reb?" one of the Federals asked.

"I swear, Mister, you all has got most as many of these-here U.S. guns as we'uns has."

Lee announced a retreat, and at dark on September eighteenth, Longstreet's men led the army from the battlefield southward, over the Potomac into Virginia. The army passed the river all night, and near dawn General Walker approached the ford. He wrote:

"I was among the last to cross the Potomac. As I rode into the river I passed General Lee, sitting on his horse in the stream, watching the crossing of the wagons and artillery. Returning my greeting, he inquired as to what was still behind. There was nothing but the wagons containing my wounded, and a battery of artillery, all of which were near at hand, and I told him so. 'Thank God,' I heard him say as I rode on."

The invasion was over.

Lee would complain to President Davis that "desertion and straggling . . . were the main causes of . . . retiring from Maryland."

And from Washington a stricken Lincoln would soon visit McClellan, and then write him in reply to a claim that weary horses prevented his chasing Lee:

"Will you pardon me for asking what the horses of your army have done since the battle of Antietam that fatigues anything?"

But nothing was to restore Lee's lost opportunity which circumstance had destroyed, and nothing was to force McClellan into serious pursuit. With the creaking of the last wagon wheel out of the Potomac ford, early on September nineteenth, the war returned to its familiar scenes in Virginia.

19

★★★ A TIME OF LEISURE

The army was not yet safe, even on the south side of the Potomac. Lee had left Jackson to watch the ford until all the men were across. Old Jack then rode to a camp near Martinsburg. At the crossing was a rear guard commanded by General W. N. Pendleton, whose thirty big guns frowned over the river.

Pendleton kept a poor watch, and at night a small Federal party, chiefly comprised of the 118th Pennsylvania, stormed the ford. Before the artillery chief knew what had happened, the bluecoats were among his guns. Firing broke out, and Pendleton fled with his men, seeking Longstreet or any one else who could give help. The frightened officer at last came to Lee.

"All of the reserve artillery is captured," he said.

"All?"

"Yes, General. I fear all."

Lee did not lose his temper. He sent Jackson an order to rectify the situation. At daybreak, some of the troops of A. P. Hill swept the bluffs, flinging the Federals into the river, slaughtering them as they struggled over the three hundred yards of water toward the north bank. The guns were reclaimed; the Federals had taken only four in the first place. Hill's men be-

341

haved as if stung by the stalemate in Maryland, the dismal end
of the campaign, and the crowning insult of pursuit by a handful
of the enemy. The artillery barrage which launched their attack
seemed to Hill the "most tremendous" of the war.

It was but a minor brush with the enemy, but it did not improve relations in Lee's command. A Richmond newspaper declared: "Pendleton is Lee's weakness. He is like the elephant, we
have him and we don't know what on earth to do with him, and
it costs a devil of a sight to feed him."

The army was glad to camp out of the sound of guns and forget
the crossing. Old Jack settled with his command on Opequon
Creek, between Shepherdstown and Williamsport, where he could
watch near-by fords. He provided an astonishment on the first
night in this camp.

A neighboring farmer had gathered Jackson and his staff in
his home for dinner on a raw evening and had appeared smiling,
carrying a big bottle of whisky and glasses. Jackson delighted—
and confounded—his young officers by breaking in on the host.

"Do you have some white sugar?"

When that was brought, and a vigorous mixing of drinks had
begun, Jackson shouted to his staff, "Come, gentlemen, let's take
a drink."

With D. H. Hill, Kyd Douglas, Dr. McGuire and Colonel E. F.
Paxton watching, Jackson poured an oversized drink and downed
it at a gulp. He sighted Douglas, who had declined, complaining
of a headache.

"Mr. Douglas, you will find it very nice," Jackson said.

Douglas explained his headache and said he had never liked
the taste of whisky. Jackson was not content to take the only
drink of liquor his staff had seen him consume by design. He
offered Douglas a bit of a lecture.

"In that I differ with you and most men," he said. "I like the
taste of all spirituous liquors. I can sip whisky or brandy with a
spoon with the same pleasure the most delicious coffee or cordial
would give you. I am the fondest man of liquor in this army, and
if I had indulged my appetite I would have been a drunkard. But
liquors are not good for me. I question whether they are much
good to anyone. At any rate I rarely touch them."

One of Jackson's visitors at this time was Jim Lane, who had been a student at V.M.I. in Old Jack's time but who had not spoken to his old professor during the war, though he had joined Jackson's command in the Seven Days battles. Lane recalled:

"I wondered if he would recognize me. I certainly expected to receive his orders in a few terse sentences. . . . He knew me as soon as I entered his tent, though we had not met for years. He rose quickly, with a smile on his face, took my hand in both of his in the warmest manner . . . familiarly calling me Lane, whereas it had always been Mr. Lane at the Institute. . . . Then, for the first time, I began to love that reserved man."

Jackson ordered Lane to take troops to the west and tear up the tracks of the Baltimore & Ohio Railroad. Stonewall told Lane that he had recommended him for promotion, and that he would soon command Branch's old brigade of North Carolinians. "He took both of my hands in his, looked me steadily in the face, and in the words and tones of friendly warmth, which can never be forgotten, again expressed his confidence in my promotion, and bade me good-bye, with a 'God bless you, Lane!' "

The irony of this budding friendship was to become clear only on a gloomy night in the spring, when, in the wilderness near Chancellorsville, Lane and Jackson were to play roles in one of the army's great tragedies.

As Jackson rested and trained his troops, more men joined the ranks. They were to swell from twenty-four thousand to thirty-five thousand this spring. People of the area showered the General with gifts, including horses, food, furniture.

He found time for church, and once wrote Anna of hearing the Reverend Joseph Stiles preach, "a great revivalist . . . laboring in a work of grace in Ewell's division." A revival was, in fact, sweeping the army, with hundreds of conversions each week and a temporary discarding of sin. But though spectacular, it did not snuff out "Devil's Half-Acre," a nest of gambling dens within a stone's throw of Jackson's headquarters, where keno, faro and chuckaluck games were constant attractions. Jackson wrote Anna after hearing Stiles: "It is a glorious thing to be a minister of the Gospel of the Prince of Peace. There is no equal position in this world."

To an officer he once said, with deep feeling, "If our officers and men were only earnest Christians, I would not be afraid to meet the world in arms."

There was another outbreak in the army—smallpox, which took thousands out of the ranks and left Lee's rolls short for the fighting to come. Jackson escaped. He was also promoted—to lieutenant general.

The army had been operating as two corps, though this was technically outside the law. Lee was determined to fight no longer with the awkward system of divisions which had caused such confusion during the Seven Days. On October thirteenth, Jackson and Longstreet were advanced to high rank and were henceforth to command their corps as the two units of the Army of Northern Virginia.

The step upward found Jackson still engaged in his trying controversy with A. P. Hill, who had begun to press the matter after Sharpsburg. Hill was determined to clear his name. His papers passed through Jackson's hands on their way to Lee, and Old Jack added a statement to them which ended: "I found that under his successor, General Branch, my orders were much better carried out."

Lee tried to pacify Hill and end the matter, but even his tactful words were to fail. He wrote:

"Respectfully returned to Gen. A. P. Hill who will see from the remarks of General Jackson the cause of his arrest. His attention being called to what appeared to be neglect of duty by his commander, but which from an officer of his character could not be intentional and I feel will never be repeated, I see no advantage to the service in further investigating this matter nor could it without detriment be done at this time."

Hill prolonged the affair with yet another appeal to Lee: "I deny the truth of every allegation made by Major General Jackson. . . . If General Jackson had accorded me the courtesy of asking an explanation of each instance of neglect of duty as it occurred, I think that even he would have been satisfied, and the necessity avoided of keeping a black-list against me."

Hill also drew up a list of charges against Jackson and forwarded them to Lee. Jackson replied, calmly but firmly: "He had ample opportunity of knowing his neglect of duty. . . . No black-list has been kept." Jackson said that Hill's continued stirring of the matter constituted further "neglect of duty."

Lee kept the papers and said nothing, hoping that the squabble would die.

Promotion of Jackson and Longstreet, and particularly of Jackson, was of greater interest. In a recommendation of Stonewall to President Davis, Lee declared: "My opinion of the merits of General Jackson has been greatly enhanced during this expedition. He is true, honest and brave; has a single eye to the good of the service and spares no exertion to accomplish that object." Fortunately, this was not a public document. Only in later years did its publication bring puzzled comment as to whether Lee had taken Jackson's abilities lightly after the Valley campaign and the Seven Days, or was simply being politic in seeking approval of Jackson's promotion from Davis, a man who had never been able to warm to Old Jack.

After praising Jackson and Longstreet, Lee added, "Next to these two officers, I consider A. P. Hill the best commander with me. He fights his troops well and takes good care of them."

A few days after he took over the official burden of the big new corps, Jackson had a letter from Anna suggesting that she take steps to publicize his career. His reply spoke volumes.

> Don't trouble yourself about representations that are made of your husband. These things are earthly and transitory. There are real and glorious blessings, I trust, in reserve for us beyond this life. It is best for us to keep our eyes fixed upon the throne of God and the realities of a more glorious existence. . . . It is gratifying to be beloved and to have our conduct approved by our fellow-men, but this is not worthy to be compared with the glory that is in reservation for us in the presence of our glorified Redeemer.
>
> Let us endeavor to adorn the doctrine of Christ our Savior in all things, knowing that there awaits us "a far more exceeding and eternal weight of glory" . . . It appears to me that it would be better for you not to have anything written about me. Let us follow the teaching of inspiration—"Let

another man praise thee, and not thine own mouth: a stranger, and not thine own lips." I appreciate the loving interest that prompted such a desire in my precious darling.

He ended by telling Anna he could not leave his post, and that it seemed impossible for them to meet in his camp. "If I only had you with me in my evenings, it would be such a comfort!"

Again, he wrote: "And so God, my exceeding great joy, is continually showering His blessings upon me, an unworthy creature."

Old Jack demonstrated little of this humility in camp. One day Stuart, the tormentor he most enjoyed, set a new tradition for Jackson; he sent von Borcke to him with an elegant dress coat of Confederate gray made by an expensive Richmond tailor. The German found Old Jack in his weather-beaten coat:

"When . . . I produced General Stuart's present, in all its magnificence of gilt buttons and sheeny facings and gold lace I was heartily amused at the modest confusion with which the hero of many battles regarded the fine uniform . . . scarcely daring to touch it, and at the quiet way in which, at last, he folded it up carefully, and deposited it in his portmanteau, saying to me, 'Give Stuart my best thanks my dear Major—the coat is much too handsome for me, but I shall take the best care of it, and shall prize it highly as a souvenir. Now let us have some dinner.'

"But I protested energetically against this summary disposition of the matter of the coat, deeming my mission, indeed, but half executed, and remarked that Stuart would certainly ask me how the uniform fitted its owner, and that I should, therefore, take it as a personal favor if he would put it on.

"To this he readily assented with a smile, and having donned the garment, he escorted me outside the tent to the table where dinner had been served in the open air. The whole of his staff were in perfect ecstasy at their chief's brilliant appearance, and the old Negro servant, who was bearing the roast turkey from the fire to the board, stopped in mid-career with a most bewildered expression, and gazed in wonderment at his master as if he had been transfigured before him.

"Meanwhile, the rumor of the change ran like electricity through the neighboring camps, and the soldiers came running by hundreds to the spot, desirous of seeing their beloved Stonewall in his new attire; and the first wearing of a fresh robe by Louis XIV, at whose morning toilet all the world was accustomed to assemble, never created half the sensation at Versailles that was made in the woods of Virginia by the investment of Jackson in his new regulation uniform."

Stuart often visited Jackson from his luxurious quarters at The Bower, home of the Stephen Dandridge family, where he held court with Sweeny and his banjo, Mulatto Bob and his bones, a fiddle player, and assorted gay young women of the region. Once during the time of rest, Stuart and about six hundred of his troopers went on a second dash around the army of General McClellan (whose command was soon to be given to Ambrose Burnside), and when the dashing horseman returned, dragging a few prisoners and carrying information for Lee, Jackson greeted him with what he thought a paralyzing jest:

"Howdy do, General. Get off and tell us about your trip. They tell me that from the time you crossed the Potomac until you got back again you didn't sing a song or crack a joke, but that as soon as you got on Virginia soil you began to whistle 'Home, Sweet Home.' "

One night soon after, Jackson and Stuart spent an uncomfortable night together. Stuart arrived late in camp, when everyone was asleep, and lay down beside Jackson. In the cold night, Stuart pulled off Jackson's blanket. He awoke to find himself in the middle of Old Jack's cot, still with his sword and spurs on. When he greeted Jackson on the outside, he got a thin drawling reply.

"Stuart, I'm always glad to see you come. You might choose better hours sometimes, but I'm always glad to have you. But General"—Jackson stooped and rubbed his legs in mock pain— "you must not get into my bed with your boots and spurs on and ride me around like a cavalry horse all night."

Jackson had planned a visit to Winchester for some time, and in November made the twelve-mile ride to see his old friends there. Mrs. Graham, the wife of the minister, wrote to Anna: "The General's little visit to us was a perfect sunbeam. I never saw him look so fat and hearty, and he was as bright and happy as possible. He spent two evenings with us . . . I don't remember ever experiencing more intense happiness than during that visit; and when I saw our dear General in his old place at the table, I could have screamed with delight."

He paid the Grahams one more visit: "He is looking in such perfect health—far handsomer than I ever saw him—and is in such fine spirits, seemed so unreserved . . . that we did enjoy him to the full. . . . He certainly has had enough adulation to spoil him, but it seems not to affect or harm him at all. He is the same humble, dependent Christian . . . we sat and talked cosily, and the evening was concluded by bowing before the family altar again. . . . Now, was not this a charming evening, and don't you wish you had been here?"

During one evening in Winchester, Jackson dined at the home of Dr. Hugh McGuire, father of his medical director. Betty McGuire, the fourteen-year-old daughter of the house, persuaded Jackson to go into the town and pose for photographs, though he insisted upon stopping en route for a haircut. Betty led him to a photographer's gallery (it is uncertain whether it was Rontzahn's or Lupton's) and literally forced him before the camera.

The photographer settled him in a chair but, as he prepared the camera, noted that Jackson's coat was untidy.

"One of your buttons is off, General."

"Hm. Yes. And here it is." He pulled a tarnished button from a pocket. "Do you have needle and thread?"

The cameraman passed the articles to him, and Jackson sat soberly, replacing the button without troubling to remove his coat. The ineptness of his handiwork was to be noticeable in the photograph. Several poses were taken, but the one destined to endure was a full-face picture, with the hint of a smile on the tiny lips and a glittering of strong light in the eyes.

Old Jack went to one of the revival meetings in camp, accompanied by Kyd Douglas. A runner hurried ahead of them, warning troops that Stonewall was coming. Candles went out in hundreds of tents at his approach, as card players concealed their games. After the service, Jackson and Douglas walked back to headquarters under a full moon. Old Jack halted.

"Are you acquainted with the Man in the Moon?"

Douglas confessed his inability to picture that phenomenon and Jackson attempted to show him with his fingers, in vain. When they reached their tents and were retiring, a vast yell broke forth from the camp, one of the Rebel Yells often raised in the Stonewall Brigade. It swept through the army. Jackson leaned on a fence, listening. When the shouts faded, he went into his tent, speaking as if powerfully moved, "That's the sweetest music I ever heard."

The two were soon parted from such intimate relations. Douglas's comrades from his old B Company, Second Virginia, asked him to take command of a unit reduced to nineteen men. He asked Jackson's advice but was gently told to make his own decision. Douglas went back into the ranks, though Jackson agreed to hold open a place for him if he wanted to return.

Jackson had for some time expected news of importance from Anna—a baby. He was so secretive about it that none of his staff knew of the coming event and were not to be told for long afterward. At last, on November twenty-third, Anna gave birth to a daughter. Her sister, Mrs. Harriet Irwin, notified Jackson from the home in Charlotte, North Carolina, writing as if the child herself held the pen:

> My Own Dear Father—. . . I know that you are rejoiced to hear of my coming, and I hope that God has sent me to radiate your pathway through life. I am a very tiny little thing. I weigh only eight and a half pounds, and Aunt Harriet says I am the express image of my darling papa . . . and this greatly delights my mother. My aunts both say that I am a little beauty. My hair is dark and long, my eyes are blue, my nose straight just like papa's, and my complexion not at all red like most young ladies of my age, but a beautiful blending of the lily and the rose. . . .
>
> I was born on Sunday, just after the morning services at your church. . . . Your dear little wee Daughter.

Jackson replied on December fourth:

> Oh! How thankful I am to our kind Heavenly Father for having spared my precious wife and given us a little daugh-

ter! . . . Now don't exert yourself to write to me, for to know that you were taxing yourself to write would give me more pain than the letter would pleasure, so you must not do it. But you must love your *esposo* in the meantime.

I expect you are just made up now with that baby. Don't you wish your husband wouldn't claim any part of it, but let you have sole ownership? Don't you regard it as the most precious little treasure in the world? Do not spoil it, and don't let anybody tease it. Don't permit it to have a bad temper. How I would love to see the darling little thing! Give her many kisses for her father.

A day or so later: "Give the baby-daughter a shower of kisses from her father, and tell her that he loves her better than all the baby-boys in the world, and more than all the other babies in the world."

He wrote to Mrs. Irwin in gratitude, ending, "I fear I am not grateful enough for unnumbered blessings. . . . I trust God will answer the prayers offered for peace. . . . Not much comfort is to be expected until this cruel war terminates. I haven't seen my wife since last March, and, never having seen my child, you can imagine with what interest I look to North Carolina."

Now Jackson was forced to look north of the Rappahannock, where the big columns of the Federals were moving, onto Stafford Heights opposite Fredericksburg. General Burnside, abandoning earlier concentrations, seemed ready to challenge Lee's army here on the river and force his way to Richmond. His guns were placed all over the hills, dominating the town. The Confederates chose even more favorable ground, a series of heights overlooking the river bottoms which, when fortified, would be impregnable to attack.

As December wore on, assault loomed as more probable, with stirrings over the river. One afternoon, as his lines quietly watched the far fires of the enemy, Jackson lay behind a battery of artillery, wrapped in a cloak and reading a Bible. A strange chaplain passed and asked, "Of what regiment are you chaplain?" He could scarcely be brought to believe that the pious Bible student was Stonewall Jackson.

On December tenth, a day which was to be the last of peace for a time, Jackson wrote Anna: "This morning I received a charming letter from my darling little daughter, Julia [he had named her for his mother, when Anna offered the opportunity]. Do not set your affections upon her, except as a gift from God. If she absorbs too much of our hearts, God may remove her from us."

That night, music swept the cold, moist fields above the river. In the Confederate camp, men sang old songs, often returning to "Annie Laurie." On the river front a fine Federal band blared patriotic tunes, and Rebel pickets called through the dark: "Now give us some of ours, and there rolled up the strains of "Dixie," and "Bonnie Blue Flag."

Jackson was ready for the campaign, if it was to come. As one last detail, his guns were ready. He had engaged in a strange controversy over them, jealously defending them from the grasp of D. H. Hill, when it was suggested that five of Old Jack's surplus Napoleons be transferred to his brother-in-law.

Stonewall wrote to Lee in restrained anger, guarding his battle spoils: "I hope that none of the guns which belonged to the Army of The Valley, before it became part of the Army of Northern Virginia . . . will be taken from it."

He had won; and tonight, on the hills above the singing boys, the brass barrels sweated in the fog, waiting.

20

★★★ MASSACRE IN DECEMBER

The night of December 10, 1862, was bitter cold. Fogs rolled up from the river. There was half-inch ice at the river's edge.

Moonrise was at eleven forty-one, but the puny sliver it brought forth was rarely visible in the mists and cast no light. Fires died in the hill trenches on either side of the Rappahannock, and the voice of the river grew louder.

There was no longer even the fugitive laughter of early evening which had rolled from the island where men of both armies had gone to drink and gamble in a mingling of enemies.

It was hours since the shivering Confederate water-front pickets had heard the last bantering call from Yankees on the north bank, just two hundred yards over the water.

Now there was another call. The voice of a woman shrilled:

"Hellloooo . . . Johnny Reb! . . . Are . . . you . . . there?"

An answering whoop echoed.

"Yanks . . . cooooking . . . big . . . rations . . . today . . . March . . . tomorrow! . . . Yanks . . . moving . . . Do you . . . hear . . . meeeeee?"

The pickets listened in silence, but there was only the surging of tidal water, and the rising wind cuffing the alders, rattling the reeds like bones. A picket slipped back to company headquarters. Before daylight it was a story they told in the Rebel trenches, and men made their profane speculations about the daring woman on the north bank and the coming of the Union army. The tale passed along the breastworks on the crescent of hills where Lee's army waited.

By two o'clock, at any rate, it was certain that fighting was near. Pickets in the Fredericksburg streets glimpsed dim figures opposite and heard crashing timbers and the ring of tools. Word went up from the Mississippi brigade holding the town: The Yanks were putting out pontoon bridges. General McLaws was shaken from sleep at four thirty, and sent out a messenger. Lee left his bed and rode toward the lines.

At four forty-five two cannon broke the stillness—the signal that the Yankees were coming. Riflemen were ready in Fredericksburg but withheld their fire. There were still civilians to be evacuated from the town. Major Robert Stiles saw them:

"I never saw a more pitiful procession than they made trudging through the deep snow as the hour drew near. I saw little children tugging along with their doll babies, holding their feet up carefully above the snow, and women so old and feeble that they could carry nothing and could barely hobble themselves. There were women carrying a baby in one arm and its bottle, clothes and covering in the other. Some had a Bible and a toothbrush in one hand, a picked chicken and a bag of flour in the other. Most of them had to cross a creek swollen with winter rains. . . . We took the battery horses down and ferried them over. . . . Where they were going we could not tell."

General Burnside served notice that he would bombard the town despite the presence of some civilians who remained, because it was occupied by soldiers. At midmorning the Federal guns burst out. The shells tore the town to pieces, street by street. It was a miracle that even small bodies of troops lived through the shelling. Three Union bridges were now under way, but progress was slow. Confederate snipers harried the workmen.

Lee's anger flashed at the shelling of the town. "These people delight to destroy the weak and those who can make no defense. It just suits them!"

He got a message to match his mood from General William Barksdale, commanding the Mississippi boys in the town: "Tell General Lee that if he wants a bridge of dead Yankees, I can furnish him with one." Barksdale thought he might try to fight some of the town's raging fires with his troops and asked permission of General Longstreet, who replied, "You have enough to do to watch the Yankees."

The Federals at last got over the stream by flinging regiments across in boats and losing many men, but opening a rapidly expanding bridgehead on the south bank of the river.

The fog lifted, but a screening woodland protected the advanced Federal troops from Lee's guns. The Yankees stormed into Fredericksburg, and the first infantrymen went mad. Soldiers cavorted in women's underwear from the abandoned houses. They dragged pianos into the streets and watered horses in them. One man stole thousands of canceled checks from an express office, under the impression he had a fortune in his arms. Francis Edwin Pierce, in the ranks of the invaders, was one who watched the goings on:

"Boys came into our place loaded with silver pitchers, silver spoons, silver lamps and castors . . . Great three story brick houses magnificently furnished were broken into . . . Splendid alabaster vases and pieces of statuary were thrown at 6 and 700 dollar mirrors. Closets of the very finest china . . . smashed onto the floor and stamped to pieces. Finest cut glass ware goblets were hurled at nice plate glass windows, beautifully embroidered curtains torn down, rosewood pianos piled in the street and burned, or soldiers would get on top of them and dance and kick the keyboard and internal machinery all to pieces . . . wine cellars broken into and the soldiers drinking all they could and then opening the faucets and let the rest run out—boys go to a barrel of flour and take a pailful and use enough to make a batch of pancakes and then pour the rest in the street—everything turned upside down. The soldiers seemed to delight in destroying everything. Libraries worth thousands . . . thrown on the floor and in the streets. . . . It was so throughout the city, and from its appearance very many wealthy families must have inhabited it."

The Confederates on their grim heights were not simply waiting. Lee could not believe that Burnside was to commit the blunder of throwing his columns against the unassailable hills. If there was a flaw in Lee's defensive position, it was that it was too good, so nearly impregnable that no sane opponent would dare attack. It was incredible that Burnside would come into the trap. Down from the semicircle of hills looked every piece of ordnance Longstreet's corps could muster—over carefully laid zones of fire. The ranges ran from fifteen hundred to three thousand yards.

Lee would wait and delay his concentration by leaving Jackson's corps scattered where it could watch the enemy. If Burnside showed his hand, Lee could rapidly bring together his army. Breastworks rose. Privates on Marye's Hill, the greatest of the heights, were uncomfortable, and over the protests of engineers they deepened rifle pits. Longstreet approved: "If you save the finger of one man's hand, that does some good."

On December twelfth, in a foggy noon lit by a half-hidden sun, Lee learned that he was to be attacked on the ground he had chosen. Lee and Jackson were staring down on the enemy when von Borcke, much excited, arrived from Stuart's headquarters. The cavalry had found the Federals massing on the right, the German said; they had gone to within a stone's throw of the enemy line. Lee asked von Borcke to lead them to that place.

The little cavalcade halted at a barn, crept through a ditch to a hillside, until Lee and Jackson, standing in the open, could sweep the Union lines with their glasses. The cautious von Borcke watched from the safety of the ditch. The enemy was just four hundred yards away, and the signs of coming assault were unmistakable. Two pontoon bridges shuddered under columns of men and wagons and guns. Infantrymen already dug rifle pits in an endless line at the riverside. In one small area, Lee counted thirty-two guns in position. The commander turned away with content on his face, and throughout the day he was in high humor and seemed always on the point of smiling. He worked to receive Burnside. "I shall try to do them all the damage in our power when they move forward," he said.

With all doubt removed, he wasted no time in concentrating the army. Jackson was ordered to bring in D. H. Hill's division from Port Royal, down-river, and Taliaferro's men from the rear at Guiney's Station. Jackson filled in the right front, below Longstreet, a front of twenty-six hundred yards for his thirty thousand troops. The first blow, it seemed obvious, would be struck against Jackson.

Most of Old Jack's front was steep and wooded, easy to defend. There was one flaw, which General Lane noted and reported to A. P. Hill, who did not correct it. A bit of marshy woodland, almost triangular in shape, left a gap of some six hundred yards between the brigades of Lane and Archer.

For once Jackson had strength to spare. Almost three quarters of his men were placed in reserve, or in a third line near the crest of the hills. He had about 125 cannon, but could find places for only 47, so broken was the ground. Hardly a soldier was to be seen on his front; officers hid them in the woods, and through the day of prodigious preparations by the enemy, the hungry troops watched and ate. Far below them the broad plain was alive with enemy regiments. An artillery duel did nothing to drive them off. Night fell with increasing coldness; Lee allowed no fires, and the men suffered. Thousands of Jackson's troops were still without shoes despite all efforts to clothe them. At least one soldier died of exposure in the freezing mists.

Morning came with Lee's line seventy-eight thousand strong, scarcely a man in exposed position. Burnside was on the point of launching his splendid army of 125,000. In snatches of bugle calls and drum rolls the army settled. A sharp wind gnawed at the hillsides; there was a brief time for breakfast. The bands played a few lively airs. It was almost as if this were a fanfare for Jackson.

Stonewall, accompanied by his aide, J. P. Smith, galloped to Lee's headquarters near the Telegraph Road. He was dazzling. Without warning or explanation he had decked himself in his gaudy finery. He wore the coat Stuart had given him; a fancy blue cap with broad gold braid, from his wife; gleaming boots from an admirer in the Valley; new saber and spurs from a cavalry officer. He did not ride Sorrel today. Jim, after long argument, had persuaded him to ride a larger, handsomer horse.

Jackson rode down cheering lines of men, but there were undertones: "Great God! Old Jack's drawed his bounty money and bought clothes."

"He don't look right—like some damned lieutenant. I'm afraid he'll not get down to work."

Longstreet and other officers about Lee baited Jackson, laughing over the glittering garments, and someone asked him why the finery was on display. "It's some of the doing of my friend, Stuart, I believe," Jackson said. Stuart and the others began teasing him in earnest, but developing battle diverted them.

Lee asked the opinion of the general officers on the day's plan. Jackson spoke instantly. Attack, he said. If men were launched down the slopes before fog lifted from the plain, the Federal guns could not reach them. The enemy could be flung into the river. Stuart agreed, and others nodded. Lee heard them in quiet, but said in a tone that brooked no questions: No. We will stand here. If the enemy is broken, there will be time enough for attack.

Jackson remained silent.

Longstreet was not content to spare Jackson further badinage. He pointed over the plain where the Federals moved without end in their grand divisions. Some men, remembering, were to couch Longstreet's words more gracefully, but J. P. Smith, who sat beside Jackson, recalled them as:

"Ain't you frightened, General?"

Jackson's face was unsmiling as he replied to Old Pete.

"Perhaps I'll frighten them after a while."

Jackson turned to go, but Longstreet called after him. "Jackson, what are you going to do with all those people over there?"

"Sir, we will give them the bayonet."

He went down the lines with Smith, drawing fire from Federal sharpshooters. Below them enemy skirmishers moved, the first of the long blue files. The Union boys all but halted as a strange chorus came from the front lines of the Confederates:

"Haaaaaa! Bring on them good breeches, Yanks! You might's well hand over the coats and shoes now as later!"

Jackson lost men from his staff as the day's work began. Kyd

Douglas, who had returned for temporary duty, was ill with a fever and was sent from the field by a doctor. Jackson passed and gave him a solemn handshake as he went rearward. Soon after, Sandie Pendleton had a close call; a bullet smashed a knife he carried in a pocket and bruised him painfully. Old Jack himself came under fire. He treated the experience as casually as ever.

He rode far to the front with only Smith at his side; a sharpshooter fired a bullet between their heads, and Jackson turned to Smith.

"Mr. Smith, hadn't you better go to the rear? They may shoot you."

The Federals were now coming in earnest. Jackson estimated their strength in his front at fifty-five thousand. And when, at ten thirty, Lee ordered the guns on the far left to fire a few test rounds, the Yankees jumped forward at Jackson's line. The rush was soon halted by a brazen young artilleryman, John Pelham, who wheeled two guns into the open and tore at the infantry in the field. He stayed there, moving his guns about like charmed pieces, daring the fire of sixteen enemy cannon. He finally retired at Stuart's third peremptory order. The enemy then clashed with A. P. Hill's troops.

Jackson watched from the hilltop, with the anxious von Borcke near by. The German fretted about the proximity of the Federals, so near and yet unchallenged.

"Major, my men have sometimes failed to take a position, but to defend one, never!"—a thought Jackson was to recall before many months had passed. He continued, "I am glad the Yankees are coming!"

Of the scene now unfolding, von Borcke recalled:

"Suddenly it seemed as though a tremendous hurricane had burst upon us . . . a howling tempest of shot and shell hurled . . . by not fewer than 300 pieces of artillery. Hundreds of missiles . . . crashed through the woods, breaking down trees and scattering branches and splinters. . . .

"And now the thick veil of mist that had concealed the plain rolled away, like the drawing up of a drop scene at the opera, and revealed to us the countless regiments of the Federal army. At this moment I was sent . . . to General Jackson with the mes-

sage that the Yankees were about to commence their advance. I
found old Stonewall standing at ease on his hill, unmoved in the
midst of terrible fire, narrowly observing . . . through his field
glass.

"The atmosphere was now perfectly clear, and from this eminence . . . afforded . . . a military panorama the grandeur of
which I had never seen equaled. On they came, in beautiful order,
as if on parade, a moving forest of steel . . . waving their hundreds of regimental flags . . . while their artillery beyond the
river continued the cannonade."

In the Union ranks things had a different look. A Cincinnati
newspaper correspondent wrote: "Our batteries . . . opened
. . . I saw with horror that at least half the shells were bursting
behind our own men, and that they were certainly killing more of
them than the enemy."

This attack came within eight hundred yards of A. P. Hill's
lines before the Confederate officers allowed their gunners to
fire. Then cannon shattered it and, with two volleys, drove the
Union troops out of range.

Now the Federals struck the left side of the line, against Marye's
Heights, where there waited crowded regiments in a sunken road,
a perfect entrenchment, with the guns and thousands of other
muskets on the hill behind. William Owen of the Washington
Artillery of New Orleans watched the enemy come:

"At last the Federal line appeared above the ridge in front of
us and advanced. It seemed like some huge serpent about to . . .
crush us in its folds. The lines advanced at the double-quick, and
the alignments were beautifully kept. The board fences enclosing
the gardens fell like walls of paper. Instantly the edge of Marye's
Hill was fringed with flame. . . . Nearer and nearer the enemy's
line advanced, came within range of canister and we gave it to
them. Now the Federals were near enough to the infantry in the
sunken road . . . for the smoke was beginning to cover the
field. . . . Great gaps appeared; we gave them canister again
and again; a few left the ranks—more followed . . . running
in great disorder toward the town . . . the field before us was
dotted with patches of blue.

"Another division now advanced in splendid style . . . and

in a little more than fifteen minutes . . . was forced back. Of
the 5,000 men led into action, 2,000 fell in the charge. . . . The
brave fellows came within five and twenty paces of the stone wall
but encountered such a fire of shot, canister and musketry as no
command was ever known to live through. . . . Another division now came up and again assailed the hill . . . but nothing
could live before the storm of lead that was hurled at them from
this distance. They wavered, broke and rushed headlong from
the field."

Lee, watching this, revealed a new side of his nature. He said
to Longstreet:

"It is well that war is so terrible—we should grow too fond
of it!"

Now the watchers on the hills saw the victorious finish of a
trying hour for Jackson: The enemy had swept through the un-
guarded bog on his front, straight into the woods, and soon had
been tearing at his center. He had calmly sent up a reserve division under General Early; but the fighting had raged in the
timber for a long and deadly interim before the bluecoats began
to drop back; and an impetuous charge followed them into the
open.

That was the only piercing of the Confederate line, and the only
sally into the open by Lee's troops. For most of the day it was
only dreadful artillery and musket practice. Once Lee became
anxious for Longstreet's lines.

"General," he said, "they are massing very heavily and will
break your lines, I'm afraid."

Longstreet was still in his expansive, confident mood of the
early morning. "If you put every man on the other side of the
Potomac in the field to approach me over the same line, and give
me plenty of ammunition, I will kill them all before they reach
my line. Look to your right; you are in some danger there, but
not on my line."

Lee was in danger nowhere. The enemy halted attacks on
Jackson's lines in the early afternoon and made but two more
drives against Longstreet, which served only to pile the bodies
deeper before the Sunken Road. It was almost dark when the
senseless frontal assaults came to an end.

With the disappearance of the enemy skirmishers, Jackson tried to launch a counterattack he had planned for hours but had not discussed with Lee. After a few moments of confusion, he got batteries into the open and had some of his brigades trailing out of their trenches. But an overpowering enemy fire lit the night, sweeping the field his men would be forced to cross, and he reluctantly canceled plans for the attack.

He had not given up without thorough preparation. He had called Dr. McGuire to him and put him through one of his painful military catechisms, seeking to pass an important order without divulging another of his secrets.

"How much bandage do you have, McGuire?"

"I can't be sure, but I have enough for another battle."

Jackson frowned.

"Why do you want to know how much we have?"

Sighing reluctantly, Jackson said, "I want to tie a yard of bandage around the arm of every man, so that they will know each other in the night attack."

McGuire said he had no such supply of bandage and suggested that the men be asked to rip their shirts and tie rags on their arms. By the time Jackson's officers had the orders—and discovered that no more than half the men had shirts—the attack had been called off.

On the enemy side of the field, General Burnside rode with his hat pulled far down on his face: "That night I went all over the field on our right; in fact, I was with the officers and men until nearly daylight. I found the feeling to be rather against an attack the next morning."

J. L. Chamberlain, who helped with the Federal wounded on this bitter night—which was lit by the flame of the aurora borealis—saw far more than his commander:

"Out of that silence from the battle's crash . . . rose new sounds more appalling still—rose or fell, you knew not which, or whether from the earth or air: a strange ventriloquism . . . a smothered moan . . . a wail . . . weird, unearthly, terrible to hear and bear, yet startling with its nearness.

"The writhing concord was broken by cries for help, pierced

by shrieks of paroxysm. Some begged for a drop of water. Some called on God for pity, and some on friendly hands to finish what the enemy had so horribly begun. Some with delirious, dreamy voices murmured loved names. . . . Some gathered their last strength to fire a musket so as to call attention to them. . . . And underneath, all the time, came that deep bass note from closed lips too hopeless or too heroic to articulate their agony. . . ."

Jackson had visitors in the evening, and though he was busy with preparations for what was expected to be a second day of slaughter, he completely relaxed at supper.

Alec Boteler had come up from Richmond, bringing, among other treasures, a pail of fresh oysters, which Jim transformed into a feast. Boteler had also brought with him an artist from Richmond, one Volck (officers did not note whether it was Frederick Volck, the sculptor, or his brother Adalbert, a caricaturist). At any rate, Jackson was persuaded to sit for sketches after dinner. Admiring staff officers watched for several minutes as Old Jack posed on a campstool, and they roared with laughter when he fell asleep. Only the outburst roused the General. It was to be five months, almost to the day, before Frederick Volck would make a far different rendering of Jackson's face.

Lee had not forgotten that Jackson was human, and after dark he sent him an urgent reminder to bring up plentiful ammunition for tomorrow. Just as Smith was lying down to sleep, an orderly called him to Jackson's tent, where Old Jack wordlessly passed him an order from Lee, directing him to send wagons to Guiney's Station for bullets and shells. There was a postscript:

"I need not remind you to have the ammunition of your men and batteries replenished tonight, everything ready for daylight tomorrow. I am truly grateful to the Giver of all victory for having blessed us thus far in our terrible struggle. I pray He may continue it."

Smith went doggedly about his task of finding Jackson's officers: "The night was dark and the troops were sleeping on the ground. Two recollections I have distinctly: One is that of finding General Early by the striking of matches by several couriers, who were trying to make a fire for the general, and his own profane abuse of his staff, who were not with him."

As Smith rode about, Jackson dropped on his camp cot, fully clad even to spurs and sword. Boteler lay at his side. After an hour or so Jackson rose, struck a light and set up a box to shade Boteler's eyes, under the erroneous impression that his silent companion was asleep. Old Jack was scratching out an order when he had a message from Dr. McGuire. General Maxcy Gregg, wounded during the day, was on the point of death and wanted to see Jackson.

The two generals had been under strained relations since their argument on the road to Harpers Ferry, in the days before Sharpsburg. Now, with Gregg near his end, their troubles were forgotten. Smith recalled: "It was nearly daybreak when I returned to headquarters and wrapped myself again in my blankets. But I was not yet asleep when an orderly at my tent door said, 'Captain, the general wants you.' Struggling into my boots once more, I found the general making his toilet, with a tin basin of water and a rough towel."

Jackson asked Smith to go with him to visit Gregg, who was in a farmhouse near by.

Gregg had a spinal injury and was in much pain. He was conscious and alert, however, and had dictated a note to the governor back home in South Carolina: "I am severely wounded, but the troops under my command have acted as they always have done, and I hope we have gained a glorious victory. If I am to die now, I give my life cheerfully for the independence of South Carolina, and I trust you will live to see our cause triumph completely."

Smith could recall the exchange between Gregg and Sandie Pendleton on the battlefield yesterday, when Pendleton had sought to send the general to the rear, saying that the enemy was shooting at him. Gregg had answered, "Yes, sir, thank you. They have been doing that all day."

Gregg welcomed Jackson. Smith recorded part of it:

"There was an affecting interview . . . Gregg . . . wished to express regret for . . . some paper he feared was offensive to General Jackson. Jackson did not know to what Gregg referred, and soon interrupted the sufferer to say that it had given him no offense whatsoever, and then [took] Gregg's hand in his."

Jackson's voice was husky with emotion. "The doctors tell me that you have not long to live. Let me ask you to dismiss this matter from your mind and turn your thoughts to God and to the world to which you go."

Gregg's eyes were tear-filled, Smith saw. "I thank you," the South Carolinian said. "I thank you very much."

Jackson rode to the front and on the way met Dr. McGuire. These two fell to discussing the overwhelming superiority of the enemy regiments. "What shall we do, General," McGuire asked, "with such vast numbers against us?"

Jackson's mood changed radically from his gentle pity of the bedside he had left so recently. "Kill them," he said. "Kill them all, sir! Kill every man!"

Lee and Jackson watched the fog lift from the Rappahannock in the morning. From the bluff that was to be known as Jackson's Hill, they saw once more the endless lines of the Union army, in battle formations. There was no sign that the enemy would attack. The armies faced each other across the acres of wounded and dead.

General D. H. Hill stood near Lee and Jackson, talking with one of his officers, Colonel Bryan Grimes of North Carolina. Hill came with the message that the enemy had gone from his front.

"Who says they're gone?" Jackson asked.

"Colonel Grimes."

Jackson turned to the colonel. "How do you know?"

"I've been down as far as their picket lines of yesterday, and I saw nothing of them."

"Move your skirmish line as far as you can and see where they are," Jackson said.

Lee and Jackson sat silently in the rain, waiting, gazing at the enemy which would no longer attack. Grimes noted bitter disappointment on the faces of the commanders.

The Federals had asked a truce in the midafternoon. Jackson received the courier and began to write a note; he tired of it and sent Smith into the open to confer with the enemy officers. Smith met men who were more or less familiar. One of them was John Junkin, a brother of Jackson's first wife.

Jackson had been firm in his orders to Smith: "If you are asked who is in command of your right, do not tell them I am, and be guarded in your remarks."

His caution went for naught, for Junkin asked to be remembered to Jackson and sent a message from Old Jack's former father-in-law. Smith said, "I will do so with pleasure when I meet General Jackson." Junkin grinned. "It's not worth while for you to try to deceive us," he said. "We know that Jackson is in front of us."

The truce went on for several hours, with men of the two armies joining on the field to remove the dead and wounded. The slaughter of the day before became clearer now. The Union had lost almost thirteen thousand troops; the Confederacy, just over five thousand. Of the losses of Lee, Jackson had suffered the vast majority—thirty-five hundred.

Even when darkness came, the Confederates could not believe that the attacks were over. A violent storm broke in the night, however, and the armies almost forgot each other. By the next morning, Lee and Jackson learned that the enemy had retreated over the river under cover of the rainstorm. Burnside's offensive was over.

Captain Blackford of Stuart's staff would not forget this morning, or his visit to ruined Fredericksburg in the foggy dawn. He and his brother, Eugene, were the first Confederates to reenter the town:

"Eugene and myself rode on into the dear old town—the town where both of us were born. In the suburbs we met our brother Charles, a captain in the 2nd Virginia Cavalry, who had been sent on the same errand.

"Our old home had been used as a hospital. The room in

which we were born was half inch deep in clotted blood still
wet, and the walls were spattered with it, and all around were
scattered arms and legs. The place smelt like a butcher's
shambles."

The news of Fredericksburg stunned the North but brought
no wild rejoicing in the South, for it seemed to promise only
a long, bloody conflict with little hope of final victory. The
Union army, however, had reeled back and was licking its
wounds on Stafford Heights.

Lee sent Jackson downstream to block a possible crossing by
Burnside; but when it became clear that the enemy would not
soon move, the army went into winter quarters.

In his last look at the abandoned enemy positions about
Fredericksburg, Old Jack said ruefully, "I did not think that a
little red earth would have frightened them. I am sorry I fortified."

There was praise for Stonewall in Lee's orders, though nc
more than for Longstreet, whose men, after all, had borne most
of the combat burden (and yet had incurred but a fraction of
Jackson's casualties). In speaking of his corps commanders,
Lee wrote:

"To Generals Longstreet and Jackson great praise is due for
the disposition and management of their respective corps. Their
quick perception enabled them to discover the projected assaults upon their positions, and their ready skill to devise the
best means to resist them. Besides their services in the field—
which every battle of the campaign from Richmond to Fredericksburg has served to illustrate—I am also indebted to them
for valuable counsel, both as regards the general operations of
the army and the execution of the particular measures adopted."

It was something of a victory message, with a generous commander able to overlook certain minor shortcomings, such as
the failure to seal the gap in Jackson's front which had cost
him so dearly in wounded. Nowhere in Lee's reports was blame
for this oversight fixed.

General James Lane, from Jackson's V.M.I. days, had made
his first battlefield appearance as a general officer, and had lost

five hundred of his North Carolinians, for it was on his right that the Yankees had poured through. But Lane got only praise for his front-line fighting.

That was not the end of the story of the gap in the front. Jackson, when he at last made his report, was to accept no part of the blame but to put it squarely upon the commander of his front lines, A. P. Hill. Jackson wrote of the enemy attack: "They continued . . . still to press forward and before General A. P. Hill closed the interval which he had left between Archer and Lane, it was penetrated, and the enemy, pressing forward in overwhelming numbers through that interval, turned Lane's right and Archer's left."

It was more fuel for the Hill-Jackson controversy, whose bitterness was to end only with death.

Jackson left the Fredericksburg battlefield on the cold, windy morning of December sixteenth, following Stuart and his cavalrymen as they hurried to dispute the crossing of the Federals, a crossing found to be based on false reports. At the moment of this discovery, the long lines of Jackson's corps wound along a forest roadway having deep pine growth on either side. The country was unsuitable for a camp, and the regiments must march to a more open area. Jackson tried to avoid the troops by finding some parallel way of passing, for he knew they would raise their yells of greeting at sight of him. He was foiled. There was nothing to do but ride through the troops.

He went for some miles among the ragged men, so near to them that the privates brushed against Sorrel in the passage. A burst of cheering followed him for an hour down the long miles of his column, and his staff officers, attempting to follow, drew the derisive hoots of the men in ranks. When he came to an open grove, Jackson dismounted and told his staff to make camp at this spot. His young officers argued. There was a fine home near by, Moss Neck, the residence of Richard Corbin. Jackson refused. The woods were the proper camp. He settled down.

He wrote to Anna before darkness.

Yesterday, I regret to say, I did not send you a letter. I was on the front from before dawn until after sunset. The enemy, through God's blessing, was repulsed at all points on Saturday, and I trust that our Heavenly Father will continue to bless us. We have renewed reason for gratitude to Him for my preservation during the last engagement. . . .

I was made very happy at hearing through my baby daughter's last letter that she had entirely recovered, and that she 'no longer saw the doctor's gray whiskers'. I was much gratified to learn that she was beginning to notice and smile when caressed. I tell you, I would love to caress her and see her smile. Kiss the little darling for her father.

His officers called Old Jack's attention to a leaping fire they had built in the bole of a hollow poplar. The staff ate under the tree and soon followed Jackson to sleep. Within a few minutes —at ten o'clock—a thunderous crash broke up the camp. The hollow tree had fallen. Jackson's officers were awake, leaping to beat out the scattered sparks and embers from the burning tree. Once more they argued that Jackson should move them into the Corbin home. He refused, but sent a captain for food; the officer soon returned with a basket of cold biscuit and part of a ham. There was a late feast, and Old Jack turned to sleep again, to the disgust of the staff.

Even loyal Captain Smith remembered his ire at Jackson's request for food: "I regret now to say that it was with extreme pleasure that I told him I had none."

The staff had its way, however, for Jackson sat up, complaining of a severe earache, and officers were hurried to Moss Neck to prepare the Corbin family for the coming of the General. Captain Hugh McGuire yelled through a keyhole to a frightened woman in the house, explaining. The house was opened, lights moved through the big halls, and Jackson was soon comfortable in bed. Captain Smith slept on a rug before the fireplace in the General's room. Old Jack had begun the hibernation of his last winter.

Book Three:

☆☆☆ *It's all right. I always wanted to die on Sunday.*

—JACKSON

Prologue:

★★★ TAKE HEART, MR. LINCOLN

In the bleak winter, with the country sickened at the butchery of Fredericksburg and the Union passing through its darkest hours, President Lincoln groped for a new commander. He liked the looks of two sturdy veterans who had fought through the war—D. N. Couch and J. F. Reynolds, both major generals. There was agreement from Edwin Stanton, his Secretary of War, but Chase of the Treasury shook his head; another of those cold, secret men whose ambitions were entwined with the schemes of the Radical Republicans. Joe Hooker, said Chase. Hooker's the man. The President accepted as if bowing to fate, for he knew well enough it was none too easy to find a good general who would not also have a strong resemblance to a Presidential candidate.

But Mr. Lincoln was not docile in this moment. He spoke his mind to his new general, and in a remarkable letter gave him to understand that the nation was not yet lost, and that an army commander bore a certain burden and had a certain place in life:

371

Executive Mansion
Washington, D.C.
Jan. 26, 1863

Major General Hooker:

General:

I have placed you at the head of the Army of the Potomac. Of course I have done this upon what appear to me to be sufficient reasons, and yet I think it best for you to know that there are some things in regard to which I am not quite satisfied with you.

I believe you to be a brave and skillful soldier, which, of course, I like. I also believe you do not mix politics with your profession, in which you are right. You have confidence in yourself, which is a valuable, if not indispensable, quality.

You are ambitious, which within reasonable bounds, does good rather than harm; but I think that during General Burnside's command of the army you have taken counsel of your ambition, and thwarted him as much as you could, in which you did a great wrong to the country and to a most meritorious brother officer.

I have heard, in such a way as to believe it, of your recently saying that both the army and the government needed a dictator. Of course, it was not for this, but in spite of it, that I have given you the command. Only those generals who gain successes can set up dictators.

What I ask of you now is military success, and I will risk the dictatorship. The government will support you to the utmost of its ability, which is neither more nor less than it has done or will do for all commanders.

I much fear that the spirit which you have aided to infuse into the army, of criticizing their commander and withholding confidence from him, will now turn upon you. I shall assist you as far as I can to put it down. Neither you nor Napoleon, if he were alive today, could get any good out of an army while such a spirit prevails in it. And now beware of rashness. Beware of rashness, but with energy and sleepless vigilance go forward and give us victories.

Yours very truly,
A. Lincoln

General Hooker colored, glowing with a charming hue of complexion that was the envy of many women and, laughing, tossed the letter to officer friends.

"He talks to me like a father," the handsomest man in the army said expansively. "I shall not answer this letter until I have won him a great victory."

And Hooker, huge, bronze-haired, master of the majestic gesture, turned upon his army. It drilled, and sweated, and suffered the mud of its camps—and it grew. Desertions slowed and halted, and none too soon, for the Army of the Potomac had a staggering figure on its rolls: eighty-five thousand men gone, vanished, most of them deserters. Hooker forbade the visits of women (though his headquarters were still notorious, a place virtuous women were warned to shun); he had his guards ferret out civilian clothing and burn it, and he brought order to the system of leaves for his men. Soon there was better food and more plentiful uniforms, and men were ordered to the tub —weekly, or there were punishments. Discipline began to return and, with it, hope and confidence.

Hooker could not contain himself, as his rolls grew to more than 130,000:

"This is the greatest army ever assembled on the planet."

"May God have mercy on General Lee—for I will have none!"

His staff took their cues from him. Staggering orders were drawn up—half a million rations, to be ready for shipment to Richmond by boat. Secret Service was to prepare detailed maps of the Richmond defenses.

Washington was advised to be ready for the day when he would overwhelm the Army of Northern Virginia and fall upon the Confederate capital.

He would need, as a starter: 10,000 shovels, 5,000 picks, 5,000 axes, 30,000 sandbags. These could be sent care of Major General Hooker, Richmond, Virginia.

As he worked, and the tons of supplies piled up, and his railroad groaned under its burdens, and his herd of mules all but outnumbered the Confederate armies, Hooker had electrifying word from Washington: The President was coming. A visit of inspection, complete with an official party—the President and Mrs. Lincoln, their son Tad, Attorney General Bates; Dr. A. G. Henry, the President's old friend from Washington Territory; and Noah Brooks, the California newspaper reporter.

Headquarters company began to clean house in a fury, dispossessing many a charming visitor—and the army made ready.

It was April fourth, a strange, dark, cold day, when the party left Washington. The President had been late, but even that did not ruffle the determined good humor of Mrs. Lincoln, who had proposed the trip as a device to give her husband a respite from the grinding anxieties of his office.

As she waited she laughed with Brooks, who was the President's favorite newspaperman.

"He's lounging around that War Office, is what he's doing. Poking about trying to find out some news before he ought."

She was correct. Lincoln liked to walk to the telegraph office at all hours and alone, though he now carried a cane to defend himself, since his wife had discovered there had been an attempt on his life. It was in the cipher room, where he looked over the shoulders of the clerks to get news from his armies, that he had written the Emancipation Proclamation. Today, at any rate, the President was late at the War Office, and his wife waited for half an hour, chatting as Brooks studied her.

This, he thought, as she rustled about the room, might be one of those four-thousand-dollar French gowns that had caused such a scandal lately. He thought of the vicious talk swirling about her head: how she was bankrupting her husband, and perhaps the country, too, to decorate the White House and her own plump figure; about her Confederate cousins and her alleged Southern sympathies. Brooks could not believe she sided with the enemy, seeing the fierce integrity of spirit on the fleshy face in which the features were pinched together a bit too closely for beauty. A Kentucky belle, aging.

It was only lately that Brooks had rescued her from one of her soothsayers, this time the seer Colchester, who had told fortunes in a darkened room, astonishing her with the sounds of twanging banjos, throbbing drums, clashing bells. But Mary Lincoln, though Brooks had exposed this fraud by yanking away a table cover, could not be shaken in her love of the occult, and yet gave her time to spiritualists. Perhaps the thought of this voyage had come from one of her mystics. In any event, it would benefit the President.

"He's so like a child, Noah," Mrs. Lincoln said. "I sometimes wonder if he understands even that he is the President. I cannot teach him—he will see them all, mere servants, washerwomen—anyone. He talks with anyone who will come, the wounded, office-hunters, women with dead or wounded boys; and the more ragged they are, the longer will he sit and hear them."

The President came at last, chuckling over a joke of the afternoon, which he stopped to tell them. Some woman had upbraided one of his staff for having told her the President was ugly—when he was, as she could see, simply beautiful. This, Lincoln said, only after he had granted the favor she asked.

Brooks recalled what some Congressman had said: "He may not be the handsomest man in the world, but we did not nominate him for ballroom purposes." Now, Brooks thought, as Lincoln passed through the room, shambling and loose-jointed, almost flapping, it is the lamentable clothing, as much as anything else, that gives him the look of a rustic clown, making the arms hang so long and the feet so enormous. The sharp-eyed could see the agility and strange free grace even in the gaunt limbs, and the limitless dignity in the face, which most thought dull and altogether ugly. As ever, he wore one of those old-style black suits which managed to look as if it were one of a dozen bought at once, already broken in as to wrinkles and all else. Like a rural undertaker.

Beneath the short beard hung the perennial black tie, a careless knot on the collar. From the collar rose the long, striking yellow neck, heavily muscled, rolling as he spoke, nodding the head with its mass of wild hair that was like a poorly chosen wig, stiff, bristling, defiant. The big nose wrinkled like a hound's as he laughed, and in a droll way he pulled at one of the broad and absurdly projecting ears. Brooks was aware that this figure —or its caricature—was now the target of hatred and ridicule for all enemies of the Republicans and the Union. He knew that a noted British newspaper correspondent had lately informed the English: "A person who met Mr. Lincoln in the street would not take him to be what is called a gentleman." Brooks saw in the face only wisdom, compassion, deep and awkward courage.

"Mother," the President said in passing greeting to his wife, and only that, as he disappeared up a flight of stairs, almost running as he spraddled three steps at once, looking like a falling man on stilts. Brooks looked to Mrs. Lincoln, who stared after her husband with tight lips, and he realized that he had been waiting for her reply, half expecting her to address even her husband as "sir," as she did all comers.

They were off at last, down to the Navy Yard, Mrs. Lincoln herding them, and Tad gamboling around them in his Federal lieutenant's uniform, slashing the air with his little saber. They boarded the steamer *Carrie Martin* and went off into the river, feeling its strong tug beneath the spasmed beat of the engine. Snow began to pelt down, to vanish in the black water. Lincoln looked back over the city and its dim spires even before the little craft had made the great bend to the southeast. The place seemed to him the aching heart of the country and stirred him so that he was seldom able to speak of it. Back there tonight the poor shaggy-haired young poet Walt Whitman, probably crazy, was wandering among the wounded back from the army, who were still in plentiful supply. And the office-seekers and gossips and traitors and the thousands of war millionaires, a world to themselves, all carried on without the President.

Brooks found his talk rather mournful. "I am surrounded by men who are more eager to make money out of the country's misery than to put a shoulder to the wheel and lift us out of the mire. Do you wonder I become depressed, and sometimes think of how hard it will be to die, unless I can make the world understand that I would be willing to die if I could be sure I am doing my work toward lifting the burdens of all men?"

After nightfall, the party was surprised by the slowing and halting of the engine, and in the silence became aware once more of the rushing of the river. The captain entered and told

Lincoln that he could not be responsible for pushing downstream in the snowstorm and the darkness; his pilot was all but blinded. The President left the problem to the boatman, and they tied up at the bank opposite Indian Head, Maryland. They spent the night without guards posted.

Lincoln became high-spirited and talkative, and when Mrs. Lincoln had retired, and Tad had fallen asleep in his arms, the President kicked off his shoes, and with his feet held to the warmth of a small stove, wiggling his great toe through a hole in the sock, he talked of the war. He told them in low tones, as if someone on the deck might overhear, of the attempt the Navy was making tonight against Charleston. Tomorrow, Fort Sumter would be bombarded. He was hopeful that it could be taken.

He spoke guardedly of Hooker. Not that Lincoln found it difficult to recall any detail about Joe Hooker; few of the swarming thousands whom he had known during the war had impressed him so forcibly as the colorful new general. The President would not soon forget their first meeting.

Hooker had been fretting away his time in the waiting rooms of Washington, seeking a commission in spite of the opposition of old General Winfield Scott, whom he had offended back in the days of the Mexican War. At last Hooker reached Lincoln, introduced as Captain Hooker.

The President liked his looks, an erect, shapely man just under fifty, with clean, precise features, a touch of whisker on his chops, a head of thick blond hair, and lively gray eyes. There was a trace of weakness about the chin, but then Lincoln was captivated by the urgent power in the voice.

"I'm not Captain Hooker, Mr. President, but lately Lieutenant Colonel of the regular army. I have been farming in California, but since the Rebellion broke out I've been here trying to get into the service, but find I am not wanted.

"I am about to go home, but before going I was anxious to pay my respects to you, and to express my wishes for your personal welfare and success in quelling this Rebellion. And I want to say one word more . . ." As Lincoln prepared to interrupt, Hooker said, "I was at Bull Run the other day, and Mr. President, it is no vanity in me to say that I am a damned sight better general than any you had on that field."

Joe Hooker could feel the settling weight of brigadier general's stars on his yearning shoulders before he went to bed that night. He was soon off on a career of army politics that was hammered out beyond Lincoln's ken. He fought a division through the Peninsular campaign, and a corps at Antietam, where he was shot in the foot, and won promotion. He had lately commanded about a third of the army at Fredericksburg.

It was late when Lincoln and Brooks went to bed, following the stolid Bates and the earnest old Dr. Henry. It was still snowing in the morning, even when they had steamed to the landing at Aquia Creek and looked out over the dismal new board shanties rising in a shabby waterside city, stretching back from docks and rail sidings and mountains of supplies. There was a pitiful greeting, a few men cheering in unison, a scattering of wet bunting aflap on the buildings, and a handful of lesser officers to meet them. The party went into the hubbub raised by the lines of Government steamers at the docks and by the terrific coming and going of trains on the maze of tracks at the waterside. Without ado, the little group walked to the tracks, mounted an open freight car into which boards had been fitted as benches, and jerked away over the desolate, rain-soaked country toward headquarters of the army.

They alighted at Falmouth Station to a more cheering sight, two hundred well-dressed horsemen waiting in a body; and Hooker's chief of staff, General Daniel Butterfield, to greet them. They rolled off in two ambulances to meet Hooker, who gave them correct, warm, but restrained greetings and installed them in three big hospital tents, with board floors and cots and all the conveniences of camp headquarters. A round of dinners introduced the leading officers, and a schedule of grand reviews was given the President, who had ideas of his own about looking at the army. A poor layman with the Black Hawk War long years behind him, he could not fathom the huge machine under Hooker's command, but he had an eye, and he knew men. He wanted to look at the enemy, and he wanted to see the wounded of his own army.

He was taken to the banks of the Rappahannock to stare at ruined Fredericksburg over the river and at the grim slopes where his army had been massacred. Hardly a building in the town had escaped. Walls lay in ruins, block after block, with trees down amid the rubble, and flaps of tin hanging from a battered church steeple. At the riverside rose a blackened chimney, alone in its clearing, and from it trailed a smudge of smoke. At its base two Confederate pickets hung over their morning fire. From Lincoln's distance they looked to be a harmless foe.

He got into all of the hospital tents within reach of headquarters and paced slowly up and down the lanes of cots, refusing to pass up any of the men who stared up at him, and touching the hands of those who seemed aware of him. Tears and smiles followed his progress; and when he came out of the hospital area, a crowd of soldiers which had gathered in the roadway and would not be forced away cheered and called after him. Lincoln shook hands with as many as he could reach.

Hooker rushed him off to review the cavalry, and there was a swift ride to the reviewing field. The cavalcade made a deep impression on Brooks:

> The President, wearing a high hat and riding like a veteran, with General Hooker by his side, headed the flying column; next came several major generals, a host of brigadiers, staff officers and colonels, and lesser functionaries innumerable. The flank of this long train was decorated by the showy uniforms and accoutrements of the Philadelphia Lancers, who acted as a guard of honor to the President. . . . The uneven ground was soft with melting snow, and the mud flew in every direction under the hurrying feet of the cavalcade. On the skirts of this cloud of cavalry rode the President's little son Tad, in charge of a mounted orderly, his gray cloak flying in the gusty wind like the plume of Henry of Navarre.

> The President and the reviewing party rode past the long lines of cavalry standing at rest, and then the march past began. It was a grand sight to look upon, this immense body of cavalry, with banners waving, music crashing, and horses

prancing, as the vast column came winding like a huge serpent over the hills past the reviewing party, and then stretching far away out of sight.

Hooker was there to mutter in the President's ear.

"Seventeen thousand men, Mr. President. Under command of General Stoneman. Now we've massed it for the first time in one corps—no more scattering it about for the Rebels to beat up piecemeal. It is the largest body of horsemen ever seen in the world, Mr. President—greater even than the famed cavalry of Marshal Murat."

Lincoln only nodded and watched the magnificent parade of horses and men, as Hooker talked on of, "When I have taken Richmond," and "When we have cut up Lee."

On other days, the President walked through the camps, and everywhere men called to him and seemed glad to see him. They crowded about his horse, anxious to see him, touch him, and hear his low voice. He grew hoarse in the afternoon after hours of being reduced to nothing but a constant chant, "God bless you. God bless you."

There was more than one collation, in which the President, with Mrs. Lincoln elsewhere, took a boyish enjoyment. Once, as the result of gay wagers, he was surprised with a sudden kiss from a lovely and genuine Oriental beauty, the Princess Salm-Salm, wife of a New York colonel. That prompted assaults by other charming ladies, until the President retreated. In the evening, in tents near by that of the Lincolns', men heard the voice of the wife, in bitter complaint over the scene at the afternoon party.

There were a few quiet moments, which Lincoln often spent with Brooks, and then he would shake his head as if mysteriously troubled at the endless spectacles to which he was being treated, and sigh, "Ah, Hooker. He speaks so of victory, of taking Richmond. That is the most depressing thing about him. It seems to me that he is overconfident."

The President seemed to enjoy himself for the most part. One night he said to Brooks, "It is a relief to get away from Washington and the politicians, but nothing touches the tired spot."

He watched his infantry—sixty thousand strong, four corps—as it wound over hills, across the fields, its bayonets a forest of gleaming spikes without end, and near the finish the eighty cannon of the reserve artillery. The sun came out during this review, and the President, though he did not return the salutes of officers, removed his worn black silk hat to the massed privates, and his eyes followed their shining flags, torn with shell, and now bearing terrible names of places he would like to forget.

Once or twice more the President laughed.

One day, when he was being hurried to a review in a rough wagon behind six striving mules, the driver began to curse violently at the roughness of the road. Lincoln touched the man on the shoulder.

"Excuse me, my friend, are you an Episcopalian?"

The astonished driver stared over his shoulder.

"No, Mr. President, I'm a Methodist."

"Well, I thought you must be an Episcopalian, because you swear just like Governor Seward, who is a churchwarden."

The driver lashed his horses without profanity, unaware that William Seward was, or had ever been, a member of the Lincoln Cabinet.

In the evening, Hooker entertained the President and Mrs. Lincoln at an elaborate dinner, and among the guests was General Dan Sickles, the lively officer in whose quarters the Princess and her escort had so freely kissed Lincoln. Mrs. Lincoln had only icy stares for Sickles. Lincoln turned his attention to the general.

"I never knew until last night that you were such a pious man, Sickles."

The officer stared and stammered. "I'm afraid you've been misinformed, Mr. President."

"Not at all. Mother says you're the greatest Psalmist in the army. She says you are more than a Psalmist, you are a Salm-Salmist." Mrs. Lincoln joined the laughter.

The show was over at last, but even then the President found only a moment for serious discussion with his commander. He loped into his tent one afternoon, interrupting Hooker's discussion with General Couch, the next in command. Hooker gave Lincoln little attention and sat rudely continuing his conversation.

Lincoln at last broke in.

"The time has come for me to go, gentlemen." Hooker and Couch rose. "I want to impress upon you gentlemen. In your next fight," and here he turned to Couch, "put in all your men."

He shook hands and left. From the opening of the tent Hooker watched him move out of sight, the awkward, long-legged haste still evident when he could see nothing but the stovepipe hat bobbing over the tops of tents.

The blue-eyed commander with the dainty little mouth had a secret look on his face, staring after the amateur who offered such childish advice. From the headquarters tents somewhere behind him came woman's laughter. Major General Hooker returned to his work.

21

The light of massed Christmas candles flickered over the men in the dining room, the most brilliant gathering of Confederate field officers the war had seen. Jackson was incredibly the host to the throng of generals and colonels in gray. He sat, flushed, head down, at one end of the long Corbin table, light gleaming on his skull through thinned hair. General W. N. Pendleton said grace, and was long at the task.

A rising chorus of talk and laughter followed. Jackson had charged Jim and Captain Smith with the dinner, and it came in such bounty that half-starved officers could not believe their eyes. A Negro boy who served the table wore a fresh white apron.

General Lee smiled at Jackson. "You people are only playing soldier," he said. "You must come to my quarters and see how soldiers ought to live."

Jeb Stuart laughed at the apron about the servant's waist, and joked elaborately with Jackson over the bottle of old wine on the table. He roared his mirth when he discovered a print of a gamecock molded on the butter.

"I swear, Jackson, it's your coat of arms," Stuart shouted.

He held up the butter to display the state of Jackson's degeneracy.

The crowd feasted on turkeys, a bucket of Rappahannock oysters, hams, biscuit, pickles and delicacies without end which Smith had gathered from houses of the region.

Moss Neck, the home of a wealthy planter, was a rambling affair reminiscent of English country houses, with the addition of long columned porches. Its knoll commanded a magnificent view of the valley of the Rappahannock, with the river about a mile away. Jackson had for a long time camped in a tent in the yard of the place, refusing to disturb Mrs. Corbin and her young children, and her husband's sister, Kate. The master of the house was absent, as Jackson had explained to Anna in a letter of December eighteenth:

> Our headquarters are now about 12 miles below Fredericksburg, near the house of Mr. Richard Corbin, which is one of the most beautiful buildings I have seen in this country. It is said to have cost sixty thousand dollars. . . . Mr. Corbin was absent, serving as a private in the Virginia cavalry, but Mrs. Corbin bountifully supplied us . . . she urged me to remain, and offered me a neat building in the yard for my office, but I declined, and am now about 500 yards from the house, encamped in the woods. She told me that if at any time I needed house room, she could let me have it.
>
> Baby's letters are read with great interest, and it does her father's heart good to read them. . . . I have much work before me, and today I expect to commence in earnest. The reports of the battles of McDowell, Winchester, Port Republic, Richmond, Manassas, the Maryland campaign, Harpers Ferry, and Fredericksburg have all yet to be written.

When his dinner party was over and the general officers had left, Old Jack returned to his tent, and the young men around him joined the women in the Corbin house. The dinner had some solemn undertones, for the matter of Jackson's reports had become pressing; and one of the diners at Moss Neck was Colonel Charles J. Faulkner, called from the adjutant general's office in Richmond to fill in the missing papers of Jackson.

Faulkner was a capable and pleasant man, with eight years'

experience in the United States Congress and three years as the Minister to France in prewar days. He was to deal with what Kyd Douglas called Jackson's "neglected reports," one of the army's serious gaps in the official records. Jackson readily acceded to the plan, but he maintained full, almost jealous control. His battles, after all, were among the most famous fought by the army, and they had been piled one on another, fourteen in eight months, so that Old Jack, bedeviled by the business of training and supplying his troops while fighting them, had scant time to deal with reports.

He demanded that Faulkner read the papers to his staff at intervals. The reports must be simple, of verified accuracy, must evade controversy, and be subject to Jackson's approval and revision. Jackson dictated most of them himself. It was the first outburst of paper work in Jackson's command.

Within a week after his Christmas dinner, Jackson caught cold and had a recurrence of his earache. On the advice of Dr. McGuire, he moved indoors to the small yard office of the plantation, a detached frame building of a story and a half which had served as the master's library and office. It was a curious setting for Old Jack:

Fine old books lined the walls, many in foreign languages, and learned works were scattered among Virginia law books, agricultural reports, horse and cattle registers, medical and scientific and sporting books—even ladies' magazines. On the walls were hunting muskets and fishing tackle, and all about, on walls and floors, were skins, deer antlers, stuffed birds. Among the prints were steel engravings of famous race horses and fine cattle, gamecocks in the pit, and purebred dogs and cats. It was a setting to give Stuart great amusement. Captain Smith recalled the cavalryman's coming:

"Stuart's first visit to the office was memorable. With clanking saber and spurs and waving black plume he came, and was warmly greeted at the door. Papers and work were all hastily laid aside. No sooner had Stuart entered than his attention turned to the pictures on the walls. He read aloud what was said about each noted race horse and each splendid bull. At the hearth he paused to scan with affected astonishment the horrid picture of a certain terrier that could kill so many rats a minute. He pretended to believe that they were General Jackson's selections; with great solemnity he looked at the pictures and then at the general.

"He paused and stepped back, and in solemn tones said he wished to express his astonishment and grief at the display of General Jackson's low tastes. It would be a sad disappointment to the old ladies of the country, who thought that Jackson was a good man. General Jackson was delighted above measure. He blushed like a girl, and hesitated, and said nothing but to turn aside and direct that a good dinner be prepared for General Stuart."

Jackson was, as Kyd Douglas said without further comment, "a frequent visitor at the house socially," but spent most of his time working in his office. The big house sent frequent offerings of food for his table.

Jackson's Christmas letter to Anna reflected loneliness and pessimism, overlaid with his firm self-discipline.

> Yesterday I received the baby's letter with its beautiful lock of hair. How I do want to see that precious baby! and I do earnestly pray for peace. Oh that our country was such a Christian, God-fearing people as it should be! Then might we very speedily look for peace. . . .
> It is better for me to remain with my command so long as the war continues, if our gracious Heavenly Father permits. The army suffers immensely by absentees. If all our troops . . . were at their posts, we might, through God's blessing, expect a more speedy termination of the war. . . .

Jackson was busy in his office. Courts-martial met daily, like factories turning out their grim decisions. Deserters were punished in wholesale lots. Jackson's ranks began to fill slowly with the return of stragglers and the small flow of reinforcements. Men settled for the winter in their huts of logs and mud, and among these poor villages rose chapels, where the revival spirit became more intense than ever. Jackson complained of intrusions upon his time, but never of those by men like the visiting Reverend Dabney and other ministers.

Richmond's daily papers were delivered to Jackson's office,

though they were read chiefly by the staff. The price, indicating inflation in the capital, was twenty cents per copy. Old Jack's officers complained now of many another pinch which robbed them of their lean army pay: apples, $2 a dozen; soap, $1.25 per cake; oysters, $5 per gallon; shoe blacking, $1 per cake.

Lafayette McLaws, one of the general officers who had performed so well at Fredericksburg, noted these troubles in biting letters to his family, and also revealed that not all was sweetness and light in the official family of Lee:

"Everything we see sold is disposed of at ten times its actual worth . . . extortion is the rule of the hour. . . . The disposition to devour or destroy is predominant. This desire for extortion is a passion, a disease which has now seized the public mind . . . overriding all previous respectability and character, all pride of birth and family."

He then turned to the generals of his acquaintance:

"Do you know there is a strong feeling growing up among the Southern troops against Virginia, caused by the jealousy of her own people for those from every other state? No matter who it is may perform a glorious act, Virginia papers give but grudging praise unless the actor is a Virginian. No matter how trifling the deed may be which a Virginian performs, it is heralded at once as the most glorious of modern times."

McLaws then got down to cases:

"Stuart carries around with him a banjo player and a special correspondent. This claptrap is noticed and lauded as a peculiarity of genius, when, in fact, it is nothing else but the act of a buffoon to get attention." (This was in strong contrast to the testimony of the Federal General Sedgwick: "Stuart is the best cavalry officer ever foaled in America.")

McLaws attacked other Virginians: "Another general gets a friend to write a ridiculously eulogistic article in a foreign paper and has it copied in the Virginia papers."

He then came to Jackson—undoubtedly Jackson:

"Another panders to the religious zeal of a puritanical church and has numerous scribes writing fancy anecdotes of his peculiarities which never existed."

While this unsuspected criticism was being penned, Jackson

was busy with the further reorganization of the army, whose improvement in the seven months of Lee's command was remarkable. The fighting had brought forty-eight thousand Confederate and seventy thousand Union casualties, even this a ratio the South could not bear. But the troops were now well-armed, mostly with captured Federal rifles and muskets. And, most striking of all, the graycoats had 155 captive cannon, and had lost but eight themselves. Excepting only Sharpsburg, the rebels had driven the Federals from every field where the armies had clashed since Lee had led them.

The troops seemed to show no optimism for the future, however, despite Fredericksburg. Except for moments of exuberant celebration, of drinking and snowballing and gambling, it was a sober encampment.

Lee himself had been less than optimistic in speaking of the victory on the Rappahannock:

> The war is not yet ended. The enemy is still numerous and strong, and the country demands of the army a renewal of its heroic efforts in her behalf. Nobly has it responded . . . in the past, and she will never appeal in vain to its courage and patriotism. The signal manifestations of Divine mercy that have distinguished the eventful and glorious campaign of the year just closing give assurance of hope that, under the guidance of the same Almighty hand, the coming year will be no less fruitful . . . and add new lustre to the already imperishable name of the Army of Northern Virginia.

In this galloping rhetoric was the rise of a new Confederate legend: the invincibility of Lee's army in its present form, with the cumbersome old divisions replaced by two corps, and with Longstreet and Jackson at hand to carry out the orders of their chief.

The enemy was little heard from in these weeks, though the Federals were in sight over the Rappahannock and once caused a stir by trying to move toward the river's fords during a siege of rain and snow—a futile attempt, to be known as "The Mud March."

Lee sent Stuart on several raids which brought loot and prisoners, but little information. Lee sent D. H. Hill to Richmond, and two brigades to meet a Federal threat in North Carolina. He finally sent Longstreet and his men below Richmond, to defend against a threatened Federal invasion of the Tidewater country.

In these days, Lee lived less ostentatiously than Jackson, in a tent near Hamilton's Crossing, with only a cot, a folding desk and camp stove inside; though beneath his cot a pet hen laid an egg for him each day. Lee and Jackson and other officers rode out one day to visit Hayfield, a near-by mansion owned by one of Lee's cousins, Mrs. W. P. Taylor. Lee spent most of the visit teasing Jackson.

"I have brought my great generals for the young ladies to see," Lee told Mrs. Taylor. And as Jackson flushed he added, "Jackson is one of the most cruel men I have known. I had all I could do at Fredericksburg, to keep him from having his men drive all those people into the river."

Jackson was further embarrassed by Mrs. Taylor's defense of him as "a good Christian man," and even more by the request of a small girl for a kiss.

Lee and Jackson once sat together on a log to hear one of the revival services in camp, a sermon by Jackson's chief chaplain, the Reverend B. T. Lacy. Captain Smith watched them with affection as the generals wept, tears streaming into their beards, staring at Lacy as he dramatically described the peaceful homes from which the Confederate soldiers had been taken by the war.

Lee's kindliness and Jackson's stern sense of duty once came into conflict. Lee ordered Jackson to come to his headquarters one night, and Jackson told Captain Smith to be ready to make the journey. There was a snowstorm in the night, and Smith, already in bed, concluded that Jackson would not go out on his ride in view of the weather. He was rudely shaken, an hour or so later, and taken out into the storm.

Lee, "surprised and quite indignant," Smith said, emerged bareheaded into the snow when the two had finished their fourteen-mile ride.

"You know I did not wish you to come in such a storm," Lee said. "It was a matter of little importance; I am so sorry that you have had this ride."

Jackson replied, "I received your note, General Lee!"

Men in ranks learned much about their commanders in the winter camp but did not materially change their estimates of Lee and Jackson. One who wrote home expressed a general feeling: "You need have no apprehension that this army will ever meet with defeat while commanded by General Lee. General Jackson is a strict Presbyterian, but he is rather too much of a Napoleon Bonaparte in my estimation. Lee is the man, I assure you."

Old Jack did not neglect his work. On most days he dictated from morning until late afternoon in his office, and then went into the woods for a ride or a walk, often alone. He would return to his chores at night. Smith saw him late at his desk: "In the evening great stacks of papers, prepared by his own direction, were brought for his signature, and he signed his name until sometimes he would fall asleep over his table; he often wrote T. J. Jakson in his haste and weariness."

Jackson's correspondence with Richmond assumed vast proportions as he sought guns, clothing, food, harnesses and horses; but despite all, thousands of his men remained inadequately clothed, and Lee was forced to write that the troops were scarcely fed at all.

One memorable day brought a visit from a group of Englishmen, including Francis Lawler of the *London Times*, Frank Vizetelly of the *Illustrated News*, and several British officers, among them the young Marquis of Hartington and a Colonel Leslie, chairman of the military committee of the House of Commons. There was also a man who was to become commander of the British army, Colonel Garnet Wolsely.

Captain Blackford took these men to visit Jackson, warning them of Old Jack's peculiarities in advance. He described Jackson's amusing habit of taking the hats of all who came to his office, though there was no place to hang them, so that in the end the General would stare around in confusion and place the hats in a pile on the floor. The visitors could hardly contain their laughter when Jackson went through the routine described by Blackford.

Lawler, who closeted himself with Jackson, tried to get from him some dramatic remarks on his campaigns, but came out in chagrin. Jackson, he said, talked learnedly of many things but could not be brought to talk of the war. He was deucedly interesting on English cathedrals he had inspected, but on the Valley campaign he was mute. Lawler ended a week with Jackson with the statement that Old Jack was the "best informed military man he had met in America," and "as perfect a gentleman as I have ever seen." But he got no reminiscences of the war for his readers.

Now and again Jackson's humor flashed, as on a unique occasion when spring was drawing near. He rose from his paper work and stretched on his cot, eyes closed, listening to the heated argument between Colonel Faulkner and Dr. Hunter McGuire, who held a learned discussion on the merits of the wines of France and Italy. To the astonishment of his young officers, Jackson asked if there was not some wine in his supply wagons. When Jim brought it out in glasses, Faulkner and McGuire and others sipped at it, nodding and exclaiming, as Jackson asked them to tell him which European vineyards had produced it. Old Jack buried his face in a pillow, giggling, as the officers debated. He at last told them, with almost uncontrollable glee, that it was a wine of the country, made by a friend in Front Royal, in the Shenandoah Valley.

As usual, however, his humor was far from brilliant, and he was prone to burst into laughter over the simplest of jokes. One day when he expected company, he asked Major Hawks, the commissary officer, to send him some chickens for lunch. Hawks replied, "We have no chickens. The *hawks* have eaten them up." The pun rocked Jackson with laughter, from which he suffered recurrences several hours afterward.

He seemed to be devising a defense against the constant teasing of Stuart and his henchmen, however. One day when he visited in a plantation house, two young women besieged him, asking for souvenirs. When they asked for some locks of his hair, Jackson bantered with them.

"You have so much more hair than I do."

And:

"My hair is gray, and your friends would think me an old man. Why, don't you know the boys call me 'Old Jack'?"

His strongest attachment of the winter was for little Janie Corbin, the six-year-old daughter of the household. Janie was free to break in upon his work at almost any hour, and she played day after day on his hearth as he droned his reports to Faulkner. When his work was done, he took Janie into his lap; he usually had an apple for her. One day, lacking a gift, he tore from his new cap the broad band of gilt which had caught the eye of Anna. Jackson tied the golden strand about the hair of the child and watched fondly as she ran to the big house. More than once, officers recalled, the General stopped his work to cut paper dolls for Janie, usually folding paper to fashion a long line of figures holding hands. The men of the Stonewall Brigade, he told Janie.

He could turn from these moments to grim duty. He once sentenced to death four soldiers of his command found guilty of desertion. Shortly before the time of their execution, a chaplain came to Jackson's office to plead that the men be released. Jackson paced back and forth, apparently disturbed, but he heard the chaplain's story. Old Jack remained quiet when the minister had finished his appeal.

"General, consider your responsibility before the Lord," the chaplain said. "You are sending these men's souls to hell."

An officer recalled that Jackson uncharacteristically strode forward and gripped the minister's shoulders, saying, "That, sir, is my business! You attend to yours."

Jackson never forgot Anna and home. One morning he was forcibly reminded of Lexington when he caught sight of a Negro boy from that town who had come to serve Captain Smith. Jackson peered closely at the Negro and said, "Why, John, is that you?" To the surprised Smith, John explained, "Oh, I know the Major; the Major made me get the catechism." The servant had been trained in Jackson's strict Sunday school.

The cold months passed. There was a grand review of Stuart's cavalry, attended by Lee and Jackson with a huge cluster of staff officers; there were numerous elaborate dinners. For the troops there was almost constant work, for Lee was developing a bristling line of earthworks south of the Rappahannock, twenty-five miles long.

There were continuing troubles of command, and feuds smouldered between officers. Few of them involved Jackson, but when he entered controversy, as ever he was implacable. His old friend, General E. F. Paxton, protested Jackson's decision that six deserters from his brigade be punished and three of them be shot. Paxton suggested that one man only be shot, and that he be chosen by lot. Jackson replied in severe language: "With the exception of this application, General Paxton's management of his brigade has given me great satisfaction. One great difficulty in the army results from over lenient courts, and it appears to me that when a court-martial faithfully discharges its duty that its decisions should be sustained."

Similarly, when General W. R. Jones was charged with cowardice in action, Jackson was inflexible in his determination to see him brought to trial, though Jones had been one of his own candidates for promotion. Speaking to the Reverend Lacy of this, Old Jack said, "I have almost lost my confidence in man. When I thought I had found just such a man as I needed, and was about to rest satisfied in him, I found something lacking in him. But I suppose it is to teach me to put my trust only in God."

While Jackson busied himself with such affairs, an important change was made north of the Rappahannock. General Burnside went out rather abruptly, and General Joseph Hooker came in. The move drew limited attention from the Confederates.

Jackson was still deep in his old feud with A. P. Hill, which neither officer seemed willing to give up. Hill continued to demand a hearing on Jackson's charges against him, and Jackson prepared by collecting eyewitnesses to Hill's alleged neglect of duty. The squabble was never to reach a decision.

At the middle of March, Jackson moved his headquarters

from the Corbin home to a tent near Hamilton's Crossing, some ten miles nearer to Fredericksburg. He was settling down there when he learned of the death of Janie Corbin, stricken by scarlet fever. He wept like a child, Smith said.

In the same week, Jackson was saddened again, this time by the death of young John Pelham, whose courage had won the praise of all at Fredericksburg. He had fallen on a raid against the enemy in a minor skirmish. Cavalrymen saved the body with a daring swoop and brought it to camp for Stuart to weep over. The army mourned.

Jackson seemed unable to forget the approaching opportunity to attack and destroy the Federal army. He sent most of the personal baggage of his officers and men to rear camps and kept his wagons ready and waiting. In conversation with an officer, he spoke with confidence of the coming battle. "My trust is in God," he said, but then, with flashing eyes and a rising voice he cried, "I wish they would come!"

Jackson had not been idle in his personal correspondence. His Lexington pastor, the Reverend White, had asked him to make a public statement on religion and the army, and drew this reply:

> This I shrink from doing, because it looks like a presumption in me to come before the public and even intimate what course I think should be pursued by the people of God. . . .
>
> Each Christian branch of the Church should send into the army some of its most prominent ministers, who are distinguished for their piety, talents and zeal. . . . A bad selection of a chaplain may prove a curse rather than a blessing.
>
> I would like to see no questions asked in the army as to what domination a chaplain belongs; but let the question be, "Does he preach the Gospel?" The neglect of spiritual interests in the army may be partially seen in the fact that not one half of my regiments have chaplains.

He wrote to Boteler in Richmond, outraged that the Congress had repealed its ban against carrying mail on Sunday, saying, "I do not see how a nation that thus arrays itself, by such

a law, against God's holy day, can expect to escape His wrath."
To a friend in Lexington:

> Let our Government acknowledge the God of the Bible as
> its God, and we may expect soon to be a happy and inde-
> pendent people. It appears to me that extremes are to be
> avoided; and it also appears to me that the old United States
> occupied an extreme position in the means it took to prevent
> the union of Church and State. We call ourselves a Christian
> people; and, in my opinion, our government may be of the
> same character, without connecting itself with an established
> Church.

To one visitor he made a forceful statement somewhat in the
vein of these letters:

> Nothing earthly can mar my happiness. I know that
> heaven is in store for me; and I should rejoice in the prospect
> of going there tomorrow. Understand me: I am not sick, I
> am not sad; God has greatly blessed me; I have as much to
> love here as any man, and life is very bright to me. But still
> I am ready to leave it any day . . . for that heaven which I
> know awaits me.

But, chiefly, he wrote to Anna. At the death of Janie Corbin,
he wrote movingly to his wife; and at news of the death of a
kinsman's child he wrote: "I wish I could comfort her, but no
human comfort can fully meet her case; only the Redeemer can,
and I trust that she finds Jesus precious."

Anna wrote that their daughter Julia had chicken pox. Jackson, worried, called in McGuire and questioned him on the
disease, and then wrote a long letter of advice and treatment to
Anna. He also wrote:

> How much I do want to see you and our darling baby! But
> . . . I am afraid since hearing so much about the little one's
> health, that it would be imprudent to bring it upon a journey,
> so I must content myself. Mrs. General Longstreet, Mrs.
> General A. P. Hill, and Mrs. General Rodes have all been to
> see their husbands. Yesterday I saw Mrs. Rodes at church,
> and she looked so happy that it made me wish I had Mrs.
> Jackson here too."

The month-old Julia was much on his mind:

> I am gratified at hearing that you have commenced disciplining the baby. Now be careful, and don't let her conquer you. She must not be permitted to have that will of her own, of which you speak. How I would love to see the little darling. . . . Can't you send her to me by express? . . . I am glad to hear that she sleeps well at night, and doesn't disturb her mother. But it would be better not to call her a cherub; no earthly being is such . . .
>
> Don't you accuse my baby of not being brave. I do hope she will get over her fear of strangers. If, before strangers take her, you would give them something to please her . . . I trust she would lose her timidity . . . I am thankful that she is so bright and knowing. I do wish I could see her funny little ways, and hear her "squeal out with delight" at seeing the little chickens.
>
> I am sometimes afraid that you will make such an idol of that baby that God will take her from us. Are you not afraid of it? Kiss her for her father.

He wrote that he was reading Hunter's *Life of Moses,* that he devoted most Sundays to meditation. "Time thus spent is genuine enjoyment." He wrote of a variety of things, always returning to the baby.

> Just to think our baby is nearly three months old. Does she notice and laugh much? You have never told me how much she looks like her mother.
>
> I tell you, I want to know how she looks.
>
> If you could hear me talking to my *esposa* in the mornings and evenings, it would make you laugh, I'm sure. It is funny the way I talk to her when she is hundreds of miles away.

At times he seemed wrapped in gloomy religious thoughts: "I think that if, when we see ourselves in a glass we should consider that all of us that is visible must turn to corruption and dust, we would learn more justly to appreciate the relative importance of the body that perishes and the soul that is immortal."

He began to urge Anna to come to visit him: "Do you remember when my little wife used to come up to my headquarters in Winchester and talk with her *esposo?* I would love to see her sunny face peering into my room again."

Finally, on April eighteenth:

> I am beginning to look for my darling and my baby. I shouldn't be surprised to hear at any time that they were coming, and I tell you there would be one delighted man. Last night I dreamed that my little wife and I were on opposite sides of a room, in the centre of which was a table, and the little baby started from her mother, making her way along under the table, and finally reached her father. And what do you think she did when she arrived at her destination: She just climbed up on her father and kissed him! And don't you think he was a happy man?
>
> I am glad to hear that she enjoys out-doors, and grows, and coos, and laughs. How I would love to see her sweet ways! That her little chubby hands have lost their resemblance to mine is not regretted by me. . . . Should I write to you to have any more pantaloons made for me, please do not have much gold braid about them. I became so ashamed of the broad gilt band that was on the cap you sent me as to induce me to take it off. I like simplicity.

A few days later he added impatiently: "Yesterday I received your letter, but you did not say a word about coming. . . . I do hope that ere this you have received mine, saying you could come, and that you at once got an escort and started. There is no time for hesitation if you have not started."

He made arrangements to put Anna and the baby in the Yerby house, a country home near his headquarters, and on gray Monday, April twentieth, at noon, he went excitedly to the railroad station at Guiney's, in a dripping raincoat, pushing his way into the coach. He found a smiling wife and a fresh, pink-faced, fat little daughter, just aroused from a nap. He had scarcely time to notice dark Hetty, Anna's lifelong maid.

Jackson and the baby grinned and cooed at each other on the journey to their quarters, Anna recalled. But he could not take Julia in his arms because of his wet coat. Once in their room:

> He caressed her with the tenderest affection, and held her long and lovingly. During the whole of this short visit, when

he was with us, he rarely had her out of his arms, walking her, and amusing her in every way that he could think of—sometimes holding her up before a mirror and saying, admiringly, "Now, Miss Jackson, look at yourself!"

Then he would turn to an old lady of the [Yerby] family and say: "Isn't she a little gem?" He was frequently told that she resembled him, but he would say: "No, she is too pretty to look like me!"

Anna admired him as he knelt by the cradle of the sleeping baby: "I often wished that the picture of that father kneeling over the cradle of that lovely infant could have been put upon canvas." But she pointed out that Old Jack was also a stern parent.

One day she began to cry to be taken from the bed . . . and as soon as her wish was gratified, she ceased to cry. He laid her back upon the bed, and the crying was renewed with increased violence. Of course, the mother-heart wished to stop this by taking her up again, but he exclaimed: "This will never do!" and commanded "all hands off" until that little will of her own should be conquered.

So there she lay, kicking and screaming, while he stood over her with as much coolness and determination as if he were directing a battle; and he was true to the name of Stonewall, even in disciplining a baby! When she stopped crying he would take her up, and if she began to cry again he would lay her down again, and this he kept up until finally she was completely conquered, and became perfectly quiet in his hands.

On April twenty-third, when Julia was five months old, Stonewall had her baptized in the parlor of the Yerby house, with the Reverend Lacy officiating and many staff officers present. Julia "behaved beautifully." On the next Sunday, Jackson took Anna to church. She was much impressed.

My husband took me in an ambulance to his headquarters, where the services were held, and on the way were seen streams of officers and soldiers, some riding, some walking, all wending their way to the place of worship. . . . We found Mr. Lacy in a tent, in which we were seated, together with General Lee and other distinguished officers.

I remember how reverent and impressive was General Lee's bearing, and how handsome he looked, with his splendid figure and faultless military attire. In front of the tent, under the canopy of heaven, were spread out in dense masses the soldiers, sitting upon benches or standing. The preaching was earnest and edifying, the singing one grand volume of song, and the attention and good behavior of the assembly remarkable.

Anna recalled that Jackson did not allow her visit to interfere with his military duties, but on one occasion her presence led him into a surprising demonstration. He rode up to show her a new bay horse, Superior, a handsome animal given by admirers, and after taking the horse to the porch of the house, "he remounted him, and galloped away at such a John Gilpin speed that his cap was soon borne off by the velocity; but he did not stop to pick it up, leaving this to his orderly behind him, who found great difficulty in keeping even in sight of him. As far as he could be seen, he was flying like the wind—the impersonation of fearlessness and manly vigor."

Anna had been in camp about a week when a traveling photographer—Minis of Richmond—appeared in Jackson's headquarters, asking that Stonewall sit for a picture. The General refused, but Anna was at his elbow. She persuaded him to sit: "As he never presented a finer appearance in health and dress (wearing the handsome suit given him by General Stuart)."

Anna herself arranged his hair, "which was unusually long for him, and curled in long ringlets." Jackson posed in a chair, seated in the draughty hall of the big country house, where "a strong wind blew in his face, causing him to frown, and giving a sternness to his countenance that was not natural."

This was one of their last moments together.

Anna wrote of this final photograph of her husband: "The three-quarters view of his face and head—the favorite picture with his old soldiers, as it is the most soldierly-looking; but to my mind, not so pleasing as the full-face view which was taken in the spring of 1862, at Winchester, and which has more of the beaming sunlight of his *home-look*."

The army had looked with curiosity at Anna Jackson, the wife of their strange, compelling corps commander. An officer left a record of the impression she made on the visit: "Slightly built and tolerably good looking, and was somewhat gaily though modestly dressed."

On Wednesday, April twenty-ninth, a booted courier ran heavily over the porch of the Yerby House, and soon there was a rapid climbing on the stairs and a rap on the door of Jackson's room.

"What is it?"

"General Early's adjutant wishes to see General Jackson."

Jackson got out of bed. "That looks as if Hooker were crossing the river," he said to Anna. He went out of the door in his hastily arranged clothes. He was back within ten minutes.

He was changed when he returned to the bedroom and spoke to Anna. He had been right, he said. The Federals had flung some of their 138,000 fine troops over the Rappahannock, and fighting was to be expected. She must take the baby southward immediately. He must go to headquarters. If his duties permitted, he would return to see them to the train. Otherwise, her brother Joseph could accompany her. He gave her a hasty kiss, and left, without breakfast.

He was hardly out of sight when artillery began to roll. Volleys shook the house and brought the Yerby family to panic. The Reverend Lacy appeared with an ambulance, saying that Jackson had sent him to get them out of danger. They went off with no more than a note from Jackson, saying that he could not leave his post.

Anna, Hetty and Julia went with their baggage into the crude vehicle just as musketry began to rattle in the area about the house. On her way to catch the train to Richmond, Anna saw "several wounded soldiers brought in and placed in the out houses, which the surgeons were arranging as temporary hospitals. This was my nearest and only glimpse of the actual horrors of the battlefield, and the reader can imagine how sad and harrowing was my drive to the station on that terrible morning!"

Jackson no longer had time to concern himself for his family's safety. He had immediately sent a message to Lee about the

Federal move; the enemy had come over a pontoon bridge and now lay in strength on the river bank, though they did not appear to be ready to attack. Jackson was forming a strong line along the railroad track parallel to the river. The message found Lee in his tent. He was notably calm.

"Well, I heard firing," Lee said. "And I was beginning to think it was time some of you lazy young fellows were coming to tell me what it was all about. Say to General Jackson that he knows just as well what to do with the enemy as I do."

Jackson went to the front, saw that two vigorous officers, Early and Rodes, were making proper plans to receive the enemy, and he returned to headquarters. Here he discovered that the movement in his front was probably a feint, and that the enemy was crossing in force above Fredericksburg, to the west, and that Union troops in great numbers were moving through the rough country toward a village called Chancellorsville.

Just as his servants were striking his tent, Jackson stepped inside for a final moment, dropping the canvas behind him. Soldiers near by were startled to hear Jim cry, "Hush! The General is praying." Within a few moments the staring men saw Old Jack emerge. There was an Old Testament look about his face.

★★★ CHANCELLORSVILLE

The Virginia spring was now in full flower, and in the woods beyond the drying roads were drifts of redbud and dogwood. Peaches and cherries were in bloom, and on the damp earth were carpets of bluets and mandrakes and bloodroot and rue anemones. Few soldiers took note of them.

North of the river, Fighting Joe Hooker was stripping for action the world's finest army, so he proudly declared. Unmistakable orders had gone out. Not a Confederate private but understood what was to come.

President Lincoln had spared nothing to give Hooker the mightiest army the Union could muster, backed by mountains of supplies. Lincoln had lately written his commander:

> . . . Our primary object is the enemy's army in front of us. . . . What then? The two armies are face to face, with a narrow river between them. Our communications are shorter and safer than those of the enemy. For this reason we can with equal powers fret him more than he can us . . . continually harass and menace him . . . If he weakens himself then pitch into him.

Hooker had made plans, several of them, but always with this central idea, which he explained to Lincoln:

402

After giving the subject my best reflection, I have concluded that I will have more chance of inflicting a heavier
blow upon the enemy by turning his position to my right
(that is, moving upstream), and if practicable, to sever his
communications with Richmond.

Hooker could keep few secrets. Lee wrote to Richmond that
the Federals were issuing ninety thousand rations, and concluded
that the enemy had seventy thousand men, at a minimum. Lee's
privates evidently knew even more. They yelled across the river,
deriding the Yankees about the eight days' rations they had been
ordered to carry.

A Washington newspaper, the *Morning Chronicle*, soon gave
Lee even more accurate knowledge of Federal strength, by blandly
publishing vital facts on the Army of the Potomac: The sick of
March 28 numbered 10,777; the ratio of sick to the entire army
was 67.64 per 1,000. Hooker wrote the Secretary of War in anger
and alarm, protesting the article, but it was too late; as he had
feared, Lee was now working out the interesting Federal arithme-
tic. He began to understand what odds he faced. Hooker over-
estimated Lee's strength but was not unaware of his advantage,
even so. The Federals had positive information that most of
Longstreet's big corps was still far away, near Suffolk.

On April twenty-sixth, a cold, gray, rainy day, the Federal
movement had begun in earnest, most of the strength moving upriver toward the fords west of Fredericksburg. The men carried
sixty-pound packs, and, as usual, littered the roads with discarded
burdens. They sang:

"Joe Hooker is our leader, he takes his whisky strong,
So our knapsacks we will sling, and go marching along."

On April twenty-ninth, the day Mrs. Jackson was rushed back
to Richmond to avoid Federal cannon fire, Lincoln wired Hooker:
"How does it look now?"
The reply:
"I am not sufficiently advanced to give an opinion. We are busy.
Will tell you all as soon as I can, and will have it satisfactory."
Hooker was entertaining guests at a review on this day, min-

isters from Sweden and Prussia, as well as a clutch of Washington politicians and officials.

By April thirtieth, Lee was positive that Hooker's main assault would come from upstream, and he began to shift some of his regiments away from the Fredericksburg area. Fog hung heavily in rear of the lines of the left. In that direction lay a vast entangled forest of black jack oaks and stunted scrub called the Wilderness. Through this unlovely country ran one good road, the Plank Road, running west from Fredericksburg and entering the Wilderness at a place called Salem Church. This highway divided in the scrub, joined again at a point some ten miles from Fredericksburg, only to separate once more. The one road thus afforded a network of trails in the Wilderness, with one of the chief junctions at the place known as Chancellorsville, which was marked by a single brick house in a clearing of about one hundred acres.

Lee and Jackson were fully aware of this country, but on April thirtieth still had to give their attention to the banks of the Rappahannock, near the old Fredericksburg battlefield. Here the Federal guns on the opposite hills commanded the bottom lands and made it dangerous to launch an attack on the enemy regiments which had already crossed to the south side. The two commanders studied the terrain with care, discussing the possibility of assault, and Lee said, "I will give orders for it, if you think it can be done."

Jackson rode out to make a further inspection, moving slowly through a sifting rain, studying the big guns. He at last concluded with regret that it would be unwise to attack here on the river. He asked Lee what remained to be done.

Lee referred him to the map, and ran a finger over the darkened area of the Spotsylvania Wilderness. He was convinced, Lee said, that Hooker would push his columns through this country to hit at the Confederate left. He gave Jackson orders to move in that direction on the following morning—Friday, May first.

With him, Jackson was to take General McLaws with the three brigades Longstreet had left behind. Early's division, with a bit of support from Mississippi troops and some good artillery, would hold the river front. Jackson must get into the Wilderness and meet Hooker's advance. The army must not fight here against the river bank.

Jackson was not surprised. He had already had Hotchkiss make detailed maps of the region which included the Wilderness, and for himself had made a copy extending the ground far to the west so that he would have wide room for maneuvering.

Just after midnight of May first, Jackson got into his new uniform and passed orders to put the troops in motion. When a warm, soft day came, the corps was well on its way to the Plank Road, where it was to turn to the west. General Rodes and his men led, with A. P. Hill and Trimble's old division, under General Colston, in their rear. It was a tiny force to throw into the path of Hooker, who was driving through the scrublands, but at about 8 A.M. Jackson settled his men near Chancellorsville, around the lines of a jaunty vanguard commanded by General R. H. Anderson. There were reports that the woods out front were acrawl with the enemy.

Reports of the enemy's approach increased, and men in the shallow trenches of the front line became anxious. One of them asked General Anderson what they would do in the face of so many Yankees. "Fight," Anderson snapped. "General Lee says so."

By the time Jackson reached the scene, McLaws and his men were also in line, and six brigades faced the enemy. Jackson robbed the men of even this comfort, for he got them up and marched forward. One column moved over the section of the road known as the Old Turnpike toward the Chancellorsville clearing, and the other moved on the Plank Road toward the same objective. The bulk of Jackson's corps, when it came up, would follow the second column.

Old Jack began the forward push at 11 A.M.; and had taken no more than a few steps when Yankee scouts noted his move. At eleven twenty the first gun of the battle of Chancellorsville sounded, and a gray shellburst hung over the tangled scrub. Jackson was riding with the southernmost wing on the Plank Road. To his right, he heard, McLaws had been caught up in a musket fight. Jackson's front also met the enemy. A battle was building up.

McLaws sent a brief message: He was faced by vast numbers of the enemy. He was waiting far short of the Chancellorsville clearing. A flank attack, McLaws thought, might be launched from the Plank Road. The Federals were alert on each road. Jackson was making plans to blast his way through with artillery, when he opened a dispatch from Stuart:

"General: I am on a road running from Spotsylvania C.H. to Silvers, which is on Plank Road three miles below Chancellorsville. . . . I will close in on the flank and help all I can when the ball opens. . . . May God grant us victory."

Jackson scratched a reply on the back of the dispatch: "I trust that God will grant us a great victory. Keep closed on Chancellorsville."

Old Jack had completed his note when Lee came up and assumed charge of the ground; he explained to Jackson that he had left Early on the river to hold off the Federals in the rear. Lee listened as Jackson described the situation in the forest. The enemy, Stonewall said, had seemed timid. In case it was needed, a flank movement could be made to the south, where the ground favored it. Lee went out of sight to reconnoiter, leaving Jackson to direct affairs.

At about 4 P.M., after hours of minor skirmishing, Jackson rode to Catharine Furnace—an old ironworks—and here met Jeb Stuart.

These two came under artillery fire when they went to a knoll to study the country, and could learn little of what lay to the west of them. Jackson rode back and forth along his line; and after a time, when the forward push halted, he went up to a South Carolina regiment in the vanguard. A shrewd line officer, Captain Alex Haskell, greeted Jackson.

"What is it, Captain Haskell?"

"Ride up here, General, and you will see it all."

Jackson and A. P. Hill and their staffs rode with Haskell a short distance to a point from which they had a view rare in this country, a clear look over miles of the stunted growth, to Chancellorsville itself. The triple lines of the enemy were in plain sight. The position of Hooker was based on earthworks and would be difficult to storm, perhaps impossible.

For the first time, it was clear that Hooker had been brought to a stand. From this point there would be serious fighting. Lee's force of 60,000 must find some means of reducing the odds held by Hooker's 130,000.

Jackson's somewhat distracted manner as he watched the enemy hinted that he was groping for the solution. He studied the Federals for a long time, as if he were not satisfied with what he saw.

He turned to Haskell: "Hold this ground until 9 o'clock to-night. You will be relieved." He then entrusted the young officer with the passwords for the night, which were "Liberty" and "Independence." Jackson went in search of Lee, whom he found in a stand of scrubby pine. It was near dark when the officers turned their horses out of the Plank Road and went under the trees to escape the fire of an enemy sharpshooter. Lee dismounted and sat on a log, beckoning Jackson.

Lee asked for a report on the left of the line. Jackson described the timorous action of the Federals throughout the afternoon and then told Lee of the fortified line in which the Federals now lay. Old Jack expressed the positive opinion that Hooker was making some kind of feint, or that his plans had miscarried. "None of them will be on this side of the river tomorrow," he said.

Staff officers watched Lee's firm shake of the head. "I hope you may be right," Lee said. "But I believe Hooker will deliver his main attack here. He would not have gone to such lengths and then give up without effort."

Jackson said once more, quietly, that he thought the enemy would fall back and cross the Rappahannock to the north bank.

Lee turned to a canvass of the possible means of attack for tomorrow. The thick tangle on the right prevented a move in that direction. Perhaps the troops should be hurled straight ahead, despite the forbidding Union rifle pits. Lee suggested a careful study of the front, and picked Colonel T. M. R. Talcott from his staff; Jackson sent Boswell with him. The two engineers left the commanders in the grove and went forward on foot, in the light of a rising moon. One of their first sights was unforgettable, the whitened face of a dead Confederate picket whose body hung on a fence.

Lee and Jackson and the other officers waited, becoming chilled. Lee asked Jackson detailed questions about the chances of a flank attack by the left. Jackson could tell him little about the roads, except that he had seen them briefly from his hill in the late afternoon. He could not be sure how good they were, nor how wide, nor whether they would hide a force from the enemy.

There was a stir in the roadway as they talked, and Jeb Stuart reported: Fitz Lee and his troopers had found an uncovered Federal flank in the woodland. Stuart said his men had been able to come quite near the enemy because Hooker had sent his cavalry on a raid to the south. The unprotected flank could be approached from the Confederate left, if suitable roads could be found.

Lee asked Stuart about the roads, and the cavalry chief was soon riding away to make an investigation. He had been gone but a short while when Talcott and Boswell returned, and they confirmed all that Jackson had said of the Yankee line in the front. It seemed impregnable. An attack there would be ill-advised. Enemy troops were still digging tonight, and the thick trees in the front would prevent artillery fire against the entrenchments.

By the light of a lantern, Lee studied his map, and the conversation became more animated. Officers crowded closer. The generals were in agreement that the enemy must be attacked as soon as possible. Lee was thinking aloud, asking himself how he might get at the enemy. Jackson spoke:

"You know best. Show me what to do, and I will try to do it."

This scrap of the conversation struck Talcott as significant at the time, before it became apparent that Jackson was receiving orders for the supreme stroke of his career.

Lee had at last made up his mind. He stood and ran his finger rather vaguely over the left-hand roads on the map. The details, he said, would be left to Jackson. He would choose the exact route, launch the troops and arrange the timing of the assault. Lee gave only one specific order: "Stuart will cover you with the cavalry."

Jackson gave a quick reply, with a salute. "My troops will move at 4 o'clock."

Lee nodded and told him to check the enemy's position in the morning. Jackson left the place.

He halted a few hundred yards away and dismounted in the woodland with Smith and Pendleton. It was becoming colder and Jackson had neither coat nor blanket. He at first refused Pendleton's offer of a cape, but under insistent pleas he pulled it about him and lay on the damp earth. He stirred after a brief nap and went to Pendleton, who slept against a tree. Jackson draped the cloak about the young aide and went back to his place on the ground. When Pendleton rose in the darkness of early morning, Jackson was asleep without cover. The General began to sneeze.

Old Jack went to a campfire near by and sat on a cracker box, holding his hands near the warmth. A tall figure came into the light, the Reverend Lacy, Jackson's chief chaplain and a man thoroughly familiar with this neighborhood, where his family owned lands. Lacy had arrived late in the night and had already conferred with General Lee on the roads of the region.

Jackson invited Lacy to sit on one end of the cracker box. There was a brief interrogation:

"Is there a road over which I could hit the enemy in the flank —either flank?"

"There is nothing on the right, but you could use several roads to the left. They lead to the turnpike beyond Chancellorsville."

Jackson gave Lacy a map and a pencil. "Draw it here for me."

Lacy marked off a road, but one which lay near by and soon crossed into the lines of the enemy.

"That one is too near. I want to get well around behind the enemy, and without being seen. You don't know of another road?" Jackson asked.

"There is none that I know of. But there must be some sort of trail from Catharine Furnace into the Plank Road, for moving the iron ore."

"Who can tell us about it?"

The owner of the smelting furnace had a young son who knew the country well, a boy named Charles Wellford, Jr. He might guide officers over the flank. Jackson was excited. He aroused Jed Hotchkiss, explained the situation and sent him with Lacy to find the elder Wellford. They were to determine whether there was such a road as he needed, and whether it would pass big guns. Hotchkiss would hurry back with the news, and Lacy would find young Wellford to act as guide.

It was still dark when the two men left. Jackson was joined at the fire by Colonel Armistead Long, and the pair sat in silence

until the shivering Jackson complained of the cold. Long brought
him a cup of coffee from a neighboring fire. While Old Jack drank,
his saber fell from its place against a tree. Long picked it up—
wondering, he later said, if this were an ill omen. Jackson buckled
the weapon about his waist.

Lee came. He sat by the fire on another of the numerous cracker
boxes the enemy had left here recently and talked with Jackson.
They speculated over whether Hooker would attack this morning
and spoil their planned maneuver. Jackson told Lee of the mission of Lacy and Hotchkiss, but said little else.

Hotchkiss arrived hurriedly. There was a road on the flank,
he reported. Wellford had shown him a covered route that would
put the army well to the enemy's rear.

"I have sketched it," Hotchkiss said. "If you would like to see
it."

He drew up a cracker box between Lee and Jackson and opened
his map. He traced a well-defined track: it was about twelve
miles long and ran southwest from Catharine Furnace until it
crossed what was known as the Brock Road. Here was a slight
detour of some two thousand feet to the south to avoid a clearing, and then back into Brock Road, going north into the Plank
Road. Lee and Jackson missed no detail, and Hotchkiss answered
their questions with clarity. The generals were soon satisfied.

"General Jackson," Lee asked, "what do you propose to do?"

Jackson put his finger on the route they had discussed. "Go
around here," he said in a calm voice.

Lee then turned to discuss the business of the day. "And what
do you propose to make this movement with?"

Jackson did not hesitate. "With my whole corps."

Lee's eyes turned briefly to Old Jack's face, and then to the
map.

"And what will you leave me?"

"The divisions of Anderson and McLaws."

In short, Jackson proposed to hurl all of his men through
the Wilderness in a vast flanking attack, leaving Lee to face
Hooker's vast force with a puny line of under fifteen thousand
men.

If Jackson's audacity surprised Lee, or made him fearful of

facing the enemy with the skeleton of an army, he gave no sign. "Well, go on."

Lee began to scratch out orders. Jackson went to prepare for the road.

Some of the troops at breakfast yelped a few cheers as he passed but soon quieted, seeing signs of trouble in Jackson's face. It was much later than he had planned—five o'clock—when the leading company left the Plank Road and wound through the Wilderness toward the iron furnace. The order of march was: Rodes, Colston (who had the old Stonewall Brigade), and A. P. Hill. The files were long and were followed by wagon trains heavy with ammunition and by jolting ambulances.

When the march had begun, and Jackson saw the first troops well along the narrow woods track, he returned to Lee. It was their last meeting. It was 7 A.M., May second.

Jackson slowed Sorrel, and after the generals had passed brief words which no one could overhear, Jackson gave a familiar gesture. He pointed down the road and glanced at Lee from beneath his cap. Lee looked after him as he disappeared in the forest.

The day was pleasant until the sun rose high, when the men became thirsty and shrugged out of their jackets. The road was firm but soft underfoot, without being either dusty or muddy. Progress was at first rapid. Few officers had been told what was planned. The inquisitive von Borcke wrote: "All was bustle and activity as I galloped along the lines . . . Jackson's corps was marching in close columns in a direction which set us all wondering what could be his intentions, but we would as soon have thought of questioning the sagacity of our admired chief as of hesitating to follow him blindly wherever he should lead."

The march was almost without incident. Jackson minimized one danger when he found an exposed stretch of roadway on heights near the iron furnace. His men had been seen by Federals, and a few shells dropped into the clearing. Jackson had them run over the ground here at double time and had swung aside the wagons into an even more remote woodland trail. Jackson placed a brigade here to guard his vulnerable column.

Old Jack constantly hurried his officers. Once, while riding with General Colston, Jackson pointed out that this was indeed a Virginia Military Institute caravan. Rodes and Colston had been assistant professors in Lexington, and Munford of the cavalry had been cadet adjutant. The others recalled more V.M.I. men who marched with the army: Stapleton Crutchfield, General Whiting, James Lane, of the class of 1854; and Lindsay

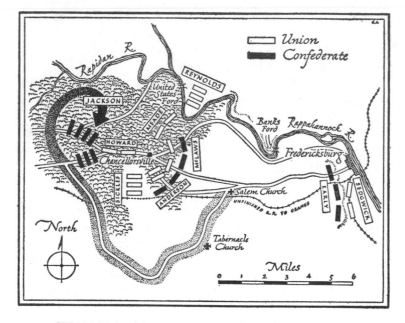

CHANCELLORSVILLE—JACKSON'S ATTACK

Walker, class of 1845. There were perhaps a dozen officers of field rank who had been comrades in Lexington.

Jackson turned to thoughts of the enemy: "I hear that General Hooker has more men than he can handle. I should like to have half as many more as I have today, and I would throw him into the river. . . . We have always had to put all our troops in fighting line, and never had enough when we needed them most."

The officers went on with the subdued rumbling of the column all about them. The march until noon seemed almost peaceful.

In the Federal lines there was no lack of warning. Jackson's secret had been known almost from the start but, because of an incredible chain of circumstances, was to be disregarded until it was too late.

It remained for Hooker to misinterpret the reports of dozens of competent officers. His mood today was not at all that of the day before, when he had timidly pulled back his advance and canceled plans to attack. One of his generals, Regis de Trobriand, recalled the morning:

"Hooker began to be troubled about what was going on in our front beyond that dense curtain of woods. He sent forward troops, and through an opening in the woods there appeared a column of Rebels marching rapidly from the left to the right. . . . This movement threatened our right . . . less disposition had been made against attack there than elsewhere. The whole 11th Corps prolonged the general line parallel to the road. A small brigade thrown back barred this road with two guns, resting on nothing, leaving our extreme right completely in the air."

Hooker, seeing the movement, instantly divined the obvious. He could see the stream of Jackson's troops from his own headquarters. Hooker spread his map on his cot and said, half to himself, "It can't be retreat. Retreat without a fight? That is not Lee. If not retreat, what is it? Lee is trying to flank me."

A Federal party went forward toward Jackson's route but was delayed in the thick scrub. This attack managed to take some of Old Jack's rear guard, five hundred men of the Twenty-seventh Georgia, who surrendered in a body.

Hooker warned his flank commander of the right, General O. O. Howard, but then appeared to forget the danger. By early afternoon, headquarters had concluded that it was retreat, and not attack, that Jackson planned.

A cavalry captain on the Federal flank near General Howard's command of Germans wrote: "The movement of Jackson's force . . . had been noticed by our pickets . . . the Confederate forces appeared to be moving away from our front, and it was believed . . . in full retreat on Richmond. . . .

"About noon General Hooker, superbly mounted, a picture of manly beauty, accompanied by a large staff, had come riding the lines. He was greeted with cheers as he passed, and we were all relieved as we felt that our position has been personally inspected by the commanding general."

For several hours diligent Federal officers begged superiors to take note of the gathering storm on the right. An Ohio colonel from the front lines took several pickets to brigade headquarters, where they told of seeing the Rebels swarming across their front. The generals were not impressed. The colonel went to division headquarters three times, and on the third was barked at by General Devens, "You are frightened, sir." The colonel went even further, to corps headquarters, where a bevy of gold-braided officers laughed at him and sent him back to his lines.

A well-known and gallant artilleryman, Captain Hubert Dilger, found the enemy swarming in on his front and tried to see General Howard. He was laughingly refused admittance. Dilger was finally defeated by reading a dispatch from Hooker's headquarters at 4:10 P.M.: "We know the enemy is fleeing and trying to save his trains." Dilger went to his post, but he was not reassured. He held his gunners ready, and would not permit his horses to be moved, even for water.

At two forty-five, a major, Owen Rice, had sent a message to the commander of his brigade: "A large body of the enemy is massing in my front. For God's sake, make disposition to receive him!" The message went up to the one-armed Howard, who laughed and said no men could push through thickets in his area.

Hooker had already made preparations for the chase of Lee's army on the morrow, in this order: "The Major General commanding desires that you replenish your supplies of forage, provisions and ammunition to be ready to start at an early hour tomorrow."

Later, the fragment of Union cavalry which Hooker had left himself brought in a few tattered prisoners. The horsemen jeered at the Confederates. One of the prisoners retorted, "You may think you've done a great thing just now—but you wait till Old Jack gets around on your right!" The Federals laughed.

Some time before the sun approached the horizon over the dense trees, the smells of cooking supper came from the far right of the Union line.

Through these hours, Jackson rode with a growing impatience, almost as if he were unconscious of the enemy's weak and belated sallies toward his line of march. Dr. Hunter McGuire recalled: "Never can I forget the eagerness and intensity of Jackson on that march. . . . His face was pale, his eyes flashing. Out from his thin compressed lips came the terse command: 'Press forward! Press forward!' In his eagerness as he rode, he leaned over on the neck of his horse, as if in that way the march might be hurried. 'See that the column is kept closed, and there is no straggling,' he more than once ordered; and 'Press on, press on!' was repeated again and again."

Jackson had placed officers behind each regiment with a guard of bayonets and orders to spear stragglers. Even so, men fell out of the ranks. A Georgia colonel wrote: "Many fell . . . exhausted, some fainting and having spasms; only a few had eaten anything since the morning before."

Far in the rear, Lee waited. In the late morning he wrote to President Davis:

"I find the enemy in a strong position at Chancellorsville and in large force. . . . He seems determined to make the fight here. . . . It is plain that if the enemy is too strong for me here, I shall have to fall back and Fredericksburg must be abandoned. . . .

"I am now swinging around to my left to come up in his [the enemy's] rear. . . .

"If I had with me all my command, and could keep it supplied with provisions and forage, I should feel easy, but as far as I can judge the advantage of numbers and position is greatly in favor of the enemy."

Lee had yet no informative report from Jackson.

Old Jack pushed on. When his vanguard came in sight of the Plank Road at about 1 P.M., the main force had not seen a Federal. A few enemy cavalrymen fled as the Rebels advanced, and Virginia troopers gave chase.

Jackson and General Fitz Lee went to the Burton Farm in the neighborhood, and looked down on the enemy. An account was left by Fitz Lee:

"Upon reaching the Plank Road some five miles west of Chancellorsville, while waiting for Stonewall to come up, I made a personal reconnaissance. What a sight presented itself to me! The soldiers were in groups, laughing, chatting, smoking . . . feeling safe and comfortable. In the rear of them were other parties driving up and slaughtering beeves.

"So impressed was I with my discovery that I rode rapidly back to the point on the Plank Road where I met Stonewall himself. 'General,' I said, 'ride with me.' He assented, and I rapidly conducted him to the point of observation. There had been no change in the picture. It was then about 2 P.M. I watched him closely. His eyes burned with a brilliant glow, lighting up a sad face; his expression was one of intense interest; his face was colored slightly . . . and radiant at the success of his flank movement.

"To my remarks he did not reply once during the five minutes he was on the hill; and yet his lips were moving.

"One more look on the Federal lines, and then he rode rapidly down the hill, his arms flapping to the motions of his horse, over whose head it seemed, good rider as he was, he would certainly go.

"Alas! I had looked on him for the last time."

Jackson soon arrived on the old turnpike. He was disappointed to find that he had not passed the enemy flank and come into the rear of the blue lines. He gave quick orders: "Tell General Rodes to move across the Plank Road; halt when he gets to the old turnpike, and I will join him there."

Fitz Lee was a bit chagrined to see Jackson leave with no word of praise for his discovery: "I expected to be told I had made a valuable personal reconnaissance—saving the lives of many soldiers—and that Jackson was indebted to me to that amount at least."

But Old Jack was in a hurry now. He gave Colonel Mumford orders to ride on the left of the column and take the road leading to Ely's Ford on the Rapidan, if possible. He added gaily, "The Virginia Military Institute will be heard from today!"

Jackson turned to the roadside; and sitting on a stump, either hurry or excitement making his handwriting shakier than usual, he wrote his last dispatch:

> Near 3 P.M., May 2, 1863
>
> General,
> The enemy has made a stand at Chancellor's which is about miles from Chancellorsville. I hope as soon as practicable to attack.
> I trust that an ever kind Providence will bless us with great success.
>
> Respectfully,
> T. J. Jackson.
> Gen'l R. E. Lee
>
> The leading division is up and the next two appear to be well closed.

He read over the message and saw that he had omitted the mileage figure in the second line, and with a swift pen he inserted the digit "2."

Within an hour his pickets had exchanged fire with the enemy, but skirmishing was light and the Federals did not take alarm. Jackson gave specific orders to General Rodes, who commanded the vanguard. Under cover of a ridge the men were brought up and spread in battle formation. Other regiments came behind them, slowly now, taking precious time to crowd into heavy files. The front now lay perpendicular to the turnpike and reached for about a mile on either side of it. At the sound of bugles, the ranks were to drive ahead at full speed.

It was getting late. Perhaps too late. At his distant position Lee had begun to lose hope.

The Federals who were within sight of Jackson's column were cooking supper.

Old Jack finally saw a bugler following a group of officers toward him. He looked at his watch: five fifteen. Major Eugene Blackford, coming from the front, said that the lines were ready.

Jackson turned to Rodes.

"Are you ready, General Rodes?"

"Yes, sir."

Jackson's voice was slow. "You can go forward then."

Bugle calls ripped through the quiet, and men rustled into the thickets. Almost at this instant there came a faint sound of distant firing in the forest. A cavalry captain turned to ask Jackson whose guns those were.

"How far do you suppose it is?" Jackson asked.

"Five or six miles."

"I suppose it is General Lee."

Before Jackson there was a crash of muskets and men began to run. The Rebel Yell rolled through the woods. Startled Federal batteries fired a few rounds. The Germans of the exposed Union Eleventh Corps looked up in terror to see, beyond the droves of fleeing deer and rabbits, the plunging lines of Confederates. The enemy turned and ran. The flank was rolled up as if made of paper. Jackson's men met momentary confusions, but overwhelmed resistance and swept everything before them.

General Howard caught his first glimpse of the catastrophe which had befallen him: "It was a terrible gale. The rush, the rattle, the quick lightning from a hundred points at once; the roar redoubled by the echoes through the forest; the panic, the dead and dying in sight, and the wounded straggling along; the frantic efforts of the brave and patriotic to stay the angry storm."

Jackson had crushed Hooker's flank, but perhaps, even so, it was too late for victory today. Within an hour, or at a little after 6 P.M., there remained of General Devens's division only wreckage and tiny pockets of resistance. Jackson's troops had obliterated Howard's first line and now held high ground on every hand. Snarls in marching orders and confusion of the swift attack had held back about five thousand men on one flank of the advance, but this did not seem to lessen the power of the charge.

At a little after six o'clock, a second charge ordered by Jackson had carried forward to a place known as Dowdall's Tavern. By now, Federal resistance had begun to organize. In some quarters there was terrific cannon fire before the Confederates. The skirmishers ran into fortified positions.

General Hooker was sitting on the porch of the house at Chancellorsville, taking his evening toddy. An officer behind him, peering westward with a field glass, shouted, "My God, here they come!" Hooker and his staff mounted and galloped along the

Plank Road, where they met flying fugitives, the first of the ambulances, and news of disaster. Hooker's generals hurriedly formed emergency lines of battle.

Captain Hartwell Osborn of the cavalry, serving with Howard, saw the rout from the Federal ranks:

"Along our front deer and wild game came scurrying . . . firing increased and soon came nearer. The right was steadily falling back . . . bullets began to hail down our line from right and rear . . . It was the most trying experience the command ever endured . . . the whole clearing became one mass of panic-stricken soldiers flying at the top of their speed . . . As we passed General Hooker's headquarters a scene burst upon us which, God grant, may never again be seen in the Federal army of the United States. The 11th Corps had been routed . . . Aghast and terror-stricken, heads bare and panting for breath, they pleaded like infants at the mother's breast that we should let them pass to the rear unhindered."

Captain R. E. Wilbourn, the chief signal officer of Jackson's staff, kept up with the commander through most of this attack, watching the General as he cheered on his men, leaning far down on Sorrel, pushing outward with his hand as if he would lift them ahead physically, shouting, "Press forward! Press forward!"

Wilbourn wrote of Old Jack as the great attack tore through the forest:

"Frequently . . . he would stop, raise his hand, and turn his eyes toward Heaven, as if praying for a blessing on our arms. The frequency with which this was done that evening attracted the attention of all with him.

"Our troops made repeated charges, driving the enemy before them every time, which caused loud and long-continued cheering along our entire line . . . and General Jackson would invariably raise his hand and give thanks to Him who gave the victory. I have never seen him seem so well pleased with the progress and results of a fight as on that occasion.

"On several occasions during this fight, as he passed the bodies of some of our veterans, he halted, raised his hand as if to ask a blessing upon them, and to pray to God to save their souls."

23

★★★ "MY OWN MEN!"

The moon rose. Not a cloud hung in the sky, and the forest lanes glittered with light. But it was pitch dark in the trees, and banks of smoke drifted everywhere. There was a stench of powder, the dead, the lowland creeks. A crazy quilt of fire blazed in the brush, and from burning thickets the wounded called, threshing, whimpering for water. There was a growing lull in the battle, broken by sporadic volleys of musketry; less frequently, when something in the night aroused the guns, the mad landscape was scourged by artillery fire. Already the two armies had strewn the wilderness with almost six thousand dead and wounded.

Men fired at the slightest motion, and the night was full of shadows. No man knew where the front lines now lay, and the forces flailed in the forest, striking fire and explosions when they blundered against each other.

Jackson's victorious troops, having run like pursuing hounds into the deep tangle, were being overcome—not by the enemy, but by darkness, thickets, the drifting apart of files, loss of officers, rupture of communications. Some companies succumbed to hunger, halting to loot overrun Federal camp sites and abandoned knapsacks, scattering, joining strange outfits. Like a dammed

420

stream the advance broadened, slowed, and halted. The forward waves ceased movement a little after seven o'clock.

Within ten minutes Jackson was aware that his onslaught was no longer. His officers had never seen him so elated, though they had to read the signs in the tones of his voice as he snapped precise answers to messengers coming and going, and in the vigorous impatience with which he went toward the front. He did not hesitate but began to prepare for a night attack in order to restore the momentum of his corps. With an ear cocked toward the happy tumult of calling by his men, he paused in the twilight by Dowdall's Tavern, beswarmed with couriers and officers.

Word from the front was that the first and second lines had halted. He must now order up the third, the division of A. P. Hill. Good news came from General Rodes, who had gone ahead to reconnoiter: No Federals lay between Jackson's lines and the vital heights at Fairview.

Someone in the confusion of the roadway saw Jackson at about that moment, there in the thronging passage of a conquering army almost, but not quite, out of control. He had halted in a familiar attitude, his face turned skyward, his right hand raised in prayerful thanksgiving.

An excited colonel, Cobb of the Forty-fourth Virginia, came to report: Confederates, as ordered, had seized the strong breastworks near Chancellorsville, without the loss of a man.

It was not yet victory, not in Jackson's mind. He gave his orders with an assurance that made him seem the only man to comprehend this bewildering field. He could not have been unaware that he had launched, and all but completed, one of the most audacious strokes of military history. But he could not rest.

The army, indeed, was in a moment of supreme peril. Its main forces were divided, and now further scattered. If, by some miracle, the Federals could recover to launch an attack, Lee's army might be destroyed in the night. He must push troops ahead to Chancellorsville itself, and in some strength.

Not even he could know the exact state of confusion among the enemy, where continuing panic had staged indescribable scenes. Far beyond him, in the Yankee-held areas of the forest, the Dutchmen of the broken Eleventh Corps yet fled like wild things, and swept almost all before them. As stout new lines were formed against the disaster by sweating, cursing officers, the tide of Dutch terror burst over them, ripping them apart. From every direction, it seemed, came this stream of wide-eyed, panting men going to the Union rear, among them beef cattle gone mad, plunging guns and their frantic teams, caissons, ambulances, wagons. Hospital stations were overrun, tents trampled, the wounded overturned. A group of doctors, up to bloody elbows in their work, stampeded and ran away with the Germans. The fleeing thousands left behind an endless debris, and where they went, they spread terror. At the least disturbance, other, smaller flights were begun. At the extreme rear, on the river, sutlers and camp followers were busily crossing.

It was a miracle that Jackson, even at his distance, could not hear the chorus of fear croaked by the unfortunate Dutchmen, who beat at their officers and clambered over road blocks. The Dutchmen were already ripping from their caps and shoulders the telltale crescent insignia of their corps, by now a badge of infamy and disgrace.

In some aisles of the forest there was great courage by the Army of the Potomac in face of the Dutch melee, and in those places the steady troops beat back their frenetic comrades and established a bulwark against Jackson. Union officers placed their men in line on their bellies, bayonets upraised, and in these steel traps caught shoals of Germans. One colonel, lying thus with his troops, snared a Dutch general, who fled into a ditch, screaming, "Sarr, you do not know who I am! I am Prigadier General" The colonel captured him with a naked saber: "You're nothing but a damned coward to me."

In the mid-current of retreat, handsome Joe Hooker sat his white horse for a time, turning about, calling encouragement in a princely voice. "Receive them with the bayonet, men!" he cried, pointing to the oncoming Dutchmen. "Receive them with the bayonet!" He seemed a rock of courage, but in the sight of the stricken faces of the disintegrating corps, he must have found something to shake him.

The stunned Howard himself, desperate at the wreckage of his corps, pottered in vain among the jostling men. He was ordered by a lieutenant colonel from Hooker's staff to turn his artillery upon the retreating mass. "I will never fire upon my own men!" he shouted. And from somewhere the brave, distraught general drew forth an American flag, and pressing it with the stump of his arm, he held it over his breast as the remainder of his men broke past him toward safety.

Though he could not witness these spectacles, Jackson could shrewdly divine what had befallen the victims of his flank attack and perceive what he must do now. He prepared orders extending his lines to Chancellorsville and then rode ahead, scouting out the dim scene, giving little attention to those who galloped with him as they threaded along the crowded tracks—men crawling in and out of the underbrush, horsemen passing, men calling to companions, companies seeking new positions, reinforcements moving up, litter-bearers, deserters, skulkers, Negro servants. At their feet along the roadsides lay the dead and wounded.

John Casler, the private in Jackson's ranks, would not forget these hours:

"The woods, taking fire that night from the shells, burnt rapidly and roasted the wounded men alive. As we went to bury them we could see where they had tried to keep the fire from them by scratching the leaves away as far as they could reach. But it availed not; they were burnt to a crisp. The only way we could tell to which army they belonged was by turning them over and examining their clothing where they lay close to the ground, so we could see whether they wore the blue or the gray.

"We buried them all alike by covering them up with dirt where they lay. It was the most sickening sight I saw during the war and I wondered whether the American people were civilized or not, to butcher one another in that manner; and I came to the conclusion that we were barbarians, North and South alike."

Jackson went impatiently through the traffic, shouting, "Men, get into line! Into line! Whose regiment are you? Colonel, can't you keep a line? Get these men under control instantly." Then on, with the disquieting knowledge that Hooker would not long delay in flooding his front with new troops, knowing that the enemy had a reservoir of men and could yet commit regiments which had scarcely heard the sound of guns during the day. If Jackson could join his own ranks with those of Lee, by pushing Lane's brigade to the front, he might prepare a fresh assault upon Hooker's rear, while Lee once more occupied the attention of the enemy. The stage might then be set for the final act, the breaking of the Union columns against the river. Jackson might have his opportunity by daylight.

Jackson halted at a busy road intersection, where the roads from Hazel Grove and Bullock's joined the Plank Road. Here he untied from his saddle his India-rubber cloak, and drew the thick wrap about him against the increasing dampness of the chilly night. Over the passing of men there was a call: "General Hill? Anybody seen Hill?"

Jackson answered. It was General James Lane who had called.

"My orders," Lane said. "You want us to draw the line about here? I can't find Hill."

Jackson flung his arm abruptly, all but shouting. "Push right ahead, Lane. Right ahead."

A group of horsemen emerged from the shadows. It was A. P. Hill and his staff, and before the officers had opportunity to exchange their triumphant gossip, Jackson was passing his order. As if impatient that it had not been anticipated, he gave Hill the command that he had been holding in his mind since sunset.

"Press them. Cut them off from the United States Ford, Hill. Press them."

"I don't know, General. I don't know. My staff is not familiar with the ground, I'm afraid."

Jackson wheeled to the party behind him, calling to Captain Boswell, his engineer. "Report to General Hill, Boswell, as soon as you can. I want you to show him how the ground lies. I want the ford cut off. You understand?"

As Hill and Jackson rode together, they followed the lead of a single mounted man, a courier named David Kyle, a native of the place who had often passed through the Wilderness trails. Jackson sent him ahead to test the paths. The scout walked his horse through a North Carolina regiment, as Jackson and his staff waited, and moved into a road. He drew fire from the enemy and returned galloping in a hail of harmless musket balls.

Hill then left Jackson, and with no more than a handful of officers and a team of signal sergeants and couriers, Jackson moved into the shadowed Plank Road. With him now were Lieutenant Joe Morrison, his wife's brother; Lieutenant Wynn; and his signal officer, Captain Wilbourn. Jackson took no particular note of them.

He led the party with caution, through a swampy depression, and onto the slope which led to high ground about Chancellorsville. He stopped to listen. Over the weakening cries of men in the darkness, Jackson heard the enemy. Axes were ringing in the front, as the Federals strengthened their works. A few orders could be heard. Jackson remained motionless for several minutes, rigidly attentive, turning in his mind the daring question: Attack?

He made his decision wordlessly and, turning, spurred off the road, heading back toward his own lines. The crackling underbrush seemed louder than the earlier thunder of hooves on the oak planks of the turnpike. Once an officer halted Jackson, with a hand on his bridle. "General, you shouldn't expose yourself. Let me take you back."

"There's no danger, sir. The enemy's routed. Go back and tell General Hill to press on."

The men with Jackson did not recognize the officer.

They were at this moment riding in dappled moonlight, in a dying storm of sound. Absurdly loud, it seemed to men of the staff, the calls of whippoorwills floated through the hot woodland. The staff itself spread ominous sounds as it crossed the front of the Eighteenth North Carolina, of Lane's Brigade.

There had been a report among the North Carolina front ranks that a Yankee cavalry attack was making up, and the men had been tense. Jackson's returning party approached the outposts of this regiment, in a light pounding of hooves and clatter of sabers—sounds for all the world like those of a party of cavalry, forming for a charge. The North Carolinians were given quiet orders: Fire, and repeat fire.

Jackson and his officers were some fifty feet distant. In the uncertain light of the moon they became darkening shadows. They had a Union look about them.

A yellow stitching of musket fire ran along the brush. The

group about Jackson was shattered. Two men fell from saddles, horses screamed and reared.

"Cease firing men!" It sounded like Hill's voice.

Joe Morrison drove toward the ranks of the Carolinians, shouting, "Stop! You're firing at your own men!"

A hurried drawl came back from the bushes: "That's a lie! Pour it on 'em boys!"

Sorrel wheeled under Jackson and carried him off to his right, skittish and rearing. They crossed the front of a second company. There was another volley. Pain staggered Jackson. Men shouted. The General lost his reins, and Sorrel plunged into the brush, in the direction of the enemy. A branch clubbed Jackson across the forehead, stunning him, knocking off his cap, raking a bloody gash. Jackson turned the horse into the open with his wounded hand and slumped in the saddle.

He did not recognize Lieutenant Wynn of his staff as the young man caught him. For a moment in the resounding blackness they stood together, the boy bolstering the hard-breathing general; they were no more than one hundred yards from Federal lines, judging from the sounds. The two listened as if the night hung on what they might hear: digging, scraping of spades, and of something else, probably bayonets and tin plates. Harsh orders in Northern voices. A company of men on the move, singing "John Brown's body lies a-mouldering in the graaaaaave! " Laughter. And the whippoorwills. A shadow approached. It was Captain Wilbourn. With Wynn he led Jackson to a spot beneath a tree.

Wynn gave the General some water and disappeared. "I'll get an ambulance," he called. Wilbourn's voice rose in the road, arguing with some troops in an effort to get litter-bearers. Somehow, General A. P. Hill was there. It was strange that the most bitter of Jackson's enemies within the army should be there to give help.

"Oh, I tried to stop their firing," Hill said. "General, are you much in pain?"

"It's very painful," Jackson said. "I think my arm is broken. I think all my wounds came from my own men." The long face was without color in the moonlight.

Wilbourn sent someone to find help, to see if Confederate lines were near by, and warned, "Don't let them know it's Jackson."

Soon Wilbourn was back at Old Jack's side. With a knife he slashed Jackson's rain cape, then the uniform sleeve and the shirt, revealing slow dark blood on the flesh. Wilbourn took the General's haversack and cape and field glasses. The haversack contained only a few papers, two of them religious tracts.

General Hill pulled off Jackson's gloves, one of them filled with blood. He took Jackson's belt and sword, as well.

Someone held out a whisky bottle. Jackson shook his head, but Wilbourn insisted that he drink, and the General drained the flask, little more than a mouthful. He then asked for more water. He seemed to revive slightly. Someone asked about the coming of a doctor.

"My own men," Jackson said.

"Dr. Barr is here somewhere," a voice said.

"Dr. McGuire," Jackson said. "I want McGuire."

"He's to the rear, General. Dr. Barr is here."

Hill now sat, having taken the wounded man's head in his lap. Jackson whispered, "Is he a skilful surgeon, Hill?"

"He stands high in his brigade. We will have him see to you until McGuire can come."

"Very good." Jackson closed his eyes and seemed to relax.

The doctor, carefully probing, found three wounds, one in the left shoulder, bleeding freely, another in the left forearm, and one in the right palm. A musket ball was lumped under the skin of the hand.

Jackson still lay outside his own lines. Two men stepped into the road near the growing cluster of the party about Jackson, bearing rifles: Federal infantrymen. Hill spoke in a quick casual voice. "Take charge of those men." Several forms went forward and, almost without a struggle, the bluecoats were led to the rear.

Men came and went. Others of the General's party were dead or dying: Boswell and another captain, a sergeant and courier were dead, three others injured. A number of horses were down, and at intervals one of them pawed and screamed in the brush near by. Sorrel had run off into enemy lines where he was to be held, unrecognized, for several days, and then returned.

Jackson stirred with the return of a form to the party, recognizing the voice of Joe Morrison.

"We'll have to move him now," Morrison said. "There's Yank gun crews moving up there on the road. They'd blow us to bits."

Morrison and two others lifted the General into a litter. Jackson's breathing was harsh and staccato. As they entered the road, a yellow explosion burst the night beyond them, and flying iron filled the air. Grapeshot shredded the trees. The party flattened on the roadway, with the young men attempting to cover Jackson. They lay for a moment, and more fire poured past them—a small storm of sparks flew from the gravel of the road as the cannon scoured the ground.

The General attempted to rise, but was pushed down. "You must lie still, General," someone said. "It will cost you your life to get up."

As the party struggled to its feet and moved the General, the litter fell once more. A bearer dropped his pole and fled into the woods in a new burst of firing. The General groaned, complaining of pain in his side. Wilbourn begged passing men to give a hand, but none would come. He finally shouted that General Jackson was hurt; two men came quickly, and the litter moved forward once more.

In the roadway more men began to gather, curious at the sight of so many forms milling about. A few pressed through the officers. "Who you got there? Who's hurt?" They did not fall back when told that it was only a wounded officer. One of the unidentified men came close enough to recognize his commander. "Great God, it's Old Jack." There was true dismay in his voice.

Excited talk spluttered through the group near Jackson: "General Hill's been shot. Who's in command?" Riders went for General Rodes and General Stuart. The litter passed out of that confusion toward the rear. It met General Dorsey Pender who, though wounded himself, went to the center of the party and dismounted, speaking to Jackson, expressing his regrets—and his fears that he must retreat. For the first time since his wounding, Jackson moved swiftly. He sat up. "You must hold your ground, Pender! Hold your ground, sir!" Pender said no more of the possibilities of pulling back his lines. The litter went out of sight, off the road, through the brush.

Captain Smith, who had now joined the party, spoke during a

halt in a moonlit clearing. He was alarmed by the pallor of Jackson's face and the pained expression. "General, are you much hurt?"

"Never mind me, Captain. Never mind me." After a pause Jackson said, "Let's win the battle first, and then worry about the wounded."

The party still was under fire, still with great difficulty carrying the General and at the same time caring for the horses; but in crossing a roadway, the men came upon an ambulance. The officers sighed with relief, but found that the canvas-covered wagon already bore Colonel Stapleton Crutchfield, chief of Jackson's artillery, as well as a strange captain. Crutchfield was moaning endlessly, and the driver said his leg was hopelessly shattered; he could not be moved. After a moment of discussion, the captain called from within, demanding that he be moved to make room for General Jackson. He began to struggle out, and the men went forward to help him; the General was placed inside, calling weakly for whisky. Several men went to find stimulants, Joe Morrison climbed into the wagon to hold Jackson's arm, and the ambulance moved slowly rearward, over the path of the afternoon's battle. An officer went ahead with a small party to locate the rougher spots in the road, leaving men to mark them for the driver. The two injured officers jolted along, Crutchfield still moaning, and evidently out of his mind. The wagon paused finally, in the yard of a house, that of the Reverend Melzi Chancellor. Here Dr. McGuire found Jackson.

McGuire leaned over him. "I hope you're not badly hurt, General."

The words of the reply were clear. "I am badly injured, Doctor. I'm afraid I'm dying. I'm glad you've come. I think the place in my shoulder is still bleeding."

McGuire found the wound in the darkness and halted the blood by pressing a finger over the great artery in the shoulder. He called for a light, and in the glow of a lantern saw that the handkerchief tourniquet had slipped. He tightened it. Jackson thanked him gravely, as if he were a stranger. McGuire looked at the General more closely than he had during all the months of riding and fighting with him.

Jackson had control of himself and was remarkably calm, almost as if he were in his own home, preparing to retire for the evening. His mind was clear despite the pain and loss of blood.

His suffering was intense, McGuire saw. Cold hands, a clammy skin, deep pallor of the face. The lips were bloodless, a thin band of ridged flesh drawn tightly over the teeth. The expression was fixed in a rigid mold, the brow furrowed. Breathing was slow.

McGuire halted the bleeding with ease and gave Jackson a bit of whisky and some morphia, which had been brought by a near-by regimental doctor. The ambulance began to move once more, this time with McGuire riding at Jackson's side. On the road, Crutchfield still groaned. Once the General pulled McGuire's ear to his lips.

"Is Crutchfield dangerously wounded?"

"No. Only painfully."

"I am glad it is no worse."

Crutchfield's groans diminished, and during a time when Jackson seemed to sleep, the colonel asked McGuire of the General's condition. The doctor's reply brought a cry from the artilleryman: "Oh, my God." Jackson stirred and, thinking his companion in greater pain, ordered the wagon halted and directed McGuire to give help to Crutchfield.

Near eleven o'clock the wagon mercifully paused, turned past the Wilderness Tavern, into a field where men and ambulances thronged, and halted at the field hospital of the Second Corps. Jackson was carried into a tent which had been warmed for his arrival; he could smell the charred wood of the camp stove. They lay him on a cot beneath clean, heavy blankets, and gave him a dram of whisky. He was greeted by Dr. Harvey Black, the chief surgeon, and two or three other doctors whom he did not know. The General drowsed.

McGuire found Jackson's pulse quickening and his body warmth returning. The others went away, and McGuire sat with Captain Smith, watching. The General lay quietly on his back, his breathing regular, with good color in his cheeks. McGuire leaned over him at intervals, but for two hours he postponed his examination. He went out of the quiet tent and left Smith alone with Jackson, but was back within an hour, bringing the other doctors—Dr. R. T. Coleman, the chief surgeon of the General's old division, Surgeon Walls, and Dr. Black. Their low talk aroused Jackson, who stared at them and then gave his abrupt smile, nodding. McGuire leaned over the cot.

"We must examine you, General."

Jackson nodded several times. McGuire absently studied his watch, noting that it was two o'clock. Sunday morning.

"We will give you chloroform so that you will have no pain. These gentlemen will help me. We might find bones badly broken, General. So that the only course might be amputation."

The General watched McGuire's face closely.

"If that is our conclusion, do you want us to go on with the operation?"

The weak voice was firm and a bit impatient. "Certainly, Mc-Guire. Do for me whatever you think best."

The doctors stirred. One of them spread a salve over the General's face to protect the skin, and Dr. Coleman folded a cloth cone. Soon there was the heavy, unpleasant odor of the anesthetic in the place. The General breathed deeply under the cloth, several times, so that it could be heard throughout the crowded tent.

"Breathe more deeply. Deeply."

"What an infinite blessing," Jackson said. His voice strayed on, lost. "Blessing. Blessing . . . Bless . . ." His words became garbled, and the listening men could not understand them. He appeared, at last, to have lost consciousness.

McGuire took up the battered right hand. Smith held the light as the doctors probed. On the back of the hand, under the dark flesh, was a round ball which had entered the palm. Two small bones were broken. McGuire lanced the skin and removed the bullet. He rolled it in his palm. "A smooth-bore Springfield," he said. "Our troops." He glanced around at the others. It was becoming clear that his own men had indeed wounded him. The Federals had long since abandoned the old muskets.

The doctors turned now to the injured shoulder, where, about three inches below the shoulder, a bullet had torn the muscle, fractured the bone and passed through the arm. It was an ugly, irregular wound. Lower, in the forearm, a second wound; the entry near the elbow, passing through the arm, emerging on the inside above the wrist. McGuire saw the decision on the faces of the others: This arm could not be saved. Gangrene was certain if they attempted to save it by treating the wounds and setting the bones. The shaken heads made a conference unnecessary. It was not a difficult decision and the operation was simple. Each of them had performed hundreds such in his time.

McGuire cut around the damaged arm and sawed through the bone; Dr. Walls tied off the arteries, working swiftly behind him, so that there was little loss of blood. Dr. Black bore on the chest with his stethoscope meanwhile, hearing the firm pounding of the heart. McGuire dressed the wound and turned his attention to Jackson's scratched face, where the cuts were superficial, requiring no more than clear plaster.

Jackson did not stir for half an hour, beyond a spasmodic turn of the head. He passed through the operation in excellent condition. McGuire ordered him to be given coffee, which he took with ease, and he fell into light slumber. An hour passed.

At about three thirty, an argument arose outside. Sandie Pendleton had come with a message for the General. The doctors told him it was impossible; Jackson was not to be disturbed until morning. Pendleton insisted. The army was in danger, he said. The troops were in disorder; General Hill was unable to take the field, and General Stuart had sent him to take orders from Jackson. The interview was imperative if the army was to be made safe in the coming hours. The doctors relented.

McGuire entered the tent with Pendleton but was not needed as spokesman. Jackson instantly recognized the visitor. "Well, Major. I'm glad to see you. I thought you were killed."

Pendleton spoke of Hill's wounding, and of Stuart's coming to the front to take command. Stuart, he said, was in ignorance of the situation on the front and had sent to Jackson for instructions.

The General was immediately interested. He asked a few pointed questions, about the terrain and location of the brigades, and the news of the enemy. When Pendleton answered, a look of quick vigorous intelligence passed over Jackson's face, but the effort was too much. He exhaled slowly and with blank features said, "I'm sorry. I don't know. I can't tell. Say to General Stuart he must do what he thinks best."

This seemed somehow to have waked the General, who turned, grinning, to Smith. "Did I have anything to say under the chloroform? Anything wicked?"

Smith shook his head and before he could reply, Jackson spoke with a rush. "I have always thought it was wrong to give chloroform when there is a possibility of death at hand. But it was the most delightful sensation, Smith. I was conscious enough to know what was going on. I thought I once heard music—I suppose it was the saw."

Jackson soon fell asleep, and with Smith at his side, rested undisturbed through the night.

At the front, during these hours, blind slaughter went on without reason or direction. A Union cavalryman looked from heights above the Rapidan at a sight he could never forget, of which he would write:

"A scene like a picture of hell lies below us. As far as the horizon are innumerable fires from burning woods . . . cannon belching in monotonous roar; and the harsh quick rattling of infantry firing. . . . It is the Army Of The Potomac . . . engaged at night in a burning forest. At our feet artillery and cavalry are mixed, jammed, officers swearing, men straggling, horses expiring."

What the cavalryman saw was the terrible, bloody and inconclusive attack of the fifteen thousand of Sickles's corps trying to get back within Union lines. The files were threshing, now against Rebels, now against Union lines. When the corps clashed with its own companions in arms, the casualties were as great as when it met the Rebels, and no one seemed able to halt the senseless affair until at last, God knew how, the men of Sickles's rushed back into their own lines and settled down, leaving uncounted casualties in the tangle behind. The rifle fire died out in the Wilderness, and soon the quiet reached even the clearing at Chancellorsville, where for so long there had been a scene of tearing men and horses, couriers driving in to Hooker's headquarters, officers attempting to rally survivors, hospital parties passing with litters, brass bands blowing madly in an effort to revive morale. The drifting smoke all but blotted out the moon.

Things had quieted when the moon sank from sight and the armies lay down for a brief sleep before the next bath of blood.

Lee had known little of Jackson's movements since his dispatch of three o'clock in the afternoon, though fully aware of the damage the assault had done to the Union flank. The commander had spent some anxious hours in the final phase of Jackson's approach to the exposed Eleventh Corps of the enemy—for shortly before, Lee had word of a disaster from his rear. There had been a misunderstanding of verbal orders, and General Early had pulled out from Fredericksburg, leaving that town to the enemy and opening the rear of the army to attack. Lee had then flung his thin lines against Hooker, even as Jackson hit the flank, and all had pressed the enemy hard. It had been a brisk, costly dusk battle, and in some quarters it flamed long after dark, particularly about the Fairview Cemetery, where the ranked Federal guns, loaded with everything from canister to trace chains, had cut great gaps in the gray columns. The battle in the dark blazed on, with neither side able to halt it, until about twelve o'clock, when it fizzled out to the southward.

Lee went to sleep in a pine copse beneath an oilcloth cover and a blanket. He had been asleep for little more than two hours when the voice of his aide, Walter Taylor, aroused him.

"Who is there?"

"It's Captain Wilbourn," Taylor said.

Lee invited Wilbourn to sit beside him. "Tell me about the fight last night, Captain."

Wilbourn, bone-weary and heavy-lidded, tried to tell Lee of the entire assault, from the moment they found the Federal flank naked, its troops unsuspecting, until the advance had halted, more than a mile beyond Wilderness Church, the enemy crushed.

He then told the story of Jackson's wounding as he scouted the enemy. Lee groaned, shaking his head, and though Wilbourn described Jackson's hurts as flesh wounds, Lee seemed deeply moved. "Ah, Captain, any victory is dearly bought that takes General Jackson from us, even for a short time."

Wilbourn spoke of the instant when Jackson was shot and his pain. Lee rose suddenly. "Ah," he said. "Don't talk about it.

Thank God it is no worse." He stood without speaking, and Wilbourn, assuming that he had been dismissed, moved to go. "I want to talk more with you," Lee said.

Under his questions, Wilbourn told him that General Stuart was now in command, Hill having been wounded, and General Rodes having bowed to Stuart's seniority. "They want you to come there yourself, General," Wilbourn said.

Lee smiled and asked where Stuart and Jackson were, so that he could write dispatches to them. Wilbourn gave the positions, and as an afterthought, "General Jackson planned to take the United States Ford road, I think, and cut them off from the river."

Lee's reaction was instantaneous. "We must press those people today," he said. He went about the business of directing his army, writing dispatches, calling in his couriers, in the midst of it pulling on his boots, and ordering breakfast for Wilbourn. The army made ready to fight once more.

On the flank where Jackson's loss had brought things to a standstill, the fate of the lean columns in the coming day was uncertain indeed. The enemy had not yet come to realize it, but they lay with the golden opportunity of the war in their hands, astride the separate wings of the Confederate army.

For his part, Stuart may not have realized the full extent of the danger. In any event, without quailing in the face of the unknown, he planned attack. A man who had never commanded infantrymen in action, assisted by general officers who themselves had never led so much as a division into battle, was to challenge the overwhelming weight of the Federals. His very hope of stinging the enemy and probing for advantage seemed dim when he discovered that Crutchfield, the artilleryman, was among Jackson's wounded officers. But for one man, Jackson's staff was missing. The cavalry chief answered the situation himself by riding up and down the front lines in the blackness, calling for silence among his men, in preparation to go forward with the dawn.

24

★★★ THE DEPARTURE

The battle could not be followed from the field hospital, but its voice came in strongly—musketry and cannon fire, too. It was a clear, sunny Sunday morning, cool at first, until the dew disappeared. A fragrance of blooming fruit trees hung in the air. The General had spent a restful night, and took a meager breakfast, smiling. "I'm going to get well," he said. The doctors smiled too, even when beyond his sight.

No one told the General of the little burial service in a near-by family graveyard, when his shattered arm was interred.

Jackson sent Joe Morrison to Richmond cross-country. He was to find Mrs. Jackson, tell her all details of the wounds, and bring her back, along with baby Julia.

Jackson then busied himself, under McGuire's careful eye. He gave Smith a dispatch to be sent to General Lee, dictating only a few lines about his wound, the victorious attack, and his passage of command of the corps.

He seemed to work from a great reservoir of strength and determination.

Suddenly he waved his one big pale hand at the men filling the tent. "Too many of us," he said. "You have me out of trouble, now. They need you there in the lines." He sent away all of the staff, excepting Smith.

Two visitors came—the Reverend Lacy was first. He entered mournfully. "Oh, General, what a calamity!"

"I'm wounded," Jackson said, "but not depressed. I believe it was according to God's will. I can wait until He makes His object known to me."

He talked with the minister in a low voice. He told Lacy he had thought he was on the point of death when he fell from the litter after being wounded. There was a good deal of spiritual talk, evidently comforting to Jackson. The staff did not listen closely.

Kyd Douglas came and Smith took his news, passing it on to the General. Jackson was moved at word of the death of General Paxton, shot down while leading a charge, and when he heard of the gallantry of the Stonewall Brigade under fire, he said, "It was just like them! A noble body of men!"

Jackson by now began to writhe slightly. There was pain on his face. McGuire came and examined the side of which the General complained. He found nothing, though he spent several minutes in a careful exploration. McGuire determined that the lungs were clear and had an ointment applied to the side. The pain had disappeared in the early evening, and Jackson seemed to revive. He asked detailed questions about the progress of the battle and about the wounded in near-by tents. When the bravery of one of his officers was described, he would give his head its characteristic shake from side to side, muttering, "Good, good." He praised the old brigade once more. "Some day men will be proud to tell their children they fought in the Stonewall Brigade. The name belongs to the men, not to me."

A note came in from General Lee. Smith, on request, read it to the General:

> General,—I have just received your note telling me that you were wounded. I cannot express my regret at this occurrence. Could I have directed events, I should have chosen for the good of the country to be disabled in your stead.
>
> I congratulate you upon the victory, which is due to your skill and energy.
>
> Very respectfully, your obedient servant,
> R. E. Lee, General.

Jackson wore an embarrassed look and, turning away, he said shyly, "General Lee is very kind. But he should give the praise to God."

McGuire, as he looked in at his patient for the last time during the evening, thought that things were going well indeed. He and Smith agreed that the General was on his way to recovery.

Jackson passed a painless, peaceful night. In the morning McGuire had a message from Lee. Jackson was to be moved if possible. The Federals were threatening to cross the Rapidan at Ely's Ford and might drive in the direction of the field hospital. The guard of infantry placed there might not hold back the enemy.

McGuire explained this to Jackson. "Don't move me if it will do harm," Old Jack said. "I would like my wife to stay in that house down the way, when she comes. If the enemy does come, I will not fear them. I have always been kind to their wounded, and I'm sure they would be kind to me."

A second note from Lee arrived in the evening, insisting that Jackson be moved to safety. McGuire prepared to take the General to Guiney's Station the next morning. There was some discussion as to whether McGuire should accompany the General. Lee had ordered him to go along, but Jackson at first demurred, insisting that he would not add to the common complaint that the general officers had always monopolized the services of leading doctors, leaving the men to suffer. When McGuire cited Lee's order, Jackson succumbed. "General Lee has always been kind to me, and I thank him."

Just after daylight, on Tuesday, Jackson was placed in an ambulance and began his day-long ride to more comfortable quarters on the Chandler farm, where he had once been invited to make his headquarters by the Chandler family. With Lacy and Smith as attendants, Jim riding at the rear, Crutchfield as his fellow patient, and McGuire to direct the party, Jackson's ambulance rolled off. Ahead of it went Jed Hotchkiss of the staff and some of his engineer troops, who sweated through the day, grubbing up roots, logs and stones, filling in ruts and sinkholes. They also ordered wagons out of the way, but until they explained to the drivers that Stonewall Jackson was on his way to the rear, they got nothing but profane defiance. The name seemed to be magic, and by magic it spread. Numbers of people waited at the roadside on the chance of seeing the General pass.

It was not long before the wagon began to overtake the walking wounded, heading back from the battle to the line of the Richmond, Fredericksburg and Potomac Railroad, and these men, discovering Jackson's identity, raised cheers around the wagon. The party now began to pass hundreds of people, among them many who wept; the men generally stood with hats in hands, the women with heads bowed, as if at a funeral. A considerable crowd halted the ambulance at Spotsylvania Court House, with people pressing close enough to see the General.

Down the road the people waited with gifts, the meager delicacies their farms could boast. Officers took their pails of milk, and cakes, pies, honey, dried fruit, bags of fried chicken and biscuit, until there was no more room. Looking back, the officers could see people going to their knees in the brush, praying for the General before he was out of sight. It was a strange spectacle that cast a gloom over the young men with Jackson.

Inside the ambulance there was idle chatter, almost cheery. McGuire had not seen Jackson so talkative; and several times he put a suspicious palm on the General's forehead to be certain that his temperature was not on the rise. Jackson explained in some detail his battle plan—that he had intended to cut the Federals from the United States Ford by sliding his files past them to the north, and then, by taking positions between them and the river, force them to attack. He defended that tactic with a smile. "My men sometimes fail to drive the Yankees from a position, but they always fail to drive us."

Someone asked if Hooker's plan of battle seemed sound to the General, and Jackson replied without pause, as if he had already pondered the problem. "It was, in the main, a good conception, sir. An excellent plan. But he shouldn't have sent away his cavalry. That was his great blunder. That enabled me to turn him, without his being aware of it, and to take him by his rear. If he had kept his cavalry with him, his plan would have been a very good one."

He spoke of several of his officers, praising General Rodes rather extravagantly, saying that he had performed flawlessly on

Saturday afternoon during the pell-mell assault, and that he hoped Rodes would be promoted soon. He said with some heat that officers should be promoted on the field for valor, as a spur to the entire army.

He spoke emotionally of the death of Paxton, and of Boswell, who died in the volley before Jackson was wounded.

He was cheerful and bright most of the way, but in the afternoon the jolting seemed to tell on him, and when the heat was at its worst he suffered an attack of nausea; the ambulance was halted for a time, and the doors were opened. A few people stared from a distance, and the hot scent of the briar-covered road banks and flowering shrubs came in. The General had suggested his old favorite remedy—cold towels on an uncertain stomach; and a soldier ran to a house near by, waited while the well windlass screeched, and returned with a bucket of icy water. The treatment appeared to comfort Jackson. "Ah, that does it," he said. "That's true relief."

At eight in the evening they came to the Chandler place, having rocked twenty-seven miles in the day. McGuire was forced to disappoint the Coleman Chandler family, which still busied itself preparing the finest parlors for the General. It seemed that some soldiers had died in "the big house," Fairview, recently, with erysipelas. The doctor thought there was danger of infection. He was immediately satisfied with the frame office near by, a plain little building under three huge oaks. He soon had Jackson bedded down.

The patient had tea and bread for supper and ate hungrily. He went off to sleep just as a spring thunderstorm broke.

There was cooler weather in the morning, and some excitement; the wagons were being hurriedly packed for a trip to safety from raiding Union horsemen, said to be on their way. Some of the staff rode off, saying good-bye to the unsuspecting Jackson as if they returned to the front lines. Lacy, Smith and McGuire privately determined to return with Jackson if captured, in order to be able to care for him. The threat hung over the party most of the day.

Lacy went in at ten in the morning and held his devotional at the General's request, a short prayer and a reading of the

Bible. Jackson said he was ready to die if God willed it, but said he did not think the time was near. The thought must have struck home to him, for during McGuire's examination of the wounds Jackson talked about his prospects, and wondered how long he might be absent from the army. He once said to Smith, "I suppose many would take these wounds as a great misfortune. To me they are one of the blessings of my life."

"All things work together for good to them that love God," Smith said.

"Yes, that's it. That's it."

The wounds were in good condition. Healing had begun on the stump of the severed arm, and no infection had attacked the wounded hand, though McGuire applied splints to prevent movement of the shattered bones. Smith once thought Jackson's mind might be wandering. He passed to the General the news that Hooker had intrenched himself north of Chancellorsville, and Jackson said, "That's bad. Very bad." Later he stirred from sleep to call out, "Major Pendleton, send in and see if there is higher ground back of Chancellorsville."

Jackson seemed suddenly to have recalled that Smith was a divinity student, and he spoke long and often of religion, sometimes in a disconnected way.

"The Christian must carry his religion into everything, Smith," the General would say. "Makes a man a better commander, a better shoemaker, a better tailor. Teaches him punctuality, fidelity . . . In the commander of an army, it calms his perplexities at a critical hour."

Or he would say, "The Bread of Heaven . . . You will find precepts for everything in the Bible, Smith. Can you tell me where the Bible gives generals a model for their official reports on battles?" Smith laughed, shaking his head.

"Look at Joshua," Jackson said seriously. "His narrative of the battle with the Amalekites; there you have one. Brevity, fairness, modesty, and it traces the victory to its proper source —the blessing of God."

Once he interrupted a long silence with, "Oh, for infinite power!" and spoke of the healing powers of Christ. He put Smith through questioning, asking him what were the headquarters of Christianity after the Crucifixion, and afterward sending the officer to his old trunk to dig up an atlas and locate the ancient city of Iconium.

His mind went back often to the army, and he spoke with great clarity of his flank attack on the enemy: "Our movement was a great success; I think the most successful military movement of my life. But I expect to receive more credit for it than I deserve. Most men will think I planned it all from the first; but it was not so. I simply took advantage of circumstances as they were presented to me in the providence of God. I feel that His hand led me—let us give Him the glory."

For another day his strength held out, but at one o'clock Thursday morning he roused, suffering from nausea, and asked Jim to get the wet towels once more. Jim said that Dr. McGuire should be consulted and that he was asleep in the next room. Jackson, saying that McGuire had not slept in three nights, refused to allow him to disturb the doctor. He asked Lacy to prepare the towels for him and lay for some hours under their cooling touch.

When McGuire rose at daylight and was told that Jackson was in severe pain, he went to the bedside and began an examination. He had not far to go before finding the trouble: pneumonia in the right lung.

There was some quiet discussion as to whether it had been brought on by the General's fall from his litter, or the cold towels he insisted upon using. In the afternoon, Jackson seemed to improve and hopes rose slightly.

Mrs. Jackson arrived, coming from a heavily armed train that was prepared to blast its way through the Yankee cavalry, if necessary. Her big-eyed, gentle face was made old with anxiety, which deepened as she met officers of the staff on the porch, who detained her, saying the General's wounds were being dressed. When she asked of his condition, one of the men said, "Pretty good." She read danger in those words.

With her was Mrs. Moses Hoge of Richmond, who was to be her companion. The Reverend Hoge was abroad on a Confederate mission, to obtain a supply of Bibles for the soldiers. Behind was the Negro woman, Hetty, carrying the infant Julia in her arms. The women stood on the porch, ill at ease as they watched a team of soldiers digging a grave. They were astounded to see a coffin exhumed, and it was explained to Mrs. Jackson that General Paxton's body was being sent to his home. It was a shock to her; Paxton was an old friend and neighbor from Lexington. It was a poor preparation for entering the sick room.

The sight of her husband stunned her, and she paused in the doorway summoning courage to approach him. She knew in that moment that she had lost him. The face was darkly flushed, and its cuts and scratches had the look of serious wounds to her. She had been told nothing that could prepare her for the shock of the missing arm and the huge bandaged hand. His face was sunken and bony. McGuire aroused him after a few gentle shakes, and when, with a remarkable recovery of his senses, he had come to himself, Jackson recognized Anna instantly. It was so unlike him, Anna reflected, to make such a demonstration of affection over her; it was as if he sought to compensate for his weakness. Finally, gravely, and with some effort, he said, "I know you would give your life for me. But I'm perfectly resigned. Don't be sad. I hope I am going to recover. Pray for me, but always remember in your prayers the old petition, 'Thy will be done.' "

Then, in a way that drained her restored confidence in his strength, he sank into a stupor and when he tried to speak, he could not be understood. He gave up, finally, to the effect of drugs.

When he swam upward to the surface of consciousness to greet her, he was uniformly cheerful. Once he said, "My darling, you must cheer up and not wear such a long face in the sickroom."

He seemed to understand her every word, and two or three times, when she suggested that the baby be brought in to him, he refused. "Not yet," he said. "Wait until I feel better."

Through most of the hours when she sat with him it was only his labored breathing that she heard, and in his rare stirrings:

"My darling, you are very much loved."

Or:

"You're the most precious little wife in the world."

McGuire had called in more doctors, and on Friday they came: Dr. S. B. Morrison, a kinsman of Mrs. Jackson (whom the General recognized with: "That's a familiar old face"), Dr. David Tucker of Richmond, and a Dr. Breckenridge. These men consulted, and tried to give Jackson relief with a blister, but with little success. His wounds, dressed Friday, were healing well, and the pain in his side had disappeared. But though even his breathing seemed easier, he complained of an overpowering exhaustion, and he weakened noticeably.

On Saturday, Mrs. Jackson, Mrs. Hoge and Hetty went in with Julia. He fondled the infant on his bed and held his wounded hand over her head, closing his eyes in silent prayer while the child cooed at him. Julia was taken away.

"McGuire," the General said, "I see from the number of physicians here that my condition is dangerous. But I thank God that, if it is His will, I am ready to go."

In the evening, he shook his head at Anna's suggestion that she read some Psalms to him, but then roused, repentant. "Yes. We must never refuse that. Get the Bible and read them." He also asked her to sing for him, and with her brother Joe accompanying, she chanted some hymns in a low voice. He fell asleep.

Early Sunday, in the first daylight, Anna told him that he must prepare himself for the worst. He looked calmly at her, without surprise or any reaction that she could see. She repeated, and asked if he wanted God to have His will with him. "I prefer it," he said. "Yes, I prefer it." This was said with some emphasis, but she could not yet be sure that he understood.

"Before today is over you will be with God."

"I will be an infinite gainer, to be translated." His breathing was swift, as if it demanded all his strength. He told her that she should go home to her father in North Carolina; and when she asked him where he would like to be buried, he said, "Charlotte." Later, under her prodding, he said, "Yes, in Lexington, and in my own plot."

Some of the men were at the doorway, and a few of them cried. Jim wept unashamedly, shaking his head to fling tears from his cheeks.

McGuire offered him brandy and water, but after a sip, with

a wry face, Jackson said, "It tastes like fire, and can't do me any good."

Before noon, Anna tried once more to tell him that the end had come, but he lifted his hand to her shoulder. "Oh, no, you are frightened, my child. Death is not so near. I may yet get well."

She flung herself across the bed, beating at the covers, weeping bitterly, and when she raised her head she told him again that the doctors had given up hope.

"Call McGuire," he said.

She went to the door and returned with the doctor.

"Doctor, Anna tells me that you have told her I am to die today. Is it so?"

"I'm afraid so, General. I'm afraid . . ."

Jackson studied the ceiling as if trying to focus his attention on the problem at hand. "Very good," he said primly. "Very good. It's all right." He told Anna he had a great deal to say to her, but his words became gibberish, and his lips finally ceased to move.

At one o'clock in the afternoon, Sandie Pendleton was admitted. The General was awake. "Who preached at headquarters today?"

Pendleton told him that Lacy had preached, and that the entire army was praying for him. "Thank God," Jackson said. "They are very kind . . . It is the Lord's day, Pendleton. My wish is fulfilled. I always wanted to die on Sunday."

Then there were only scraps of conscious talk, a wandering mind, babbling, as if he commanded on the field, or sat with his wife and child in Lexington, or held prayers with his staff, or sat at the mess table.

At one thirty, the doctors told him he had two hours to live, and he seemed to understand. Feebly he said, "All right. Very good. It's all right."

A short time later he shouted: "Tell A. P. Hill to prepare for action! . . . Pass the infantry to the front! . . . Tell Major Hawks . . ."

Soon a faint smile, almost sweet, passed across the pale lips under the beard. Anna and the men leaned forward to the bed.

"Let us cross over the river, and rest under the shade of the trees."

He was gone. It was three fifteen in the afternoon.

In the bloody Wilderness, where he had fought his last, was the ruin of the greatest of American battles. For four days now, Joe Hooker had been back in his camps across the Rappahannock, looking down on Fredericksburg, his files badly torn. President Lincoln was recovering his composure from the bad moment when he had got the word of defeat from Chancellorsville: "My God, what will the country say?"

It was victory for Lee and Jackson and Stuart and the young commanders of the army, but it was another of those inconclusive blood baths with which the army was so familiar. It had fought, and it had won, and taken heavy toll of the enemy. But everything was as before.

In the six fierce days the Union had lost over seventeen thousand men, almost six thousand of them captured or missing. The Army of Northern Virginia had lost twelve thousand.

Yet the wail that went up in the South at the news from Guiney's Station drowned out the mourning for the dead of Chancellorsville, as well as the shouts of victory. Something had now been lost that could not be replaced by conscription. It was not only Lee, saying with his grave flourishes, "I have lost my right arm," or, "Such an executive officer the sun never shone on . . . straight as a needle to the pole he advanced to the execution of my purpose." There was much more in the dirge that went up over the South. The unlettered in the ranks and back home knew unerringly that the greatest Yankee-killer of them all had gone, and they feared the future without him.

After Jackson, on the field at Chancellorsville, had been nothing for the Confederates but fierce refusal to be whipped. Disaster indeed fell upon Joe Hooker, but it was by no means fatal, though it exposed his lack of courage and his betrayal of his gallant brigades. He had become timorous in the midst of his grand design, partially, perhaps, because he had been stunned when a Rebel cannonball clipped a column at the Chancellor Mansion, where the Federal commander leaned smoking, playing the Viking warrior. In the end, though without accomplishing his purpose, Lee had caught Joe Hooker in his own trap.

There were moments, after Jackson was carried away, when the war might have hung in the balance. When, for example, John Sedgwick came lumbering in on the flank, having been loosed by Early's retreat from Fredericksburg. If Hooker had been equal to his rhetoric, he would not then have dug himself into his trenches before Lee, but would have attacked in cooperation with Sedgwick, crushing the Confederates between two wings. Instead, his own troops crawled behind the breastworks, and Lee, thankful, put a small guard on them and turned to deal with Sedgwick alone. For a bad day and night, Sedgwick's men were hemmed against the river by the Rebels, hammered on every hand, losing forty-seven hundred men. Sedgwick at last, with little help from Hooker, escaped over the river, and by then Hooker was ready to be frightened by his shadow.

It began to rain on May fifth, and the Wilderness was gloomy. Behind were still the pontoon bridges over the Rappahannock to safety; the supply trains were already there. During the day, a false report came in that Longstreet's corps had come up from the east, reinforcing Lee. Unfortunately for Hooker, it was a Rebel trick, a planted rumor brought by pretended deserters Longstreet was still in the Tidewater beyond Richmond.

But this was enough for Hooker. He called for a retreat, in fact sternly ordered it, overriding his generals in an unhappy council of war which found Couch, Reynolds and Meade openly hostile and speaking for an attack. Hooker still outnumbered Lee by two to one, but he marched away, his troops slow in the rain, committing more depredations than usual and deserting in droves. Hooker's guards and provost marshals could not even keep account of the hundreds who streamed away north through Alexandria and homeward.

Jackson's attack had done it—overcome the Yankee host— but as he fell, the army somehow had faltered and slowed, the country thought. From Richmond southward men did not debate the courage or cowardice of the Union troops; they began to understand for the first time in the months of blood the true worth of a general who knew how to hurl his columns like saber sweeps, and how to make weapons of the men in ranks. The general had been found, and was now gone, at the very moment when he was showing the nation that the little victories of the Valley were only the most elementary phases of warfare.

At Guiney's Station the staff officers prepared the body in a suit of civilian clothes Jim had found, for the once-splendid coat Stuart had given the General had been slashed to shreds. Jackson was wrapped in a dark military cloak and placed in a coffin. Anna went to him in the parlor of the Chandler house; she sobbed most of the night, slept toward dawn, and then rose to see the body once more. The General's face showed fewer traces of suffering now than in his last hours, she thought. The men had covered the casket with spring flowers and banked lily of the valley about the head.

The funeral party left for Richmond on Monday, with most of the General's staff and Mrs. Jackson, Mrs. Chandler and Mrs. Hoge in a special car. Kyd Douglas went to Lee, asking permission for the Stonewall Brigade to march in the funeral procession. Lee refused sadly:

"I cannot even leave my headquarters long enough to ride to the depot and pay my dear friend the poor honor of seeing his body placed upon the cars. . . . Those people over the river are showing signs of movement."

The commander in chief wrote his wife:

. . . In addition to the death of officers and friends . . . you will see that we have to mourn the loss of the great and good Jackson. Any victory would be dear at such a price. His remains go to Richmond today. I know not how to replace him; but God's will be done! I trust He will raise up someone in his place. The papers will give you all the particulars. I have no time to narrate them.

On the same day, Lee issued an order to the army:

General Orders No. 61.
With deep grief the commanding general announces to the army the death of Lieutenant General T. J. Jackson, who expired on the 10th instant, at a quarter past 3 P.M. The

daring, skill, and energy, of this great and good soldier are now, by the decree of an all-wise Providence, lost to us.

But while we mourn his death we feel that his spirit still lives, and will inspire the whole army with his indomitable courage and unshaken confidence in God as our hope and strength. Let his name be a watchword to his corps, who have followed him to victory on so many fields. Let his officers and soldiers emulate his invincible determination to do every thing in the defense of our beloved country.

Douglas boarded the train as it was leaving for Richmond. Along the route, at every station, and at points between, crowds hailed the train, and at Ashland a group of women entered to place fresh flowers and wreaths on the coffin. By three o'clock the train reached Richmond, and at the station a procession of dignitaries and soldiers took over the casket. One of the new Confederate flags was draped over the coffin—the one which was to have flown from the Capitol flagstaff—and the line of march moved to the Executive Mansion, where Governor Letcher met the widow. For two miles the streets were thronged with people, all, evidently, having left their work for the day. Minute-guns boomed over the wailing of army bands.

During the night the body was embalmed. Two men made a plaster death mask of the face: the sculptor, Frederick Volck, and his assistant, Pietro Zamboggi. A few people came later. One was General Garnett, who came to peer at the shadowed features. Tears welled in his eyes, and two young men of Jackson's staff observed him, a little incredulous. Garnett approached, taking Douglas and Pendleton by the arms and walking to a window, staring out into the dark city. "You know the trouble between Jackson and me," he said. "I can never forget it. But I tell you no one can lament his going more than I do. I believe he did me a great injustice, but I know he acted from pure motives. He is dead. Who is there to fill his place? Who?"

The next day the body went on display in the reception room of the Executive Mansion, where many came to peer through the glass pane at the famous General, whose face wore a grave, firm expression, and was very much as in life, except that the features were a bit smaller. President Davis and the Cabinet came, and the pallbearers—all of whom were generals except for Commodore French Forrest—Longstreet, Ewell, Winder, Garnett, Kemper, Corse. Garnett had come only at the insistence of Douglas and Pendleton, and at last had come gratefully.

The procession went down Governor Street into Main, and up Main to Second, thence from Grace down into Capitol Square, and into the Hall of the House of Representatives.

The troops marched with reversed arms. First there was a brass band, the Nineteenth Virginia Infantry, the Fifty-sixth Virginia; General Pickett and his staff, mounted; six pieces of artillery; a squadron of cavalry; the hearse, drawn by four white horses and draped in black bunting; the pallbearers; one of Jackson's horses, well groomed and shining, led by a servant; a few soldiers of the Stonewall Brigade who were in the city; General Elzey and his staff; Richmond officials; President Davis in a carriage; his Cabinet on foot; Governor Letcher and his aides and a number of Virginia and Richmond politicians.

The casket went into the Hall of the House and was put on a white-draped altar before the Speaker's bench, with the flag still over it. More than twenty thousand people streamed through the place in the afternoon and evening, most of them taking their first look at the General. Flowers were piled about the bier until some had to be taken away to make room for spectators, still coming in after dark. Officials made several attempts to close the doors and clear the hall, but they were shouted down.

An old man once yelled from the rear, waving aloft an empty sleeve. "I give my arm for him, damn ye, and I'm agoing to see him, too!" Governor Letcher ordered the doors left open until all who wanted to come had filed by.

Douglas was one of the last to see him. He looked into the room about midnight when the doors were closed and only the sentries were about. Roses literally buried the casket, and in slowly stirring candlelight a sentry stepped back and forth. The General's face looked as if it were done in marble. Douglas took a few flowers and left the place.

Mrs. Jackson had numerous visitors during the early evening, some of them ministers who had known her husband. There was much weeping, and a good deal of scripture was read. Mrs. Jackson was particularly comforted by the Reverend T. V. Moore, a stranger to her, who quoted from the fourteenth chapter of the Gospel according to John: "Let not thy heart be troubled; ye believe in God, believe also in me."

The crowds sought out Julia and would not leave the baby alone, longing, apparently, to touch her. Hetty finally retreated to the rear of the house, finding a haven beneath a window, where she held the child until the people had gone. "They won't give my baby no rest," she said.

On Wednesday, the final journey began. Anna boarded the train, which went by way of Gordonsville to Lynchburg. At every stop, people gathered under the windows and remained until she went out to take the flowers and wreaths they handed up. More often than not, the crowd called for Julia. "The baby!" they would shout outside the dirty pane. "Stonewall Jackson's baby!"

Hetty handed Julia out the window to be kissed, dozens of times. At Lynchburg the party pushed through a crowd of people and boarded a canal boat with the casket. They moved on, more slowly now, to Lexington, behind straining mules on the towpath.

Cadets of the Institute took over the casket in Lexington. It went to Jackson's old lecture room, which, they told his widow, had not been used since he left. The casket remained through a day in the midst of the passing of hushed, staring people and the slow firing of guns on the campus.

On Friday morning, Jackson's old pastor, the Reverend White, preached a simple service at the Presbyterian Church. A hymn, "How Blest the Righteous When He Dies," was followed by a reading from the fifteenth chapter of First Corinthians, then the sermon. The procession to the cemetery was brief.

Anna saw that the cemetery looked down upon a spreading view of the valleys and blue hills, with the mountains beyond. But the country they had loved looked strange. As she left, sobbing afresh, she did not look back.

★★★ *Appendix*

Prologue, Book One

The account of John Brown's hanging is drawn from those of eyewitnesses, especially Major J. T. L. Preston and Jackson himself. Conversation is authenticated by numerous unquestioned sources. Though minor details of this and other Prologues of this book [which are not always chronological with the story] are drawn with a freer hand than is the case in the text itself, the effort has always been to render accuracy in both fact and spirit.

Chapter 1

Jackson's clear expressions of fatalism, cited on page 13, were reported by an intimate of field service, Colonel John D. Imboden, and by Mrs. Jackson, who quoted a letter from her husband to a Presbyterian minister.

Literature of the Valley campaign is almost endless. Colonel William Allan, who was with Jackson throughout, left a factual record; a reliable synthesis is in D. S. Freeman's *Lee's Lieutenants*. Details of this account come from General Richard Taylor, who left valuable and charming memoirs; Colonel T. T. Munford of the cavalry and Colonel James A. Walker of the infantry, and numerous soldiers of lesser rank.

Some highly regarded works on Jackson must be used warily. See *Lee's Lieutenants*, Volume 2, pages 330, 332, 344, 362, for examples of Dr. Freeman's comments on serious errors by Colonel G. F. R. Henderson, a Jackson biographer, in matters of official orders, time sequence, dates, geography. Colonel Henderson's misconceptions of the opening of the Valley campaign unfortunately distort subsequent events.

Chapter 2

Front Royal, first of the sensational victories upon which Jackson's military reputation rests, was in fact the opening skirmish of a lengthy running battle which may be understood only by comparison of the sources, which are frequently at variance. This simplified account, though seen largely through

Confederate eyes, attempts justice to both adversaries—but the chief concern was to offer the layman a clear view of the dramatic opening of the campaign. The quoted testimony of General G. H. Gordon is evidence that Federal commanders miscalculated affairs in and near Front Royal from start to finish.

Chapter 3

The battle of Winchester may be accurately reconstructed without consulting official records, for the informal accounts of many Confederate participants offer richly detailed scenes of the field. Among the most valuable are those of Henry Kyd Douglas, Richard Taylor, William Allan, and the Reverend R. L. Dabney. They share a quality common with many reminiscences of Jackson in that they bear more directly on his striking character than on direction of troops.

There may be room for doubt that Jackson actually led his army in its first Rebel Yell (though Kyd Douglas reports it convincingly); there can be no doubt that he paused, while under dangerous fire, to chide General Taylor for use of profanity.

Jackson's military failures were almost universally neglected by early biographers, though they serve only to dramatize his victories. The fighting from Front Royal to Winchester illustrates his lack of control over artillery and cavalry at this stage of his career.

Chapter 4

Many phases of Jackson's military personality, unique in American annals, seem to have been forced upon him by circumstance. His consuming love of secrecy, for example, grew from the failures of subordinates who were timorous, like Colonel Conner, or who failed to follow the cryptic orders of Jackson. Though he retreated from Winchester with the unerring skill of a tactical genius, Jackson learned more than one lesson during these marches.

Chapters 5 and 6

The intricate movements of the twin battles of Cross Keys and Port Republic reveal Jackson at the peak of his skill in improvization on the field. The picture offered by his first biographers, however, in which he appears as something of an omnipotent war god, is out of focus. For all the delicacy of Jackson's timing at the end of his Valley campaign, much of the credit for the triumphant conclusion must go to General Ewell, who appeared at a fortunate instant, leading reinforcements. Early in the battle, by all existing evidence, Jackson seems to have attacked injudiciously.

Chapter 7

Jackson's early life, though lost in legend and romanticized by his contemporaries, is preserved in spirit by Jackson himself in his remarkable and unstudied letters. His career from West Point forward may be traced with confidence, for his correspondence leaves little to the imagination. The modern reader will be struck by the similarities of Jackson's expressions on sex, war and religion—a phase which escaped early biographers.

The impossibility of achieving absolute accuracy in the myriad affairs of the Civil War is illustrated by the minor errors concerning Jackson by even so careful a historian as Dr. Freeman, whose work will long remain the most valuable guide to the military affairs of the Confederacy in the Virginia theater. Dr. Freeman, for example, misread his source (T. J. Arnold's *Life & Early Letters of General Thomas J. Jackson*) and gave the impression that R. E. Lee recommended Jackson to Virginia Military Institute—when in fact his backing was given him some years later, when Jackson sought a post at the University of Virginia.

Chapter 8

Jackson's ten years in Lexington seem the most important formative period of his life. In this account of that period, village legends of his peculiarities have been largely discounted, and chief reliance is placed on the memoirs of his widow, the testimony of his shrewd sister-in-law, Margaret Preston, and recollections of fellow officers and faculty members.

Readers should take note of the spiritual climate of the middle nineteenth century in the United States. Religious sentiment was expressed in fulsome terms, in letters, diaries, and, evidently, in conversation. Jackson may thus appear as the incredible figure of a religious fanatic to modern eyes, though he seemed nothing of the sort to most people of his day.

Jackson's early persuasion as "A Union man" must be judged with similar caution. The evidence consulted for this account is found chiefly in letters from Jackson. Like many another prominent Confederate who had served with the United States Army, Jackson gave lip service to the principle of the Union. He betrayed the fragility of the tie, however, in: "I am strong for the Union at present, and if things become no worse I hope to continue so"—and in telling V.M.I. cadets that if sectional conflict became a reality, "draw your swords and throw away the scabbards."

At a distance of almost one hundred years it is impossible to judge the moralities involved when the choice of State or Nation fell upon military men of conscience. Most of Jackson's Virginia contemporaries seem to have found the problem even less perplexing than he.

Full details of the strange household routine of Jackson in Lexington may be found in the memoirs of his widow, chiefly in letters whose revelations seem to be utterly unconscious.

Chapter 9

The death scene of the Widow Henry at Bull Run follows the account of General Charles F. Walcott, published by the Military Historical Society of Massachusetts in 1883. It describes a visit to the field and a conversation with Mrs. Henry's son. Frank B. Sarles, Jr., historian of the National Park Service at Manassas National Battlefield Park, regards this as the most reliable account, but adds, "A completely authentic account of Mrs. Henry's death is rather difficult to find."

The bestowing of the nickname "Stonewall" upon Jackson has a small literature of its own. Readers with a thirst for details should consult Freeman's *Lee's Lieutenants,* Volume 1, page 733, for a display of evidence on the incident. Yet another version is found in Southern Historical Society Papers, Volume 19.

Chapter 10

A legend flourishing in the Valley of Virginia to this day, and occasionally published, is that the German general, Erwin Rommel, toured Virginia in the 1930's, in particular studying the military trail of Jackson—and that Old Jack's surprise thrusts and flank attacks were reincarnated in the North African tank fighting of the Afrika Korps during World War II.

Monroe F. Cockrell of Evanston, Illinois, investigated the persistent tale and concluded that it was wholly untrue. Rommel did not visit the United States. The man possibly mistaken for him was General Friederich von Boetticher, military attaché to the German Embassy, who often motored to the Virginia battlefields with his family.

Prologue, Book Two

Official records on the Richmond bread riots are scanty, and the attitude of the Confederate Government in suppressing news of it may be read in the appeals to the Richmond press and orders to the telegraph officials. The account of this significant protest rests largely on the entry of J. B. Jones in his *A Rebel War Clerk's Diary,* and on brief accounts in Richmond newspapers. A slight change in chronology has been made here as an aid to the Jackson narrative.

Chapter 11

It is all but incomprehensible to modern soldiers that Jackson should have attempted a major transfer of his troops from Western Virginia to the Richmond fighting while keeping his destination secret from all but two or three officers; yet this is almost the exact truth.

Perhaps more important in Jackson's career is the increasing sternness of his nature through this and subsequent operations. General Taylor, who looked on his commander with a sophisticated eye, left important lines:

"Observing him closely, I caught a glimpse of the man's inner nature. It was but a glimpse. The curtain closed, and he was absorbed in prayer. Yet in that moment I saw an ambition as boundless as Cromwell's, and as merciless."

Taylor spoke as an intimate. This was perhaps the first of

the voluminous lore comparing Jackson to Cromwell—a superficial similarity at best. That Taylor did not overstate the dimensions of Jackson's ambitions is revealed in the unmistakable language of Jackson's letters.

Chapters 12, 13 and 14

The confusions of the swamp fighting of the Seven Days endure in the literature of the campaign. From it all, Jackson emerges as the most inscrutable of the strange figures on the smoky landscape. His failures of the week probably will never be fully illuminated, but a narrative of the battles, with attention focused on Jackson through testimony of eyewitnesses, speaks more eloquently than the massive commentaries, which often serve to bog the casual reader in infinite complexities.

Among the lesser errors in the accepted history of this fighting is an example in the work of Dr. Freeman, who perhaps understood this conflict more fully than any other student. The error, of importance in relation to Jackson, was in recording that Jackson and Jefferson Davis, in a stiff, hostile confrontation during this week, had never before met. Jackson's published correspondence reveals a letter to his wife shortly after the battle of Bull Run, describing a meeting with Davis, when the two discussed details of affairs in Western Virginia.

Chapters 17 and 18

Jackson's famed mount, who bore the names Sorrel and Fancy, lived to an age of more than thirty, dying at the Old Soldiers' Home in Richmond in 1886, after a number of years on the family farm of Mrs. Jackson in Lincoln County, North Carolina. His history is vague during the campaign against Pope and in the invasion of Maryland. At some point before Second Manassas, Sorrel was stolen—or perhaps strayed. Not long after Antietam, he was returned; there seems no reliable record of details.

After Jackson's wounding at Chancellorsville, in May, 1863, Sorrel ran into Federal lines, remained unrecognized for some days, and was returned to the Confederates. Governor Letcher of Virginia saw to it that he was sent to Mrs. Jackson. The horse's stuffed skin and skeleton are in the museum of the

Virginia Military Institute. The skeleton, owned by Pittsburgh's Carnegie Museum for many years, was sent South "as a gesture of good will" in 1949.

Chapter 18

The Lost Order of Antietam, basis for one of the most melodramatic stories of the Civil War, is a matter of minor controversy. Private Mitchell, whose version of the discovery of Lee's order in Frederick has long been accepted as accurate, is followed here. Mitchell published his account at an early date and packed it with greater and more convincing detail than did Sergeant John Bloss, who recalled that he found the order with no assistance from a private.

A copy of this order in Jackson's handwriting—the document which precipitated the incident and ended the Confederate invasion of 1862—is in the Department of Archives and History, Raleigh, North Carolina.

Prologue, Book Three

The account of Lincoln's visit to his army before Chancellorsville is drawn chiefly from Noah Brooks in *Washington in Lincoln's Time*.

Chapters 22 and 23

There is hardly a reasonable doubt that Jackson was slain by his own men, and it is almost certain that the fatal shots were fired by men of the Eighteenth North Carolina.

A North Carolina story, scarcely more than a legend, is that two young riflemen of the Eighteenth North Carolina, Stuart Dixon and Robert Smith, fired the fatal shots. Kerr Scott, an ex-governor of the state, on whose farm Dixon's home still stands, recalls stories from a hunting companion of the two men—stories which always ended: "I wonder which one of us really killed him."

The sketch of the Federal panic at Chancellorsville, limited almost entirely to the Eleventh Corps, is based chiefly on Bigelow's *Campaign of Chancellorsville*, General O. O. Howard's autobiography, and Livermore's *Days & Events*.

The narrative of Jackson's wounding is a composite from

myriad sources and is fuller than most because, with minor exceptions, all testimony is weighed and used in the light of companion sources. There are conflicts of long standing over the details, but these seem of little importance. The narrative of Jackson's last hours does not halt to consider these controversies. A typical example: Captain R. E. Wilbourn and Captain James Power Smith each claimed to have slit Jackson's sleeve and tended his wound.

The indispensable source is D. S. Freeman, in both *Lee's Lieutenants,* Volume 2, and *R. E. Lee,* Volume 2; this synthesis, though it does not attempt to underline the drama of the situation, reliably sifts and clarifies earlier testimony.

The death mask of Jackson, now in the Valentine Museum, Richmond, was made by the sculptor, Frederick Volck, with the probable assistance of one Pietro Zamboggi. The museum has correspondence between Volck and Edward V. Valentine in which Volck writes of the mask: "It is the same I took at the Governor's Mansion when the body of Jackson was brought thither. . . . The mask . . . is the only one in existence." In Valentine's papers, however, is a note: "Pietro Zamboggi, the man who made the cast of Jackson's face." Museum researchers have concluded that the two men worked together.

Volck's brother, Adalbert, a caricaturist, may have made the drawing of Jackson after the battle of Fredericksburg, though Jackson's aide, Captain J. P. Smith, identified the artist only as "Sculptor Volke"—which would seem to point to his brother Frederick.

Though no liberties have been taken with testimony on Jackson's last hours, an effort has been made to reduce the air of pious unreality which marks the recollections of attending ministers and other friends. This was done for no other reason than that these ring falsely in modern ears, and the use of all the original conversation (or purported conversation) robs Jackson of some natural dignity and his death of its moving drama.

The Missing Anecdotes

No character on the Civil War stage seemed to attract as many anecdotes as did Jackson, and veteran hobbyists of the

war will note many of the most familiar stories of Stonewall
are not included in this narrative. Almost invariably, the decision to omit was based on probable fact—external evidence
proved or hinted that the tale was untrue. In many instances,
omission was a matter of taste or intuition.

Dr. Hunter McGuire, Jackson's physician, left as many interesting stories of his commander as any officer; yet his tales
and their versions seem to vary over the years and, like the
recollections of most soldiers, are often demonstrably inaccurate. An example of his testimony which is not questioned
seems in order:

"Listening to Jackson talk of Napoleon Bonaparte, as I often
did, I was struck with the fact that he regarded him as the
greatest general that ever lived. One day I asked him something about Waterloo. He had been over the field, inspected the
ground, and spent several days in studying the plan of battle. I
asked who had shown the greatest generalship there, Napoleon
or Wellington. . . . He said, 'Decidedly, Napoleon.' I said,
'Well, why was he whipped, then?' He replied, 'I can only explain it by telling you that I think God intended him to stop
right there.' "

McGuire also left unique accounts of Jackson at the first
battle of Bull Run, including one of the wounding of Jackson's
hand:

"On his way to the rear the wound pained him so much that
he stopped at the first hospital he came to, and the surgeon there
proposed to cut the finger off; but while the doctor looked for
his instruments and for a moment turned his back, the general
silently mounted his horse, rode off, and soon afterwards found
me."

Though these have the ring of truth, and come from a generally reliable witness, they are not so compelling as to lead
the narrative from the safer ground of already full reports.

★★★ Select Critical Bibliography

Allan, Elizabeth Preston, *The Life & Letters of Margaret J. Preston.*
Allan, William, *Jackson's Valley Campaign.*
Arnold, T. J., *Early Life & Letters of General Thomas J. Jackson.*
Avirett, J. B., *Memoirs of General Turner Ashby & His Compeers.*
Bigelow, John, Jr., *The Campaign of Chancellorsville.*
Brooks, Noah, *Washington in Lincoln's Time.*
Casler, John O., *Four Years In The Stonewall Brigade.*
Chesnut, Mary Boykin, *A Diary from Dixie.*
Cooke, John E., *Stonewall Jackson.*
Dabney, R. L., *Stonewall Jackson.*
Freeman, D. S., *R. E. Lee,* four volumes.
Goss, Warren Lee, *Recollections of A Private.*
Hamlin, Percy G., *Old Baldhead.*
Hamlin, Percy G., *The Making of A Soldier; The Letters of R. S. Ewell.*
Henderson, G. F. R , *Stonewall Jackson & The American Civil War.*
Howard, McHenry, *Recollections of A Maryland Soldier & Staff Officer.*
Hunter, Alexander, *Johnny Reb & Billy Yank.*
Longstreet, James, *From Manassas to Appomattox.*
Lonn, Ella, *Foreigners in the Confederacy.*
Moore, Edward A., *The Story of A Cannoneer Under Stonewall Jackson.*
Owen, William M., *In Camp & Battle with the Washington Artillery of New Orleans.*
Polley, J. B., *A Soldier's Letters to Charming Nellie.*
Russell, William Howard, *My Diary North and South.*
Sherman, William T., *Memoirs.*
Stiles, Robert, *Four Years Under Marse Robert.*
Taylor, Richard, *Destruction & Reconstruction.*

461

von Borcke, Heros, *Memoirs of the Confederate War for Independence.*
Welch, S. G., *A Confederate Surgeon's Letters to His Wife.*
Wiley, Bell I., *The Life of Johnny Reb.*

In addition these major sources gave help beyond quotation of passages, and were invaluable as guides and interpreters of background:

Battles and Leaders of the Civil War.
Blackford, W. W., *War Years with Jeb Stuart.*
Douglas, Henry Kyd, *I Rode With Stonewall.*
Freeman, D. S., *Lee's Lieutenants.*
Jackson, Mary Anna, *Memoirs of Stonewall Jackson.*
Southern Historical Society Papers.
Townsend, G. A., *Rustics in Rebellion.*

Index

463